"A PITIFUL, UNHOLY MESS"

Titles in the series

"NO ONE AVOIDED DANGER"
NAS KANEOHE BAY AND THE JAPANESE ATTACK OF 7 DECEMBER 1941

"THIS IS NO DRILL"
THE HISTORY OF NAS PEARL HARBOR AND THE JAPANESE ATTACKS OF 7 DECEMBER 1941

"THEY'RE KILLING MY BOYS!"
THE HISTORY OF HICKAM FIELD AND THE ATTACKS OF 7 DECEMBER 1941

Pearl Harbor Tactical Studies Series

J. Michael Wenger, Robert J. Cressman, and John F. Di Virgilio, editors

More than three-quarters of a century has passed since 7 December 1941, and yet no comprehensive tactical history exists for the Japanese attacks on the island of Oʻahu. Much of the material and documentary evidence relating to the attacks has become generally available to historians and researchers only within the last two decades. This material not only spans far-flung repositories in the United States and Japan, it also bridges a vast chasm separating two very different cultures, complicating the material's use.

The Pearl Harbor Tactical Studies series seeks to fill this wide gap in military history by exploring the deepest levels of practical, personal, and tactical details. The goal of these works is to promote a deeper understanding of the events of 7 December 1941 and to convey the chaos and magnitude of the disaster on Oʻahu as experienced by individuals. A careful survey of the available records and accounts from both sides has resulted in comprehensive accounts that document the epic American-Japanese struggle on and over Oʻahu and the intensely human tragedy of that day.

THE HISTORIES OF WHEELER, BELLOWS, AND HALEIWA FIELDS
AND THE JAPANESE ATTACKS OF 7 DECEMBER 1941

"A PITIFUL, UNHOLY MESS"

J. MICHAEL WENGER, ROBERT J. CRESSMAN, AND JOHN F. DI VIRGILIO

NAVAL INSTITUTE PRESS

Annapolis, Maryland

Naval Institute Press
291 Wood Road
Annapolis, MD 21402

Library of Congress Cataloging-in-Publication Data
Names: Wenger, Jon Michael, 1950– author. | Cressman, Robert, author. | Di
    Virgilio, John F., author.
Title: "A pitiful, unholy mess" : the histories of Wheeler, Bellows, and
    Haleiwa Fields and the Japanese attacks of 7 December 1941 / Jon Michael Wenger,
    Robert J. Cressman, and John F. Di Virgilio.
Other titles: Histories of Wheeler, Bellows, and Haleiwa Fields and the
    Japanese attacks of 7 December 1941
Description: Annapolis, Maryland : Naval Institute Press, [2022] | Series:
    Pearl Harbor tactical studies series | Includes bibliographical
    references and index.
Identifiers: LCCN 2022017317 | ISBN 9781682476024 (hardcover)
Subjects: LCSH: Pearl Harbor (Hawaii), Attack on, 1941 | Wheeler Army Air
    Field (Hawaii)--History. | World War, 1939-1945--Hawaii--Oahu. | Oahu
    (Hawaii)--History, Military--20th century. | BISAC: HISTORY / Wars &
    Conflicts / World War II / General | HISTORY / Military / Naval
Classification: LCC D767.92 .W4638 2022 | DDC
    940.54/26693--dc23/eng/20220629
LC record available at https://lccn.loc.gov/2022017317

30 29 28 27 26 25 24 23 22   9 8 7 6 5 4 3 2 1
First printing

CONTENTS

PREFACE

The story of the attacks on Wheeler, Bellows, and Haleiwa Fields on 7 December 1941 is well known to those interested in the history of the Pacific War and at least vaguely familiar to many Americans. Wheeler Field, south of Schofield Barracks and the largest of the three American pursuit bases on Oʻahu, suffered horrific losses in men and aircraft. Although the base had existed for only nineteen years, the airmen who served there and their dependents had developed a great affection for the facility. Bellows and Haleiwa Fields, on Oʻahu's windward and leeward shores respectively, were still comparative backwaters. Although Bellows was undergoing expansion at the time of the attacks, Haleiwa was virtually unchanged since the barnstorming days of the 1920s. In late 1941, both fields were used as gunnery training camps by the squadrons of Wheeler's 14th Pursuit Wing.

Regardless of which pursuit base they called home, the airmen played prominent roles in the fierce defense of their bases on 7 December. Pilots and aircrews attached to squadrons at all three fields had but one thought: take to the air, search for the Japanese attackers, and destroy them.

Well before we began work on this volume, the authors were keenly aware that the full story of Wheeler, Bellows, and Haleiwa Fields from 7 December 1941 had yet to be told. It was not until we delved into the voluminous materials bequeathed to history by the defenders (and attackers) that we appreciated the intricacy of the full story and the difficulties we would encounter in writing it. Our desire to do justice to the defenders of Oʻahu's pursuit bases led us to take on this daunting task. It is our hope that readers will remember the courage and heroism of those men on that infamous day.

J. Michael Wenger

Robert J. Cressman

John F. Di Virgilio

ACKNOWLEDGMENTS

book such as this is necessarily the product of the supporting labors of many, from trained archival specialists, to friends and colleagues in the field, to those who lived through these momentous events. Some of those we wish to thank no longer work in the archives in which we began our research more than forty years ago, but our debt to them remains. And nearly all the veterans with whom we talked or corresponded have since died.

In particular, this work stands on the shoulders of three individuals without whose resources any work dealing with the attacks on Oʻahu would fall woefully short of the mark. Dr. Gordon W. Prange's papers remain an unparalleled source of information. We especially thank Jennie A. Levine at the University of Maryland and Dr. Donald M. Goldstein, Marianne Kasica, and Michael Dabrishus of the University of Pittsburgh for making Dr. Prange's materials available. Similarly, Walter Lord's work is practically synonymous with Pearl Harbor studies. Access to his interviews, questionnaires, and correspondence came to us via archivist Curtis Utz of the Naval History and Heritage Command. The papers of aviation historian David Aiken include personal accounts, notes, maps, photography, and voluminous correspondence with many of the participants in the air battles over Oʻahu. Access to his staggering accumulation of historical material came to us via Chris McDougal, Director of Archives and Library at the National Museum of the Pacific War in Fredericksburg, Texas.

Archivists and reference specialists at a number of institutions and repositories provided help and guidance. The National Archives and Records Administration in College Park, Maryland (NARA II), has provided access to records over the course of many years, and we thank Jim Trimble, Holly Reed, Theresa Roy, and Sharon Culley of the Still Picture Branch; Nathaniel Patch of the Textual Branch; and Andrew Knight and Alice Rosser of the Cartographic Branch for their assistance. The generous staff at the Naval History and Heritage Command (formerly the Naval Historical Center) in Washington, D.C., helped us over the span of a generation, particularly Charles R. Haberlein, Agnes F. Hoover, and Mike Walker. Lisa Fox of the University of North Texas supplied copies of interviews from that institution's oral history program. Our research at the National Archives and National Personnel

Records Center in St. Louis, Missouri, would not have been possible without the energy and advice of Scott A. Levins, Bryan McGraw, Barbara Bauman, Whitney Mahar, Eric Kilgore, Dean Gall (who provided a set of general orders that detailed firefighting activities), Donna Noelken, Jennifer Moll, Amy Reckmann, Angela Miller, Mary Parker Biby, and Jaclyn Ostrowski. Randy Hackenburg of the U.S. Army Military History Institute at Carlisle Barracks, Pennsylvania, provided access to the Denver Gray Collection. James Tobias provided access to Army regulations held by the U.S. Army Center of Military History at Fort McNair in Washington, D.C. We also thank Bradley D. Cook, Photograph Curator at the Indiana University Archives, and Clara Snyder, Digital Archivist at the National Museum of the Pacific War in Fredericksburg, Texas.

The following individuals assisted with translation of Japanese documents, books, articles, and monographs: Dr. Kataoka Hiroko (formerly of North Carolina State University), Oka Akio, Sugahara Kan, Dr. Kawamoto Minoru, Tagaya Osamu, and D. Y. Louie. In particular, Mr. Sugahara was instrumental in evaluating our translation of the Japanese aircrew rosters from the attacks on Oʻahu.

Shibata Takehiko and Kageyama Kōichirō at the War History Office of the Japanese Defense Agency offered expertise, documents, and analysis and served as our liaison with Japanese veterans.

Fellow historians and researchers extended generous offers of assistance. Capt. Roger Pineau, Cdr. Chihaya Masataka, Capt. Uesaka Yasushi, Sugahara Kan, Shimizu Ikuo, and Kamada Minoru aided our research in Japan.

Other individuals provided documents, materials, and valuable advice, including Fr. James F. Garneau, John B. Lundstrom, James C. Sawruk, John W. Lambert and Sam Smith (the latter two individuals via Mark Stevens), Mark R. Wenger (who assisted with architectural terminology), Mark Frey, Geoff Gentilini, Randall Asherbranner, Kathleen Lang, William M. Cleveland, Todd Pederson, Jeffrey Dodge,

James Lansdale, Ron Werneth, Yoshida Jirō, Louis Bontya (who helped us reconstruct Wheeler's flight line at the time of the attack and provided insights into the design of the base's hangars), and our late friend Richard F. Barnes, who provided much-needed encouragement in the latter stages of our work. Capt. Charles B. Gillman, USN (Ret.), provided invaluable guidance in helping us craft our narratives regarding the American pursuit pilots and their combats. Dr. Timothy P. Mulligan made available copies of the fragmentary codebooks recovered from Japanese aircraft wreckage. Ray Emory provided admission records of the General Hospital at Schofield Barracks from 7 December 1941. Institutions and individuals in Japan supplied documents and photographs: War History Office of the Japanese Defense Forces, Yoshino Yasutaka, Murooka Yasuo of Maru magazine, Todaka Kazunari, Tanaka Shōichi, Kamada Minoru, Makino Akihisa, Matsumura Hirata, Hori Kenji, and Fujita Iyozō. Tagaya Osamu assisted with translation issues and secured pictures of Japanese aircrews from Dr. Izawa Yasuho.

Extended families and acquaintances of American veterans provided accounts, photographs, and other personal papers (with the veteran's name and 1941 rank in brackets): Michael Bloom [1st Lt. Wallace Bloom], Fr. Greg Andrews, Beth Ford, and Julie Welsh [Pfc. Carroll T. Andrews], Carolyn Borozny [SSgt. Lowell V. Klatt], Virgil R. Henderson [Capt. Charles C. Cunningham] via Jessie Higa, Paul Hibel [Cpl. Franklin Hibel], Ken Cooke and Frank Holmes [2nd Lt. Besby F. Holmes], Gayle Kent [2nd Lt. George A. Whiteman], Georgia Lambert [2nd Lt. Jean K. Lambert], Patricia Lee [SSgt. Stephen J. Koran and Flora Belle Koran], Rosemary Melton [Pfc. Vernon C. Rubenking], Doug Nelson [Maj. Hilmer C. Nelson], Robert B. Plybon [2nd Lt. Paul C. Plybon], Susan Robinson [Pvt. Guy Messacar Jr.], Rex Russell [Pfc. Edmund H. Russell], James W. Spinney [Lt. Col. Edmund C. Sliney], and Robert S. Turk III and William R. Turk IV [SSgt. Robert S. Turk Jr.].

Other individuals provided photographs: Randall Asherbranner, Michel Beckers, Dana Bell, Mark Stevens, Ernest Arroyo, Gary Asher, William Bartsch, William M. Cleveland, Dan Hagedorn, Jessie Higa, James Lansdale, Walter Lord (via the Naval History and Heritage Command), Al Makiel, Todd Pederson, Dr. Gordon W. Prange (via Dr. Donald M. Goldstein and the University of Maryland), Philip M. Rasmussen, Satō Zen'ichi (via the Pearl Harbor Aviation Museum), Susan Stanaway (from the collection of her deceased husband, John Stanaway), and Kathy Weeks. Authors J. Michael Wenger, Robert J. Cressman, and John F. Di Virgilio also provided photographs. Because we began concerted work on this volume relatively recently, we came in sustained contact with few veterans and had to rely on articles, reminiscences, interviews, and materials passed to us by their families.

The following Japanese aviators contributed materially to our understanding of Japanese ordnance, tactics, and the events of 7 December 1941: Fujita Iyozō, Harada Kaname, Hori Kenji, Matsumura Hirata, Satō Zen'ichi, Tamura Heiji, Ushijima Shizundō, Yoshida Jirō, and Yoshino Haruo.

World War II Valor in the Pacific National Monument and Pacific Historic Parks have supported our research and work for many years. Our thanks to Tom Shaw, Marjorie Shaw, Patty Brown, Scott Pawlowski, and Stan Melman for providing hundreds of statements and narratives from Pearl Harbor Survivors Association membership applications; Patty Brown and Daniel Martinez provided insights, advice, and key documents.

We could not have completed this work without the assistance of historian Jessie Higa of Honolulu. Her knowledge and advice, and the materials she provided, have enhanced the narrative substantially. Her unexcelled research into the Wheeler Field community and the families and dependents from 7 December 1941 aided us in our understanding of the civilian side of the story. Higa and her extended family have deep roots in the islands, and her familiarity with and reverence for the cultural history of the Hawaiian people helped us gain a deeper understanding of the events of 1941 than would have been possible otherwise.

We would like to express gratitude to our families for their suggestions, patience, and support as we made our way toward completion of this work.

Finally, we wish to thank Adam Kane, Glenn Griffith, and Robin Noonan of the Naval Institute Press, our copy editor, Mindy Conner, and former press members Richard Russell, Emily Bakely, and Rachel Crawford, for their encouragement and continued interest in our work, specifically in the Pearl Harbor Tactical Studies series.

NOTES ON NAMES AND TERMINOLOGY

Aircraft Names

The Imperial Japanese Navy designated its types of aircraft in a very particular way, and we refer to them as it did. The reader thus will not find the anachronistic "Val" or "Kate" in the text because those names were not introduced until November 1942.

IMPERIAL JAPANESE NAVY

▷ Aichi D3A1 Type 99 carrier bomber (*kanbaku*) (Val)
▷ Mitsubishi A6M2 Type 0 carrier fighter (*kansen*) (Zero)
▷ Nakajima B5N2 Type 97 carrier attack plane (*kankō*) (Kate)

U.S. ARMY AND CIVILIAN

▷ Airspeed AS.6A Envoy I
▷ Boeing B-17C/D/E Flying Fortress
▷ Boeing P-12B/C/E Hawk
▷ Boeing P-26A/B/C Peashooter
▷ Curtiss A-12 Shrike
▷ Curtiss JN-4
▷ Curtiss P-36A Hawk
▷ Curtiss P-40B/C Tomahawk

▷ De Havilland DH-4A
▷ Douglas A-20A Havoc
▷ Douglas B-18 Bolo
▷ Douglas BT-2CI
▷ Douglas C-33
▷ Fokker C-2
▷ Fokker D.VII
▷ Fokker F.VIIb/3m
▷ Grumman OA-9
▷ Keystone B-6A
▷ Lockheed 10E
▷ Lockheed Vega 5b
▷ Martin B-10/B-12 Flying Whale
▷ Morane-Saulnier monoplane
▷ Nieuport XXVII C.1
▷ Nieuport XXVIII C.1
▷ North American AT-6
▷ North American O-47B
▷ Royal Aircraft Factory S.E.5a
▷ Sikorsky OA-8
▷ Sopwith Camel
▷ SPAD S.VII
▷ SPAD S.XIII
▷ Stinson O-49

U.S. NAVY
▷ Boeing F4B
▷ Consolidated PBY Catalina
▷ Curtiss SOC-1 Seagull
▷ Grumman F4F-3A Wildcat
▷ Vought SB2U-3 Vindicator

U.S. Navy Ship Names

Unless otherwise specified, U.S. Navy ship names will be understood as being preceded by USS (United States Ship); the alphanumeric identification number will be used only at the ship's first mention. All times and dates are those observed locally by a ship or station unless otherwise specified and are rendered in military fashion (e.g., 1000 for 10:00 a.m., 1300 for 1:00 p.m., etc.).

Personal Names

We follow the Japanese fashion for names, with the surname first and the given name last. Romanization of Japanese names from kanji characters is an inexact science, so after translating the names herein we consulted historian Sugahara Kan of Japan, who offered corrections and alternative readings. The nature of Japanese personal names precludes a last word in this matter, but with Mr. Sugahara's help the rosters of the Japanese participants are as authoritative as practicality allows.

American servicemen whose legal names included "empty" initials in place of given names are referred to in accordance with military documents of the time, enclosing the initials in quotation marks (e.g., AvnCdt "G" "C" Beale).

Hawaiian Place-Names

Except for the names of military bases and public buildings, and quotes from contemporary correspondence, Hawaiian place-names are rendered in the orthography of that language.

Japanese Terms

chūtai: Japanese aviation unit of six to twelve aircraft, usually comprising three *shōtai*s

kanbakutai: Japanese aviation unit of Type 99 carrier bombers

kankōtai: Japanese aviation unit of Type 97 carrier attack planes

kansentai: Japanese aviation unit of Type 0 carrier fighters

Kidō Butai: (literally, "mobile force"): any Japanese naval force that contained an aircraft carrier and was capable of independent operation. In terms of the Hawaiian Operation, *Kidō Butai* was a euphemism for "Carrier Striking Force."

kōkūtai (often abbreviated as *kū*): a large, land-based group of Japanese naval airplanes. In theory, the group could encompass hundreds of aircraft of generally one mission type, such as fighters or bombers. A *kōkūtai* was roughly the equivalent of an American air group but also included all administrative functions dealing with base facilities, personnel, and aircraft maintenance—functions Americans usually assigned to air base commands. The term was not used when referring to carrier air groups.

shōtai: Japanese aviation unit of two to four aircraft

Miscellaneous Terms

girt: a horizontal structural member in a framed wall, used to provide lateral support to the wall panel and wind resistance

Lufbery Circle: a defensive air tactic in which aircraft enter a string formation and turn in a semicircular pattern, or arc, with each plane protecting the aircraft in front of it

National Personnel Records Center

For two generations, the term "National Personnel Records Center" was synonymous with the former

Page Avenue facility in St. Louis, Missouri, that held all the Official Military Personnel Files (OMPFs) from the World War II period and other eras. In recent years, as the volume of records being released for public use increased, the facility in St. Louis became two institutions in one building operating under the National Archives and Records Administration, each with its own separate research room, staff, and procedures. The National Personnel Records Center administers nonarchival records (those closed to the public), and the National Archives administers archival records (those open to the public).

Primary sources accessed through the research room in the Records Center are cited as residing in "NPRC, St. Louis." Open material accessed through the research room in the National Archives is cited as residing in "NARA, St. Louis." The custody of records in St. Louis relating to World War II changes daily, passing increasingly to the National Archives. The citations herein refer to the custodian of records at the time of the authors' research and may no longer be valid.

ABBREVIATIONS

AA	antiaircraft	ComPatWing	Commander Patrol Wing
AC	Air Corps	ComScoFor	Commander Scouting Force
AFB	Air Force Base	CoPlt.	copilot
AFCC	Air Force Combat Command	DAR	detailed action report
AFHRA	Air Force Historical Research Agency, Maxwell AFB	Fr.	Father (chaplain)
		HAD	Hawaiian Air Depot (USAAF)
AFHSO	Air Force History Support Office, Bolling AFB	HAD	History and Archives Division (Naval History and Heritage Command)
AG	adjutant general		
A-V(N)	commissioned aviation officers designated naval aviators and qualified for general duty afloat or ashore	HAF	Hawaiian Air Force
		HD	Hawaiian Department
		HQ	headquarters
BOQ	bachelor officer quarters	IFR	individual flight record
CCC	Civilian Conservation Corps	kg	kilogram
CG	commanding general	MAG	Marine Aircraft Group
CinCPac	Commander in Chief, U.S. Pacific Fleet	MC	Medical Corps
		NARA	National Archives and Records Administration
CinCUS	Commander in Chief, U.S. Fleet		
CNO	Chief of Naval Operations	NAS	Naval Air Station
CO	commanding officer	NASPH	Naval Air Station Pearl Harbor
Com14	Commandant, 14th Naval District	NCO	noncommissioned officer
ComAirBatFor	Commander Aircraft, Battle Force	NHHC	Naval History and Heritage Command
		NTU	North Texas University
ComCruScoFor	Commander Cruisers, Scouting Force	OMPF	Official Military Personnel File

OpNav	Office of the Chief of Naval Operations
PHA	*Pearl Harbor Attack* Hearings
PHSA	Pearl Harbor Survivors Association
PX	post exchange
QM	quartermaster
QMC	Quartermaster Corps
ROTC	Reserve Officer Training Corps
SOP	standard operating procedure
TF	task force
T.H.	Territory of Hawai'i
UNTOHC	University of North Texas Oral History Collection
USAAC	United States Army Air Corps
USAAF	United States Army Air Forces
USAT	United States Army Transport
USS	United States Ship
VFW	Veterans of Foreign Wars
VMF	Marine Fighting Squadron
WD	War Department
WPA	Works Progress Administration
YMCA	Young Men's Christian Association

STANDARD NOMENCLATURE FOR U.S. NAVY SHIPS

BB	battleship
CV	aircraft carrier
DD	destroyer

U.S. ARMY RANKS

Gen.	general
Lt. Gen.	lieutenant general
Maj. Gen.	major general
Brig. Gen.	brigadier general
Col.	colonel
Lt. Col.	lieutenant colonel
Maj.	major
Capt.	captain
1st Lt.	first lieutenant
2nd Lt.	second lieutenant
AvnCdt.	aviation cadet (after June 1941)
F/C	flying cadet (prior to June 1941)
MSgt.	master sergeant

1stSgt.	first sergeant
TSgt.	technical sergeant
SSgt.	staff sergeant
Sgt.	sergeant
Cpl.	corporal
Pfc.	private first class
Pvt.	private

U.S. NAVY RANKS AND RATINGS

Adm.	admiral
Rear Adm.	rear admiral
Capt.	captain
Lt. Cdr.	lieutenant commander
Lt. (jg)	lieutenant (junior grade)
Ens.	ensign

JAPANESE RANKS AND RATINGS

The Imperial Navy's aviation ratings did not correspond with those of the U.S. Navy. For commissioned ranks, American equivalents are used. For the sake of simplicity, Japanese noncommissioned and enlisted ranks are presented as follows: WO (warrant officer), FPO1c, FPO2c, FPO3c (petty officer first, second, third class), and F1c (seaman first class). The table below lists corresponding Japanese terminology and translation.

Adm.	*taishō*	admiral
Vice Adm.	*chūjō*	vice admiral
Rear Adm.	*shōshō*	rear admiral
Capt.	*taisa*	captain
Cdr.	*chūsa*	commander
Lt. Cdr.	*shōsa*	lieutenant commander
Lt.	*tai-i*	lieutenant
Lt. (jg)	*chū-i*	sub-lieutenant
Ens	*shō-i*	ensign
WO	*hikō heisōchō*	flight warrant officer
FPO1c	*ittō hikō heisō*	flight petty officer first class
FPO2c	*nitō hikō heisō*	flight petty officer second class
FPO3c	*santō hikō heisō*	flight petty officer third class
F1c	*ittō hikōhei*	flight seaman first class

PHOTO CREDITS

Many of the photographs and illustrations in this book are official U.S. Army/Army Air Forces/Navy documents from the collections of the National Archives and Records Administration and National Personnel Records Center. Photos marked 18-PU, 71-CA, RG 77, RG 80, 80-CF, 80-G, 111-SC, 342-FH, and RG 407 can be found at NARA II in College Park, Maryland. Photos marked 15WHO are from the 15th Wing History Office at Joint Base Pearl Harbor–Hickam. Photos marked AFHRA are from the Air Force Historical Research Agency at Maxwell AFB. Photos marked BAFB are from Barksdale AFB. Photos marked BKS are from the War History Library (Senshi bu) of the Japan Defense Agency, War History Section (Bōeichō Kenshūjo Senshishitsu). Photos marked HSA are from the Hawai'i State Archives. Photos marked HWRD are from the *Honolulu Star-Advertiser* in the Hawai'i War Records Depository at the University of Hawai'i. Photos marked NARA, St. Louis are from the National Archives and Records Administration in St. Louis, Missouri. Photos marked NGEF are from the National Guard Educational Foundation. Photos marked NMPW are from the David Aiken collection in the National Museum of the Pacific War. Photos marked PHAM are from the Pearl Harbor Aviation Museum. Photos marked TLM are from the Tropic Lightning Museum, Schofield Barracks. Photos marked IUA are from the Indiana University Archives. Photos marked USAFM are from the National Museum of the U.S. Air Force. Photos marked USAMHI are from the U.S. Army Military History Institute in the U.S. Army Heritage and Education Center at Carlisle Barracks, Pennsylvania. Photos marked USAR are from World War II Valor in the Pacific National Monument.

Photos loaned or given by individuals are indicated by the donor's surname.

Chapter One

"SITUATED ON THE ELEVATED PLAINS OF MAGNIFICENT OAHU"
The Development of Wheeler Field

On 6 February 1922, the Army authorities on Oʻahu formed a detachment of twenty men from the 4th Squadron (Observation), 5th Observation Group and placed them under the direct command of the Hawaiian Department. The men reported for duty with the Hawaiian Division Air Service at Schofield Barracks under the command of 2nd Lt. William T. Agee, formerly the assistant operations officer for the 5th Observation Group. Agee's men grubbed brush and undergrowth along the southern limits of Schofield's military reservation, on the site of a former drill field used by the Hawaiian Division's 5th Group Observation Cavalry. Their objective: prepare the site for construction of a new airfield.[1]

Agee's training and operational experience in both ballooning and heavier-than-air flight had prepared him well for observation duty with the Hawaiian Division. Certainly he was no stranger to danger in the air. Following a free ballooning ascent from Fort Sill, Oklahoma, with two fellow officers and NCOs, he endured a harrowing overnight flight in a runaway balloon that ended with a bumpy, out-of-control landing in the desolate Texan landscape near Wichita Falls.[2]

The detachment from the 4th Observation Squadron cleared the location for the new landing field quickly, thankful for the cool trade winds blowing over the scrubby terrain. Within a few weeks the soldiers "had leveled a strip sufficiently smooth for takeoff and landing of the relatively slow and light aircraft of 1922." Accommodations for the men and aircraft still to come were as primitive as the new landing strip. The as-yet-unnamed airfield's first buildings were five Bessonneau hangars—wood-framed canvas structures that resembled oversized tents—that were not well suited for the breezy conditions between the Waiʻanae and Koʻolau mountain ranges. The hangar line lay along a nearly east–west axis, with openings facing south. The northeast corner of the structures was adjacent to Kamehameha Highway (relocated later due to Wheeler's development during the 1930s), which ran north-northwest into Schofield Barracks. Truck parking, an area for tents and tent flies, and an apron for the eleven De Havilland DH-4As assigned to the 4th Observation Squadron all lay farther south.[3]

When they were finished, the men had transformed the site "situated on the elevated plains of magnificent Oahu" from "a mass of guava bushes

The Cavalry Drill Field at Schofield Barracks, looking northeast, as photographed from an aircraft of the 5th Observation Group at 1034 on 15 September 1921. It was this area—taken over by the airdrome at Schofield Barracks—that became Wheeler Field. Note the tracks and courses for use in exercise and close-order drill. **NARA II, RG 77**

The Schofield Airdrome, looking north, on 8 April 1922, seven months prior to the naming of Wheeler Field. The five Bessonneau hangars open to the south are ready to service the eleven De Havilland DH-4As of the 4th Observation Squadron. **NARA II, 342-FH-3B-21797**

and scrub trees" into Hawai'i's newest landing field. The sweeping vistas of the mountains to the east and west, and of the broad plain extending from O'ahu's shore to the north and Pearl Harbor to the south, did not, however, make up for the lack of amenities and permanent facilities. The Bessonneau hangars rested on turf and dirt floors and were "not weather proof."[4]

On 11 November 1922 the new airfield received its name. Hawaiian Department General Orders No. 47 announced: "The airdrome at Schofield Barracks, Hawaii, is named 'Wheeler Field' in honor of Major Sheldon H. Wheeler, who perished in an airplane accident July 13, 1921, at Luke Field, Hawaii, of which field he was in command at the time of his death." While Major Wheeler was attempting to land, his aircraft went into a spin, crashed, and burst into flames. The accident also killed Wheeler's passenger, Sgt. Thomas A. Kelly of the 4th Observation Squadron.[5]

The major's contemporaries described "Sam" Wheeler as one of the Air Service's "ablest officers and veteran flyers." Born on 6 April 1889, the Vermont native attended that state's university for two years before entering the U.S. Military Academy, from which he graduated on 12 June 1914. After a year of service with the 25th Infantry Regiment, Wheeler's interest in aviation led him to the Aviation Section of the Signal Corps at Rockwell Field near San Diego, California. He received the rating of junior military aviator on 2 September 1916, was attached to the 1st Aero Squadron, and participated in the Punitive Expedition in Mexico. When America entered World War I, his billet was Kelly Field as commanding officer of the 8th Aero Squadron. Following service in other stateside assignments, in August 1918 Wheeler received orders to France, where he commanded Orly Flying Field south of Paris. He returned to the United States in April 1919, and after a short stint of duty at Hazelhurst Field on Long Island transferred to the Hawaiian Department for his final assignment at Luke Field. Wheeler's death occurred only three months before he was to depart for the Field Officers' School at Langley Field. A tribute in the *Air Service News Letter*

Maj. Sheldon H. Wheeler, American Expeditionary Force, circa August 1918. **15WHO**

voiced high praise: "It is indeed regrettable that this young officer should be cut off in the midst of a promising Army career, and the Air Service, the Army as a whole, and those individuals who were fortunate to know Major Wheeler, keenly feel his loss."[6]

Wheeler's First Permanent Buildings

The War Department addressed the need for permanent buildings at Wheeler Field in early 1922. The Hawaiian Department took delivery of "material for the erection of six steel airplane hangars for the Air Service" during March, only days after 1st Lieutenant Agee's detachment finished erecting the temporary facilities. Dockworkers landed the buildings' components—which arrived in one shipment—and loaded the ponderous cargo onto flatcars bound for O'ahu's interior. Anticipating the need for ground transport farther inland, the constructing quartermaster laid a rail spur from the main line of the Oahu Railway and ran the tracks as close to the construction site as possible, thus saving three thousand feet in truck transportation. Formal authorization of construction followed on 11 April.[7]

Although the new buildings were designated "hangars," the Air Service decided that four of them would be used for purposes other than aircraft maintenance. Confusing matters further, the Army specified three hangar types, with a trio of Type 1 hangars designated as "open storage facilities," which the Air Service used as follows:

1. Barracks: dormitory space, mess and kitchen, storage, toilets, recreation/day rooms, and classrooms
2. Group and squadron headquarters: officer assembly rooms, dispensary, armory, photographic laboratory, and supply room
3. Garage: toolroom, storage, and office space

A single Type 2 building supplied space for "war reserve storage," and the remaining pair of Type 3 structures were used as typical aircraft hangars.[8]

There were other challenges in addition to the logistical problems of shipping the structural components inland, namely water and sewer connections, and routing of electrical service to the new airfield. The scrubby area south of Schofield Barracks presented headaches as well. The sloping terrain required further clearing and grading of the grounds, which "were in a comparatively wild state." The construction crews who assembled the hangars were hampered by damaged corrugated sheathing in shipping containers that they reported were "broken through rough handling in transit." Some of the sheets could not be repaired; others required heavy applications of caulk to make the joints water resistant. Having weathered all these difficulties, the project's engineers wrote the completion report for the six buildings and stated enthusiastically: "At the completion of this project Wheeler Field can be said to be an independent unit."[9]

Although contractors officially completed the $133,600 project on 30 June 1923, Wheeler's men had occupied the hangars several months earlier when the 17th Composite Group was organized at the

base, with the group's Headquarters Detachment, the 4th Observation Squadron, and the 19th Pursuit Squadron as component commands. Meanwhile, Wheeler's officers and men resided at Schofield Barracks, not a great distance away from the aviation activities at the field, but far enough to impose considerable inconvenience and wastage of the gasoline required to transport the 15 officers and 252 enlisted men to the flight line.[10]

The six new steel hangars erected immediately south of the Bessonneau hangars stood in two rows of three structures each. From east to west, the southernmost row that faced the landing field consisted of the headquarters building for the group and squadrons, two airplane hangars, and a concrete apron that opened to the south. Behind and to the north lay the barracks, garage, and storehouse buildings. Four of the five Bessonneau hangars were used for storage, although they were eventually replaced with three smaller corrugated steel buildings for bomb storage and other uses. Completing the suite of permanent structures were two sets of oil storage tanks with a capacity of 80,000 gallons. After additional units were assigned to Wheeler by 1930, the Army erected two small "cities" of pyramidal tents, latrines, and mess facilities on each end of the hangar group.[11]

Recommendations for Further Development

Plans for further expansion at Wheeler outside the limits of the original "Schofield Barracks Aerodrome" had to await the decision of a board of officers appointed on 10 November 1926 by the commanding general, Hawaiian Department, "to study the needs of the Department in connection with the Air Corps Five Year Program." On 21 February 1927, the board recommended that Wheeler Field be expanded by 400 acres that adjoined the old landing field and extended to the northwest at an estimated cost of $107,450, excluding the purchase cost of the land. In 1928 Congress passed HR11134, which provided $597,000 for hangars, warehouses, shops,

Hangars at Wheeler Field, home to the 17th Composite Group, circa 1927, looking southeast. The building in the foreground is the group barracks. The two buildings to the left are the garage and storehouse, with one of the group's two airplane hangars at far right. **NARA II, RG 77**

The first-floor bunk area inside Wheeler Field's barracks (Building 3101) following the former hangar's conversion from February through July 1927. **Sam Smith, via Mark Stevens**

Tents erected to house the 230 men of the 75th Service Squadron. The additional units assigned to Wheeler caused a shortage of quarters early in the field's history. View taken circa December 1930. **NARA II, RG 77**

A temporary mess hall built to accommodate men of the 75th Service Squadron. View looking northwest toward the eastern end of the Storehouse in the background to the left. **NARA II, RG 77**

Aerial view looking northeast of the buildings at Wheeler near the end of the early field's heyday, on 14 May 1931. Note the tents on either end of the complex, with the 75th Service Squadron on the right. All three buildings on the south side were used as airplane hangars. In the distance is Wheeler's first baseball field (*left center*); beyond it is the original Kamehameha Highway. **NARA II, 342-FH-3B-21831**

an operations building, a photo laboratory, a parachute building, gasoline storage, and an improved landing field. The actual appropriations exceeded $650,000. Subsequent outlays for quarters and barracks dwarfed the earlier expenditures and totaled almost $1,750,000. In one of his last official acts prior to his retirement, Quartermaster General Maj. Gen. Benjamin F. Cheatham approved the final layout plan for Wheeler Field on 20 January 1930.[12]

Decisions regarding Wheeler's layout were followed by discussions about designs for the base's hangars and enlisted barracks. The Air Corps was developing Albrook Field in Panama at the same time, so it seemed economical for the new hangars in Hawai'i to share the same design as those at Albrook—a proposal that met with approval on 7 July 1930. An additional proposal that the Hawaiian Department adopt the design of the eight barracks at Albrook received some support as well. Albrook's roof design incorporated deep eaves and soffits intended to carry water from tropical rains away from the exterior walls and to provide shade from the hot sun. Lower floors also incorporated eaves that projected outward from deck level to protect the

NCO married housing area north of Hangars 3 and 4, looking north, on 7 May 1935. The lack of variation in architectural design is apparent. Schofield Barracks is in the distance. **NARA II, 342-FH-3B-21827**

floors below. Oʻahu's more moderate weather probably drove the Army's decision to retain the Hawaiian Department's barracks design, which was still a departure "from the type of barracks heretofore constructed by the War Department."[13]

Construction: 1931–1933

By 17 September 1930 the stage was set for Wheeler's expansion to begin. The first phase of the 1931–33 Wheeler project moved forward with construction of quarters for married officers and noncommissioned officers, and housing for bachelor officers. Although work on all the quarters commenced in February 1931 and proceeded in parallel, contractors completed the forty sets of NCO quarters and the bachelor NCO quarters first under the terms of contract W-60qm93, wrapping up construction on 7 March 1932. Both NCO and officer residences shared a common design with quarters at Schofield Barracks. All NCO married quarters were "single-storied and of modified Spanish

design," with stucco exterior walls and a built-up roof that featured five plies of roofing felt topped with a bituminous coating and a layer of gravel. The quarters incorporated steel window sashes (as protection against Oʻahu's voracious termites), electric kitchen appliances, and gas water heaters. Except for four units that had reversed floor plans, all of the NCO units were identical.[14]

Apparently, the flat roofs—a notoriously bad design choice for a region with heavy rainfall—proved unsatisfactory with regard to water leaks, so at some point prior to October 1941 contractors replaced the flat roofs with conventional hip roofs that shed rainwater more effectively.[15]

Bounded by Strieber and Haley Avenues north and south, and Eastman Avenue to the east, the Bachelor Quarters (Building 267), which also served as an NCO Club, could accommodate twenty-one noncommissioned officers, with the prospect of adding a northern wing that would double the residential

NCO Quarters 211 on the inside of Langley Loop, with characteristics typical of the Pueblo architectural style employed in the older residential structures from the early 1930s. Quarters 213 (with its reversed floor plan) is off to the right. **NARA II, RG 77**

Wheeler Field's NCOs' Club, looking northwest, on 11 November 1941. Reassignment of the 26th Attack Squadron to Hickam Field in December 1939 (marking the conversion of Wheeler to primarily a pursuit base) likely prompted the removal of the bomb and propeller formerly suspended over the main entrance. **NARA II, 342-FH-3B-48700**

capacity. The building material arrived promptly, chiefly via truck with the occasional help of the Oahu Railway. Following two construction extensions totaling fifty-one days, the Army accepted the completed sets of NCO quarters on 7 March 1932. Situated west of the Kamehameha Highway's original trace, the forty-two units (with one exception) faced two concentric loop roads—Eastman Road and Langley Loop. The two thoroughfares terminated on Wright Avenue, which ran parallel to and one block north of Wheeler's soon-to-be-constructed hangar line.[16]

The progress of forty-two married officer quarters proceeded similarly. Work started on 25 February 1931, and all units were accepted on 21 May 1932. Though differing in appearance from the NCO quarters, the officers' accommodations employed nearly identical construction materials and methods. As with the NCO residences, the quarters were of a single design, with six of the units having reversed floor plans for a modicum of variety. Plans also called for a Bachelor Officer Quarters (Building 302), which also functioned as a service club. The building provided accommodations for sixteen bachelors, who entered their quarters from inside the building through an attractive arcade. Eight "community garages" with spaces for fifty-eight vehicles served

the officers, with similar facilities offered to married and bachelor NCOs.[17]

As dazzlingly modern as the new quarters might have been, the "concrete houses stood bleakly . . . amid the bare red dirt plains of Wheeler Field." Although the contractors planted grass lawns before the government formally accepted the buildings, the lots were devoid of other vegetation. Some families purchased and planted their own trees and shrubs, but did so in a haphazard and generally unattractive manner. As early as October 1931, Maj. Ernest Clark— commanding the 18th Pursuit Group—called upon the services of then–1st Lt. Donald G. Stitt, an ardent landscape gardener. At March Field in Riverside, California, Stitt had been in charge of beautifying grounds and quarters in addition to his regular Air Corps duties. Put to work by Major Clark at Wheeler, Stitt's talents literally bore fruit. He secured and planted an estimated five thousand shrubs and young trees. In addition to native flowering trees and plants, he set out three or four different types of fruit trees and thirty-five shrubs at each set of quarters. Wheeler soon gained fame for its "natural" horticultural beauty.[18]

Four large barracks completed the final residential portion of the construction project from 1931 to 1933. Barracks Nos. 1 and 2 (Buildings 69 and 66), each

Married officer housing area at the east end of the base, looking north, on 7 May 1935. Six of the forty-two units had reversed floor plans. The five field officer residences at the northern apex of the inner Curtis Loop (Quarters 364–368) were larger, and their two wings extended farther to the rear. Although Curtis Loop was named for aviation pioneer Glenn H. Curtiss, the misspelling was never corrected. **NARA II, 342-FH-3B-21828**

Quarters 305 for a company-grade officer on Wright Avenue, looking north, one of thirty-seven such residences completed and accepted on 21 May 1932. Quarters 304 (facing west) and Quarters 306 (facing east) are in the background on the left and right, respectively. **NARA II, RG 77**

The opulent living room in one of the five field officer quarters on Curtis Loop. **NARA II, RG 77**

The Officers' Club and Bachelor Officer Quarters (Building 302), looking northwest, on 27 April 1932. The main entrance into the lounge (*at far left*) opens off Wright Avenue, which runs left to right across the bottom of the photograph. Wright intersects with Curtis Loop, which passes north alongside the officer apartments. **NARA II, RG 77**

The residential arcade to the rear of the lounge and dining facilities at the Officers' Club, looking north, on 15 July 1932. This architectural feature was most in keeping with the modified Pueblo Style adopted for the earlier buildings at Wheeler Field. **NARA II, RG 77**

The lounge in Wheeler Field's Officers' Club, looking west, 15 July 1932. Note the baby grand piano in the distance at right center and the dining room beyond, with double swinging doors leading into the kitchen. **NARA II, RG 77**

Officers' Garage (Building 308), which serviced Quarters 304-306 and 309, circa September 1933, view looking southwest just off Vought Avenue. The garage had a capacity of six vehicles. Quarters 304 (*left*) and 309 (*right*) are in the distance. **NARA II, RG 77**

accommodating 200 men, had a footprint of 75 by 181 feet. Barracks Nos. 3 and 4 (Buildings 68 and 71), each accommodating 100 men, were half that length. The Construction Division at Fort Shafter drew up the plans for the striking three-story structures, which featured subdued buff stucco exteriors and a resplendent color contrast "secured by [a] red tile roof, apple green trim and polychrome panels in the tower-like corners of the buildings." The solid modernity of the buildings contrasted sharply with the colonialist architectural design at Albrook Field. The four barracks formed a quad at the midpoint of the planned hangar line between Santos-Dumont Avenue to the south and Wright Avenue to the north. The enlisted men of the 75th Service Squadron, the 6th and 19th Pursuit Squadrons, and the 26th Attack Squadron looked forward to residing in Wheeler's state-of-the-art facilities once they were completed in June 1932.[19]

The quarters constructed during the earlier 1930s all evoked the Pueblo style, with rounded arches and exterior stucco walls. The arcaded entrance to the Bachelor Officer Quarters was particularly successful in that regard, although the exteriors of the quarters were less convincing, particularly the 100-Man

One of four permanent barracks built during the early 1930s, 200-Man Barracks No. 1 (Building 69) lies just beyond Santos-Dumont Avenue, looking west across the street from Hangar 2. Two small parking lots (one of them at the front left) served the entire barracks quadrangle. 200-Man Barracks No. 2 (Building 66) is in the background to the right. **NARA II, RG 77**

100-Man Barracks No. 4 (Building 71), across from Santos-Dumont Avenue in the foreground, 23 May 1932. 100-Man Barracks No. 3 (Building 68) is to the north, behind and to the right, on slightly higher ground. **NARA II, RG 77**

and 200-Man Barracks, which merely applied arches and stucco to a more modern design.[20]

As Wheeler's quarters and barracks neared completion, a second building phase commenced on 7 December 1931, to include construction of technical buildings and miscellaneous improvements to the landing field, as follows:

Hangars	(Buildings/Hangars 1–4)
Air Corps Warehouse	(Building 21)
Air Corps Machine Shop	(Building 23)
Air Corps Assembly Shop	(Building 24)

Wheeler's hangars were first in the queue. As noted earlier, the design of the hangars (Hangars 1–4, west to east) was identical to those at Albrook Field. Each hangar had two aircraft bays, one on each side, separated by a wide passageway called the "central office core." Each building had a steel framework covered by tinted and waterproofed exterior masonry and plaster. The roof was made of corrugated metal sheeting, and side "walls of steel sash extend[ed] from the eaves girt down to somewhat below mid-wall height." Concrete blocks formed the lower wall. Though the hangars were sufficient for the diminutive pursuit ships of the early 1930s, the two bays and

the connecting passageway measured only 120 by 243 feet. The two-story central core provided office space and storage. Stairs accessed a second-floor mezzanine with an operations office facing the landing field and a series of interior observation windows to observe activities in the aircraft bays. The pockets for the hangar doors on the front of the buildings lacked the ornamental Art Deco features the hangars at Hickam Field would exhibit later in the decade; Wheeler's quartet of hangars definitely embraced function over flair. The hangars' rear doors did not open completely, and thus required no pockets.[21]

The Air Corps Warehouse, Machine Shop, and Assembly Shop—apart from being of a single-bay design and having different entrances and compartmentalization—were "similar to other plans for buildings of like nature constructed at other flying fields throughout the country." The three buildings were substantially larger than the hangar pairs and had a third again as much square footage. A two-track spur from the Oahu Railway serviced the shops and warehouse.[22]

On 12 February 1932, two months after work started on the new hangar line, contractors broke ground on a second group of support buildings:

Hangar 1—patterned after identical structures at Albrook Field in Panama—lies at the western end of Wheeler's hangar line, looking northeast, 7 January 1933. Note the awning over the entry to the two-story central office core between the aircraft bays on either side. Unit storage, offices, and squadron/group operations occupied the core, which also featured a second-floor mezzanine with windows looking into the aircraft bays. Pockets on the right and left held the hangar's doors, which rolled east and west, away from the central office core. **NARA II, RG 77**

The Air Corps Machine Shop (Building 23), one of a pair of buildings at the west end of the hangar line. Along with its companion building—the Air Corps Assembly Shop (Building 24; out of view to the right)—the Machine Shop is often misidentified as an oversized hangar with pockets and doors opening onto the flight line to accommodate aircraft. The window glazing that extends nearly to ground level and the standard entryways cut into the sides and rear of the buildings are distinctive. The third building in the background to the left—the Air Corps Warehouse (Building 21)—had no hangar-type rolling doors. **NARA II, RG 77**

Dispensary	(Building 67)
Radio Building	(Building 29)
Parachute Building	(Building 25)
Fire Station/Guard House	(Building 64)
Quartermaster Garage	(Building 61)
Quartermaster Utilities Shops	(Building 62)
Air Corps Warehouse	(Building 21)

By year's end all the structures were complete. Except for the large garage and the utilities shops, the buildings were of "modified Spanish design"—in some instances quite heavily modified, with only the tile roof and stucco exterior indicative of such a style. With its rounded arches, Wheeler's Dispensary resembled the style more than the other buildings.

Wheeler's Dispensary (Building 67), looking south across Wright Avenue, circa May 1933, shortly after completion. Barracks No. 1 and Hangar 2 are in the background to the right. The rounded arches are typical of the Pueblo Style. **NARA II, RG 77**

The Fire Station/Guard House (Building 64), looking northwest, on 5 January 1933. The second floor included dormitory space for the firefighters and guards; prisoner cells for serious offenders were in the annex to the rear. The back end of the Air Corps Utilities Shops is at the far left. **NARA II, RG 77**

The component buildings of Wheeler's Post Exchange complex (Building T-70) at the corner of Chanute Road and Santos-Dumont Avenue, looking southeast, in early 1941. A spacious restaurant with a lunchroom (and probably the beer garden) is at the center. The two-story store is to the right, and a tailor shop, barbershop, and shoe shop are in the building at the far right. The structures show the cobbled-together nature of the facility. Barracks No. 4 is in the background to the left. **NARA II, RG 77**

Its footprint of 5,380 square feet restricted its use to minor surgeries and illnesses; more serious cases were transferred to the General Hospital at Schofield Barracks. The Fire Station/Guard House was similar to the one that would be built at Hickam Field, in that the engine house for two trucks was in front and cells for thirty-one prisoners were in the rear wing.[23]

The last major building project from the earlier 1930s was the Administration Building (Building 75). Begun on 12 December 1932 and completed ten months later, the structure lay on the south side of Wright Avenue, centered between the officer and noncommissioned officer residential loops. The Hawaiian Department's engineers at Fort Shafter prepared a design that called for "a two-story structure with a partial basement development under the west end for transformers and night lighting equipment and a meteorological room in a penthouse on the main roof." A twelve-foot-wide ambulance garage sat on the east end of the building. The first floor housed an assembly room, base operations, and other office space. The second floor featured a courtroom and

The Headquarters Building (Building 75) at Wheeler Field on 22 August 1939, looking southeast from Wright Avenue. Note the revolving beacon atop the large penthouse on the main roof. To the right of the beacon is a weather data collection station and a glassed-in observation tower. **NARA II, 342-FH-3B-21838**

offices for the base commander, executive officer, and adjutant.[24]

Wheeler's early development also included efforts to "facilitate and coordinate the use of the hangars with the landing field." Accordingly, contractors poured a concrete apron of variable width along the hangar line and in front of the shop buildings west of the hangars. "Runways" measuring 150 feet by 275 feet connected the aprons in front of each hangar pair to the turf landing field. The project also provided aircraft wash racks at the rear entrance of each hangar.[25]

Even before the construction projects of the early 1930s were completed, the Hawaiian Department recognized the need for illumination at Wheeler Field. After the department's air officer modified plans submitted by the Material Section at Wright Field, Ohio, installation of a night lighting system moved forward on 7 January 1933. The system consisted of field boundary and obstacle lights, a neon-lit wind tee, floodlights, a rotating beacon atop the third-story penthouse roof of the Administration Building, and an electrical equipment room in the basement. A desk for remote control of the night

A field boundary light at Wheeler. **NARA II, RG 77**

The control table for the night landing system, 1 September 1933, located at the south end of the second floor of the central core in Hangar 4. Note the wind direction indicator on the left side of the control table. **NARA II, RG 77**

Wheeler Field, looking northeast, on 21 August 1933, shortly after completion of the field's expansion. The presence of the technical buildings, aircraft on the aprons along the hangar line, and "runways" leading from the hangars onto the turf landing mat indicate that the transition of men and equipment from the original buildings (out of the picture at right) is already under way. The first row of structures on the flight line (*left to right*) are the Air Corps Machine Shop; the Air Corps Assembly Shop; the Parachute Building; and Hangars 1, 2, 3, and 4. In the second row are the Air Corps Warehouse, the Quartermaster Garage, the Utilities Shops, the Photo Laboratory, the Fire Station, and the quadrangle with the four barracks and Dispensary. Note the tents to the west and the Headquarters Building far to the east. In the rear is the NCO and married officer housing. Schofield Barracks lies beyond. **NARA II, 342-FH-3B-21809**

The last components of Wheeler's lighting system, 2 October 1935, looking west. The zone bars atop the ridgelines of Hangar 4 were also affixed to Hangar 3 (just out of the picture at the upper left). Together with the octagonal array of "safe and danger" landing lights (visible at the upper left center), the zone bars provided a clear signal as to the orientation of the hangar line and its position relative to the landing mat. **NARA II, 342-FH-3B-21830, cropped**

One of the floodlight arrays erected in the vicinity of Hangar 4 (out of the picture to the left), looking north toward the Headquarters Building, 8 August 1933. Note the beacon atop the penthouse and the ambulance garage just visible on the right side of the building. **NARA II, RG 77**

View looking past the east bay of Hangar 4, probably during the 1930s. Note the NO SMOKING sign and the 19th Pursuit Squadron sign at center, and the field illumination floodlights in the distance. **Cressman**

landing system was installed in the second-floor operations office in Hangar 4.[26]

Although the primary night-lighting system was complete as of 19 July 1933, the signal lights were not operable until 14 March 1935. The lights consisted of four "zone bars" mounted on the roof ridgelines on each of the four bays of Hangars 3 and 4. Contractors also erected a safe/danger "landing circle" of thirty alternating red and green lights mounted on an octagonal pipe framework atop the roof of Hangar 4. Controls for the signal lights were in Hangar 4 and in the penthouse of the Administration Building. The Army added other system controls and enhancements to the floodlight array during the summer of 1937.[27]

The expansion of Wheeler Field recommended by the Hawaiian Department's board of officers in 1927 was finally complete. The base, although still part of Schofield Barracks administratively, was far removed from the primitive 1921 facility of blimpy

Bessonneau hangars that evoked America's early barnstorming era. Expansion of Army aviation on Oʻahu and the threat of war foretold more changes to come for the Hawaiian Department's principal pursuit base.

First Permanent Buildings Demolished: 1932–1936

For the rest of the 1930s the men at Wheeler Field and their families enjoyed a welcome respite from the noise and clutter of building construction. With the completion of the greatly enlarged base (except for the Administration Building) in December 1932, the way was clear for men and matériel to move across the field to the modern new installation. Demolition then commenced, with the northwest building of the old six-hangar array the first to be removed. By October 1933 the Army had razed all the old structures to the south except for the easternmost pair of hangars, leaving behind four concrete platforms where the buildings had been. The pace of demolition slowed

during 1934, leaving the last two orphaned hangars intact—though on borrowed time—as warehouses.[28]

In 1936, the need to free space for the grass landing mat in front of Wheeler's new hangar line mandated removal of the base's two remaining steel-framed hangars, which sat some five hundred yards from the east terminus of the parking apron. A general contractor—the Russian Art Metal Shop— salvaged a portion of the steel framework from the hangars for possible use at Hickam but reserved the corrugated roofing and siding, along with some of the steel sash and supporting members, for use at Wheeler. By 7 May, the demolition was complete and the steel had been delivered to Hickam Field, which was then in the initial stages of construction.[29]

Construction: 1939–1941

Amid rising concern over Japan's aggression in the Far East in the latter 1930s, the War Department decided to modernize and expand the air forces and aviation establishments in the Philippine and

Steel girders and uprights salvaged from Wheeler Field's two remaining original hangars lie along the shore near Iroquois Point on the west side of the Pearl Harbor Entrance Channel in early 1936. View looks northeast toward the Pearl Harbor Navy Yard's Coaling Plant, Radio Masts, and Lower Oil Tank Farm on the opposite side of the channel. **NARA II, RG 77**

The Cantonment, looking northwest, circa October 1939. Barracks T-90 and T-89 are out of the picture at left, and Barracks T-81 through T-87 (*left to right*) are in the background at the center right. The Mess Hall (Building T-88) is the T-shaped structure in the foreground, and the Latrine (Building T-96) is in the background at left. Grading for the NCO quarters is under way in the far background at right, dating this image to the fall of 1939. **NARA II, RG 77, collage**

The Cantonment, looking east, on 10 October 1941. Thirty-six tents—housing more than two hundred *additional* men in a cantonment designed for just over three hundred—clog the formerly open area beside Barracks Nos. 1 and 2 at top, putting pressure on the limited mess and latrine facilities. **NARA II, 80-G-279373, cropped**

Hawaiian Departments. Although Wheeler Field had been updated earlier in the decade, further expansion of operations would require additional facilities. Accordingly, via the Supplemental Military Appropriation Act (FY 1940) and other legislation, Congress authorized $1,713,607 for Wheeler's expansion. The Army expended just under $1,373,000 from August 1939 to January 1941 on projects ranging from new quarters (both temporary and permanent) to a new fuel storage system.[30]

The first substantial project during Wheeler's 1939–41 expansion was construction of a cantonment to house three hundred troops just west of Barracks Nos. 1 and 2. The Cantonment consisted of fourteen wooden barracks—each housing twenty-two men—a latrine, and a kitchen and mess hall. All the buildings had screened doors and windows and rested on footings of concrete blocks. The buildings were designed to be broken down in ten-foot sections "for reuse later at airfields on the outlying islands." The project proceeded with amazing celerity; the Cantonment was completed in just over five weeks.[31]

Only five days after work on the Cantonment began, crews with earth-moving equipment commenced a three-month project of grading and

Grading for the married NCO duplexes was well under way in late 1939, as seen from the corner of Strieber Avenue (*lower right*) and Chanute Road (out of the picture to the left). The automobile in the background at left is parked on Haley Avenue—the east–west thoroughfare separating the two blocks of future housing. In the distant background at left are Hangar 1 and the Cantonment. Other support buildings (*left to right*) are the Fire House, the Parachute Building, the Assembly Shop, the Quartermaster Garage, and the Air Corps Warehouse. **NARA II, RG 77**

Quarters 279-A/B on Strieber Avenue, looking north—one of thirty-seven NCO duplexes completed in 1940. Wheeler's boundary with Schofield Barracks lies just beyond the quarters' backyards. **NARA II, RG 77**

leveling the terrain east and west of the existing officer and NCO housing, respectively, to prepare for construction of additional married housing in those two areas. Contractors also overlaid portions of the two graded sites with courses of crushed rock in preparation for extending the residential road net. Work on thirty-seven sets of duplexes for married NCOs started on 25 October 1938 and was completed on 20 August 1940. The interiors of the duplexes had painted concrete floors and plastered walls, and the exteriors were painted cinderblock. Each unit featured "an entrance porch, kitchen, breakfast nook, living room, two bedrooms, and a connected bath." The grading for the officers' quarters on the east end of the base was completed as well, although the Army delayed construction on that portion of the project.[32]

NCO duplexes, looking east, 28 December 1941. Quarters 279-A/B is the duplex closest to the left edge of the photograph. **NARA II, 342-FH-3B-48707, cropped**

When Wheeler Field first opened for business in 1921, it operated without a control tower, deemed superfluous owing to the lack of competition for the nearby airspace and the relatively low level of aerial activity. By 1940, however, the prospect of additional units and air operations mandated a tower to regulate departures and arrivals. Construction on the Control Tower commenced on 20 February 1940 and was completed exactly two months later. The finished structure consisted of "a steel framework supporting [a] wood floored, glass inclosed [sic] control tower on the roof of the existing A.C. Operations Hangar [Hangar 4]." There was sufficient space in the tower for a "mechanism controlling the landing lights [and] flood lights on [the] runways." The tower operators, who had an excellent field of view of the entire landing mat, gained access via a stairway rising from the upper floor of the central core that bisected Hangar 4, a walkway, and a series of ladders to enter along the east face of the tower. The plans called for commercial-grade glass in the window glazing and quarter-inch glass in the sixteen skylight panes.[33]

Wheeler Control Tower atop Hangar 4, looking southwest, circa 20 April 1940. Note the covered stairway that accesses the roof from the office area in the central core and the "safe and danger" landing lights on their supporting framework. **NARA II, RG 77**

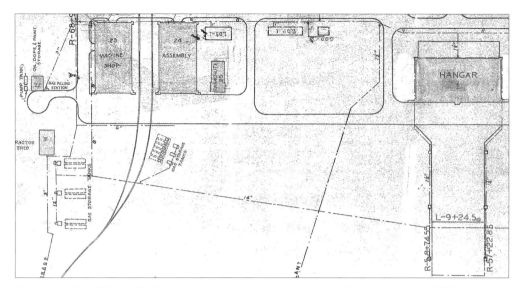

A portion of the Hickam Field water map showing the components of the underground Air Corps Gasoline Fueling System. At the far left are the six 50,000-gallon fuel storage tanks, the tanks of the old 100,000-gallon system just below the Assembly Shop (Building 24), and the six metered fueling pit boxes (three on each side) along the edge of the "runway" extending from Hangar 1, all fed by underground pipework running east from the storage tanks. Also depicted are the water lines underground in the vicinity of the fueling system to safeguard the apron and hangars from gasoline fires. The figure on page 118 shows the location of the pit boxes in an overhead view of Hangars 3 and 4 in later 1941. **Higa**

The additional aircraft that began arriving in 1939 and 1941 taxed Wheeler's facilities, because the Curtiss P-36s and P-40s required far more aviation gasoline than the old Boeing P-12s and P-26s. This in turn led to construction of a new underground Air Corps Gasoline Fueling System to augment the original 100,000-gallon system of ten tanks that had been placed just south of the Assembly Shop at the far western end of the base. The new gasoline storage facility, similar in concept and design to the "Aqua system" already in place at Hickam Field, had a capacity of 300,000 gallons supported by an array of six 50,000-gallon tanks. The new fuel system routed aviation gasoline to six metered "pit boxes" on each of the four "runways" in front of the hangars, for a total of twenty-four distribution points along the

Excavation is under way and forms are in place to pour the concrete-lined valve pits to contain the controls for regulating fuel flow to and from the six 50,000-gallon fuel tanks. **NARA II, RG 77**

Several valve pits with large access doors await backfilling operations in mid-1940. Note the two workmen standing in the structures and other valve pits in the distance to the right. **NARA II, RG 77**

hangar line. Although the system, including fueling pits, was "complete" by September 1940, it is unclear when the pits in front of the hangars went into operation. Nonetheless, the system provided Wheeler with at least the potential for the rapid refueling critical for effective fighter defense.[34]

A more visible construction project was the base's flagpole, which workers completed on 3 September 1940, exactly three months after the Von Hamm–Young Company signed the contract. Located two hundred feet directly north of the Headquarters Building, the seventy-five-foot pole was visible from all points of the base.[35]

The activation of the 14th Pursuit Wing in October 1940, and of the 15th Pursuit Group shortly thereafter, potentially doubled the aircraft and airmen Wheeler had to accommodate and forced further reassessment of Wheeler's facilities. In addition to the permanent quarters then under construction and scheduled for completion in May 1941, a temporary camp for the 15th Pursuit Group's enlisted men was begun in November 1940. Although the camp was ready for occupancy shortly before Christmas, the Mess Hall (Building T-57), three latrines (Buildings T-54, T-55, and T-56), and sixty-four tent floors—the latter fabricated from salvaged lumber—were not completed until 21 January 1941. Unfortunately, the

lack of sufficient real estate near the hangar line forced the builders to place the tents and the mess facilities in two separate areas. The tents and latrines were in the open area immediately behind the Fire House, while the Mess Hall was 350 yards away, across the street

Flagpole near the Headquarters Building, looking south, January 1941. **NARA II, RG 77**

A view of Wheeler's flight line, looking northeast, 26 August 1941, illustrates the difficulties experienced in quartering Wheeler's enlisted population. Three congested tent cities are visible. On the left (behind the Fire Station/Guard House) is the temporary camp intended to house 384 men of the 15th Pursuit Group. Moving up and to the right, another eighteen tents (thirty-six by October) crowd the Cantonment. On the right, large garrison tents and several temporary buildings fill the cramped gap between Hangar 2 and Hangar 3 (the latter just out of the picture to the right). **NARA II, 80-G-279360, cropped**

from and east of the two 100-Man Barracks. Although more permanent quarters were planned, about a thousand men were living in tents in early 1941. During late 1940 or early 1941, and roughly concurrent with erection of the 15th Pursuit Group's camp, an expanse of large tents also sprang up along the flight line in the open area that separated Hangars 2 and 3.[36]

The construction schedules for the two residential building projects still under way in 1940 called for their completion in May 1941. The first of those projects was the Air Corps Barracks (Building 72). Although the three-story "600-Man Barracks" was small in comparison to the enormous, consolidated barracks at Hickam Field, it was nonetheless a massive building exceeding 111,000 square feet, excluding the basement. The barracks lay on Santos-Dumont Avenue just north of Hangars 3 and 4, with a mirror-image structure planned for an adjacent site

The completed three-story, 600-Man Air Corps Barracks (Building 72) looking east from Wright Avenue, 28 October 1941. **NARA II, 342-FH-3B-48703**

just to the east. Completion of the new L-shaped barracks relieved crowded conditions for airmen packed into the Cantonment, other temporary barracks, and still living under canvas. The 15th Pursuit Group's camping area behind the Fire Station was vacant by the first week in October, with some of the tents being moved to the Cantonment and other areas.[37]

Although the 600-Man Barracks was complete, the complex of thirty-eight officer quarters planned for the opposite end of the field was not. Bounded north, south, east, and west by Fenander Avenue, Wright Avenue, Lilienthal Place, and Frutchey Road, the residences occupied two blocks along Wright Avenue. The array of quarters encompassed three ten-unit officer apartments, twenty-five company officer duplexes, and ten field officer quarters of many different designs—accompanied, of course, by the required network of utilities and water/sewer connections. As with the new NCO Quarters to the

west, the Army borrowed liberally from the engineering plan files at Hickam Field to facilitate speedier construction and save on design costs. Although it is uncertain when construction on the project ended, the contractors had a scheduled completion date of 16 May 1941; aerial photographs show all structures in place by 26 August.[38]

Other Wheeler Field Enhancements

During early or mid-1941, one or more companies from the 804th Engineer Aviation Battalion (probably Capt. George E. White Jr.'s Headquarters Company and 1st Lt. Alfred O. Jones' Company A) reported to Wheeler Field from Schofield Barracks to commence work on an extensive network of aircraft revetments, or bunkers, at the eastern and southern limits of the reservation—a reflection of growing concern regarding potential aerial attacks on O'ahu's bases. At least some of the revetments were in place by mid-June.

Wheeler's new married officer housing, completed circa mid-1941, looking northeast, 26 October 1941. Most easily distinguishable are the three U-shaped, ten-unit apartment buildings at left. The remaining structures are a mix of duplexes for company-grade officers and two-story field officer quarters, all built using architectural plans and specifications borrowed from Hickam Field. At far right are two wood-framed bachelor officer barracks for the junior officers transferred during the fall of 1941. Note the baseball grandstand at the lower left. **NARA II, 80-G-279360, cropped**

Wheeler's aircraft revetments, 26 October 1941. The earthen bunkers paralleled Wright Avenue and the recently constructed officer housing at left, turned and hugged the west side of Kamehameha Highway, and then followed the Oahu Railway spur that serviced Wheeler's Machine and Assembly Shops. Note the alternative design of the revetments at the upper left, consisting only of parallel excavations rather than U-shaped berms.
NARA II, 80-G-279372, cropped

By 21 August, 109 revetments of various configurations and construction ran south along the new Kamehameha Highway from its intersection with Wright Avenue, then turned southwest and west, following the Oahu Railway's serpentine right-of-way south of the landing field. Most of the revetments accommodated a single aircraft, although twenty-six were designed to provide space for two. Almost all were three-sided berms opening toward the west and north. A limited number appear to have been parallel excavations that allowed aircraft to enter at one end and exit from the other.[39]

During the early summer of 1941, paving contractors began extending Wheeler's parking aprons southward from the hangars toward the landing mat, and to the west from Hangar 4 toward the Assembly Shop and Machine Shop. Not only were the areas between the old hangar runways of March 1933 to be filled in by the westward extension, but the pavement was also—as originally envisioned during the early 1930s—to extend south four hundred feet from the hangar line. By late summer the new apron was approximately half finished and fronted Hangars 3 and 4, extending west to the midpoint of Tent City at the center of the hangar line. By mid-October, portions of the new pavement stretched past Hangars 1 and 2 to the Parachute Building. Although it is uncertain how far the apron reached by December 1941, aerial photographs suggest that it extended to the Assembly Shop west of the hangar line.[40]

During the last six months of 1941, barracks for both enlisted men and bachelor officers, office space,

warehouses, theaters, and chapels were constructed on the formerly open spaces on the base. By the end of the year, following expenditure of millions of dollars, Wheeler's prewar development was largely in place. The primitive backwater "amid the red dirt plains" of central O'ahu had become "an ideal spot." Attractive quarters, tropical breezes, and lush vegetation notwithstanding, however, the degree to which Wheeler Field might fulfill its mission of protecting O'ahu would depend on more mundane operational considerations that would come to a head during 1941.

Paving of Wheeler's parking aprons is nearly finished on 10 October 1941. The most recently paved area stops just short of the Assembly and Machine Shops at the bottom of the photograph. Note the location of the valve pits for the six underground 50,000-gallon gasoline storage tanks, just to the right of the checkerboard-roofed building at the bottom center. **NARA II, 80-G-279373, cropped**

Layout of Wheeler Field showing the status of the base, the aircraft parking apron, and its prominent landmarks on 7 December 1941. **Di Virgilio**

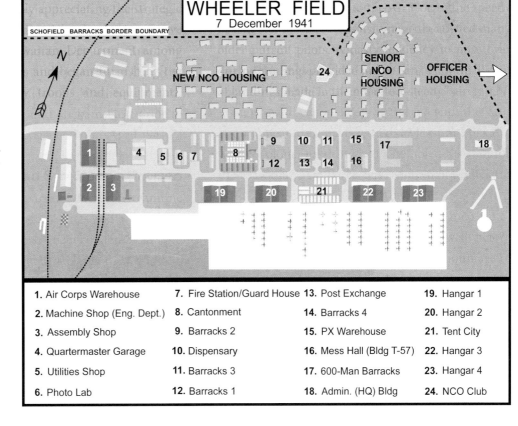

WHEELER FIELD
7 December 1941

SCHOFIELD BARRACKS BORDER BOUNDARY

NEW NCO HOUSING

SENIOR NCO HOUSING

OFFICER HOUSING

1. Air Corps Warehouse	7. Fire Station/Guard House	13. Post Exchange	19. Hangar 1
2. Machine Shop (Eng. Dept.)	8. Cantonment	14. Barracks 4	20. Hangar 2
3. Assembly Shop	9. Barracks 2	15. PX Warehouse	21. Tent City
4. Quartermaster Garage	10. Dispensary	16. Mess Hall (Bldg T-57)	22. Hangar 3
5. Utilities Shop	11. Barracks 3	17. 600-Man Barracks	23. Hangar 4
6. Photo Lab	12. Barracks 1	18. Admin. (HQ) Bldg	24. NCO Club

Chapter Two

"NOTHING BUT A PROFUSE GROWTH OF SUGAR CANE AND GUAVA BUSHES"

The Development of Bellows and Haleiwa Fields

On 31 January 1917, with the Great War in its third year, the heretofore neutral United States broke diplomatic relations with the German government three days after Germany declared unrestricted submarine warfare. The "grace period" lasted only until U-boats sank four unarmed American merchantmen in mid-March of that year.[1]

President Woodrow Wilson quickly signed several executive orders related to the defense of the United States. Executive Order 2565, "Order of Withdrawal of Certain Public Lands for Military Purposes; Waimanalo, Hawaii," signed on 28 March 1917, purchased approximately "1,510 acres of 'Crown lands' [from Kamehameha III] at Waimanalo, District of Koolaupoko, Island of Oahu, Territory of Hawaii." The land, designated the Waimanalo Military Reservation, was "set aside for military purposes." Five days later, President Wilson appeared before a joint session of Congress and requested a declaration of war, and on 6 April a state of war existed between the United States and the Central Powers.[2]

Early History and Development of Bellows Field

The Waimanalo Military Reservation, located along the shore of Waimānalo Bay, occupied "a nearly level stretch of white coral sand (with some coral rock) varying from 10 to 20 feet above the level of the Pacific Ocean." A knoll at the center of the reservation rose to a height of 55 feet, and an elevated ledge of volcanic rock near the reservation's northern boundary jutted into the sea to form Wailea Point. The area's most prominent geographical feature, the "jagged and picturesque" Koʻolau Mountain Range, rising from 1,600 to 3,100 feet, lay off the reservation to the west about 3 miles inland. The rich and fertile plain that stretched from the shore, through the reservation, to the mountains proved ideally suited for sugarcane cultivation. The abundant rainfall on the island's windward shore created a lush environment far different from the dusty conditions that prevailed on the leeward coast of Oʻahu west of Pearl Harbor.[3]

Existing documents do not indicate how the Army initially utilized its new real estate. Six years after the executive order that set aside the land, however, the Waimanalo Sugar Company still cultivated sugarcane on a 229-acre parcel leased from the War Department. The site was first mentioned in Army Air Service newsletters in a June 1926 announcement that "the new gunnery range at the Waimanalo Military Reservation . . . was officially opened by the 6th Pursuit Squadron on April 19th last." The Air Service constructed a line of targets and, at some point, a "large emergency field" where pilots could land and clear jammed guns. Previously, pursuit aircraft from Wheeler Field had used "a curved sandpit near Fort Kamehameha" for target practice—an arrangement deemed "very unsatisfactory" because of the poor visibility and high winds there.[4]

Although the conditions near Waimānalo Bay were an improvement over those at Fort Kamehameha, the early aerial gunnery runs were not altogether without incident. On 26 April 1926—only a week after the range opened—2nd Lt.

Harry C. Wisehart experienced engine failure while attempting to clear a gun jam. Wisehart survived a water landing and swam back to the beach. The fact that Wisehart had not tried to land before clearing the jammed gun implies that the construction of the "large emergency field" likely followed that mishap. The date when the strip came into use for pilot training is unknown.[5]

In addition to training, the landing strip proved useful for the Air Corps men who used the reservation as a summer rest camp. The first such recorded use came in October 1928 when squadrons of the 5th Composite Group at Luke Field began two-week rotations to Waimānalo. First to make the trip east was the 23rd Bombardment Squadron, with all 116 men and their "tents, poles, rolling kitchens and mascots" being ferried to the windward shore by air. The 72nd Bombardment Squadron and other units followed, with the 23rd Squadron's Martin bombers providing transportation. The squadrons

Waimanalo Range Landing Field, the original emergency landing strip that supported the reservation's gunnery range, looking north, 1 June 1933. **AFHRA**

The Air Corps Range Camp at Bellows Field, circa 1936, looking north. The short runway that replaced the emergency strip is out of the image at the upper left. The Mess Hall adjoins the tent city on the right, with the Latrine at the lower center, and the Officers' Building atop the hill at the far left. Note the pursuit squadron from Wheeler Field—mostly P-12s—along the photograph's upper margin. **NARA II, RG 77**

One of thirty tents (No. 15) erected on platforms in the Air Corps Range Camp, looking south toward the parking area and the Ko'olau Mountains. A course of siding rises from the floor to keep the worst of the windblown rain out of the four-man tent. **NARA II, RG 77**

traveled light, so the evolutions—landings included—consumed only three hours.[6]

The Air Corps began constructing facilities to support regular air operations at the reservation in the spring of 1931, establishing a temporary work camp with "soldier labor." Difficulties with moving lumber over the "steep Pali grade" delayed the project, but construction of the Air Corps Range Camp finally began on 29 April 1931. The camp was completed in July, and the department's pursuit squadrons immediately began "gunnery practice season[s]" there.[7]

The Air Corps Range Camp consisted of a tent city, kitchen, mess hall, latrines, and an officers' barracks. The tent city of thirty pyramidal tents on wooden platforms was in two rows (Buildings 1–30), with each sixteen-foot-square tent resting on eight concrete piers. The thirty-by-sixty-foot Officers' Building (Building 33) sat atop the reservation's

Parking lot at the former Air Corps Range Camp. Bellows continued to use the tents as quarters for squadrons engaged in gunnery practice during the months just prior to the war. The trees contrast sharply with the camp's otherwise desolate appearance circa 1940 or 1941—judging from the light-colored, late model Plymouth convertible (*lower left*) and Buick coupe (*lower center*). **Aiken, NMPW**

The Officers' Building (Building 33) nearing completion in January 1936, looking north toward the sea from the brow of the hill that overlooks the runway off to the left. The windows wrapping around the right face of the quarters and turning left along the east side ensured the occupants had a sea breeze. **NARA II, RG 77**

The enlisted Mess Hall and Kitchen (Building 31), January 1936, down the hill and upwind from the Latrine, looking north. Note the kitchen's three chimneys at the structure's far right. **NARA II, RG 77**

central knoll overlooking the tent city from the west. The Kitchen and Mess Hall for the enlisted airmen (Building 31) lay at the southern end of the U-shaped tent area. A temporary latrine (Building T-32), thoughtfully placed downwind from the residential/mess areas, completed the camp. The Kitchen and Mess Hall, each of the tents, and the Officers' Building all had electricity, and all structures except

the tents had water connections. The camp accommodated 16 officers and 120 enlisted men—sufficient to support deployment of a squadron.[8]

Late in the summer of 1931, the 50th Observation Squadron deployed to the reservation for two weeks of training that emphasized low-altitude bombing. Periodic rain squalls and the trade winds whipping in from offshore made it necessary to stake down

The new runway at Bellows Field in its original configuration (as indicated by the inked lines on the original print), looking northeast toward Waimānalo Bay, circa 1935. To the right, construction of the tent platforms in the camp is nearing completion, though without tents or palm trees. **NARA II, RG 77**

aircraft at night behind the line of sand dunes. During the deployment, department commander Maj. Gen. William Lassiter visited the camp and witnessed an "attack" on the shore of Waimānalo Bay by the entire 18th Composite Wing.[9]

While the airfield was still awaiting a name, a small but significant spate of construction took place in early 1933, having been authorized more than a year earlier in October 1931. The first of two projects to reach completion in January 1933 was a new runway (Building 49) south of the old emergency strip. The new strip, 983 feet long and 75 feet wide, was built atop 10 inches of coral rock and had a rolled, oiled surface. Five weeks later, contractors finished a small shop and storeroom (Building T-37) with space for aircraft repairs. For the time being, the construction of tactical buildings at the Waimanalo Reservation was complete.[10]

On 19 August, per General Orders No. 8 (1933 series), the War Department named the landing field

Barren, windswept Bellows Field during its early years. **Cressman**

Bellows' Shop and Storeroom (Building T-37) in November 1935, looking north along the road passing west of the tent camp. The building's modest size reflects the base's equally modest maintenance requirements in 1935. Note the peaks of the Ko'olau Mountains in the distance on the left. **NARA II, RG 77**

at the Waimanalo Military Reservation Bellows Field after a World War I aircraft observer and recipient of the Distinguished Service Cross.[11]

Second Lt. Franklin Barney Bellows of the 50th Aero Squadron and his pilot, 2nd Lt. David C. Beebe, took off on a morning reconnaissance mission on 13 September 1918 on the second day of the St.-Mihiel offensive in northeastern France. Weather

2nd Lt. Franklin Barney Bellows, circa 1918. **15WHO**

conditions were exceedingly poor, with "clouds, high wind and mist," but Beebe held fast at nine hundred feet, flying without the protection of accompanying fighters. Although German batteries in and behind the lines subjected the low-flying aircraft to heavy fire, the Americans penetrated five miles into enemy territory before Beebe reversed course and returned behind friendly lines with a severely damaged engine. Although Beebe survived the mission, 2nd Lieutenant Bellows had suffered mortal wounds from the German fire and died shortly after Beebe landed. For their "extraordinary heroism in action," each of the officers received the Distinguished Service Cross.[12]

The Army used Bellows—known semiofficially as Waimanalo Military Reservation, Bellows Field—for purposes quite apart from aviation in the following years. Infantry units bivouacked on the site, as did the Coast Artillery. "A line of 90 [millimeter] guns along the beach, usually 14 to 25," likely fired at targets placed offshore to avoid putting the tents set up "on the opposite side of the road" in the line of fire. Apart from the landing strip and targets for strafing and bombing practice, the reservation remained "nothing but a profuse growth of sugar cane and guava bushes."[13]

Later Development at Bellows

A series of extensions to the runway proved to be a turning point in Bellows Field's prewar development. Although the skimpy documentary evidence provides no detailed chronology, aerial photographs from the period demonstrate that most of the runway extensions took place prior to January 1938, as the results of at least three separate paving projects are visible in aerial photographs from 1938 and October 1941. These extensions brought the runway to its configuration of late 1941: approximately 2,800 feet long and 150 feet wide.[14]

Additional development during 1935–38 included quarters for noncommissioned officers, the Dispensary (Building T-38), the Operations Office (Building T-43), and the Post Exchange (Building T-59). All the buildings were temporary wooden structures, in keeping with the transitory and limited nature of assignments

Bellows Field, 10 January 1938, looking southwest, as the project of lengthening the runway neared completion. The original Air Corps Range Camp (*far left*) is visible, augmented by additional buildings at the base of the hill, facing the runway at the center. Note the Waimānalo Plantation Village on the upper left, with the sugar mill at top left center. **AFHRA**

The somewhat primitive Operations Office (Building T-43), circa March 1938, looking south. The building, about two hundred feet from the runway, faced northwest. By 1941, two longitudinal additions extended the structure southwest and more than doubled its size. Note the wind tee behind the unidentified building at the upper right. **NARA II, RG 77**

Post Exchange (Building T-59), located down the hill and in front of the Officers' Building. View looks west. **NARA II, RG 77**

Bathhouse at the officers' beach. **NARA II, RG 77**

at Bellows Field. New and improved amenities along the reservation's beachfront enhanced the site's reputation as a tropical paradise, with beach umbrellas, pergolas, barbeques, and bathhouses dotting the shore along Waimānalo Bay. The officers' beach was just south of Wailea Point, and the enlisted men's beach was farther south.[15]

Construction from 1939 to 1941 introduced the first permanent buildings at Bellows Field, beginning with the Entrance Gate (Building 55), completed in April 1939. A far cry from the Art Deco splendor of the entrances at Hickam Field and Schofield Barracks, the gate's characteristics reflected the function-oriented, no-frills atmosphere at Bellows. The native volcanic

Typical beach umbrella on the enlisted men's beach at Bellows. **NARA II, RG 77**

A thatched pergola on the enlisted men's beach provides shade from the midday sun. **NARA II, RG 77**

Bellows Field Entrance Gate (Building 55), June 1940. Sentry boxes on either side of the entrance have two small ornamental bombs atop two taller columns. The location was just north of a T intersection of a primary road leading west to the Waimānalo Plantation Village that ran south of the airfield. The sign just right of the entryway reads, NO ONE ADMITTED TO OFFICERS' BEACH WITHOUT A PASS. **NARA II, RG 77**

The Main Camp Storehouse (Building 45), circa June 1940, looking southwest. Completed in December 1938, this structure built of native stone was one of very few prewar buildings at Bellows intended to be permanent. The aerological apparatus on the roof indicates that the Storehouse and the adjoining structure on the right might already have been in use as the base headquarters. **NARA II, RG 77**

As other storehouses and barracks were erected at Bellows Field, the Detachment Barracks (Building 59, seen here) and the Main Camp Storehouse were converted to the base headquarters, with a gabled breezeway connecting the two buildings. View looks southwest, June 1940. **NARA II, RG 77**

Bellows Field Control Tower (Building T-63), looking south, June 1941, with the west corner of the Officers' Building along the image's left margin. The tower's limited height was not critical because the building stood atop the hillside overlooking the airfield. **NARA II, RG 77**

rock incorporated into the Storehouse (Building 45) and the Detachment Barracks (Building 57)—finished in late 1938 and April 1940, respectively—represented a departure from the wood and canvas typical of Bellows' "architecture" for most of the 1930s. The field's Control Tower (Building T-63), however, completed on New Year's Day 1941, was a return to the flimsy but functional conventions of earlier years.[16]

More changes and upgrades for the Waimanalo Military Reservation were in the wind for 1941. On 5 April, Lt. Gen. Walter C. Short, commanding general, Hawaiian Department, sent a letter to the War Department via "'Clipper' Air Mail" requesting funds for several construction projects at Bellows Field. Among other items, Short proposed a permanent control tower and an Aqua aviation fuel–delivery system. Enlargement of the field's runway

to 3,400 feet and construction of a second, longer runway measuring 5,000 by 300 feet, however, constituted the most pressing requirement.[17]

In the spring of 1941, the Hawaiian Air Force transferred the O-47Bs of the 86th Observation Squadron to Bellows to open space on Wheeler Field's aprons. The B-18s of the 58th Bombardment Squadron followed three days later, arriving on 9 March at 0700. Both movements were supposed to be permanent transfers for the squadrons, but the crews from the 58th discovered that the landing speed of their new Douglas A-20As was too hot for the length of Bellows' runway, and the squadron moved to Hickam Field on 29 April.[18]

Until the summer of 1941, Bellows Field still existed as a satellite of Wheeler Field, with airmen on detached service from Wheeler and Hickam Fields performing the administrative functions at Bellows. The first commanding officer (or NCO-in-charge, under the 18th Air Base Group) of Bellows Field was TSgt. Salvatore Torre, who would be moved permanently to Bellows Field with the 86th Observation Squadron in November 1941.[19]

On 22 July 1941, General Orders No. 42, Headquarters, Hawaiian Department activated Bellows Field as a "separate permanent Military Post." The first officer in command of Bellows as an independent base was Col. William V. Andrews, per Bellows Field General Orders No. 1 issued 25 July 1941. Large-scale physical changes at that time partially displaced the "profuse growth of sugar cane and guava bushes" of the old Waimanalo Military Reservation. By October 1941, earthmoving and grading had begun for a new runway more properly aligned with the prevailing winds. The 5,000-foot runway was set on a line running approximately from 315 degrees to 45 degrees. Two large tent camps and a multitude of temporary buildings went up south of the runway. Elsewhere, south of the old runway's windward terminus there were 16 barracks for 416 enlisted men, 3 mess halls, a post exchange, a 600-man theater, 2 administration

Bellows Field on 10 October 1941. On the left, earthmoving and grading are under way for the new runway that passes at an oblique from far left center toward the lower portion of the image. The oval array of new barracks, storehouses, mess halls, and other buildings at upper right was the last prewar construction at the base. A new tent camp lies to the right of the runway's center point, and housing for the Waimānalo Plantation Village is at bottom right. Note the P-40s of the 78th Pursuit Squadron in the parking area at upper center, to the right of the runway. **NARA II, 80-G-279365**

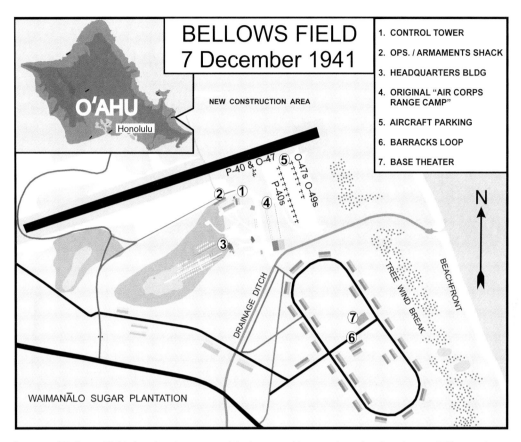

Layout of Bellows Field showing the status of the base and its prominent landmarks as of 7 December 1941. **Di Virgilio**

buildings, an infirmary, a firehouse, a bakery, and 11 storehouses.[20]

Thus, by late 1941, much of the infrastructure at Bellows was either complete or in process, enabling the Hawaiian Air Force to use the base as a relief valve for dispersal of pursuit assets from Wheeler Field—Oʻahu's principal fighter base. The changes could not come quickly enough.

Early History and Development of Haleiwa Field

In addition to enlarging Bellows Field, the Hawaiian Air Force also had plans to transform a small airstrip north of Haleʻiwa Town on the western shore of Oʻahu into a permanent installation. Around the turn of the twentieth century, the old sugar plantation settlement of Waialua adopted the name of the nearby Haleiwa Hotel, which lay near the narrow-gauge Oahu Railway owned by Hawaiian businessman

Benjamin J. Dillingham. After extending his railroad around Kaʻena Point and beyond in order to service a future freight customer just around the northern tip of Oʻahu (the Kahuku Sugar Mill), Dillingham conceived of the hotel as a "planned destination resort" and a way to increase ridership on the railroad. The hotel opened for business in 1899. Eventually, a small landing strip one mile up the coast took its name from Haleʻiwa Town.[21]

The diminutive airfield began as a private landing strip for civilian flight instruction and barnstorming. At some point during 1920s the Army leased the strip, which was first used as a gunnery range in 1928. The 18th Pursuit Group's history notes that "the major portion of the flying training for December 1928 was confined to aerial gunnery on tow targets on ranges Number 1 and 2 at Haleiwa." It is unclear when military aircraft first employed Haleiwa as a landing field, although an Air Corps photograph from 27 April

The Haleiwa Hotel, built by Hawaiian entrepreneur Benjamin J. Dillingham. Despite the locale's natural beauty and the hotel's amenities and sumptuous architectural features, the resort had difficulty competing with the new hotels built in downtown Honolulu and Waikīkī. **Wenger**

1933 shows five Keystone B-6A twin-engine bombers operating from the grass strip. The strip, aligned with the shore and Oʻahu's northeasterly trade winds, was anchored on the northeast shore of Waialua Bay on the south and ran northeast from Puaʻena Point.[22]

The first textual military reference to Haleiwa as a landing field came in August 1935 when, after the Hawaiian Department's maneuvers, two of three flights from the 6th Pursuit Squadron encamped at the little strip while the third flight stayed at the Navy Mooring Mast on the old Cecil Hemp Plantation west of Pearl Harbor. The primitive conditions at Haleiwa were in keeping with the maneuvers' supposed simulation of wartime conditions, but the cool breezes

The earliest known image of Haleiwa Landing Field, looking northeast, at 1030 on 27 April 1933. The area looks much as it would in photographs taken in late 1941. Note the five Keystone B-6A twin-engine bombers present—four on the landing field at the center, and one airborne in the distance. By 1941, units sent to Haleiwa for gunnery practice used the area at lower center (just left of the trees) for their temporary camp. **15WHO**

there proved far more pleasant than the conditions on the dry plains "ewa" (west) of Pearl Harbor. An *Air Corps News Letter* correspondent compared the landscape at the Mooring Mast with "Texas mesquite country," with "Scorpions, Tarantulas and Centipedes substituted for Rattlesnakes." The Haleiwa Landing Field, the correspondent continued, in the field's earliest known description, "is the smallest on Oahu, being about fifty feet wide and a thousand feet long. All the men in 'C' Flight feel that they can land on the Navy Carriers without much trouble." Supplemented by strips of painted tent canvas, the lush vegetation surrounding the field provided effective concealment for the freshly camouflaged Boeing P-12C/E pursuit craft. They proved so difficult to locate from the air, and even the ground, that when department commander Maj. Gen. Hugh A. Drum inspected Haleiwa during the maneuvers, he had to ask, "But where are the airplanes?" Wheeler Field's 6th and 19th Pursuit Squadrons continued their use of Haleiwa as a gunnery training facility during the later 1930s.[23]

On more than one occasion the field's proximity to the beaches of Oʻahu's North Shore prompted airmen to intervene in swimming and boating mishaps offshore to the west, an area renowned for its high waves and rough seas. On 15 February 1936, a boat carrying two soldiers and a civilian "capsized in the rough and shark-infested waters about a mile from shore, placing them in imminent danger of drowning." When the first attempt to rescue the craft's occupants failed, Pvt. Howard N. Bossert of the 19th Pursuit Squadron and SSgt. James W. Mitchell of Company C, 3rd Engineers, from Schofield Barracks took a fourteen-foot outboard boat (probably the field's crash boat) and motored through the rough surf "at great danger to themselves and with much difficulty." Both Bossert and Mitchell received the Soldier's Medal for their initiative and heroism in rescuing the swimmers. On 26 December 1937 Cpl. Paul W. Stone of the 6th Pursuit Squadron swam out alone to rescue an exhausted civilian swimmer amid

"squally weather," and likewise received the Soldier's Medal for his heroism.[24]

Through 1941, Haleiwa had "no permanent detachment . . . no paved runways, and no installations other than boundary marking lights." As early as March 1941, however, the War Department recognized the need to alleviate the crowded conditions at Hickam and Wheeler Fields with "additional first-class airports." Lieutenant General Short proposed enlarging the unimproved facilities at Haleiwa by grading and extending the runway to 4,000 by 300 feet and constructing an operations building and control tower, gasoline storage for 100,000 gallons, an Aqua system for fuel delivery, and a small warehouse for oil storage. Since the Hawaiian Department envisioned "a small permanent detachment to refuel and handle planes on the ground and to operate radio and control installations," Short also requested a combined barracks/mess hall. The price tag for bringing Haleiwa up to standards was $450,000. On 25 June, the War Department authorized Maj. Gen. Henry H. Arnold, chief of the Air Corps, to proceed with the project.[25]

Haleiwa Field, 1941 Development

Although no available records indicate whether material changes had occurred at Haleiwa by the first week in December 1941, such improvements definitely lay ahead. In early November, 1st Lt. Christian R. Meckler, technical supply officer for Wheeler Field's 18th Air Base Group, visited the field to determine the feasibility of a planned "distribution point" there. The air base group devised the setup to facilitate movement of supplies and transform Haleiwa from a mere outpost into a base that could support more robust operations. Specifically, plans called for the 45th, 46th, and 47th Pursuit Squadrons from the 15th Pursuit Group to commence a rotating schedule of two-week stints at Haleiwa.[26]

When squadron rotation from Wheeler kicked off with the arrival of the 45th Pursuit Squadron on 3 November, the 15th Pursuit Group almost certainly provided Meckler with assistance and advice, with

Overhead view of a seemingly vacant Haleiwa Field on 4 September 1941, although close examination reveals intriguing details. The highway and rail line coming from Hale'iwa Town (far out of the image to the left) run from the far lower left to far right, with the railroad below the line of trees and the highway on the opposite, north side. The highway was part of the direct route from Wheeler to Haleiwa Field. At left center, a natural metal Curtiss A-12 (barely discernible) sits about 150 feet from the highway. Left of the A-12 there are numerous discolored patches on the ground in straight lines and at regular intervals—positions where ground crews fueled or maintained aircraft. The photograph of the field from 1933 shows aircraft parked in this very position. **NARA II, 80-G-279357**

help arriving in the form of four aircraft from Wheeler Field on 4 November. Two men from the group's headquarters squadron—Maj. Paul W. Blanchard Jr. and 2nd Lt. Archie L. Roberts Jr.—arrived in a P-36A and an AT-6, accompanied by 2nd Lt. Fred B. Shifflet and 2nd Lt. Jerome R. Sawyer, two P-36A pilots from the 46th Pursuit Squadron. The maintenance requirements of the 45th's P-36As, officers, and men served as an ideal test for Lieutenant Meckler. Apparently, the supply arrangements were satisfactory, with 1st Lt. Edward D. Curry Jr.—the technical supply officer with Wheeler Field's 24th Material Squadron—reporting on 13 November as "Officer-in-Charge of the Distribution Point . . . at Haleiwa Landing Field."[27]

Haleiwa Field, circa mid-to-late 1942, looking west toward Waialua Bay from the highway that passed east of the field. The western tip of the Wai'anae Range trails off at the center of the image, and two P-40Ds or -Es are at the left center; aircraft 373 is in the foreground. The planes occupy the same parking area used by the P-36s and P-40s of the 47th Pursuit Squadron during the first week of December 1941. At that juncture, the tent area for the officers and men was at center just beyond the end of the tree line. Note the undeveloped nature of the field. **Pederson**

Chapter Three

"FERRYING OF NEW AIRCRAFT . . . ASSUMED THE PROPORTIONS OF A MAJOR PROBLEM"

Genealogy of Wheeler Field's Units

Wheeler's air organizations evolved in tune with the field's physical transformation. The days of the 4th Observation Squadron as Wheeler's only tactical unit ended on 1 May 1923. A complicated series of unit arrivals and departures followed, but matters stabilized on 11 January 1927 when the 6th and 19th Pursuit Squadrons reported to Wheeler from Luke Field. Thirteen days later, Hawaiian Department General Orders No. 2 redesignated those two squadrons as the 18th Pursuit Group, which became synonymous with Wheeler Field over the next sixteen years. Another important change to the tactical mix occurred on 1 September 1930 with activation of the 26th Attack Squadron and its attachment to the group. The 75th Service Squadron provided logistical support for the new pursuit group and eventually was elevated in status and designated the 18th Air Base Group, being responsible for overall base administration. This new organizational structure carried the base through the end of the 1930s.[1]

The End of the Biplane Era

The initial deliveries of the Hawaiian Department's last biplane pursuit aircraft predated the construction of the "modern" Wheeler Field in the 1930s. The Boeing Company's P-12 Hawk pursuit ships began arriving on Wheeler's aprons in 1930 and operated there for eight years. The planes' astonishing longevity on Oʻahu resulted from the War Department's failure to reinforce the Hawaiian Department properly during the Great Depression, but also from steady improvements in the P-12's design, with three variants making their appearance over the years.[2]

Delivery of Boeing P-12 Pursuit Planes to Wheeler Field

Variant	First Delivery	Total Delivered
P-12B	25 April 1930	18
P-12C	5 January 1931	20
P-12E	30 November 1931	34

Boeing's P-12 biplane, called "one of the best known fighter series of the between-wars years," was standard equipment for most of the Army's pursuit squadrons during the early 1930s, as well as for many Navy and Marine Corps fighting squadrons (as the F4B). The P-12's armament consisted of either a pair of .30-caliber machine guns or one .30-caliber and one .50-caliber gun. An engine ring-cowl and improved landing gear distinguished the P-12C from the earlier P-12B. The most widely known version of the Boeing fighter was the P-12E, which incorporated a redesigned vertical stabilizer and a tail wheel rather than a skid. The new Panama headrest stored a life raft and protected the pilot in

the event of a land crash in which the aircraft nosed over completely.[3]

Two batches of P-12Bs arrived on Oʻahu in April and May 1930, and twenty P-12Cs followed on 5 January 1931. The P-12s eventually replaced the old PW-9s that Boeing had delivered to the Hawaiian Department in October–December 1925. The thirty-eight P-12B/Cs had an attrition rate of 42 percent for the period ending in August 1936: sixteen crashes resulted in total losses, plus other write-offs. Augmenting the two earlier variants was the later P-12E, which arrived on Oʻahu in dribs and drabs, starting with six new aircraft coming in late 1931, some as cargo on board the SS *Admiral Perry*.[4]

Wheeler Field at the zenith of the biplane era. Approximately twenty-one Boeing P-12E Hawks of the 18th Pursuit Group form an impressive lineup on the apron, facing south in front of the hangar line at the far right. Note the aircraft of the group commander (probably Lt. Col. John C. McDonnell) in the foreground, distinguished by the three diagonal stripes on the fuselage and the group's "Fighting Cock" emblem below the tarpaulin that shields the cockpit from the morning sun. Two aircraft from the group headquarters flight lie to its right, followed by the 19th Pursuit Squadron with the twin-striped squadron commander's aircraft and those of the flight commanders, with single stripes. The Hawks of the 6th Pursuit Squadron lie beyond at the end of the line. Assuming that all the fighters are the P-12E variant, the image dates from April 1936 or later. Along the Waiʻanae Range in the distance, clouds at center enshroud Mount Kaʻala, the highest point of Oʻahu at 4,025 feet. **TLM, P.000,353**

Boeing's Model 218—considered to be the P-12E's prototype—played a role in the Shanghai crisis of 1932. While ferrying a Model 218 from Hongqiao Airport to Nanking on 19 February 1932, American volunteer pilot and adviser to the Chinese Air Force 2nd Lt. Robert McCawley Short ran into a formation of three Japanese fighters and shot down one of them. Three days later he encountered fighters and bombers from the carrier *Kaga*. Short engaged three Mitsubishi B1M Type 13 three-place bombers and killed the Japanese flight commander before he perished in low-altitude combat with Nakajima A1N2 Type 3 fighters.[5]

When Wheeler's eleven surviving P-12Bs were declared obsolete on 1 May 1935, pressure mounted on the War Department to make up the losses. The "new" aircraft, however—two deliveries totaling fifteen additional P-12Es—did not reach the Hawaiian Department until April and July 1936. Nine of the aircraft came from March Field in Riverside, California, presumably owing to the field's proximity to California's port facilities.[6]

Earlier in 1935, finally appreciating the strategic importance of the Hawaiian Islands, the Army gave top priority to the Hawaiian Department among all its overseas garrisons and began furnishing the islands "with necessary troops and equipment."

With respect to Hawai'i's aerial assets, the subsequent steps by Washington came not a moment too soon. By mid-1937, Wheeler had only thirty-four operational fighters on its books. While the percentage of machines down for maintenance at any given time is unknown, it seems reasonable to assume that the Hawaiian Department could count on only twenty-five of the aging fighters being available at any given time to blunt an aerial assault against the islands.[7]

The Monoplane Era Begins: Boeing P-26

The Air Corps decided to replace the increasingly depleted P-12s on O'ahu with another offering from Boeing—the P-26A Peashooter, which by the mid-1930s was standard equipment on the mainland. Boeing's dominance in fighter development for the Army and Navy ended with the P-26A. The sleek, all-metal fighter bridged the gap from the biplane era to the modern aircraft of the immediate prewar years—a period of astonishing advances in military aviation. Although considered a radical departure when it was introduced to the Air Corps, the speedy Peashooter's lack of responsiveness dissatisfied many older pursuit pilots. A nasty tendency to nose over during landings provided more than "a few thrills out of landings made in the none-too-steady" aircraft.[8]

P-26s of the 18th Pursuit Group face north on Wheeler's apron, circa 1938, looking west toward the Wai'anae Range approximately five miles distant. The colors of aircraft PR/39 (18th Pursuit Group, 39th aircraft) in the foreground appear more restrained than those of paint schemes from the earlier 1930s. **TLM, P.000,347**

Even with the tentative decision made to ferry substantial numbers of P-26As to Hawai'i, their transition to O'ahu was agonizingly slow. The Air Corps prepared three recently overhauled P-26As (A.C. Serial Nos. 33-38, 33-60, and 33-83) drawn from units at Barksdale Field, Louisiana. The three disassembled and crated fighters reached Hawai'i on 14 July. Engineers at Wheeler reassembled the Peashooters and "assigned them to squadrons for test[s] to determine their suitability for use in the Hawaiian Department."[9]

With the presumptive go-ahead in hand from the authorities in Hawai'i, in 1938 the Air Corps issued orders for movement of the P-26s to commence from airfields in the continental United States. Other than three planes that originated at Selfridge Field, Michigan, the aircraft came from the 1st and 20th Pursuit Groups at Barksdale Field. In order to pass the best machines available to the Hawaiian Department, the Air Corps selected airplanes that had undergone overhaul at the San Antonio Air Depot an average of less than four months prior to their departure for O'ahu. Upon learning that a large portion of Barksdale's P-26 inventory would soon be a distant memory, the men there "expressed regret over seeing these excellent little planes go" but were consoled by "the rumors of [a] new type of Pursuit ships [P-36As] to be delivered in the future." With the impending equipment upgrade to Curtiss P-36As, busy days lay ahead at Barksdale.

Eventually, forty-two P-26s destined for surface transport from San Diego to Hawai'i arrived on the West Coast. Available records indicate that pilots from the 20th Pursuit Group ferried many of the fighters to the West Coast, with the 77th and 79th Pursuit Squadrons under Maj. Milo N. Clark and Maj. Armin F. Herold shouldering the task for the earlier deliveries. The authorities first gathered the aircraft at Duncan Field near San Antonio, close to the depot's overhaul facilities. Many of the ferry pilots reported from Barksdale Field via Douglas C-33 transport, although Major Clark made the

Maj. Armin F. Herold, commanding officer, 20th Pursuit Group, at Barksdale Field, Louisiana, circa 1937. Herold led the ferry flights to the West Coast for many of the P-26s that made their way to the Hawaiian Department in March 1938. **BAFB, cropped**

three-hour hop in a BT-2CI two-place biplane. After spending the night at Duncan Field the pilots departed on 12 January 1938 for a very full day of flying: from San Antonio to Midland, El Paso, Tucson, and finally March Field, California, where they rested overnight and thawed out from the brutal cold in the open-cockpit fighters. They ended their journey on 14 January with a short leg into Rockwell Field, just across the bay from San Diego. Major Herold led six aircraft on a more leisurely ferrying mission six weeks later, leaving on 28 February and arriving on 5 March.[10]

The Hawaiian Department took delivery of the first batch of twenty aircraft on 9–10 March 1938, and six more arrived on 30 March. A six-month hiatus in deliveries to O'ahu followed. In late July, fourteen P-26s emerged from overhauls in San Antonio and were ferried to California, and the Hawaiian Department accepted delivery on 26 September. The aircraft were processed at the Hawaiian Air Depot at Luke Field and then forwarded to Wheeler.[11]

Although pursuit commanders in Hawai'i welcomed the latest batch of Peashooters—P-26Bs with fuel-injected Pratt and Whitney R-140-33 Wasp engines—the Boeings had been in the Air Corps' inventory for more than three years. The type's service life had reached its zenith and was now tracing a downward trajectory. Further deliveries of new aircraft—specifically the Curtiss P-36A—lay far in the future as tensions rose in the Far East.[12]

Lt. Col. William E. Lynd Takes Command

Five days subsequent to Wheeler's final P-26 delivery, a new commander arrived to replace Maj. Bernard J. Tooher, a short-timer who held the reins for six months in mid-1938. The *Honolulu Star-Bulletin* announced on 13 September 1938 that the incoming commander—Lt. Col. William E. Lynd—was due to arrive on the USAT *Republic* on 1 October. Lynd traveled in company with "noted airmen" Col. Walter H. Frank (incoming commander, 18th Wing) and Lt. Col. Shepler W. Fitzgerald (incoming commander, 5th Bombardment Group), representing a clean sweep of the Hawaiian Department's air leadership.[13]

Born in 1893, William E. Lynd hailed from the west-central Kansas town of Santa Fe. Prior to World War I he attended the University of Washington in Seattle, studied law, and gained admittance to the Idaho bar. He enlisted in the Idaho National Guard on 16 December 1915 and entered federal service with the 2nd Idaho Infantry. Following assignments in North Carolina, New York, and New Jersey, Lynd received a commission in 1917 as a 2nd lieutenant of field artillery; he sailed for Europe late in the year. At a critical juncture in his career in 1918, he entered the Air Service to receive training as an observer and was eventually assigned to the 135th Aero Squadron in France. First Lieutenant Lynd was awarded the Silver Star for his repeated (though unsuccessful) attempts to complete a photographic reconnaissance of a ten-mile-long stretch of the German lines from Montsec to Viéville-en-Haye. Lynd and his pilot made three flights in the face of enemy fighter opposition, abandoning their attempts only when darkness forced them to halt.[14]

After gaining a regular commission in 1920, Lynd completed primary and advanced flight training in 1922 and proceeded through various training commands before receiving orders in 1930 to duty in the Office of the Chief of the Air Corps in Washington. Following a brief tour of duty as the commander of Crissy Field near San Francisco, he took over the 20th Pursuit Group at Mather Field east of Sacramento. During the 1930s Lynd attended the Command and General Staff School, the Army War College, and the Naval War College, graduating from the latter in July 1938, only two months prior to assuming his duties with the 18th Pursuit Group.[15]

Lieutenant Colonel Lynd inherited the 18th Pursuit Group at a time when pursuit aviation in Hawai'i was declining, recent P-26 deliveries notwithstanding. In the year following the arrival of the P-26Bs in September 1938, five operational losses

Lt. Col. William E. Lynd, commanding officer, 18th Pursuit Group (note the group's pin on his shoulder strap), while visiting Hickam Field, circa 1940. The medals on the flap of Lynd's left shirt pocket are the Silver Star (*left*), Mexican Border Service Medal (*center*), and World War I Victory Medal with 3 clasps (*right*). **AFHRA**

reduced Wheeler's P-26 roster to forty planes. The number plummeted to thirty in November after ten planes were transferred to the Philippine Department. By the following spring, the obsolete P-12Es were no longer available even as a stopgap after the remaining twenty-three aircraft were shipped back to the mainland for use as drones and trainers. Aircraft maintenance and overhauls depressed the number of available fighters still further. With yet another shipment of ten P-26As due to depart Hawai'i for the Philippines in early November 1939 and diplomatic relations deteriorating with both Germany and Japan, the Air Corps finally set plans in motion to bolster the island's fighter defenses, although organizational changes within the Hawaiian Department were to occur first.[16]

Wheeler Separates from Schofield Barracks

From its inception through the 1930s, Wheeler Field remained a part of adjacent Schofield Barracks. Although "under the command of the 18th Composite Wing," Wheeler depended on Schofield for "disciplinary, recreational and administrative functions and for all supply except air corps supply." In 1939, however, the Hawaiian Department cut the cord between the airfield and the immense complex to the northwest that had birthed and nourished it. General Orders No. 14 issued by Headquarters, Hawaiian Department on 30 August 1939 established Wheeler "as a permanent military airfield." The next day, Wheeler hosted a separation ceremony in which Maj. Gen. William H. Wilson, commanding the Hawaiian Division, handed the ceremonial key to the base to Brig. Gen. Walter H. Frank, commander of the 18th Wing, who in turn entrusted the token to Lt. Col. William Lynd, Wheeler's commanding officer.[17]

Wheeler did not immediately become self-sufficient. Schofield continued to provide nontactical support services (financial, quartermaster, and medical facilities) during the transition period, although at the time of separation Wheeler established its

own medical unit. By late October, Schofield was still in charge of maintaining Wheeler's quarters, as evidenced by Lieutenant Colonel Lynd's letter of 24 October to Schofield's post commander regarding the ill-conceived flat roofs on the NCO and Officer Quarters. Lynd complained that there was "not a single quarters on Wheeler Field that do not leak badly in several rooms."[18]

The First Curtiss P-36As Arrive

As the aircraft situation at Wheeler grew increasingly critical, the authorities in Washington approved transfer to the Hawaiian Department of twenty Curtiss P-36A Hawks, with fifteen originating from Langley Field in Virginia and five from Selfridge Field, Michigan. The twenty aircraft arrived at the Sacramento Air Depot between 4 and 15 August 1939. Once cleared for overseas service, they were transported to Hawai'i, arriving on 23 October.[19]

Even though the Hawks were roosting at the fringe of obsolescence, the Wheelerites were impressed with planes "reputed to exceed 300 m.p.h. in level flight and to dive at 500 m.p.h." The dazzled correspondent for the *Air Corps News Letter* reported that the sleek metal birds "put the old glint in many an eye." The pilots, accustomed to the outdated P-26s, "were thrilled at their performance." A common complaint regarding the aging Boeings was that their relatively high landing speed did not "lend itself to landing on a sidewalk," an obvious reference to the narrow runway at Bellows Field. The P-36s required less landing space, prompting predictions that "the difficulties experienced at Bellows Field will undoubtedly be diminished."[20]

When war broke out in Europe in September 1939, the War Department decided against sending further fighter reinforcements to Hawai'i, choosing to emphasize American bases in the North Atlantic and Caribbean rather than the Pacific. O'ahu's air assets again stagnated and resumed the slide toward obsolescence. The temporary patch of twenty P-36As delivered in late October would have to suffice, even

Ground crews roll an 18th Pursuit Group P-36A (PR/71)—one of twenty delivered from the mainland in late October 1939—on Wheeler's parking apron, circa 1940. The attractive natural metal finish as much as the type's performance in the air undoubtedly "put the old glint in many an eye." **TLM, P.000,349**

as the aerial forces in place on Oʻahu slipped further behind the curve with each passing month.[21]

A Purely Pursuit Base and a New Pursuit Group

At the close of 1939, the 18th Pursuit Group's dual character—possessing both attack and pursuit squadrons—ended. On 7 December 1939, a letter from the War Department announced that Wheeler's 26th Attack Squadron was to change its designation to the 26th Bombardment Squadron, and the men were to change station "to Hickam Field which building has progressed sufficiently to accom[m]odate

them at that place." The squadron "ceased its tactical flying" the following day after returning at 1045 from a deployment to Bellows Field. Capt. George R. Acheson, a former squadron commander, led the aircraft on a final, though unofficial, review over the base in a Lufbery Circle formation. Each of the crews fired a signal flare in a final salute to their soon-to-be defunct squadron. Pvt. John Woronuk, a passenger on one of the A-12s (A.C. Serial No. 33-213), accidentally discharged his flare into the fuselage, and the plane caught fire. Woronuk and the pilot, 2nd Lt. Rolle E. Stone Jr., bailed out as the A-12 went down "in a blaze of glory." With the departure and

A Curtiss A-12 Shrike attack bomber (AR/52) on the apron at Wheeler Field, circa 1939. By 1941 only a few of these aircraft remained at Wheeler and Hickam Fields in training and liaison roles.
TLM, 06.18.03-12

reassignment of the men, the 18th Pursuit Group's era of "pursuit only" aviation began.[22]

For Americans still struggling to emerge from the Great Depression during 1939 and 1940, threats posed by the widening European war and continuing Japanese aggression in the Far East presented a disquieting prospect. To protect its interests in the Pacific, the United States needed to expand its air power in Hawai'i and the Philippines. The authorities in Washington realized that concentrating the Hawaiian Department's air assets into one air wing could not "meet the problems created by any great expansion," thus setting the stage for far-reaching changes on O'ahu.

Effective 19 October 1940 the Hawaiian Department's old 18th Wing—comprising the 5th and 11th Bombardment Groups, the 18th Pursuit Group, and two reconnaissance squadrons—passed into history. Per Hawaiian Department General Orders No. 37, on 1 November the newly constituted Hawaiian Air Force replaced the old 18th Wing. The new force's tactical units were split among two organizations: the 18th Bombardment Wing (the former 18th Wing renamed) and the newly constituted 14th Pursuit Wing.[23]

The components of the new pursuit wing consisted, initially, of the 18th Air Base Group (which supplied the wing's cadre) and the 18th Pursuit Group, with only the 6th, 19th, and 78th Pursuit Squadrons in place. On 28 November, General Orders No. 44 activated the 15th Pursuit Group effective 1 December 1940. The group's component commands were a headquarters squadron and the 45th, 46th, and 47th Pursuit Squadrons. The Hawaiian Department would activate three additional pursuit squadrons to further populate the groups in 1941.[24]

Maj. Gen. Frederick L. Martin Arrives

Concurrent with the organizational changes came a new commander. On 1 October 1940, Frederick Leroy Martin received a temporary promotion to major general and orders to depart his billet at

Brig. Gen. Frederick L. Martin at Mitchel Field, 20 September 1940. The ribbons above Martin's left pocket are for the Distinguished Service Medal (*left*) and the World War I Victory Medal (*right*). **NARA II, via Cressman, cropped**

the 3rd Wing, General Headquarters Air Force at Barksdale Field to take the reins of the newly formed Hawaiian Air Force. One month and a day after his promotion, on 2 November 1940, Martin disembarked from the USAT *Leonard Wood* in Honolulu Harbor. Shortly after reaching O'ahu, Martin opened a letter from Maj. Gen. Henry H. Arnold in Washington dated 16 October telling him, "it is quite probable that new equipment [aircraft] will be available for assignment to Hawai'i not later than the first of July, 1941."[25]

Although Arnold's letter sought to reassure the new Hawaiian Air Force head that the aircraft pipeline would be open again by mid-1941, that news did not reassure Martin. Over the previous five years the War Department had been very slow in taking appropriate steps to remedy Hawai'i's aerial deficiencies. A thorough assessment substantiated Martin's dismay, particularly regarding the lack of modern pursuit aircraft. Although the equipment rosters at Wheeler Field showed thirty-five aircraft on hand at the end of 1940, Martin discovered that sixteen of that number—45 percent—were obsolete Boeing P-26s that could not possibly hope to meet a modern enemy force on even terms.[26]

Martin's response to Major General Arnold on 17 December stressed the importance of modern aircraft for defense in the Pacific:

> In my opinion we have in the past and are still practicing a very faulty policy with reference to providing our foreign possessions with modern equipment [i.e., aircraft]. The importance of these stations from the standpoint of national defense dictate[s] that they receive first consideration in the assignment of modern equipment and the full quota of personnel for its operation. We have been satisfied in the past to supply our units in foreign possessions with obsolescent equipment until organizations in the States had been equipped with modern types. This to me is very faulty and could, in these times of uncertainty, be very detrimental to our scheme of national defense. Our foreign possessions are outposts of great importance and should by all means receive *first consideration* as to quantity and quality of equipment.[27]

Lt. Gen. Charles D. Herron—the commanding general of the Hawaiian Department—was also aware of the cumulative and negative effects that Washington's shift in priorities had exerted on his department's preparedness. On 31 December 1940, two weeks after Martin's letter to Arnold, Herron echoed Martin's concerns in a radiogram to the War Department, stating that the Army possessed insufficient aerial strength to ensure an adequate defense of O'ahu. The Air Corps' inventory in the islands stood at a paltry 117 planes—most of them antiquated and obsolete. Responding to Herron's and Martin's alarming missives, the War Department agreed to upgrade the Air Corps' assets in Hawai'i and to institute a buildup of modern aviation equipment on O'ahu. After a year of playing second fiddle to the war in Europe, the Hawaiian Department was finally to receive a much-needed infusion of modern aircraft.[28]

Maj. Gen. Charles D. Herron (*left*) confers with Maj. Gen. Henry H. Arnold (*right*) during the latter's visit to the Hawaiian Department in circa January 1940. **AFHRA**

Ferrying Operations

P-36As, FEBRUARY 1941

The infusion would not be instantaneous. In his direct reply to Martin on 3 February Arnold expressed his sympathy but emphasized the many competing and conflicting priorities affecting the assignment of new aircraft coming off the assembly lines at Boeing, Curtiss, and Lockheed. The view on the pursuit side at Wheeler Field was encouraging, however, as the War Department arranged a February delivery of a portion of the fighters promised earlier. Secretary of War Henry L. Stimson provided a rough outline of the planned aircraft transfers for "the Hawaiian Project" in a letter to Secretary of the Navy Frank Knox: 148 pursuit planes, to include a shipment of P-36As to augment the number already in place, and additional deliveries of new P-40Bs to follow.[29]

Knox was involved because the Navy had agreed to use its aircraft carriers to transport the fighters, having proved the evolution feasible when the *Wasp* (CV 7) launched twenty-four P-40s and eight O-47As off the Virginia Capes in twenty-three minutes on 14 October 1940. On 6 February Adm. Harold R. Stark, the Chief of Naval Operations (CNO), ordered Adm. Husband E. Kimmel, Commander in Chief, U.S. Pacific Fleet (CinCPac), "to direct 1 carrier to be at San Diego on Feb. 13 for the purpose of transporting to Hawaiian Area 31 P-36 Army pursuit planes." Stark stated that Army pilots would fly the fighters off the carrier, that he expected the aircraft to arrive in San Diego on 14 February, and that Kimmel would need to supply a second carrier to ferry fifty more aircraft (P-40s) around 15 March.[30]

By late 1940, however, "the ferrying of new aircraft to depots or to units had assumed the proportions of a major problem." Policy dictated that "the receiving unit . . . ferry its own allocation of new aircraft from the factories or from depots." The policy worked a hardship even within the continental United States, as units throughout the country had to train new pilots or use pilots who were inexperienced in the operation of the newest types emerging from the factories. The high level of inexperience and the ramping up of production rates at various aircraft manufacturers "were problems of critical concern" throughout the spring of 1941. In December 1940, a pilot other than a flight leader needed a minimum of "one years [*sic*] experience as an active Pursuit Pilot" to ferry an aircraft from the manufacturer to its destination.[31]

Records from individual units reveal a less than satisfactory picture in that regard. Taking Wheeler Field's 47th Pursuit Squadron as an example, of the unit's twenty-one officers, only nine men (just over 40 percent) had three or more months of experience as a pursuit pilot in November 1941. Only six men—squadron commander Capt. Gordon H. Austin, the four 1st lieutenants, and 2nd Lt. George S. Welch (just short of 30 percent of the officers)—had the requisite pursuit experience to qualify for single-engine ferry service. With the Army Air Force's flight schools cranking out fresh graduates as frantically as factories were rolling out new airplanes, it is doubtful whether the situation regarding experience was much better elsewhere in 1941.[32]

With the situation growing more critical by the day, on 6 February 1941, Col. William O. Butler—chief of staff of the Southwest Air District (4th Air Force)—received a telephone call from Lt. Col. Victor H. Strahm at General Headquarters Air Force at Langley Field. Strahm told Colonel Butler "to prepare for the immediate dispatch of aircraft and crews to board the carrier *Enterprise* (CV 6) at the North Island Naval Station, San Diego." The planes and their crews were to gather no later than 11 February at March Field at Riverside. Pilots, aircraft, and crew chiefs from Selfridge Field were to report under similar instructions.[33]

Written orders that amplified—and sometimes contradicted—the earlier telephoned orders called for the officers, crews, and airplanes to arrive at NAS San Diego on North Island no later than 0900 on 12 February to prepare for boarding the aircraft carrier that same day for transport to the Hawaiian Islands.

Planned Fighter Reinforcement of O'ahu

Airfield	P-36s	Pilots	Crew Chiefs
Hamilton Field	19	19	15
Selfridge Field	14	14	15?
TOTAL	31	31	30?

While in transit, the crew chiefs were to service the fighters "for the eventual fly-off from the carrier after docking in Hawaii." Two pilots and P-36s from Hamilton Field would accompany the group as alternates in case of accidents or mechanical difficulties, but with instructions to return to Hamilton Field as soon as the *Enterprise* sailed.[34]

Immediately, shortfalls in men, matériel, and time threatened delays. Although the authorities stated a preference for as many of the pilot positions as possible to be filled with Air Reserve volunteers from Hamilton's 20th and 35th Pursuit Groups (with Regulars from the 35th to occupy the remaining openings), a jumbled mix of pilots originated from a far broader swath of pursuit groups—four from Hamilton and two from Selfridge. The schedule left little or no time to spare, and the pilots and planes were forced to depart Hamilton and Selfridge only one to three days after the movement was announced.[35]

In addition, the overall quality of the Air Reserve pilots left much to be desired; some had as little as seven hours of transition training in P-36s. Even experienced pilots tended to fall short on gunnery training, most with only seven to thirty hours. The majority of the volunteers—perhaps eager for an assignment overseas—had been "checked off" on P-36s, but many had still been flight cadets as late as November 1940. To counterbalance this shortcoming at the last minute, the 4th Air Force assigned as many Regulars as possible from the 20th Pursuit Group at Hamilton Field.[36]

The quality of the aircraft destined to depart from (and those to remain at) Hamilton Field also set off alarm bells. The base's commander stated flatly that the exodus to the Hawaiian Department

would leave him with "not a P-36 in flying condition" on the aprons. Although the state of the departing airplanes was better, four of the fighters were at the extreme limit on engine time, with not enough hours left to reach North Island and O'ahu. Other aircraft required installation of machine guns, parachutes, oxygen delivery equipment, and radio receivers.[37]

Maj. George R. Tourtellot—commander of the 35th Pursuit Group at Hamilton Field—was selected to lead the flight of P-36As from the *Enterprise* to O'ahu. Tourtellot was already at Hamilton and thus well placed to coordinate the mission's details, a fortunate happenstance as the movement of men and aircraft toward San Diego was already in process when he received his orders from 4th Air Force Headquarters in Riverside.[38]

Tourtellot possessed a wealth of experience in pursuit aviation accrued over a period of twenty years. In France during the Great War and afterward, he flew many of the aircraft types used by Germany, France, and Great Britain during the conflict: Curtiss JN-4s, Nieuport XXVII C.1s and XXVIII C.1s, Morane-Saulnier monoplanes, SPAD S.VIIs

1st Lt. George R. Tourtellot in his formal Army Air Corps portrait, circa 1932. **NARA II, 342-FH-4A-12445**

and S.XIIIs, Sopwith Camels, Fokker D.VIIs, and S.E.5as. He won his wings as a second lieutenant on 14 January 1920. Further, he was no stranger to the Hawaiian Department. As a 1st lieutenant Tourtellot had served in the 19th Pursuit Squadron at Wheeler Field, flying all three variants of Boeing's P-12 during 1932–33. Circa March 1940, following duty at Selfridge, Maxwell, and Sherman Fields, then-Major Tourtellot took over the 35th Pursuit Group at Moffett Field. By the time he transferred with his group to Hamilton Field in October, Tourtellot had accumulated many hours in the P-36A and P-40 and held the rating of command pilot. The authorities could hardly have selected a more able and qualified leader for the flight into Wheeler Field.[39]

The pilots at Hamilton Field found out about the move to Hawai'i very soon after their commanders did. In a letter to his parents, 2nd Lt. George A. Whiteman of the 20th Pursuit Group, 55th Pursuit Squadron related, "This afternoon our group commander [Col. Ira C. Eaker] called us together and asked for 18 volunteers to go to Hawaii. Sixteen of us stepped up and the list went to Washington tonight." Whiteman offered some general details that probably did little to alleviate his parents' anxiety, such as the prospect of flying his plane off an aircraft carrier. The need to write two other letters and pay his bills prior to his departure dictated the unaccustomed brevity of Whiteman's letter. Time was indeed short: word was that he would be leaving Hamilton Field in two or three days.[40]

At Selfridge Field, 2nd Lt. Lewis M. Sanders also mustered among the men slated for transfer to the Hawaiian Department. The move was sudden and very much a surprise: "I received a call asking me if I wanted to go to Hawaii. A few days later I was aboard the USS *Enterprise* leaving San Diego for the Hawaiian Islands. While I had no experience taking off from an aircraft carrier, I managed to make it, and soon I was stationed at Wheeler Field."[41]

A complex series of ferry flights that commenced on 7 February brought thirty-one P-36As to NAS San Diego by 12 February. The planes arrived from two widely separated locations: twenty aircraft from Hamilton Field and eleven from Selfridge Field. The aircraft from Hamilton had passed though the hands of various units at Barksdale Field in Louisiana and Moffett Field near Sunnyvale, California—the former base of the 20th Pursuit Group before its migration to Hamilton in late 1940.[42]

Each of the originating fields launched the P-36s in two batches on 7 and 9 February. From Hamilton, 2nd Lt. John M. Thacker (20th Pursuit Group, 79th Pursuit Squadron) and 2nd Lt. Everett W. Stewart (54th Pursuit Group, 42nd Pursuit Squadron) commenced the movement toward San Diego with a two-hour hop to Bakersfield, California, where they waited for the remaining eighteen pilots and aircraft from Hamilton to arrive on 9 February.

The transition from Selfridge Field was more complex because it had six intermediate destinations. From the 1st Pursuit Group, Capt. Paul W. Blanchard Jr. (94th Pursuit Squadron) and 2nd Lt. Lewis Sanders (27th Pursuit Squadron) flew to Scott Field, near Belleville, Illinois. Blanchard stayed overnight, but Sanders continued the same day to Post Field at Fort Sill, Oklahoma. The balance of the pilots departed for Scott Field two days later, with all present at Post Field by 9 February. The flights continued the next morning with refueling stops at Midland Field (Midland, Texas) and Biggs Field (El Paso) before reaching Tucson Army Airfield, where the men rested for two nights.[43]

From Bakersfield and Tucson, most of the thirty-one aircraft flew into March Field near Riverside, where Army and Navy aircraft mechanics checked over the P-36As and made minor modifications "to insure [*sic*] proper hoisting in boarding and later in flying off the [*Enterprise*]." The two alternate aircraft came along for the trip to Hawai'i after one aircraft from Selfridge Field sustained landing gear damage and one from Hamilton developed engine trouble. Although various portions of the group finished the ferry missions on different days, by 12 February

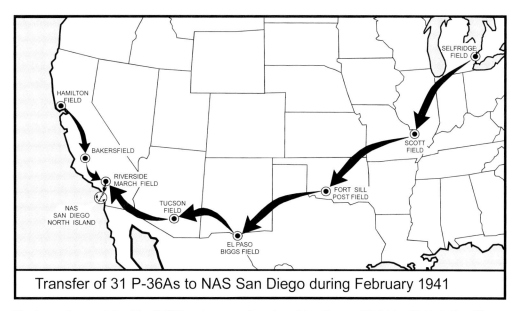

Transfer of 31 P-36As to NAS San Diego during February 1941

Routes and waypoints of the P-36 ferrying operations from Hamilton and Selfridge Fields to San Diego. Although far shorter than the journey from Selfridge Field, the flights from Hamilton nevertheless involved considerable distances. **Di Virgilio**

thirty of the aircraft and pilots were in place at North Island. The only hiccough in the schedule involved 2nd Lt. James O. Beckwith Jr. (94th Pursuit Squadron), who delayed at Yuma Army Airfield and did not arrive at North Island until 13 February.[44]

As the thirty-one P-36s converged on San Diego, the Navy prepared to transport them and their crews to Hawai'i. The *Enterprise* got under way from Pearl Harbor on 7 February, the same day the fighters began leaving Selfridge and Hamilton Fields. Following the six-day voyage to San Diego, in company with the destroyers *Farragut* (DD 348) and *Aylwin* (DD 355), the carrier moored at North Island on 13 February, just in time to embark the pilots, crew chiefs, and aircraft waiting there. The last of the P-36s was on board by 15 February, and the carrier, having also

The *Enterprise* off Honolulu, 12 February 1940, in the configuration in which she would appear during her aircraft ferry mission from San Diego to Pearl Harbor in February 1941. The identification letters EN (painted in chrome yellow) are just discernable on the right, at the forward end of the flight deck. **NARA II, 80-G-410093, via Cressman**

embarked 10 officers and 369 enlisted men of the 1st Defense Battalion, U.S. Marine Corps, departed San Diego, again in company with the *Farragut* and the *Aylwin*, that same day.[45]

As the *Enterprise* closed on Oʻahu early on the morning of 21 February, the flattop turned into the wind and launched the "Air Corps Detachment, USS *Enterprise*" in ten three-plane elements. The thirty-one Army pilots arrived at Wheeler Field after flights that varied from forty minutes to just over an hour. Capt. Arthur R. Kingham and 2nd Lt. Charles M. Parrett were exceptions—perhaps forming a two-plane element that hovered near Oʻahu to ensure that all thirty-one pilots arrived safely. Kingham and Parrett finally landed after two hours in the air. Col. Harvey S. Burwell, commander of Wheeler and the 18th Pursuit Group, "strode to the side of [Tourtellot's] plane to offer his aloha and his post's grateful hospitality to its new fighting detachment." Twenty-four of the pilots beefed up the 15th and 18th Pursuit Groups—twelve to each—and the remaining officers transferred into other organizations at Wheeler, including the recently formed 58th Bombardment Squadron. Major Tourtellot was the only pilot not to be absorbed into the Hawaiian Air Force; he had orders to return on the *Enterprise* when it departed Pearl Harbor for the Puget Sound Navy Yard for "an interim overhaul." Upon arrival on the West Coast, Tourtellot returned to Hamilton Field to resume command of the 35th Pursuit Group.[46]

P-40Bs, MARCH 1941

On 3 March—ten days after the delivery of the P-36As to Wheeler Field—CNO Admiral Stark sent a dispatch to Admiral Kimmel and reiterated that fifty P-40s would be arriving in San Diego for transport to Hawaiʻi on an aircraft carrier of Kimmel's choosing. Army pilots and enlisted mechanics would accompany the planes and fly them off the carrier at their destination. The men were not to remain on Oʻahu, however, but would return to the States at the earliest opportunity, preferably on an eastbound aircraft carrier.[47]

The War Department's insistence on ramping up the number of aircraft being sent to Hawaiʻi forced changes in the template that had been established by the February mission. Admiral Kimmel's response to Stark on 8 March advised his chief that the increase in the number of aircraft being ferried (fifty rather than thirty-one) made it impossible for Army pilots to launch from the aircraft carrier under consideration (the *Lexington* [CV 2]). Even if the carrier's entire air complement were struck below, there would be insufficient space on the flight deck forward of the Army "air group" to ensure a safe launch. Hence, there would be no grand fly-off such as occurred in February, and thus no need for a complete complement of Army pilots to board in San Diego; only the crew chiefs, maintenance men, and four to eight pilots would ride as guests of the Navy.[48]

The P-40B Tomahawks that made their way to Hawaiʻi in March 1941 were a lot of fifty-one aircraft with consecutive serial numbers, all produced at Curtiss-Wright's manufacturing plant in Buffalo, New York, and originally all intended for the pursuit groups at Hamilton Field. The fighters rolled off the assembly line in batches of one to seven over a sixteen-day period during late February and early March. Pilots from the 8th Pursuit Group at Mitchel Field, Long Island, picked up the fighters at the Buffalo plant and ferried them to the Fairfield Air Depot at Patterson Field, Ohio, where the Army accepted delivery. While details regarding the movement of the aircraft to California are uncertain, pilots from Mitchel Field probably ferried them to Hamilton Field. The movement from Hamilton to San Diego occurred during 14–16 March.[49]

When they reached North Island, the pilots and maintenance crews probably saw an aircraft carrier for the first time in their lives—and what a sight it must have been. The Lady Lex—age, recalcitrant elevators, and poor ventilation notwithstanding—was still an object of wonder, the largest American warship (along with her sister ship, the *Saratoga*)

The *Lexington* transiting the Panama Canal, circa February 1939. The carrier was in the same configuration during her March 1941 ferry mission from San Diego to Pearl Harbor. Note the flight deck forward, which was widened during a refit concluded in 1937. **Cressman, cropped**

U.S. shipyards had ever built. The *Lexington*'s cranes began hoisting the olive drab and neutral gray P-40s on board, and two days later, at 0500 on 18 March, the *Lexington* lit off boilers three, four, five, and six, and at 0837 was under way. The destroyers *Lang* (DD 399), *Benham* (DD 397), *Ellet* (DD 398), and *Wainwright* (DD 419) formed the carrier's antisubmarine screen. The voyage west to Hawai'i proceeded uneventfully, though under blackout conditions.[50]

The midwatch of 25 March brought the welcome sighting of the lighthouse on Moloka'i and O'ahu's light on Mokapu'u Point. The *Lexington* passed Diamond Head at 0524 and at 0810 moored at interrupted quay F-2 along the southern shore of Ford Island. The choice of the mooring was not coincidental. Not only were the two quays designed to accommodate an aircraft carrier, but the design of the southernmost quay (F-2-S) also facilitated hoisting out aircraft to be rolled down onto the naval air station, a necessity for the fifty-one P-40Bs because they could not be launched from the *Lexington* as she closed on O'ahu.[51]

As the tedious and time-consuming evolution of unloading the P-40Bs proceeded, the pilots and maintenance men who had accompanied them were likewise discharged onto Ford Island. At least four pilots from the 8th Pursuit Group, all second lieutenants—George R. Bickell, James J. Flood, Ingram C. Connor Jr., and Raymond K. Gallagher—left the ship, presumably with instructions to familiarize the men at Wheeler with the operation and handling characteristics of the Curtiss P-40. All four men joined the Headquarters Squadron, 18th Pursuit Group that same day, as did MSgt. Olsen K. Fields, who was destined to become the squadron's lead aircraft mechanic. The seventeen other crew chiefs and maintenance personnel also received assignments within the group's squadrons.[52]

One last sizable task remained: the P-40s had to be ferried north from NAS Pearl Harbor to Wheeler Field. The four pilots just in from the West Coast ferried thirteen of the aircraft up to their new home. Perhaps eight to ten other pilots from Wheeler—among them 2nd Lt. Henry E. Thompson (46th

Four Curtiss P-40s from the 19th Pursuit Squadron parked on the turf of a Hawaiian airfield in 1941, most likely Wheeler Field. **Makiel**

Pursuit Squadron) and 1st Lt. Woodrow B. "Woody" Wilmot (45th Pursuit Squadron)—participated in the fifteen-minute hops from Ford Island to Wheeler, setting a precedent that would be repeated during the final delivery in Secretary of War Stimson's "Hawaiian project" one month hence.[53]

P-40B/Cs, APRIL 1941

On 12 March, two days before the first shipment of P-40Bs flew from Hamilton Field to San Diego, Admiral Stark wired Admiral Kimmel's headquarters advising him that "it is desired to transport by carrier from San Diego to Hawai'i [Utility Squadron] VJ-2 and fifty-five additional Army P-40 planes in late April or early May." Stark inquired which carrier might be available for such a mission and on what date. He again asked whether Kimmel wished to have Army pilots on board to fly the aircraft into O'ahu. The next day, Kimmel responded that the *Enterprise*—having commenced an interim overhaul in Bremerton only ten days earlier—would be available during the period that Stark had requested but left unaddressed the issues of VJ-2 and the Army pilots.[54]

Meanwhile, the Curtiss-Wright plant in Buffalo continued rolling out P-40s. Following a ten-day hiatus in production in support of the "Hawaiian project," fifteen deliveries of one to nine aircraft

per batch took place from 19 March to 6 April, netting fifty-three more aircraft for the Hawaiian Department. The new aircraft included the latest variant from Curtiss, the P-40C, which was outfitted with self-sealing internal fuel cells and "fittings for a 52-gallon drop tank below the fuselage." Although details are unavailable, the Air Corps almost certainly employed the pursuit pilots at Mitchel Field to ferry the P-40s to the Fairfield Air Depot, and thence through various waypoints to Hamilton Field.[55]

Toward the end of March, Admiral Stark stepped up pressure on CinCPac to provide a hard date regarding the *Enterprise*'s availability for the April mission to O'ahu. The need to transfer VMS-2 (Marine Scouting Squadron 2) to the Ewa Mooring Mast Field on O'ahu was another pressure point. Stark had received word that the squadron would be fully equipped with Vought SB2U-3 Vindicators and was needed to bring MAG-21 (Marine Aircraft Group 21) up to strength. In his dispatch to Admiral Kimmel on 28 March, Stark stated that the Army fighters could be made available anytime after 21 April but queried his fleet commander whether it would be advisable to ship the Marine aircraft on board with the Army fighters. Kimmel, waiting for the *Enterprise* to emerge from overhaul at Bremerton on 31 March, responded that the carrier planned on taking only the load of P-40s to Hawai'i and that the

The interrupted mooring quays of Berths F-2 (*center right*) and F-3 (*upper left*) adjacent to NAS Pearl Harbor toward the southern tip of Ford Island, 10 October 1941, looking northeast. The *Enterprise* is moored in F-2, port side to, while the other berth is empty. According to their deck logs, the *Lexington* and *Enterprise* moored in F-2 during March and April of 1941. This facilitated offloading the P-40s atop the southernmost platform (F-2-S), which was connected to the naval air station. On 7 December 1941, the battleship *California* (BB 44) occupied Berth F-3. **NARA II, 80-G-279375, cropped**

Marines at Ewa would have to wait until mid-May for delivery of their aircraft.[56]

The *Enterprise* moored starboard side to the Naval Air Station dock in San Diego at 1622 on 3 April and awaited the arrival of the Army contingent from Hamilton Field. The schedule indicated that aircraft would arrive at North Island during 19–20 April, with maintenance men and two pilots to arrive on the latter date. After loading the men and aircraft, the carrier got under way from San Diego at 1325 on 21 April, crossed the Pacific toward Hawai'i in company with Destroyer Division Seven plus the

Patterson (DD 392) as an antisubmarine screen, and moored in Berth F-2, port side to, at Ford Island following a passage of six days.[57]

MSgt. Charles C. Cunningham on the grounds of the Consolidated Barracks at Hickam Field, probably in March 1940 around the time of his promotion to master sergeant. As a noncommissioned officer pilot, Cunningham was something of a rarity. By January 1940 he had amassed an astonishing number of flying hours as a pilot—nearly 1,000 hours each in bombardment and observation, and most recently about 700 in cargo. In December 1940 Cunningham finally received a commission as a first lieutenant. **Henderson**

A Douglas C-33 cargo plane on the pavement in front of Wheeler Field's Hangar 3 (*out of frame at right*), circa 1939. By late 1941, 1st Lt. Charles Cunningham operated a pair of C-33s of the 19th Transport Squadron out of Hickam Field. **TLM, P.001,801**

A dozen or more pilots from Wheeler were shuttled south to Ford Island to help the two Army pilots who arrived on the *Enterprise* to deliver the P-40s. Air transportation to Ford came courtesy of 1st Lt. Charles C. Cunningham flying a C-33 from Hickam's 17th Air Base Group with seating for fourteen men. Capt. Kenneth P. Bergquist used the 18th Pursuit Group's Grumman OA-9 with seating for six. Cunningham and Bergquist each made four shuttles between the two airfields on 26–27 April, and each of the pursuit pilots made one or more ferry flights north into Wheeler.[58]

The delivery of the additional fifty-three P-40B/Cs during the last week of April—"without undue incident," Major General Martin noted—helped to reequip the 14th Pursuit Wing. Martin's comment did not take into account the vexing issues and difficulties that the Air Corps had faced and surmounted to get the planes there, including using two of the Pacific Fleet's three aircraft carriers to effect final delivery of the fighters to Wheeler Field.[59]

The months following the deliveries were no time for complacency. As of 1 May 1941, more than a third of Wheeler's available pursuit planes—fifteen obsolete P-26s and forty-six nearly obsolete P-36s—were nearing the end of their days of frontline service. There was also word from the War Department regarding pursuit aviation in the Hawaiian Department. Although the Air Corps earmarked twin-engine Lockheed P-38 Lightnings to modernize the 15th Pursuit Group and replace all the P-36s, the newer aircraft would not be available for twelve

Capt. Kenneth P. Bergquist, circa late 1941, while assigned as an engineering officer to the headquarters squadron of the 14th Pursuit Wing. **USAR 1234**

Grumman OA-9 amphibian PR/39 assigned to the 18th Pursuit Group's headquarters squadron, circa 1939. Although he was commanding officer of the 44th Pursuit Squadron, Captain Bergquist flew one of the 18th's two OA-9s that shuttled pilots from Wheeler Field to Ford Island after the *Enterprise* delivered the fifty-three P-40Bs and -Cs. **TLM, P.001,666**

months, an eternity in the Pacific Basin, where Hawai'i represented the last major advanced outpost (save for the Philippines) facing a bellicose adversary in the Central Pacific. The leadership at Wheeler Field had to make do with the improved equipment at hand and accelerate the pace of training to ensure that the pilots would be ready to take advantage of the new fighters when the War Department delivered on its promise in early to mid-1942.[60]

Admiral Kimmel's Confidential Letter 2CL-41

As planning proceeded for the promised infusion of aircraft into the 14th Pursuit Wing, the new commander of the Pacific Fleet was exerting considerable pressure on the already weak resources of the Hawaiian Air Force. Two weeks after assuming command as Commander in Chief, U.S. Fleet (CinCUS) on 1 February, Adm. Husband E. Kimmel issued Pacific Fleet Confidential Letter No. 2CL-41, which established the Naval Base Defense Force and named Rear Adm. Claude C. Bloch, Commandant, 14th Naval District, "Naval Base Defense Officer." By the end of the month Bloch had distributed Naval Base Defense Force Operation Plan No. 1-41, which

outlined the principal threats Pearl Harbor faced: sabotage, mines, surprise submarine attacks, and air attacks. Five subsequent annexes to the plan contained detailed operational instructions.[61]

On 28 February, Rear Adm. Patrick N. L. Bellinger (ComPatWing 2)—commander of the Navy's patrol squadrons in Hawai'i—forwarded Naval Base Defense Air Force Operation Plan No. A-1-41 (as Annex B to Bloch's plan). The annex set in place the interservice order of battle for the air assets defending Hawai'i. A Search and Attack Group under Bellinger included the Navy's patrol squadrons and the Hawaiian Air Force's bombardment and reconnaissance units. The Search and Attack Group was to (1) locate, report, and track all hostile surface ships in a position to take or threaten hostile action; and (2) destroy hostile ships by air attack.

An Air Combat Group, which was to "operate as directed by the Commanding General Hawaiian Air Force," included all shore-based Army pursuit squadrons, all shore-based Navy and Marine fighters, and one division of shore-based scout bombers. The fighters were to (1) intercept and destroy hostile aircraft; and (2) identify and report type of attacking aircraft. The scout bombers were to (1) trail attacking carrier type planes to their carriers; and (2) report the carriers' location to the commander of the Search and Attack Group.[62]

Maintaining the highest practical degree of readiness was a key component of the ability of the fighter force to blunt a Japanese carrier-based attack. In their Addendum I to the operation plan of the Naval Base Defense Air Force, Martin and Bellinger outlined the concepts of the required readiness for each unit. They defined five levels of "material readiness," with level A denoting that all aircraft were available, and E denoting that none were available. Similarly, Martin and Bellinger designated five "degrees of readiness," with 1 meaning that all fighters were ready for takeoff within four minutes, and 5 denoting that the aircraft would require four hours prior to takeoff. The two officers noted that maintaining higher states of readiness for extended periods would result in deterioration of personnel fitness and interfere with the transition training of new pilots and crews, while "conditions C or D, 4 or 5 [could] be maintained without unduly curtailing normal training work." With new pilots arriving in the Hawaiian Department with only two hundred hours of flying under their belts, the liabilities of maintaining high levels of readiness for any extended period were never far from the minds of Wheeler's leadership.[63]

Brig. Gen. Howard C. Davidson Takes Command

After Col. Harvey S. Burwell relinquished command of the 14th Pursuit Wing to accept an assignment as special inspector of the Hawaiian Air Force with headquarters at Hickam Field, Brig. Gen. Howard C. Davidson reported to Wheeler from Hickam on 7 April 1941 to take over Burwell's erstwhile command. Howard Calhoun Davidson was born in Wharton, Texas, on 15 September 1890. He left home in 1907 to attend Texas Agricultural and Mechanical College but left there in January 1909 to take the entrance examination for the U.S. Military Academy

in West Point. He received an appointment from the 9th Congressional District of his home state.[64]

Davidson did not have an easy time at West Point, but "after a hard struggle" he managed to graduate 85th in the 1913 class of 92 cadets. Shortly thereafter he was commissioned a 2nd lieutenant in the 22nd Infantry Regiment, 2nd Infantry Division at Texas City, Texas. He deployed with the regiment near the U.S.-Mexican border during the Mexican Revolution of 1914—a conflict in which the United States was supposedly neutral. The 6th Brigade (including the 22nd Infantry) under Brig. Gen. Clarence R. Edwards was operating at that time on the flank of the Mexican army in support of the Federales. Fortunately for 2nd Lieutenant Davidson, he requested a transfer to the Philippines in 1915, well in advance of Francisco "Pancho" Villa's cross-border raid into Columbus, New Mexico, and the resulting Punitive Expedition into Mexico by the United States. Freed of the "mosquitoes and mud in Texas City," Davidson rode a motorcycle to the West Coast and arrived in San Francisco "in a state of exhaustion due to the difficulty of crossing the desert . . . with nothing but sand tracks for roads."[65]

On the way to San Francisco, Davidson stopped in San Diego to visit some fellow officers undergoing flight training. That stopover marked a turning point in his career. When he arrived in the Philippines he asked for permission to take the flight examination. After passing the exam in Manila he received orders back to San Diego, took training, and received the rating of junior military aviator in January 1916. With the outbreak of World War I, the Army assigned him as officer in charge of training at the 2nd Aviation Instruction Center at Tours, France. Davidson just missed getting into action near Verdun before the Armistice ended the war.[66]

Following service in the occupation forces, now-Major Davidson returned to the United States. During the 1920s he served in various billets at Mitchel and Bolling Fields, and with the Air Corps Tactical School at Maxwell Field. The 1930s saw Davidson

Brig. Gen. Howard C. Davidson, commanding general, 14th Pursuit Wing, attending a sports event at Wheeler Field in August 1941. **NARA II, 111-SC-125880, cropped**

steadily advance. Having attended the Command and General Staff School at Fort Leavenworth he took command of the 19th Bombardment Group, and of the Training and Operations Division in the Office of the Chief of the Air Corps. After a course at the Army War College, he transferred in July 1940 to Hickam Field, where he commanded the base headquarters, 17th Air Base Squadron, and Hickam Field prior to his promotion to brigadier general on 7 April 1941.[67]

The Pursuit Command Structure Is Revised
In late October 1941, as part of efforts to streamline the administration of the air wings and airfields on Oʻahu, the Hawaiian Department rotated command of its principal airfields on the island among the three field commanders. Effective 27 October 1941, Col. William J. Flood assumed command at Wheeler Field, having arrived from Hickam where he had served as assistant chief of staff (G-4, Supply) under Major General Martin.[68] Col. William E. Farthing moved from Bellows to Hickam, and Lt. Col. Leonard D. Weddington went from Wheeler to Bellows.

These changes represented no mere game of musical chairs. Underlying Short's special order was the accompanying General Orders No. 68, which significantly altered the structure of leadership at the airfields. Previously, the wing commanders—Brig. Gen. Jacob H. Rudolph at Hickam and Brig. Gen. Howard C. Davidson at Wheeler—exercised administrative base authority as well as tactical command over their respective air groups and squadrons. The commanders of the air base groups at the respective fields served as "caretakers" under that scheme, though reporting directly to the wing commanders. On 27 October, however, the base commands separated entirely from the air wing commands. Hence, Colonel Flood took over command at Wheeler from Brigadier General Davidson and now reported to the commanding general, Hawaiian Air Force.[69]

Despite the effective dates in the two orders, the changes took time to implement because the files of the wings and bases had to be separated and moved. At the end of November, the transition was not yet complete; Colonel Flood still appeared on the roster of the 18th Air Base Group as its commander, with paperwork lagging far behind the nominal reassignments. Indeed, as Davidson indicated in late December, well over a month passed "before the complete separation of the Base[s] and Wing[s] had been effected." At year's end, the situation appeared to have settled, at least at Hickam, where Colonel Farthing had assembled his staff for the Hawaiian Air Force Base Command, Hickam Field, which HAF General Orders No. 26 activated on 25 December. The officers thus assigned functioned in their prescribed capacities well before Christmas, although the sorting of the mountain of paperwork from the files of the bombardment and pursuit wings continued at least through the end of the year.[70]

By the last months of 1941, Wheeler Field seemed to have entered the "modern" era, arguably more so than Hickam Field. Although Wheeler was considerably older than Hickam, it boasted both up-to-date facilities and, importantly, earthen revetments to safeguard its aircraft—an enhancement the newer Hickam lacked. With respect to aircraft, 103 of the most advanced Army fighters in general service—the Curtiss P-40B/C—had arrived at Wheeler during March and April 1941. Wheeler's greatest weakness was its untried pursuit pilots, but the aggressive training regimen in place would gradually ameliorate that problem. On balance, it would have been difficult to dispute anyone at Wheeler who maintained that the base was prepared to defend itself—and the island of O'ahu—against all comers.

Organization of Hawaiian Air Force (Wheeler and Bellows Fields)

Maj. Gen. Frederick L. Martin, commanding

Hawaiian Air Force, Headquarters
and Headquarters Squadron (Hickam Field)
    19th Transport Squadron
    7th AC Squadron, Communications
    7th AC Squadron, Weather
    Tow Target Detachment
    Hawaiian Air Depot

14th Pursuit Wing (Wheeler Field),
Brig. Gen. Howard C. Davidson, commanding
    15th Pursuit Group, Headquarters
    and Headquarters Squadron
        45th Pursuit Squadron
        46th Pursuit Squadron
        47th Pursuit Squadron
        72nd Pursuit Squadron

    18th Pursuit Group, Headquarters
    and Headquarters Squadron
        6th Pursuit Squadron
        19th Pursuit Squadron
        44th Pursuit Squadron
        73rd Pursuit Squadron
        78th Pursuit Squadron

    307th Signal Company, Air Wing
    674th Ordnance Company, Aviation
    696th Ordnance Company, Aviation
    Signal Section, Headquarters 14th Pursuit Wing

Wheeler Field, Col. William J. Flood, commanding

18th Air Base Group, Headquarters
and Headquarters Squadron
    17th Air Base Squadron
    24th Material Squadron
    25th Material Squadron
5th Chemical Service Company, Aviation, Detachment
39th Quartermaster Company (L/M), Detachment
45th Signal Platoon
741st Ordnance Company, Aviation
Detachment Quartermaster Corps, Wheeler Field
Detachment Financial Department, Wheeler Field
Detachment Medical Corps, Wheeler Field
Ground Defense Battalion (men organic to tactical units)

Bellows Field, Lt. Col. Leonard D. Weddington, commanding

Headquarters and Headquarters Squadron
Detachment Headquarters, Bellows Field
Air Support Command
86th Observation Squadron
Detachment Quartermaster Corps, Bellows Field
Detachment Financial Department, Bellows Field
Detachment Medical Corps, Bellows Field
Hawaiian Air Force, Casual Detachment
Ground Defense Unit (men organic to tactical units)

Chapter Four

"IT WAS A PARADISE . . . A QUIET PEACEFUL LIFE"
Life at O'ahu's Fighter Bases

The airmen assigned to Wheeler and Bellows Fields represented a diverse cross-section of America's population. They came to serve their country from a broad range of educational, social, and economic strata. Their motivations for joining the Army varied widely, although economic circumstances during the 1930s led many young men to choose the military as a career.

Ernest A. Brown, born to sharecroppers on 6 February 1916 in Crisp, Texas, worked on the farm until he was sixteen. When the family moved to Waco, he worked in the cotton mill with his parents. Though he knew he was fortunate to have work, he quit the mill for health reasons and joined the Civilian Conservation Corps (CCC). Brown worked in a CCC camp in Santa Fe, New Mexico, during the day and pulled night shifts as a projectionist in one of the town's movie theaters. With the Great Depression still ravaging America, finding work that supported a comfortable lifestyle was next to impossible. It seemed increasingly likely that America would be drawn into the war in Europe, so it was a blend of patriotism and dismal economic prospects that led Brown to an Army recruiter in El Paso, Texas.[1]

In 1928, Wisconsin native Henry C. Brown was living with his grandmother, who "had taken him in" at the age of six. She and the boy moved to Stanley in northwest Wisconsin, about one hundred miles due east of Minneapolis. Henry Brown wanted to go into the military after he graduated from high school in 1940, but his grandmother and uncles convinced him to enter the CCC instead. He remained in the corps only until December 1940, when he ran away from the camp and hopped a freight train heading south to Madison. He made his way to an Army recruiter's office and presented himself as an orphan. After signing his "adoption papers," Brown left for Jefferson Barracks, Missouri, for basic training.[2]

Clarence W. Kindl, born on 17 June 1916 in western Pennsylvania, graduated from high school and found a job but was laid off during the late 1930s. His widowed mother had no other means of support, so he and a friend looked for work in Norfolk, Virginia. Finding none, Kindl stopped in Washington, D.C., on the return trip to Pennsylvania, saw an Army recruitment office, and enlisted on 17 June 1940. Fortunately, enlistment in the Air Corps was not difficult if one was willing to sign up for foreign service.

Seeing plentiful openings in Hawai'i, Kindl selected "Air Force, Unassigned, Hawaiian Department."[3]

During the Depression, Fred R. Runce worked in a laboratory associated with a WPA frozen food development program in addition to several other odd jobs. During the winter of 1940, with the draft coming and rumors regarding the lab's possible closure, Runce "thought of getting out in the Pacific [to] miss the initial part of the war in Europe." Out of curiosity he walked into the Army recruiting office in the government building where he worked. Somewhat to his surprise, the affable recruiting sergeant asked, "Where do you want to go?" Although the question caught Runce off guard, he opted for the Hawaiian Department and within four hours was on a train headed for San Francisco to be inducted into the Air Corps.[4]

Milroy L. Richardson, born in the Minnesota town of Clarkfield, grew up twenty-five miles to the southwest in Canby near the South Dakota line. Richardson's father was unable to work, and the family lived off surplus commodities from the government as well as the wild game that Milroy hunted. After high school graduation in 1939, he entered the CCC, Camp 712, in Grand Marais, Minnesota. All but three of the boys who graduated in his class joined the CCC. Richardson left the CCC in August 1940 and enlisted in the Army, volunteering for the 1st Cavalry. Before he completed basic training, the Army dispensed with the horses and put the men in vehicles. When Richardson objected, "That ain't what I enlisted for," the Army offered him his second choice—the Air Corps.[5]

Born in Shelby County, east Texas, on 6 December 1906, Will Roy Sample was reared on the family farm. He left home during the Depression and drifted to various locales between California and south Texas. Unable to find employment, he returned home and announced his intention to enlist in the military, because "I won't be running around here with nothing." He joined up in 1939, telling the sergeant that he wanted to get as far from the United States as possible. Since there were no slots open for the Philippines (his first choice), Sample chose the Hawaiian Department.[6]

John J. Springer, born on 19 November 1919 about ten miles southeast of Minneapolis in Rosemount, Minnesota, moved to San Francisco during his childhood. He lived in a foster home after his parents separated, but economic conditions forced Springer to drop out of school. With times desperate and jobs impossible to find, he felt that a career in the military was his only option.[7]

Everett W. Stewart, born on 18 July 1915 near Talmage, Kansas, grew up on the family farm 150 miles west of Kansas City. He attended Kansas State College of Agriculture and Applied Science and was in the ROTC from 1933 until 1936. Stewart graduated with a reserve commission in the infantry in 1937. With the approach of war, he decided that he wanted to be a fighter pilot ace, so he applied to flight school. Stewart graduated from Kelly Field in June 1939 and went on active duty. He reported to Barksdale Field, Louisiana, on 8 June, joining the 20th Pursuit Group, 79th Pursuit Squadron. In December the entire group transferred to Moffett Field near Sunnyvale, California. Stewart eventually joined the 35th Pursuit Group, 21st Pursuit Squadron at Hamilton Field, where he remained until February 1941.[8]

The Airmen Arrive in Hawai'i

Many thousands of American servicemen made their way to the Territory of Hawai'i in the years before America entered World War II. Their experiences during the crossing from the West Coast to Honolulu Harbor were as varied as their backgrounds. Some voyages proved relatively uneventful. The crossing of Pvt. Henry Brown—eventually destined for the 47th Pursuit Squadron at Wheeler Field—was typical. After receiving some minimal training at Jefferson Barracks, Missouri, he left for Angel Island in San Francisco Bay in late 1940. There he boarded the USAT *St. Mihiel*, headed for Hawai'i. When he reached O'ahu, Brown reported to Schofield Barracks.

USAT *St. Mihiel*, venerable troopship and transporter of livestock, circa 1930s. **Wenger**

Only half of the men he was with at the time even had uniforms; Brown still wore his CCC clothing.[9]

The crossing on the *St. Mihiel* was not uneventful for everyone. Pvt. Milroy L. Richardson's voyage was memorable for all the wrong reasons. On at least one of her preceding voyages, the aging Army transport carried nine hundred mules from the West Coast to Alaska. Following that Arctic adventure, workers flushed the transport's hold with saltwater to remove the malodorous evidence of her last cargo and then installed berthing for troops. Unfortunately, the "sanitization" of the ship did not eliminate the manure residue from the cracks and crevices in the berthing area.[10]

Five days prior to his departure for Hawaiʻi on the *St. Mihiel*, Richardson married Viola Sanders from Denver, Colorado, enjoyed a brief honeymoon, and made reservations for 4 December to bring her to the islands. About three days after the transport was "cleaned up," Richardson and the other men queued up for boarding. They could smell the manure when they turned onto the street leading to the gangway.[11]

In the July heat, it was "hotter than a pistol" belowdecks and the stench was unbearable.

Richardson reported to his assigned bunk and vomited immediately. Along with several other men, he struggled topside to gulp down a breath of fresh air, but the ship "still smelled to high heaven." He and his bunkmate crawled atop one of the canvas-covered lifeboats, "sicker than dogs." When the *St. Mihiel* set sail, Richardson and his friend were still on top of the lifeboat, having missed roll call and been declared missing. The pair spent an enjoyable two days on their little boat before being discovered. "Jesus, did we get our butts chewed!" Richardson did not go below for the rest of the voyage except to retrieve his bag for disembarkation in Honolulu.[12]

Cpl. Clarence W. Kindl made his own unwelcome discovery at the end of his passage on the USAT *Leonard Wood*, which arrived in Honolulu at night. The men discovered that despite the promises of recruiting sergeants stateside, an NCO at the foot of the gangway was arbitrarily dictating unit assignments. As Kindl walked down toward the pier, the sergeant at the bottom sang out "left-right . . . Wheeler Field–Hickam Field." Kindl had set his heart on going into bombardment aviation but found himself sent to Wheeler instead. When he objected,

Soldiers on board an Army transport approach Honolulu Harbor (*at left center*) while looking back to the east toward Diamond Head, the first major landmark they encountered after departing the West Coast. **Cressman**

The transport carrying the soldiers proceeds into Honolulu Harbor, with men peering at the slips and wharves of U.S. Naval Station, Honolulu at center right. In the distance, note the tug moored alongside Wharf No. 2, and four of the naval station's warehouses beyond. **Cressman**

"I don't want to go to Wheeler," the sergeant snapped back, "I didn't ask you."[13]

SSgt. Stephen J. Koran's difficulty involved getting his fiancée, Flora, to Honolulu. When he discovered that claiming government travel subsidies would lead to a substantial delay, Koran decided to pay for Flora's passage on the SS *Lurline* out of his own pocket. When the *Lurline* arrived in Honolulu,

Koran rode out with the harbor pilot to meet the boat, planning to surprise Flora. Unfortunately, a swell threw him off balance when he tried to mount the rope ladder on the *Lurline*'s beam, and he fell into the water between the pilot boat and the ship. He was uninjured but "looked like a drowned rat" when he finally boarded. To bypass the three-day waiting period, Koran enlisted Rev. Raymond M. Squire to

New Army arrivals in the Hawaiian Department await transport from Honolulu Harbor to various bases on Oʻahu, circa September 1940, in this view looking west. The men are in Irwin Memorial Park near Halekauwila Street (present-day Aloha Tower Drive). The Aloha Tower looms in the distance. **NARA II, 111-SC-123475**

perform the marriage ceremony on 29 January 1941 at the Community Methodist Church in Wahiawā. The couple spent a ten-day honeymoon at the Moana Hotel in Waikīkī.[14]

Officers sometimes had a better, or at least a more exciting, time during the crossing to Hawaiʻi.

Having remained at Hamilton Field until February 1941, 1st Lt. Everett W. Stewart was one of thirty-one pilots—seventeen from Hamilton and fourteen from Selfridge Field—who made the crossing on the *Enterprise* and then flew his P-36 off the ship and on to Wheeler Field on 21 February. At the time he

The SS *Lurline* awaits a pilot from Honolulu Harbor prior to entry and berthing on 22 June 1933. Among the passengers waiting to disembark was Rear Adm. Harry E. Yarnell, the incoming commandant of the 14th Naval District. **NARA II, 80CF-797.2-59**

was not certain whether he would be staying there or proceeding on to the Philippines.[15]

2nd Lt. Phillip L. Willis volunteered for service in Hawai'i after winning his wings on 15 August 1941. He and his fiancée planned to be married there on Christmas Day. As an officer, Willis was allowed to take his car with him, and he was pleased to see the crew of the *President Coolidge* cover the car after lashing it down on the deck in San Francisco. He was sure that good times lay ahead. "Let me have that paradise of the Pacific!" was all he could think during the four-and-a-half-day passage.[16]

Impressions of Wheeler and Bellows Fields

During the late 1930s and the months leading up to December 1941, Wheeler and Bellows Fields were as different as two bases could be. The commander of the 14th Pursuit Wing, Brig. Gen. Howard C. Davidson, thought Wheeler Field "a beautiful place, nicely constructed and well kept," although he did not particularly care for its proximity to Schofield Barracks. Also, the base's exposed position left it open to incursions by outsiders.

Col. William J. Flood, who commanded the field itself, agreed wholeheartedly with Davidson's assessment. Wheeler was neat, tidy, beautiful, and well run, but its greatest drawback was its openness, which made espionage almost inevitable. As Davidson put it, "It lay there like a fish on a beach." His efforts to erect fencing about the base failed when he ran into opposition from the Hawaiian Department.[17]

Although the type and quality of Wheeler's quarters varied considerably, many of the men (and their wives) seemed satisfied. Their living conditions at Wheeler were far superior to the endemic poverty of rural America and the privations of the Great Depression.

Because the barracks at Wheeler Field were already filled to capacity, the base assigned many enlisted men to temporary quarters under canvas

pending completion of permanent housing. After joining the 696th Ordnance Company, Pvt. Fred R. Runce moved into Tent City between Hangars 2 and 3, which served as a holding area for the service troops and several pursuit squadrons while contractors completed the 600-Man Barracks. Surprisingly, the men enjoyed living in the tent barracks, finding the smaller number of men quartered in a tent preferable to the more spacious but crowded squad rooms of the older concrete barracks. Runce was fortunate that his tent was right off a street and got breezes that not all the tents enjoyed. "Oh, how we liked the barracks area!" he remembered. The men adjusted quite well to life under canvas in the pleasant Hawaiian weather.[18]

NCOs (staff sergeants and above) had the option of moving into Wheeler's detached housing. Among those fortunate NCOs was Staff Sergeant Koran. Flora Koran, who had worked outside her home for twelve years prior to her marriage to Stephen, was happy as a lark cooking up recipes that she had clipped from magazines in her single years. The twenty-seven-year-old woman who had lived in dreary apartments for all her adult life thought "keeping house was just marvelous." As an added advantage, the breakfast nook window offered the Korans one of the most beautiful sunset views on O'ahu.[19]

Flora acquired considerable skills as a baker, and the smell of her pineapple upside-down cakes wafted down the streets and brought in the boys for impromptu "inspections." Sometimes the stream of young men who came in for a taste of her cooking made her feel as if she were running a restaurant.[20]

While Flora was at home baking, Stephen Koran was on duty at Wheeler as a chief aerial photographer, working mainly with the 86th Observation Squadron until that unit transferred to Bellows Field. He was in the air quite a bit during the week, sometimes flying to the other islands, but he tried to keep his wife informed regarding prospective dinner plans. His pilot helped by agreeing to fly the aircraft directly over the Korans' duplex and revving

Stephen and Flora Koran in Waikīkī with Diamond Head as a distant backdrop, circa 1941. Staff Sergeant Koran, a professional photographer at Wheeler, probably set a delayed shutter release before running back to his perch on the sea wall, ensuring a beautifully composed photograph for posterity rather than a mere snapshot. **Lee**

Quarters 257, the duplex in which Stephen and Flora Koran are thought to have set up housekeeping after their marriage on 29 January 1941. The Korans probably lived in 257-A at left. View looks northeast toward the boundary between Wheeler Field and Schofield Barracks. Quarters 289 is in the background at the far right, and Quarters 283 is on the far left. **Lee**

Flora Koran shows off her dream kitchen in the couple's duplex at Wheeler Field, circa 1941. **Lee**

the engines three times as a signal that Koran would be home for dinner.[21]

In March 1941, Margaret "Sunny" Stewart joined her husband, 1st Lt. Everett Stewart, in Quarters 434-A, a duplex on Vought Avenue. The duplex was sparkling new when Sunny arrived, with two bedrooms, one bathroom, and a living room complete with a fireplace, "whether you needed it or not." The new housing complex itself still looked like a construction project—no lawn, sidewalks, or shrubbery—although the quarters had been provided with garbage cans. The lack of vegetation was not that upsetting with practically a twelve-month growing

season, because "anything'll grow later." More disturbing was that their furniture was still on the slow boat to Oʻahu. Happy to be together again, the Stewarts purchased a card table, requisitioned two Army cots, and borrowed four wooden "GI chairs" from one of Wheeler's offices.[22]

The Stewarts knew very well how fortunate they were to have on-base housing, which was exceedingly difficult to obtain. Had Sunny arrived any earlier, the couple would have had to search for housing in town, probably in Wahiawā. The unmarried officers suffered from the housing pinch as well, although contractors had almost completed a pair of BOQ apartment buildings on Lilienthal Place. By mid-to-late 1941, wooden BOQ "barracks" had been erected at the far eastern end of the base for unmarried 2nd lieutenants.[23]

The attractions of life in Hawai'i extended far beyond the new, modern quarters. Pvt. Will Roy Sample was sure he had landed in paradise. The soft climate and the natural beauty of the flora, with orchids and ferns growing wild, were a far cry from the dreary privations of east Texas. First Lt. Everett Stewart agreed. "It was a paradise . . . a quiet, peaceful life." In retrospect, however, enlisted men and officers alike acknowledged that the relatively slow pace of island life and the practice of keeping "tropical hours" quite likely hampered readiness.[24]

With more education than most airmen at the field, Pvt. Mannie E. Siegle landed an office job with the base's Quartermaster Detachment. Within two months he was in charge of ordering all supplies for Wheeler Field. He enjoyed his work but recognized that the base was a "leisurely place." The men knew their jobs and were well trained, but everyone seemed "more interested in sports than . . . going off to war." Except during alerts, it was customary at Wheeler on Wednesday afternoons to have quiet time in the barracks or to engage in organized sports.

First Lt. Everett Stewart's daily routine is a prime example of "tropical hours." Barring extenuating circumstances, a pilot's day started with flying at 0700, but he had *every* weekday afternoon off for golf and other leisure activities. There was no question that the lax routine had a corrosive effect on the units' overall preparedness.[25]

If Wheeler Field exemplified solid modernity, Bellows Field expressed just the opposite, although it had come quite a way from its humble beginnings as a gunnery range. The buildings within the newly constructed "Barracks Loop" were two-story affairs with sand-colored clapboard siding. The barracks for Pvt. Byron W. Kolbert and Bellows' Headquarters Detachment was only about one hundred yards from the shore in "a great spot, [with a] beautiful view."

On that eastern corner of the base, however, trouble loomed in paradise. Although the array of sixty-three-man barracks and the support buildings of "standard cantonment construction" were complete, the contractors had failed to provide sewerage connections. Half of the buildings sat on ground so low that even cesspools were infeasible, although the rest were able to use the existing septic system until the sewerage hookups became available.[26]

Other than the new construction, Bellows was a bit rough. Surrounded as it was by sugarcane fields and with a single road leading to it that ran through the township of Waimānalo, "You couldn't say that this base had the look of permanency to it." The only permanent structure was the "rock-solid" Headquarters Building atop the promontory in the center of the airfield, the lone high spot on "a base that was nothing but sand dunes."[27]

Visiting Dignitaries and Aviators

Through the 1920s and 1930s, Wheeler achieved some fame for hosting foreign dignitaries. With Capt. Horace N. Heison in temporary command of the field, Wheeler sent aloft a portion of its pursuit ships to take part in a thirty-plane "aloha flight" welcoming Prince and Princess Takamatsu of Japan (the prince was the younger brother of Emperor Hirohito) as they arrived at Honolulu on board the liner *Chichibu Maru* on 2 June 1931. In mid-September, thirty-four aircraft from Wheeler performed similar duties for the king and queen of Siam. One of the 18th Wing's utility aircraft—a Sikorsky C-6A twin-engine amphibian—squired the royal pair on an aerial tour of O'ahu on 17 September.[28]

Some famous military and civilian aviators used Wheeler Field during the same period as a waypoint on their attempts to cross the Pacific and set endurance records. From an Air Corps perspective, 1st Lt. Lester J. Maitland and 1st Lt. Albert F. Hegenberger carried out the most important of these flights—from the mainland to the Hawaiian Islands in June 1927. Although the Army had expressed interest

Nobuhito, Prince Takamatsu, the younger brother of Emperor Hirohito, sometime after his promotion to captain in the Imperial Japanese Navy in November 1942. **Prange**

Maj. Gen. Mason M. Patrick (the chief of the Air Corps) stressed that the timing of the Army's flight was "purely a coincidence" and was in no way connected to the Dole Derby—civilian enthusiasts competing for the $25,000 prize offered by James D. Dole for the successful first aerial voyage between the West Coast and Hawai'i. Patrick declared that "under no circumstances will the two aviators selected for this flight be permitted to accept any prize money or other awards."[31]

With modifications that included an extended wingspan and augmented fuel capacity, the lumbering Fokker had to use the seven-thousand-foot runway at the Oakland Municipal Airport because the Army field in San Francisco was too short for the fully loaded C-2. At 0708 Pacific Time on 28 June 1927, the trimotor craft carrying the two Army aviators—Maitland as pilot and Hegenberger as navigator—lifted away from the Oakland runway. The aircraft encountered a strong crosswind for the first five hundred miles and a very strong tailwind thereafter. Complications soon arose when Hegenberger's earth-inductor compass failed and the radio receiver "went bad several times." With little room for error and without his two advanced means of navigation, Hegenberger had to rely on old-fashioned dead reckoning. The weather refused to cooperate with Hegenberger's efforts to check the wind drift, because meaningful examination of the water below was almost impossible. Rain squalls forced Maitland into a nighttime ascent above the clouds to ten thousand feet so that Hegenberger could shoot the stars.[32]

in flights from the West Coast to Hawai'i for some years, the chain of command rebuffed Maitland's and Hegenberger's repeated requests, concluding that "the time was not yet ripe" for such a venture.[29]

Things started looking up in late 1926 when Hegenberger, considered "probably the best navigator the Air Corps had in uniform," proposed using a radio beam to navigate to far distant destinations. Tests at Dayton, Ohio, using such a "beacon" had proved very successful. In addition, the Air Corps had a new plane capable of making a flight over extreme distances—the Fokker C-2 transport, an aircraft with "splendid capacity, not alone for getting off the ground, but also for climbing at a good pace." To facilitate an extended flight, engineers increased the fuel capacity to 1,100 gallons.[30]

Secretary of War Dwight F. Davis approved the venture on 24 June 1927 with the proviso that "care be taken to avoid any rush in preparations for the flight." The Air Corps regarded the planned flight "as strictly an Army project" intended to "test newly developed navigational instruments and methods."

As if navigational woes were not enough, all three of the engines gave Maitland "a bit of trouble." The center engine ran rough in the frigid air and eventually failed due to an iced carburetor intake. Maitland descended to three thousand feet, managed to restart the engine, and ascended to seven thousand feet, where the stars were visible. At about midnight, the radio receiver started working and the beam indicated that *Bird of Paradise* was dead on course, testimony to Hegenberger's navigational skills.[33]

The *Bird of Paradise*, an Atlantic-Fokker C-2 (A.S. 26-202) piloted by 1st Lt. Lester J. Maitland with 1st Lt. Albert F. Hegenberger as navigator, takes off from Oakland Municipal Airport at 0708 on 28 June 1927, bound for Wheeler Field. **USAFM**

As the stiff tailwind pushed the aircraft west, Maitland decreased the speed to seventy miles per hour. Almost twenty-three hours after leaving Oakland he spied a faint light in the gathering dawn that the two men identified at 0600 as the Kilauea Point light on Kaua'i. The white cylindrical tower rising 216 feet above the water also emitted a radio beacon for 10 minutes every half hour. Although heavy clouds cloaked the island, Maitland and Hegenberger considered the sunrise on Kaua'i "the most beautiful sight they [had] ever seen." Rather than risk landing at Wheeler in the darkness, Maitland and Hegenberger circled Kaua'i, crossed the channel toward O'ahu, and finally touched down on Wheeler Field's turf at 0629 after an almost twenty-six-hour flight. Exhausted and hungry, the men discovered that the coffee, soup, and sandwiches provided for the flight (but that they could not find) had been covered by a tarpaulin.[34]

As for the civilians attempting the flight to Hawai'i, the $25,000 Dole Derby was still on. Luck ran out for all but two of the crews. Of the four that started out, two turned back and only two finished: Arthur Goebel and Navy lieutenant William V. Davis in first place, and Martin Jensen and Paul Schluter in second. An estimated throng of 20,000–30,000 people descended on Wheeler Field on 17 August to

A welcoming party greets Maitland (*left*) and Hegenberger (*right*) after their landing on the morning of 29 June 1927. **USAFM**

A throng of civilian aviation enthusiasts awaits the arrival of the Dole Derby winner on 17 August 1927.
TLM, 94.01.01-17

witness the Derby's conclusion, depleting the Post Exchange's inventory of popcorn and hot dogs.[35]

The real value of the race to Hawai'i (actually "won" by the Army) was that it demonstrated the efficacy of using radio beams to navigate over the vast expanse of the Pacific Ocean—a method that would be put to good use in the spring of 1941 when other Army pilots and their crews delivered twenty-one B-17D Flying Fortresses to the Hawaiian Department.

Some better-known aviators passed through Wheeler in the mid-to-late 1930s as well. Capt. Sir

Charles E. Kingsford-Smith, a decorated Australian aviator from the Great War whose postwar aerial exploits entertained people in the United States and the British Commonwealth, stopped at Wheeler in his Fokker F.VIIb/3m trimotor, the *Southern Cross*, on 1 June 1928 while attempting the first crossing of the Pacific from Oakland to Brisbane. Six years later, he passed through Wheeler again during a series of flights from Brisbane to San Francisco, this time in a fast two-seater monoplane—a Lockheed Altair dubbed the *Lady Southern Cross*. The west-to-east trans-Pacific crossing was yet another first in aviation

The *Lady Southern Cross*, the blue-and-silver Lockheed Altair flown to O'ahu by Capt. Sir Charles E. Kingsford-Smith on 29 October 1934, rests on the apron at Wheeler Field. **TLM, P.001,100**

Capt. P. O. Taylor (with beard, copilot) and Kingsford-Smith (pilot) mug for the camera after landing the *Lady Southern Cross* at Wheeler Field. **TLM, P.000,369**

history. About five thousand people were on hand at Wheeler Field to watch Kingsford-Smith land on the second leg of his flight from Suva, Fiji. In early November 1935, while attempting yet another series of record-breaking flights to Australia, Kingsford-Smith disappeared over the Bay of Bengal.[36]

A year before Kingsford-Smith was lost, Captain Charles T. P. Ulm, who had flown with Kingsford-Smith in his 1928 appearance at Wheeler Field, scheduled a stopover at Wheeler in 1934 in the *Stella Australis*, an Airspeed AS.6A Envoy I. Ulm and his copilot/navigator/radioman had planned to take off from Oakland on Saturday, 1 December 1934, but the weather bureau advised them to wait for a day. The men waited until Monday, 3 December, to depart, hoping for better weather near the Hawaiian Islands, but conditions worsened as they flew west. Unable to check for wind drift or to shoot stars to verify their position, Ulm and his partner became more and more concerned, as did the people waiting for their arrival at Wheeler. Various newspapers carried the flash messages and distress calls from the plane as the men became disoriented in the bad weather. An extremely strong quartering tailwind from the southeast blew them well past Oʻahu, and Ulm was forced to ditch. To save weight on the long flight, the *Stella Australis*

had not carried a life raft, as Ulm believed the aircraft capable of floating for days. His last message, received at 0930 (Hawaiʻi time) on 3 December, indicated that the *Stella Australis* was still afloat. Despite searches by "18 submarines, 3 mine-layers, and two Coast Guard vessels, supplemented later by some 35 airplanes from the Army and the Navy," Ulm and his partner vanished without a trace.[37]

In the 1930s few aviators—except for Charles A. Lindbergh—had more name recognition than Amelia Earhart Putnam. Her transoceanic and endurance flights brought her to Wheeler Field twice. At the end of one of its many voyages between the West Coast and Hawaiʻi, the *Lurline* arrived in Honolulu Harbor on 27 December 1934 with 246 passengers on board. Although many—if not most—were seeking rest and relaxation in the islands, one small group was intent on completing an entirely different quest. Amelia Earhart stepped down onto the pier near the Aloha Tower accompanied by her husband, George Putnam. Also present were close friend (and fellow pilot) Paul Mantz and his wife, Myrtle. The presence of Earhart's red Lockheed Vega 5b monoplane fueled speculation that the famed aviatrix was about to embark on another of her epic long-distance flights. The party attempted to tamp down the frenzy, insisting that the aircraft—still secured to the *Lurline*'s deck—was for interisland flights only.[38]

Earhart's true intention, however, was to use O'ahu as the springboard from which to complete the first solo flight from Hawai'i to Oakland. Tight security surrounded the group because George Putnam wanted a minimum of public attention. Before going on to the Queen's Surf Hotel, Earhart and Mantz went to Wheeler Field and consulted with 1st Lt. George H. Sparhawk, a radio expert and communications officer with the 18th Pursuit Group.[39]

As days passed and Earhart's Lockheed Vega remained parked at Wheeler, she and her advisers completed their preparations. At about noon on 11 January, George and Catherine Sparhawk hosted a luncheon for Earhart, her husband, the Mantzes, Maj. Ernest Clark (Wheeler's commanding officer), and Navy aerological officer Lt. Emory W. Stephens. After lunch, Earhart retired for a nap while Mantz went to the hangar to make last-minute checks on the Vega.[40]

Earhart's takeoff came as a surprise even at Wheeler Field, as George Putnam had insisted that the flight "not be announced publicly until Miss Earhart was in the air." William H. Ewing, chief of the Associated Press bureau in Honolulu, happened to be at Wheeler at the time of Earhart's departure. Ewing

estimated that only two hundred people (almost all military) had gathered at "the service hangar" hoping to watch a rumored test flight. The weather and the condition of the field were not good, with "low rain clouds . . . over [the] Waianae mountains stretching between Schofield plateau and the sea."[41]

At about 1600, Paul Mantz warmed up the Lockheed Vega's engine. Prior to 1630, a sedan driven by 1st Lieutenant Sparhawk drove up in front of the hangar and a smiling Earhart emerged wearing a fur-lined flying suit. At that point Putnam announced that his wife would take off for Oakland in half an hour. With the aircraft warmed up, Earhart entered the cockpit, gunned the engine, and allowed it to idle while she checked her instruments. When all was to her satisfaction, she waved at the ground crews to remove the Vega's wheel chocks, pushed the throttle forward, and taxied onto the landing field at "rain-soaked Wheeler."[42]

Although an aircraft soaring into the heavens is usually the picture of elegance, Earhart's takeoff was as ugly as they come. As described by Ewing: "The ship started slowly and appeared heavy and cumbersome. The field evidently was rough and the plane lumbered from side to side with its nearly two tons of gasoline. . . . [M]ud, in which the wheels sank

Amelia Earhart's red Lockheed Vega 5b arrives at Wheeler Field after being ferried to the base from the docks in Honolulu, circa December 1934. **TLM, P.001,604**

Amelia Earhart and her associate Paul Mantz pose atop Earhart's Lockheed 10E Electra at Wheeler, circa March 1937. **AFHRA**

several inches, was flung by the propeller in a stream behind, spattering the fuselage and tail." Despite the less than glamorous takeoff, Earhart arrived in Oakland eighteen hours and sixteen minutes later to a tumultuous welcome, having attained yet another landmark achievement.[43]

On another visit to Hawai'i, Earhart and her associates arrived by air rather than by sea. Accompanying her were copilot and assistant navigator Fred J. Noonan, navigator Harry Manning, and technical specialist and supervisor of maintenance Paul Mantz. Earhart landed her Lockheed 10E Electra at Wheeler Field on 18 March 1937 at 0545, setting a new record for the crossing to O'ahu of fifteen hours

and fifty-one and a half minutes. This time, however, the flight from the West Coast was not about breaking time records. Rather, it constituted the first leg of a flight around the world. Perhaps remembering the rough nature of Wheeler's landing field from two years previous, Earhart decided to depart for Howland Island from Luke Field on Ford Island.[44]

Earhart planned to take off from Ford Island on 20 March following a day's rest for herself and her crew. At 0553 she pushed the throttles forward and the Lockheed rolled up the runway. Approximately one thousand feet into her run, the plane blew a tire and the landing gear collapsed. The aircraft veered sharply and ground to a halt, but not before the

Earhart's Electra parked in front of Hangar 1 at Wheeler, circa March 1937. **AFHRA**

Electra sustained heavy damage, including a cracked engine, a punctured fuel tank, a badly damaged right wing, and a torn fuselage.[45]

Earhart and company wasted little time lamenting the mishap, but instead booked passage to the West Coast on the *Malolo* for that same day, leaving the Electra marooned on Ford Island. The plane was "removed from the flying field and stored in the [Hawaiian Air] Depot's final assembly hangar [probably Hangar 78] pending further instructions." At 1000 on 25 March—five days after the crash—Earhart sent instructions for shipment of the battered Electra stateside. The depot handled the disassembly, crating, and transfer of the wreck to a commercial barge for shipment on board a commercial vessel. Meanwhile, Earhart laid the groundwork for another attempt on 2 June. On this flight, however, Earhart would follow an equatorial route heading east rather than west. Somewhere between New Guinea and Howland Island, Earhart, Noonan, and the Electra disappeared.[46]

Entertainment and Morale on Base

Apart from the infrequent novelty of visiting dignitaries, entertainment opportunities at Wheeler Field proper were somewhat sparse until shortly before the war, largely because Wheeler remained a part of Schofield Barracks until 30 August 1939. The field did provide a Post Exchange with a beer garden and soda fountain, as well as activities at the service clubs. Separation of the base from Schofield brought welcome changes. The new movie theater that opened in the fall of 1941 relieved the need to visit Schofield Barracks to watch films. Other diversions, however, still required the ten-minute walk north to Schofield, where there was plenty to do: outdoor sports, a boxing arena, roller skating, bowling, a huge library, theaters, and numerous beer gardens. The town of Wahiawā, just northeast of Wheeler, was all too willing to host the men who were up for the fifteen- to twenty-minute walk out Wheeler's back gate. In addition to an outside roller/ice-skating rink there were the customary taverns and restaurants. A lively brothel "trade" gave the little town a somewhat unsavory reputation.[47]

The relatively slow pace of life at Wheeler to some degree made up for the lack of on-base amenities. Sporting events were just as popular in the military as in civilian life, and Hawai'i had it all; boxing matches, baseball, basketball, and football games were always well attended, particularly the interservice games between the Army and the Navy. Because Wheeler was "rather isolated from the activities of downtown Honolulu," the men tended to spend a lot of their free time in sports-related activities on base, with a very heavy emphasis on basketball. The 46th Pursuit Squadron had an excellent basketball team that competed regularly with squads from Schofield Barracks, although Wheeler's cagers suffered from the lack of a gymnasium for practice. Boxing was a

Happy airmen line up to enter the beer garden at Wheeler Field's old Post Exchange, 1939. **TLM, P.001,657**

The Library at Schofield Barracks. **NARA II, 111-SC-123483**

favorite spectator sport. Schofield Barracks promoted and hosted tremendous fights, with unit matches balancing the standalone bouts that were indicative of the men's high level of competitiveness and fighting spirit. O'ahu's summerlike climate fostered the popularity of baseball as well.[48]

Advancement, Pay, and Gambling

As volunteers, the men felt a sense of community and unity of purpose. All were on a path to become professional soldiers, and all were there because they wanted to be. Rank advancement in those years, however, could be very slow. A man felt lucky to have earned a corporal's stripes by the end of his first enlistment. NCOs ruled the roost. The sergeant was "like a little God," and when no commissioned officers were present, the NCO's word was law. Rank truly mattered in those days, and there was little interaction between lower ranks and the NCOs, which most agreed was a good arrangement.[49]

A baseball game in progress on 9 July 1934 at Wheeler Field between the base's team and the 35th Infantry Regiment's team visiting from Schofield Barracks. The Wheeler Fliers defeated the 35th Infantry's Cactusmen behind the pitching of Maury Jungman. The baseball field would eventually give way to a complex of NCO duplexes. **TLM, 93.14.07-26**

Presumably on payday, gaming and gambling (having spilled over from the dayrooms) proceed in earnest on the balconies and verandas of Wheeler's 600-Man Barracks.
TLM, 95.16.06

To circumvent the dilemma of rank advancement, the Army devised specialist ratings, whereby a 2nd class specialist received a sergeant's pay, but not the stripes. The men appreciated this system because they could advance and make more money without having the responsibilities of being a noncommissioned officer. The use of specialist ratings helped maintain morale as well, because a man with initiative could always better himself. Pvt. Will Roy Sample, for instance, eventually attained the status of a "first and first"—the rank of private, first class and the rating of 1st class specialist with the pay of a staff sergeant.[50]

On payday at the end of the month, soldiers and airmen settled debts and rushed to the PX to purchase items they would need for the next month, such as soap and razor blades, while they still had money in their pockets. Although Army pay was comparable to Navy pay, the Navy paid its men twice a month. The Navy men's advantage in that regard added to interservice animosity and jealousy. As Pvt. John J. Springer noted, "They had it over us which we didn't like."[51]

Gambling was widespread at Wheeler, fueled in part by the extra pay specialists received. It commenced on payday. Airmen gambled until their money ran low or they scored a jackpot and could bow out of the game with extra cash. At about 1900 or 2000 hours, most took off with their winnings (or what was left of their pay) and blew everything on a big time in Honolulu. By the fifteenth of the month, many were broke until the next payday came around.[52]

At both Hickam and Wheeler Fields, the authorities realized that gambling was impossible to eradicate and decided instead to closely regulate the activity. The bases tended to confine gambling to the units' dayrooms, which had pool tables for craps and smaller tables that could be used for poker and blackjack. The dayroom "casinos" were open for business during the weekend and on payday Fridays. An armed guard was present to prevent altercations—a position much coveted for the "rake-off" of the winnings. A percentage of the rake-off went to the squadron, but the balance went to guards, who were reputed to have cleared $300 to $500 per month.[53]

Social Life for NCOs and Officers

The NCOs on base had a very pleasant social life, with NCO clubs at both Wheeler and Schofield Barracks available to them. Schofield boasted at least four base theaters and bowling alleys as well. There was a variety of sporting events to attend and wonderful beaches for swimming. Married couples went to dances on Saturday nights, then retired in groups to someone's quarters for a late-night snack, chitchat, and the latest gossip. There were "a thousand and one stories going around"—but Wheeler "was just like a happy family."[54]

Sunny Stewart had a one-word description for social life on prewar O'ahu: "Lovely!" The natural center of such activities was Wheeler's Officers' Club. Everyone looked forward to the informal "Nineteenth Hole" gatherings on Friday nights, when drinks were fifteen cents. Saturday nights were formal occasions, with the women in gowns and the men in mess dress. Even in quarters, one dressed up when hosting more than one couple. Mess dress uniforms were obligatory in theaters and even at boxing matches, where the officers and their wives *always* dressed appropriately after 1800. Women had no difficulty finding dresses for these occasions. The multitude of Japanese and Chinese seamstresses in Wahiawā made it easy to obtain multiple outfits. A woman could purchase "material for fifteen cents a yard and the silk was dirt cheap." She need only bring in a picture of a dress, "and they'd make it for practically nothing."[55]

Going to Town

Passes to go into Honolulu and Waikīkī for one or more days were very easy to obtain before the war, although men needed to apply through the section head, the company's adjutant, and the 1st sergeant. The schedule for weekend passes called for men to be released at 1200 on Saturday—presumably after inspection—and to return by 1800 on Sunday evening. The coveted "Class A pass" enabled a soldier to leave Saturday at noon and return at 0600 on Monday. As long as the airman was back for reveille, all was well.[56]

The policy for weekday passes was also lenient. One could leave the base at 1800 and stay away until 0600 the following morning. The frequency of visits into Honolulu and Waikīkī depended on the amount of money in a soldier's pocket. The men in the lower ranks commonly went every two weeks.[57]

The Hawaiian Department's very liberal policy toward issuing passes was not without limits, however. The customary proportion of men retained on base on any given weekend was about 50–60 percent. At a bare minimum, about 25 percent of the men at Wheeler Field stayed on base to serve as guards or to perform critical functions such as mess duty. Certain individuals were ineligible for passes owing to disciplinary problems. For those men obliged to stay on base there was always entertainment available at Schofield Barracks.[58]

The principal disadvantage of going into Honolulu and Waikīkī on a Saturday or Sunday was the sheer volume of visitors; there were queues outside every establishment. Some airmen limited trips to the middle of the week and the last of the month to avoid the weekend crush. Inevitably, the Army-Navy competition continued in town. Pvt. John Springer reminisced that Honolulu was certainly a "Navy town." The sailors were easy to spot because uniforms were mandatory in the Navy. Soldiers could wear civilian garb while on pass, which made it easier to blend in with civilians in town. Many airmen shied away from Honolulu when sailors were out in force. It was not that most of the trouble started with sailors, but rather the frustrating congestion in the city was such that it took far less to set tempers flaring.[59]

Wheeler's inland location made the ride into Honolulu both long and expensive. A thirty-mile cab ride into town cost fifty cents, nearly a half-day's wages for a buck private. Five Wheelerites sometimes crammed a taxi to capacity and contributed ten cents each to lessen the expense. But despite the high costs of going into Honolulu, the city and its amusements— from the wholesome to the prurient—drew the American servicemen like bees to honey. Moreover, perhaps owing to the vast economic benefits, people in Hawai'i seemed genuinely happy to have them there, unlike the mainland, where the public often displayed hostility toward servicemembers.[60]

With the $10 to $15 an airman might accumulate during the week he could stay at the YMCA downtown for about $2.25 per night and still have money left for a good time. But the YMCA was usually filled to capacity with sailors unless one happened to win the race with the Navy's liberty boats. The YMCA's proximity to the Black Cat Café was considered a big plus as well. Some men pooled their funds to rent a cottage; others found a bed in a rooming house in

The Black Cat Café was across Hotel Street from the YMCA in Honolulu. **USAR 1592**

Honolulu or Waikīkī—a much cheaper option than booking a room at a hotel. Once a man had a place to sleep, he could move on to the bars or the beach. [61]

Selecting a restaurant was among the most important things to do after arriving in Honolulu. The food at Wheeler wasn't bad, but a nice sit-down meal with table service was a welcomed relief from the mess hall lines. Restaurants in Honolulu offered many affordable alternatives: coffee cost five cents and hamburgers fifteen, while a great steak dinner could be had for about a dollar. Chinese and Japanese restaurants offered a wide selection of exotic food at very reasonable prices. [62]

Hotel Street was "where all the action was," and the tawdry thoroughfare had it all: tavern after tavern, theaters and restaurants, and houses of prostitution seemingly on every street corner. With all the "attractions" jammed so close together it was "easier for a serviceman to part with his money." Pvt. Henry Brown and his buddies in the 46th Pursuit Squadron tended to "blow it all" on Hotel Street's cottages, rooming houses, and bars. When the money ran out or the men were sufficiently "stewed," no choice remained but to return to Wheeler. Most of the airmen were not in town simply to get drunk, though. It was fun just to walk the streets, see a movie, chase girls in town, or go to lūʻaus and the beach. [63]

High times in Honolulu were not the only outlet for servicemen on Oʻahu. For those with an automobile (or a friend who owned one) the natural wonders of the entire island became accessible. There was fishing, tours around the island, and alternative pastimes such as the swimming and relative solitude available at Soldiers Beach and the "off the beaten path" intimacy of the Sea View Inn, both just above the town of Haleʻiwa on the North Shore. Private Sample, who was fifteen years older than most of the airmen, generally had a quieter time on passes. Sample relished day trips to Soldiers Beach just to walk in the surf, pick up seashells, and relax with a beer or two at the Sea View Inn. [64]

Locations closer to Wheeler had their own appeal. The adjacent town of Wahiawā, just a short bus ride or an extended walk away, offered beer and ice cream. While a man flush with cash generally headed for Honolulu, Wahiawā offered simpler pleasures for a modest price. West of Wahiawā, the excellent restaurant at Kemoʻo Farms offered superb

Tourists, sunbathers, and swimmers crowd Waikīkī Beach during the 1930s. The twin wings of the Moana Hotel are in the background. **Cressman**

food without the inconvenience of going all the way to Honolulu.[65]

Pvt. Milroy L. Richardson of the 6th Pursuit Squadron searched out wholesome activities for when his wife arrived at the end of the year. Physical activities such as swimming, horseback riding, and roller-skating met that criterion, but like most other soldiers Richardson enjoyed the occasional beer as well.[66]

Officers such as 2nd Lt. Phillip Willis considered Hawai'i "the nicest thing in the world." Wearing a tuxedo and going to the Officers' Club "was just the thing to do on Saturday night." The officers cruised the Royal Hawaiian and Moana Hotels and the bars

up and down the beach. "We made the town just like you'd expect a pilot to do," Willis remembered, although an officer who knew he was to fly the next day went easy on the drinks. "He knew better than to get out of line." Willis could hardly wait to fly his fiancée to O'ahu to share in the fun.[67]

Bellows Field was a long way from the happy times in Honolulu, though not in air miles. One either had to traverse the Ko'olau Mountains via the Pali Pass in a bus or taxi, which was slow going, or go around the southeast corner of O'ahu on a twisting, narrow, two-lane road behind slow-moving traffic. And on arrival, "wall-to-wall 'white hats'" impeded

Soldiers Beach north of Hale'iwa Town—seen here circa the mid-1930s—had separate areas for enlisted men and officers. The Sea View Inn is just visible in the distance at the upper right. **Wenger**

The Sea View Inn—thought to date from the 1920s—was a popular place for homestyle dining. It had several dining rooms for guests and groups, and was convenient to Soldiers Beach, out of view behind the building. **HSA**

access to restaurants and bars. Hence, a substantial number of men stayed home and enjoyed fishing, swimming, and diving—for which beautiful Bellows Beach was perfectly suited.[68]

Visitors from the Mainland

Although most servicemen on O'ahu could not expect visits from friends and family (apart from the arrival of spouses), there were happy exceptions. Second Lt. George S. Welch had not seen his mother, Julia Schwartz, since he was transferred from Hamilton Field in February 1941. On 8 October, however, she boarded the *Matsonia* in Los Angeles for the six-day voyage to the islands, arriving on 14 October. Sources for the *Honolulu Advertiser*'s "Tourist Tattler" spotted

her in the lobby of the Royal Hawaiian Hotel, so she may have stayed there during her visit. George took no leave while his mother was there, but with "tropical hours" in force he was free to spend time with her in the afternoons and evenings, and during the weekends of 17, 24, and 31 October. Mrs. Schwartz's visit to the islands certainly ended on a high note. When she departed for the West Coast on 7 November on board the *Lurline*, her son treated her to a special farewell. Welch scheduled a forty-five-minute "aerobatic flight" out of Wheeler in P-40B "155," its stated purpose being to "Buzz Mothers [*sic*] Boat." Prior to her departure, like the mother of any pilot, Julia Schwartz probably begged Welch to be careful, and like any dutiful son, he probably assured her that all would be well.[69]

Waikīkī Beach and its two prestigious hotels: the Royal Hawaiian (*left*) and the Moana (*right*). **Cressman**

Chapter Five

"A RATHER CAREFREE LOT WHO HAD TO BE KEPT IN CHECK"

Duty at Oʻahu's Fighter Bases

Ranks and Specialties

Although enlisted men in the pursuit units of the Hawaiian Air Force performed a wide variety of duties, the distribution within specialties at Wheeler differed considerably compared with that of the bombardment and reconnaissance units at Hickam Field. The table below compares Wheeler's 46th Pursuit Squadron with Hickam's 4th Reconnaissance Squadron in November 1941. The reconnaissance unit at Hickam was more than 60 percent larger than its Wheeler counterpart due to the aircrew requirements for twin- and four-engine aircraft.

Enlisted Rank Distribution in Pursuit versus Bombardment Squadrons

Ranks	46th Pursuit Squadron	4th Recon Squadron
MSgt.	1	4
1Sgt.	1	1
TSgt.	7	6
SSgt.	5	22
Sgt.	18	27
Cpl.	19	19
Pfc.	38	50
Pvt.	49	92
Totals	138	221

The 4th Reconnaissance Squadron divided its airmen among twenty-four specialties, whereas the 46th Pursuit (with fewer airplane mechanics, armorers, and clerks) had six other specialties: radio operators and electricians, battery electricians, toolroom workers, cooks, and truck drivers. Again, the disparity was due to the increased size and complexity of maintaining and operating multi-engine bombardment aircraft. In addition, squadrons at Hickam Field had a far larger number of specialized airplane engine mechanics. Wheeler's squadrons had only three men rated in that specialty but more than six hundred rated as *airplane mechanics*, some of whom certainly performed double duty and maintained aircraft engines as well.

The headquarters squadrons for Wheeler's group and wing commands had far more clerks assigned, proportionately, than purely tactical squadrons. Of 165 men in the headquarters squadron of the 15th Pursuit Group, 31 (19 percent) had clerical duties, as opposed to 10 men (7 percent) in a tactical unit such as the 46th Pursuit Squadron. Clerks applied the administrative grease that maintained headquarters functions at all levels of command. One need only examine the blizzard of paperwork required at a group or even squadron level to appreciate the magnitude of the tasks these men performed behind the scenes. Paperwork included morning reports, monthly rosters, orders, assignments, and schedules, plus forms for administration of personnel, maintenance of equipment, and engineering files.

Wheeler's tactical units had an abundance of airplane mechanics and armorers, with almost two-thirds of the 46th Pursuit Squadron's enlisted men working in those two specialties. The mechanics were by far the most visible enlisted men at Wheeler. They not only kept the P-40s and P-36s flying every day, they held the pilots' lives in their hands. Proper maintenance was the mechanics' highest concern. One particular crew chief quizzed his pilots each time they landed, taking notes on the trim required for a particular aircraft and ensuring that his men made the proper adjustments before the plane's next flight. Engineers and mechanics fretted when pilots were overdue and walked down to the flight line to wait for late arrivals, who did not always return. Although there was always the hope that a missing pilot had ditched successfully and been picked up, Cpl. Edward J. White recalled that "some were and some weren't, but we always kept track of them."[1]

Armorers maintained a similarly high visibility within the squadrons. Each P-40 fighter was assigned four armorers. Pvt. Milroy Richardson of the 6th Pursuit Squadron shared the responsibility for maintaining and arming the two .50-caliber machine guns atop the P-40's engine and two .30-caliber machine guns in each of the wings. He also made sure the three-roll cam that prevented the guns from firing if the propeller blades were directly in front of the muzzles was functioning properly; improper calibration could be fatal to both pilot and plane. Armorers cleaned the guns following flight operations, running an oiled patch down the machine-gun barrel to prevent rust. On Saturday afternoons, they removed the guns and broke them down for a more thorough cleaning. When loading ammunition for aerial target practice, the armorers dipped the rounds in different colors of paint to determine which of the pilots hit the target sleeve.[2]

The Impact of Revetment Construction

The array of aircraft revetments the 804th Engineer Battalion completed in June 1941 altered the character and appearance of Wheeler Field as well as the daily life and routines of the field's mechanics,

A revetment at Hickam Field, circa mid-1942, showing two camouflaged P-40s and a P-36A under camouflage netting. P-36A "708" (A.C. Serial No. 38-22) at center and P-40B "702" (A.C. Serial No. 41-5304) were both survivors of the Japanese attack on 7 December 1941. **NARA II, RG 407**

armorers, and pilots. The new earthen berms on the eastern and southern fringes of the field partly obstructed the view of Wheeler from points east along the Kamehameha Highway as well as views from the field looking south and east. The revetments further concealed the camouflaged P-40s that had arrived during late March and April, although P-36As with a natural metal finish still stood out. By November, camouflage netting was available for placement atop the revetments, and a number of the P-36s had been painted olive drab.[3]

When squadrons deployed to "the bunkers" for the first time during the Hawaiian Department alert of mid-1941, new routines and responsibilities awaited the men who accompanied them. The procedure for any alert commenced with maintenance crews towing aircraft south and east to the revetments. The crew for each aircraft—working in shifts—lived out there and returned to the barracks only to do laundry or to enjoy an occasional hot meal.[4]

A four-man defense squad led by an armorer was responsible for the security of each plane during the period of the alert. Armorer Milroy Richardson headed the four-man squad that operated a .50-caliber machine gun to defend their revetment against attack. A second airman was responsible for ammunition, with the additional pair as general helpers. Squads set up their machine guns behind the revetments in sandbagged positions facing outward from

the field approximately one hundred feet apart, or at every revetment. An opening in the rear allowed crews to pass back and forth to either man the machine gun or maintain the aircraft. A tent fly over the gun position deflected the sun and protected the men from the daily rainstorms. Bug spray was a necessity, as were cots for all the crewmen who were in the revetments but *not* manning the machine gun.[5]

Obviously, plane maintenance during the alerts placed additional pressures on Wheeler's armorers and mechanics. Aircraft had to be kept armed, fueled, and ready to take off at a moment's notice. Engines and radios underwent constant checks. The crew chiefs—who stayed with the aircraft around the clock—started the engines every half hour to ensure that the pilots could take off immediately.[6]

Wheeler's Aircraft

The various aircraft maintenance personnel at Wheeler, Bellows, and Haleiwa Fields were there for a crucial reason: to support the aircraft charged with the defense of Hawai'i. The most important airplane types at the three fields were the Curtiss P-36 and P-40 and the North American O-47. The P-36A had its origins in the Model 75, the Curtiss Aircraft Company's entry in the Air Corps' competition for pursuit aircraft. The Model 75 suffered from "powerplant problems" and lost out to Seversky's entry, which took on the Army's P-35 designation.

Lt. Col. William E. Lynd, commander of the 18th Pursuit Group, above the western slopes of the Ko'olau Range in PR/1, his personal Curtiss P-36A Hawk, 8 February 1940. Lynd's aircraft was one of a small batch of P-36As ferried to O'ahu long before the shipments of P-36s and P-40s arrived from February through April 1941.
NARA II, 342-FH-3B-29018

Curtiss received a consolation order after agreeing to upgrade the Model 75's engine and won a subsequent completion in 1937. The order for 210 fighters that followed represented the Army's largest acquisition of pursuit ships since the Great War. The P-36A remained the Army's principal fighter aircraft until deliveries of the Curtiss P-40 commenced in 1941.

With only two machine guns firing through the propeller arc—one .50 caliber and one .30 caliber—the P-36A had insufficient firepower, but it was rugged and maneuverable, and it "gave an excellent account of itself in the hands of dedicated pilots."[7]

Aviation historian Peter M. Bowers considered the Curtiss P-40 "obsolete by European standards before

41/18P, a Curtiss P-40B of the 18th Pursuit Group's 6th Pursuit Squadron, off O'ahu, 1 August 1941, subsequent to its delivery to the Hawaiian Department in either March or April. This view shows the fighter's armament: two .50-caliber machine guns firing through the propeller arc and two .30-caliber guns in each wing. **Makiel, via Arroyo**

The right bulkhead of P-40C (A.C. Serial No. 41-13377). The airframe's serial number appears on the data plate above the vertical centerline of the map case, right of the pilot's seat. Note the charging handles for the two right-hand .30-caliber machine guns at the lower left. **USAFM**

Instrument panel of a Curtiss P-40C, 29 March 1941. The panel is recessed forward of the cockpit opening. The gun-charging handles for the two outboard .30-caliber wing guns are at lower center, just below the instrument panel. Handles for the inboard guns are just out of view along the bottom margin of the image. **USAFM**

The left bulkhead of a P-40C, 10 May 1941. The throttle quadrant, with the controls for engine revolutions, fuel mixture, and propeller pitch, is at upper center; the electrical control box is at lower center; and the elevator and rudder trim tab controls are on the left. Note the charging handles for the left-hand .30-caliber machine guns at the lower right. **USAFM**

the prototype ever flew." The fact that the P-40 was not designed from scratch but was simply a re-engineered P-36 airframe supports that view. But the P-40 has had its admirers, too. It held the line against the Japanese in China, Hawai'i, and the southwest Pacific during 1941 and early 1942, and until 1943 was available in greater numbers than any other American pursuit plane.[8]

Air Corps specifications were responsible for some of the P-40's initial shortcomings: specifically, its inadequate armor and armament, and lack of self-sealing fuel cells. The P-40's relatively poor performance against Axis fighters early in the war was due to its design as a low-altitude fighter rather than a high-altitude interceptor. In the aircraft's defense, the P-40Bs of the American Volunteer Group in China claimed to have destroyed 286 Japanese aircraft in combat with a loss of only 12 of their own. Although dogfighting with the Mitsubishi A6M2 Type 0 carrier fighter was to be avoided, the P-40 excelled in North Africa against the Messerschmitt Bf-109 at low altitude. Like its P-36 progenitor, the rugged P-40 "could absorb terrific punishment from enemy gunfire and . . . return to base when a lesser structure would have been destroyed."[9]

The P-40Bs and P-40Cs present in Hawai'i in 1941 had two .50-caliber machine guns firing through the

The two .50-caliber nose guns on a P-40B. The windscreen is just out of the picture at left, with the twin bins for the ammunition at upper left center between the two guns. The gun barrels point out to the right. **Bell**

A pair of stainless-steel .30-caliber ammunition boxes for the guns for *one wing* of a P-40B. Subtle differences in the shapes of the boxes (and their ammunition capacity) meant that the boxes were not interchangeable. Note that the armorer set the right end of the right-hand box next to the machine gun, with the same applying to the left end of the left-hand box. **Bell**

A view of the underside of the left wing on a P-40B, with access doors dropped open to allow insertion of the ammunition boxes. The long tabs on the bottoms of the boxes are positioned toward the guns. **Bell**

A view of the upper side of the wing on a P-40B, with the access doors opened to allow the armorer on top of the wing to insert the ammunition belt's lead cartridge into the gun breech. **Bell**

propeller arc, and two .30-caliber machine guns in each wing. The ammunition supply for the nose guns was stored in a stainless-steel subdivided bin positioned between the two guns, with 380 rounds per gun. To load the weapons, the armorer opened the gun breeches, set in the lead cartridges from the two belts contained in either side of the central bin, and closed the breeches. Loading the .30-caliber wing guns was more complicated in that two armorers were required, one above the wing and one below it. Two oblong hatches below each wing—one inboard and one outboard for each pair of guns—dropped open, and the armorer lifted the stainless-steel ammunition boxes into the pair of underwing receptacles. The boxes for the two guns were not interchangeable; the inboard gun carried 500 rounds, and the outboard gun carried 480 rounds. The armorer atop the wing opened two small ports, set the lead cartridges from the ammunition belts into the breeches, and then closed them.[10]

Bellows Field's Aircraft

As of late 1941, the North American O-47B was the principal aircraft in the roster of the 86th Observation Squadron at Bellows Field. Although two smaller Stinson O-49s were at the field during the first week in December, the O-47 was the 86th's mainstay. Approximately six were present at the field at that time, with three others under repair in the Hawaiian Air Depot.[11]

The O-47 resulted from a design project at North American Aviation to replace two older observation biplanes from the late 1920s and early 1930s—the Thomas-Morse O-19 and the Douglas O-38. One of the unusual characteristics of North American's offering was the observation compartment in the belly below the wings, designed to provide the observer/photographer with an unobstructed view of the terrain below. The type carried a crew of three—pilot, observer, and rear gunner. The Army maneuvers of 1941 highlighted the O-47's shortcomings,

A Stinson O-49, piloted by 2nd Lt. James T. Lewis, flies over Wheeler Field on 7 August 1941. In known images of 86th Observation Squadron aircraft, none of the O-49s appears to have a tail number. **AFHRA**

A North American O-47B assigned to the 86th Observation Squadron at Wheeler Field, circa 1939–40. All the squadron's O-47s had their natural metal finish camouflaged prior to the war. **AFHRA**

as other lighter and more nimble aircraft proved more suitable for the Army's photoreconnaissance needs. Consequently, the Army Air Force eventually employed O-47s as target tugs and as inshore patrol planes, particularly in an antisubmarine role.[12]

Pvt. Byron W. Kolbert of the 86th Observation Squadron described the North American O-47Bs as "very heavy, very clumsy," and "unmaneuverable." His description was very much in keeping with the plane's status as the heaviest single-engine aircraft in the Army Air Force's inventory. When he reported to Bellows Field on 17 September 1941, 2nd Lt. Phillip Willis had neither seen nor heard of an O-47, but he

was soon calling it "the Pregnant Pigeon . . . a big, old, fat single-engine airplane."[13]

Training
BASIC TRAINING
Although Army recruiters were far more selective in signing recruits for the Air Corps than for other branches of the Army, physical fitness was not necessarily the most important quality. Most Air Corps enlistees would have described their training as more mental than physical. Following enlistment in San Francisco, Fred R. Runce was processed at Fort McDowell, an old coast artillery installation on Angel

Island in San Francisco Bay. After arriving in Hawai'i in mid-April 1941, he drew an assignment at Wheeler Field. The "basic training" there was hardly the rigorous affair experienced by the infantry recruits at Schofield Barracks just to the northwest. "Very seldom was there any pressure put on us" in the ninety days of basic training, he recalled. Being restricted to base on weekends was the worst part of it.[14]

The 25 November 1939 edition of the *Air Corps News Letter* included a description of basic training as administered by the Hawaiian Air Force. On 14 September, Wheeler Field received a sizable number of recruits whom the authorities placed under the care of nine commissioned officers in addition to NCOs. The day after their arrival the men marched to Schofield Barracks to receive uniforms and bedding. Recruits rose at 0600, made their bunks, policed their barracks, and then reported to breakfast at 0715. Training in the morning consisted of marching and close-order drill under the direction of 2nd Lt. Frederick R. Terrell. Between periods of drill the men listened to lectures by the commissioned officers: 2nd Lt. Charles W. Dahlberg discussed Wheeler Field's regulations; 2nd Lieutenant Terrell gave instructions on military courtesy (when in doubt, *salute!*); 2nd Lt. Clemence P. Tokarz lectured on the Articles of War; and Capt. Alfred A. Grebe of the Medical Corps gave a presentation on military hygiene "imparted

in plain language and, consequently, made clear." Various NCOs took charge of chemical and gas mask training as well as calisthenics each morning. On 26 September the young men had their first firearms lesson following a march to Waikele Gulch. Most of those who were handed a Colt .45 automatic pistol had never handled a firearm. Afternoons were reserved for recreational athletics, mostly volleyball.[15]

Upon the conclusion of the afternoon period at 1500, the article noted, "our youthful soldier has had his share of exertion." Infantrymen at Schofield Barracks—not to mention O'ahu's Marines—would have found it difficult to muster sympathy for the poor Air Corps recruits undergoing such training, which fed their animosity and disdain for the soft "aviator types."[16]

A NEW TRAINING MEMORANDUM

It was amid this somewhat lax state of affairs that Brig. Gen. Howard C. Davidson took charge of the 14th Pursuit Wing in April 1941. And the laxity he

2nd Lt. George S. Welch stands beside a P-40 that is undergoing bore-sighting of its .50-caliber machine guns during the 47th Pursuit Squadron's deployment to Bellows in June 1941. **Aiken, NMPW**

View from the cockpit of a P-40 at Bellows Field during the 47th Pursuit Squadron's deployment in June 1941. **Aiken, NMPW**

perceived extended upward into the ranks of the commissioned officers, particularly the junior pilots. Although the authors are unaware of any document in which Davidson recorded his private thoughts regarding the lack of general readiness when he arrived, a synopsis in staff meeting notes of the 15th Pursuit Group for that period probably reflects his mood. The group historian for the 7th Fighter Command juxtaposed disciplinary issues within the group with the increasingly critical international situation and concluded: "It is evident that in spite of the tension [elsewhere in the world] the pilots were still a rather carefree lot who had to be kept in check."[17]

While Davidson and his staff studied how best to address the lack of preparedness in the 14th Pursuit Wing, on 4 June 1941, in anticipation of orders from the general regarding the need for rigorous gunnery training, the 15th Pursuit Group's 47th Pursuit Squadron received orders to commence a month-long deployment to Bellows Field, perhaps as a test to ensure the feasibility of such a move. Haleiwa Field was not yet capable of supporting such a lengthy deployment, so Bellows was the only option for the

intense training that Davidson envisioned. That vision notwithstanding, the 47th's stay at Bellows was apparently more recreation than work. The squadron historian's description is reminiscent of a summer camp.

This was an event eagerly anticipated as flying started about 0500 and generally concluded by 1000 for the day. The remainder of the day was spent swimming, playing baseball, volley ball or merely resting. In the evenings the Squadron ran a truck to nearby Kailua where the men could go to the movies, dance, or find other amusement. Both the officers and men lived in tents pitched next to the beach. The Squadron messed from field ranges, but the food was surprisingly good.[18]

As the 47th Pursuit Squadron whiled away the hours at Bellows prior to its 28 June return to Wheeler, Brigadier General Davidson was preparing to issue "Training Memorandum No. 1" on 1 July—a directive for the first quarter of the 1941–42 fiscal year. The eight-page document outlined Davidson's

P-40 "266" with a tail code of 46/18P (46th aircraft/18th Pursuit Group) being bore-sighted at Bellows Field, circa late summer or early fall 1941. Bore-sighting involved raising the tail so that the aircraft was perfectly level and then adjusting the guns so that fire would be level and bullets would converge at a set range. **Stevens**

vision of the pursuit wing's mission, and the training objectives and programs necessary to fulfill that mission, in sections addressing combat training, ground training, and military intelligence.[19]

Section I described the pursuit wing's primary training objective: to "attain a degree of combat efficiency so that all units will be able to fly, navigate and shoot effectively." This objective fed into the pursuit wing's mission to destroy "hostile aircraft operating over or in the immediate vicinity of the Territory of Hawaii." Davidson called upon the groups and squadrons of his command to submit their own training directives by 15 July. These lower-level directives would outline individual training for new pilots and combat/maintenance crew specialists.[20]

Section II addressed the need for individual combat training to ensure each pilot's proficiency by day or night and in all kinds of weather. Davidson emphasized the importance of "familiarization with the Hawaiian Archipelago during hours of darkness" and the ability to identify aircraft and naval vessels, both hostile and friendly. Unit combat training stressed the "tactics and techniques of mass operations." Specific pursuit training aimed to ensure the ability to deliver aerial attacks against enemy aircraft and ground personnel, and to support bombardment operations. The new "Gunnery Camp at Bellows Field" would alternate between the wing's two groups, starting with the 18th Pursuit Group in July. Deployments to Bellows were to be one month in duration, and other gunnery ranges would be made available when procured or developed.[21]

Section III dealt with ground training for new officers and flying cadets for both administrative and combat duties. Coursework included squadron duties of junior officers, airplane and engine maintenance, navigation, meteorology, correspondence, and air tactics and technique. The hordes of enlisted recruits then pouring into the base were also in Davidson's crosshairs. In addition to the "standard basic training," the new airmen were to receive "such additional training as necessary to fit them for service with the

ground defense battalions," which was to include grenade, machine-gun, and bayonet instruction.[22]

Davidson's preoccupation with training was driven by a massive influx of new pilots assigned to the Hawaiian Department following the creation of the 15th Pursuit Group. Davidson would testify at length before the Roberts Commission in late December 1941 regarding his pilots' lack of experience. Many of the new men arrived at Wheeler Field straight from flight school with only two hundred hours of flying time; none "had been in pursuit aviation [or] . . . had ever fired a machine gun." Very few had even sat in a modern pursuit plane.[23]

In mid-August yet another group of fifty-eight new pilots arrived at Wheeler's main gate—all sorely needed, but all in need of advanced training before they could join the established combat crews. In addition to lacking flight experience, the new pilots lacked military discipline, due in part to insufficient emphasis on drill and discipline in the primary flight schools, which in turn reflected their compressed training schedules. Davidson suggested instituting ground schools in the States at the colleges and universities that fed the various flight schools as a partial remedy.[24]

The new training regimen for pilots ran from 0730 until 1600 and put an end to lazy afternoons of swimming and golf. On alternating weeks, one of the two pursuit groups had the field reserved for night flying—the alternating schedule mandated by congestion at the base.[25]

ACCIDENTS AND PILOT MORTALITY
The general lack of experience among newer pilots and insufficient time in the cockpits of specific aircraft types resulted in accidents involving seventy-five aircraft from January through November 1941, ranging in seriousness from "fender-benders" to the loss of fifteen aircraft and six pilots. By far the most common accidents (nearly a third) involved ground loops and nose-overs during landings; taxiing accidents, midair collisions, and landing gear

"malfunctions" (some pilots simply forgot to lower their gear) constituted the rest. Only one accident involved engine failure—testimony to Wheeler's conscientious mechanics. Second lieutenants made up about 75 percent of the flying officers in the 15th and 18th Pursuit Groups but accounted for nearly 90 percent of the accidents—a sure indicator of pilot inexperience.[26]

A random selection of twenty-two Air Corps/Army Air Force accident reports from 1941 revealed that 80 percent involved pilot error. Nearly all those accidents were attributed to errors in judgment, poor technique, or carelessness, and in one case to a pilot's willful disobedience of orders. The two incidences of landing gear failure reflected a problem inherent in the P-36A's design, and was probably among the reasons why the Air Corps wanted to replace that type.[27]

THE BROWN INCIDENT

One of the more remarkable accidents involved Pvt. Henry C. Brown, an armorer with the 47th Pursuit Squadron with ambitions to become an Army pilot. Prior to his enlistment, Brown took flight lessons and logged almost thirty solo hours. On Monday, 8 September 1941, he and some friends were on the way to see a movie at Schofield Barracks when he mentioned that he knew how to fly and thought he could fly a P-40. When his friends laughed at him, he decided to prove it.[28]

The next morning Brown strode down the flight line to his squadron's parking area southwest of Hangar 1 and boarded a P-36. He intended to study the controls, but the aircraft's mechanic ordered him out because "he was in the way." Brown moved on to a P-40 but was unable to start the engine, which turned over but "smothered on him," sputtered, and stopped. Giving up on the P-40, Brown walked all the way down to the end of the flight line to another P-36, 97/15P (A.C. Ser. No. 38-98).[29]

Brown climbed into the P-36A's cockpit, started the engine successfully, revved it, and initiated a right turn to take the aircraft out onto the field. Pfc. Nelson

A. Vona, who was nearby, heard a bang, turned to see what had caused it, and saw the P-40 adjacent to Brown's P-36 pivot to the left after being struck. The force of the blow bent the P-36's rudder and vertical stabilizer and damaged the right wingtip. Oblivious to, or ignoring, the damage, Brown made two or three attempts to get airborne. By this time he had attracted the attention of ten to fifteen airmen, who attempted to stop the "runaway" P-36. Brown's erratic movements also alerted drivers of the base's crash truck, an ambulance, and a patrol car, who took off in a ragtag Keystone Cops pursuit. Unable to take off due to the bent stabilizer, Brown finally rolled to a stop, whereupon his pursuers tackled him and placed him under arrest.[30]

Capt. Gordon H. Austin, Brown's squadron commander, went to the Guard House to speak with him, but the interview did not go well. Austin

Damage to the rudder and vertical stabilizer on 97/15P, Pvt. Henry C. Brown's P-36A (A.C. Serial No. 38-98), 9 September 1941. The aircraft was still assigned to the 46th Pursuit Squadron on 7 December and survived the attack, though it was out of service in first-echelon maintenance at the time.
NARA, St. Louis

asked Brown if he was familiar with the case of Pvt. Rufus York, who on 16 June 1941 had taken off in an A-12 from Bellows Field during the squadron's late deployment and had been sentenced to two years' hard labor and a dishonorable discharge. Brown admitted that he was aware of what York had done but maintained "that he could fly and wanted to fly and that if the opportunity presented itself he would try to fly again."[31]

Ten weeks later, on 14 November, the Hawaiian Department proceeded with Henry Brown's trial. Although Brown pled "not guilty," the evidence against him was overwhelming. After the unanimous guilty verdict, the young man from Wisconsin was sentenced to a dishonorable discharge, forfeiture of all pay and allowances, and one year of confinement at hard labor, leaving him to stew in a predicament of his own making and wonder whether he might ever redeem himself.[32]

TRAINING EMPHASIS SHIFTS IN SEPTEMBER 1941

In early fall, Brigadier General Davidson adjusted the thrust of his training directive at Wheeler. Through most of the first quarter of the fiscal year, the 18th Pursuit Wing had concentrated on individual training to make "all pilots proficient in the handling of the P-40 aircraft." Davidson was guardedly optimistic about how his program was proceeding, as the base was not having "much difficulty . . . in teaching these officers how to fly." The headquarters squadrons of the two pursuit groups carried out this training, as reflected in the postings of incoming pilots to the group headquarters rather than to the pursuit squadrons.[33]

Three squadrons had completed intensive air-to-ground gunnery training at Bellows Field by 30 September: two units from the 18th Pursuit Group (6th and 19th Pursuit Squadrons) and one from the 15th Pursuit Group (46th Pursuit Squadron). Group training, however, had been limited to reviews and "a small number of interception problems" because

so many aircraft were out of service due to lack of spare parts. A similar lack of planes capable of towing targets retarded training in air-to-air gunnery. Davidson made it clear that the emphasis would change for the second quarter of the fiscal year (October through December), with the squadrons conducting gunnery exercises *against towed targets*. Training in interception problems in cooperation with the new Aircraft Warning System and its radar detection capabilities would pick up as well.[34]

The back-and-forth monthly rotation in and out of Bellows Field by Wheeler's two pursuit groups ended in September, when Bellows became the exclusive gunnery training venue for squadrons of the 18th Pursuit Group, and Haleiwa Field became the "property" of the 15th Pursuit Group. Although efforts to enlarge and enhance the infrastructure at Haleiwa had barely started, the training situation was sufficiently critical that the authorities felt they had to make Haleiwa a supply point for Wheeler's 18th Air Base Group. Accordingly, on 3 November, the 45th Pursuit Squadron became the first unit to make the ten-mile journey west to the coast. For the time being, however, deployments were to last for only two weeks, contrasting with the monthly rotation at Bellows.[35]

14th Pursuit Wing Deployments to Bellows and Haleiwa Fields, June–December 1941

Field	Dates	Squadron/Group
Bellows	4 Jun–28 Jun	47th Pur Sq/15th Pur Grp
Bellows	5 Jul–30 Jul	6th Pur Sq/18th Pur Grp
Bellows	1 Aug–30 Aug	46th Pur Sq/15th Pur Grp
Bellows	2 Sep–30 Sep	19th Pur Sq/18th Pur Grp
Bellows	1 Oct–7 Nov	78th Pur Sq/18th Pur Grp
Bellows	7 Nov–12 Dec	44th Pur Sq/18th Pur Grp
Haleiwa	3 Nov–15 Nov	45th Pur Sq/15th Pur Grp
Haleiwa	15 Nov–3 Dec	46th Pur Sq/15th Pur Grp
Haleiwa	3 Dec–22 Feb 42	47th Pur Sq/15th Pur Grp

Any comprehensive study of tactical activity at Wheeler Field during this critical time is nearly impossible because the Air Force destroyed most of the unit orders that governed day-to-day operations. Without question, the most important of these documents were the operations orders that scheduled tactical activity and training at the squadron level. Fortunately, stray copies of these orders have survived (almost by accident), intermingled as mere supporting documentation within other records. One of the best surviving examples of such an operations order is from the 46th Pursuit Squadron, dated 31 October 1941. No other document known to the authors allows such extraordinary visibility into day-to-day functions in one of Wheeler Field's pursuit squadrons.

With the exception of two experienced pilots making solo test flights, the schedule for 31 October sent up men in groups of two or three. Ten of the squadron's eighteen pilots were on the list for the day's flight operations. Two other pilots—Capt. Morton D. Magoffin and 2nd Lt. Fred B. Shifflet—were "visitors" from the 15th Pursuit Group headquarters, and one other man—2nd Lt. Henry E. Thompson—was from the 45th Pursuit Squadron. Eight of the squadron's pilots (all junior 2nd lieutenants) were idle. Entries from their individual flight records (IFRs) suggest that the junior pilots flew on alternate days, probably due to lack of aircraft availability.[36]

Most of the flights were to depart between 0800 and 0900, with a smaller batch of takeoffs between 1000 and 1100. When making up the schedule, the

46th Pursuit Squadron
Operations Order No. 86, Annex No. 1, 31 October 1941

Aircraft Type & Plane No.		Pilot	Scheduled	Mission Code	Remarks	Actual TO/Land
P-40C	41-13366	1st Lt. Sanders	0800–1200	O-5	To Hickam Field—Transition flying in	0845–1055
P-40B	41-13304	1st Lt. Moore	0900–1200	O-5	A-20 type airplane	0905–I055
P-36A	38-86	Capt. Magoffin	0830–0945	P-5	One hour instrument	0830–0945
P-36A	38-76	2nd Lt. Cords	0830–0945	O-5	Safety observer for Capt. Magoffin	0830–0945
P-26B	33-184	2nd Lt. Toole	0815–0945	O-5	Tow target at 15,000'	0820–0930
P-36A	38-32	2nd Lt. Norris	0830–0915	O-1	100 rds. .30 cal. fire on sleeve target	0820–0915
P-36A	38-83	2nd Lt. Thompson	0900–0945	O-1	100 rds. .30 cal. fire on sleeve target	0900–
P-36A	38-169	1st Lt. Moore	0830–compl	O-5	Test hop	0830–0905
P-40B	41-13304	2nd Lt. Sawyer	0830–compl	O-5	Test hop	0830–0915
P-40B	41-5239	2nd Lt. Woodruff	0830–0945	U-5	Begin combat at 20,000'	0830–0945
P-40B	41-5255	2nd Lt. McCabe	0830–0945	U-5	Cease at 15,000'	0830–0945
P-26B	33-184	2nd Lt. Woodruff	1000–1130	O-5	Tow target at 15,000'	Mission
P-36A	38-32	2nd Lt. Wilkins	1015–1130	O-1	100 rds. .30 cal. fire on sleeve target	called
P-36A	38-83	2nd Lt. Thacker	1015–1130	O-1	100 rds. .30 cal. fire on sleeve target	off
P-36A	38-86	2nd Lt. Shifflet	1015–1130	P-5	One hour instrument	Mission
P-36A	38-82	2nd Lt. McCabe	1015–1130	O-5	Safety observer for Lt. Shifflet	called off
A-12	33-229	2nd Lt. Thacker 2nd Lt. Norris	1100–1200	O-5	To Kahuku Point in search of Lt. Thompson	1105–1245
0-478	39-85	2nd Lt. Cords 2nd Lt. Rasmussen	1100–1200	O-5	To Kahuku Point in search of Lt. Thompson	1105–1230
A-12	33-229	2nd Lt. Cords Pvt. Sheridan	1455–1600	O-5	First priority flying time	1445–1600
BT-2BI	31-112	2nd Lt. Sawyer Sgt. Turner	1445–compl	O-5	To Bellows Field	1445–1630

Copy of Annex 1 to Operations Order No. 86, 46th Pursuit Squadron from 31 October 1941. **Asherbranner**

squadron's commander—1st Lt. Lewis M. Sanders—anticipated that all flight activity would conclude at 1200. The squadron probably had eight of its own aircraft—two P-40Bs and six P-36As—ready for service but had to borrow two P-40s from the 47th Pursuit and a P-26B from the 44th for use as a target tug. Hence, the scheduled sixteen flights required some doubling up by both pilots and aircraft.[37]

One of the more interesting features of the schedule was that 1st Lieutenant Sanders and 1st Lt. Malcolm A. Moore—the squadron's two senior officers and most experienced pilots—departed for Hickam Field for transition training in the Douglas A-20As of the 58th Bombardment Squadron. Such cross-training was routine and prudent given the chronic shortage of experienced pilots in the Hawaiian Air Force. On 31 October, more experienced pilots in the squadron honed their gunnery skills firing .30-caliber ammunition at a target sleeve towed behind a P-26B flown by 2nd Lt. Richard A. Toole and, later, by 2nd Lt. Jasper W. Woodruff, both only three or so months out of flight school. As consolation for the mundane task of towing target sleeves, Toole and Woodruff took part in high-altitude combat training to develop the tactical skills required to survive against a proficient and determined foe.[38]

While the target practice flights proceeded during the early morning of 31 October, four P-36 pilots of the 45th Pursuit Squadron flying in the same general vicinity—offshore near the Kahuku Golf Course—engaged in simulated combat. Second Lt. William J. Feiler lost control of his aircraft and went into a spin approximately two miles offshore and crashed into the sea. The crash attracted the attention of the flight from the 46th Pursuit Squadron, and 2nd Lieutenant Thompson, 2nd Lt. Othniel Norris, and 2nd Lieutenant Toole descended in an apparent search for the plane and pilot. Thompson spotted Feiler swimming near the downed plane and circled above him as a spotter for one of Wheeler's Grumman OA-9s, piloted by the 45th's commanding officer, Capt. Aaron W. Tyer. Second Lt. Robert A. Kaempfer from the group headquarters squadron, who had been part of the combat training flight, rode with Tyer to guide him to the crash scene. As the OA-9 approached, Thompson waggled his wings to indicate Feiler's position. Most likely having throttled back to remain above Feiler, Thompson pulled up sharply, stalled at about five hundred feet, "and hit the water before [he] could recover control." The aircraft burst into flames as it struck the ocean about five hundred yards offshore. A pair of two-man crews—one in an A-12 flown by 2nd Lt. John M. Thacker and another in an O-47B under 2nd Lt. Howard H. Cords—took off to search for Thompson but found no sign of him.[39]

GUNNERY PRACTICE AT BELLOWS

Meanwhile, the 44th Pursuit Squadron was preparing for its impending deployment to Bellows Field for gunnery practice. First Lt. Wallace P. Mace from group headquarters went ahead on 3 November to iron out logistics pending the 44th's arrival; he was joined three days later by 2nd Lt. Hans C. Christiansen of the 44th. On 7 November the squadron descended on Bellows for its last peacetime deployment there, close on the heels of the departing 78th Pursuit Squadron, which had trained there from 1 October through 7 November. The 44th (excepting fifty enlisted men) "left for Bellows Field T.H., at 6:30 A.M. by air and motor convoy." The squadron's aircraft arrived between 0650 and 0700, and the convoy plodded into Bellows at 0845, having covered the forty-eight miles that separated the two bases in two hours and fifteen minutes. The tedious road trip had done nothing to diminish the enlisted men's enthusiasm for the change in scenery, and their morale was described as "excellent." Upon seeing that the squadron's transition was under way, 1st Lieutenant Mace flew his P-40B back to Wheeler. The squadron began flight operations on 10 November.[40]

The experience level of the 44th Pursuit Squadron was relatively high—substantially higher than that of the 46th Pursuit Squadron, which was to move out to Haleiwa a week later. The 44th's commander, Capt. Arthur R. Kingham, was a veteran pilot with more than ten years' experience—mostly in pursuit aviation—and 2,300 hours of flying time inked into his logbooks. Along with squadronmates 1st Lt. Cecil J. Looke Jr. and 2nd Lt. George A. Whiteman, Kingham had taken part in the P-36 flight from the *Enterprise* on 17 February 1941. The squadron had six very experienced 1st lieutenants, and its eight 2nd lieutenants averaged five months of pursuit experience since flight school; only one of them had less than four months' experience.[41]

By mid-November the squadron had established a routine of flying during the weekdays and on Saturdays and taking Sundays and either Tuesdays or Thursdays off. Saturday work aside, the 44th's schedule was less aggressive than that of the 46th Pursuit Squadron across the island at Haleiwa. While the pilots at Haleiwa logged about two and a half hours in the air per day, an average workday at Bellows consisted only of one and a half hours of flying time, perhaps owing to the 44th's higher level of experience.[42]

GUNNERY PRACTICE AT HALEIWA

On 15 November the 46th Pursuit Squadron loaded up trucks and prepared its aircraft for its inaugural trip across the island to Haleiwa. The squadron's planes and vehicles departed Wheeler Field at 0645. The aircraft drifted in at staggered intervals from 0655 to 0730, giving crews time to pull planes aside and clear the small strip for subsequent landings. After lumbering west along the narrow, winding road from Wheeler into Waialua and then past Hale'iwa Town, the squadron's ground echelon crossed the bridge over Anahulu Stream, motored northeast for less than a mile, and made the left-hand turn into the field near the aircraft parking area at 0745.[43]

It is likely that all of the unit's pilots reported to Haleiwa, joining 2nd Lt. Fred B. Shifflet and 2nd Lt. Jerome R. Sawyer, who had been at the field since the first week in November. From Wheeler, the pilots ferried over the squadron's P-40s and P-36s, plus a P-26A and A-12 for target towing and liaison duties. The A-12 came in handy in short order, as 2nd Lt. Gordon H. Sterling Jr. probably transported the two newest pilots (2nd Lt. Eldon E. Stratton and 2nd Lt. Alec B. Streete) in the venerable A-12's rear seat during the first flights

2nd Lt. Gordon H. Sterling Jr. enjoys a cigarette and soaks up the afternoon sun during the 46th Pursuit Squadron's deployment to Haleiwa Field in November 1941. **Stevens**

1st Lt. Malcolm A. "Mike" Moore strikes a relaxed but serious pose during downtime in the tents behind Haleiwa's flight line (*out of the photo to the right*). View looking west. **Stevens**

Hijinks at Haleiwa. An eastward-looking cameraman catches Gordon Sterling "tightening the cords" on the informal wear of Howard Cords while squadron commander Lewis Sanders grins approvingly at right. The three other officers in the background are (*left to right*) 2nd Lt. John M. Thacker, 2nd Lt. Robert F. McCabe (*to the left of Cords*), and Mike Moore (*just visible behind Cords*). Note that the tents at center and the automobiles at left are visible in the right background of the previous photograph.
Stevens

into Haleiwa. Although the lack of operations orders for the period makes analysis of specific activities difficult, it is clear that the squadron operated at a pace that was not particularly grueling, although the pilots flew more hours per day than did the 44th's pilots at Bellows. After resting on 16 November (Sunday), the pilots began their normal flight schedule of two or three days on and one day off, with no flight operations on Thursdays and Sundays. The nature of their activities on their off days is unclear, although ground training and indoctrination cannot be ruled out. Nearby Soldiers Beach and Haleʻiwa town presumably lured some portion of the men away from the field.[44]

The squadron mounted eight days of flight operations prior to the alert of 27 November. The flight operations on 17 November probably involved takeoff and landing practice, a prudent measure given the short length of Haleiwa's landing strip. Beginning on 18 November, the men engaged in eight days of aerial gunnery training in two-to-one ratios (two pursuit craft and one target tug, with the A-12 and P-26B used for the latter function), exactly the proportion spelled out in Operations Order No. 46 from 31 October. Although more seasoned men such as the newly promoted 1st Lt. Howard H. Cords occasionally performed "tow target" duty, less-experienced pilots usually shouldered that task. By 25 November one of the Wheeler's Grumman OA-9s had arrived, possibly to provide co-piloting experience to young Stratton and Streete, who had just arrived from flight school. The compiled flight schedule shows the OA-9 in service as a target tug.[45]

Wheeler's Ground Defense Battalion

An additional training issue arose during the spring and summer of 1941 when Lt. Gen. Walter

Short, commander of the Hawaiian Department, announced his desire to have the airfields provide Ground Defense Battalions as part of a "proper employment of all military personnel in a last stand defense of Oahu" during foreign invasion. Short first broached the idea during the Hawaiian Department's maneuvers of 12–24 May. Maj. Gen. Frederick L. Martin, the chief of the Hawaiian Air Force, attempted to dissuade Short, arguing that such an arrangement would impede and complicate the training of combat crews, but to no avail. A special report prepared by Col. Harvey S. Burwell (Davidson's predecessor as Wheeler's commander) that pointed to security problems at O'ahu's airfields reinforced Short's opinion that detachments organic to the airfields were at least a partial answer to such problems. Despite Martin's last-gasp appeal in late August, Short issued orders directing the establishment and training of three five-hundred-man battalions of four companies each. Two battalions from Hickam would guard that base and also be on call with the Hawaiian Department's provost marshal to counter sabotage activities in and around Honolulu. A similar arrangement was in place at Wheeler Field, with its single defense battalion on call to provide security in the vicinity of Schofield Barracks.[46]

Wheeler's leaders were certainly no strangers to the concept of ground defense, as, "pursuant to instructions from higher authority," Colonel Burwell had already authorized platoon-sized Airdrome Defense Units—one from each squadron—on 8 April 1941. Each platoon was to have five NCOs and twenty privates, with Schofield Barracks providing target ranges, and officers and NCOs guiding the training. Including Wheeler's air base command (but excluding headquarters squadrons), Burwell's manpower demands were relatively modest—approximately two hundred men. The Ground Defense Battalions that Short mandated, however, would be more than twice that size, with the additional responsibility for Wheeler of providing security at Schofield Barracks. Wheeler's new battalion activated for training and deployed whenever the department went on alert.[47]

Training for the new Ground Defense Battalion started as early as July but came at a steep price with respect to supply, engineering, and transportation functions. Brigadier General Davidson's S-4 (supply officer), Lt. Col. Russell L. Williamson, sent a letter to his chief that outlined the disruptions. The inability to arrange transportation to the Hawaiian Air Depot to pick up spare parts was among the more disturbing of those. The absence of seventeen qualified drivers caused a ripple effect that severely hampered Base Engineering's ability to properly maintain aircraft during an emergency.[48]

Despite Martin's misgivings, however, the training continued. On 10 November 1941 Wheeler's base commander, Col. William J. Flood, submitted a provisional defense plan that gave form to Short's version of the new base defense scheme to repel enemy attacks. Prompted by a five-minute blast on the post's fire siren, the men would assemble in their squadron areas with weapons, ammunition, helmets, and light

Wheeler Field Ground Defense Battalion

Unit	Assembly Point	Coverage
Battalion HQ Platoon	1st Floor, 18th Air Grp Barracks	N/A
Company A	Guard House	South & east side of the field
Company B	Ordnance Magazines	West side of the field
Company C	Fire Station	North of the field
Company D	Transportation Park	Battalion main reserve

Note: The Wheeler Field Guard maintained regular posts and functioned as auxiliary reserve.

packs, and then rush to one of four designated company commanders (see table on preceding page).[49]

The Pace of Training Accelerates

In the final months of 1941, the pace of training at Wheeler picked up. The men had less free time, and passes off the base became more difficult to obtain. In another noticeable departure from the norm, all of the men engaged in calisthenics every morning alongside the recruits. The tempo of flight operations accelerated as well, increasing the mechanics' workload as they struggled to keep their airplanes in flying condition.[50]

As 1941 slipped away, SSgt. Stephen Koran noted a gradual shift in the character of his daily photographic routines. The increased rates of gunnery training and bombing practice drove similar increases in demands for reconnaissance and aerial photography, because the bombing range on Moloka'i required a photographic record of strike results. The pilots who flew Wheeler's B-18—the base's target tug—likewise flew more hours to tow the ten-foot target sleeve on its two-hundred-foot wire.[51]

One should exercise care when leveling criticism at Major General Martin and Brigadier General Davidson—and the other leaders at Wheeler trying to prepare their commands in 1941 for the conflict they knew was coming. Davidson had to overcome three enormous obstacles in his attempts to institute rapid and thorough change: (1) a lax mentality among the rank and file (and even the officers) instilled by the culture into which they were inserted, reinforced by practices such as "tropical hours"; (2) weak leadership at the department level; and (3) ignorance regarding Japan's intentions and timetables.

With the benefit of hindsight, it appears that leaders in the 18th Pursuit Wing were aware of the deficiencies in those areas but did not view them in terms of an imminent threat that would cast them into the ring with a savvy, shrewd, and well-trained opponent. What is *very* clear is that no one realized how little time remained to prepare for such a confrontation.

Chapter Six

"CONCERNED WITH PREPARING OURSELVES, AND COME WHAT MAY"
The Last Weeks of Peace

The officers and enlisted men at Oʻahu's pursuit bases differed in their attitudes toward the Japanese as potential adversaries. Although more senior officers and pilots were confident in their own abilities, they tempered that confidence with a dose of reality—even fatalism. It is noteworthy that the pilots at Wheeler were unaware of overall Japanese aerial capabilities and received no briefings on the subject. Despite the lack of specific intelligence, however, 1st Lt. Everett Stewart felt that in any one-to-one confrontation with an opposing air force, the Americans would be well matched in terms of pilot quality: "Fighter pilots are fighter pilots, and from any country [they would be] well-prepared and pretty well-trained." While the men at Wheeler were vaguely aware of the capabilities of Japan's Mitsubishi Type 0 carrier fighter and Germany's Messerschmitt Bf-109, Stewart believed that American equipment would prove comparable, observing, "We primarily were concerned with preparing ourselves, and come what may."[1]

Other men were less confident than Stewart. The Japanese were already seasoned, battle-hardened veterans of the war in China, and that was a cause for concern. "We knew that if we got [into a] war with them we were going to have a rough deal . . . against pilots that'd already been where we hadn't." Second Lt. Phillip Willis and the other O-47 pilots in the 86th Observation Squadron at Bellows Field also knew that the powerful Japanese navy and air force might be lurking just over the horizon. "When we went on these dawn patrol missions, we knew damn well we wasn't looking for Germans!" Willis' concerns were tempered by his uninformed optimism that no one was going to whip the United States; and in any case, Oʻahu was impregnable.[2]

When the pilots and men talked among themselves about the approaching war, most agreed that American involvement would most likely be in the European conflict. Few felt that Hawaiʻi faced imminent danger from the outside. Threats from within were another matter. Various directives along with the scheduled alerts during 1941 brought home the fact that "they might blow up our planes . . . from within Hawaii." As months slipped by and no external threats materialized, the alerts and the Hawaiian Department's suspicion of the local Japanese population reinforced the men's notion that the real threat to Hawaiʻi was already present.[3]

The relaxed atmosphere on Oʻahu and the frequent alerts led the men to assume that their superiors had taken precautions to guard against surprise attacks. "I couldn't say I really expected [the Japanese] to come over there and knock us out," Willis later said. Along with many others he assumed that someone in power would simply declare war, "and then we [would] all get going." The more immediate threat seemed to be in the Philippines, and certainly no one expected the Japanese to strike both places at once.[4]

Beer-fueled bull sessions in the enlisted quarters likewise revealed few worries regarding direct military attacks on the Hawaiian Islands. Those who followed international events mirrored the opinions of their officers and focused on Europe. Although there was general anxiety regarding Japan's intentions in the Far East, a direct attack on O'ahu was simply unthinkable. The presence of augmented guard details addressed internal security matters and reinforced the men's chief worry: acts of sabotage by the "shifty" Japanese on O'ahu—a misplaced concern by all measures.[5]

When young couples gathered in quarters or the Officers' Club, conversations were usually social in nature or on the general topic of flying. The subject of world tensions and conflicts entered conversations occasionally, but the topic of warfare generally did not. Unpleasant topics such as war and America's possible involvement in it did not make for "polite" conversation, particularly among officers and wives who just wanted to pass a pleasant evening.[6]

The Dangers of Military Aviation

Despite the stereotypical view of Army Air Force pilots as a "carefree lot," the flyers themselves knew the dangers associated with military aviation, even in peacetime. Local newspaper coverage and the Air Corps' own documents are evidence that fatal flying accidents occurred far too frequently. Particularly in the prewar years, these tragedies inculcated strict adherence to established procedures and the practice of honoring fallen fliers by naming facilities in their honor.

Tulsa, Oklahoma, native 2nd Lt. Millard C. Shibley Jr. came to Bellows Field with nineteen other

F/C Millard C. Shibley Jr. during flight training, circa 1941. **Beckers**

The aircraft in which 2nd Lt. Millard C. Shibley lost his life—an O-47B, 10/86O (A.C. Serial. No. 39-84)—parked at Bellows Field during the late summer or fall of 1941. **USAR 1765**

newly minted lieutenants on 17 September 1941. Texan 2nd Lt. Phillip Willis arrived under the same orders, and over the coming weeks the two midwesterners became fast friends. Their relationship ended abruptly at 0450 on 17 November when, just after taking off on a dawn patrol in O-47B 10/86O (A.C. Serial No. 39-84), Shibley crashed into the sea not far from shore.

He and Pvt. Warren F. French, his observer, died in the crash. Although injured, Pvt. Harry B. Addleman, the rear gunner, cleared the wreckage and managed to swim ashore. An aircraft dropped flares and life rafts, and several soldiers swam out to the wreck to look for Shibley and French, but to no avail. Later, a crash boat from NAS Kaneohe Bay arrived and retrieved their bodies. The aircraft suffered severe damage, and although workers attempted to salvage the wreck, they abandoned the effort and routed a survey voucher condemning the aircraft on 26 November. The authorities named the main gate at Bellows Field to honor 2nd Lieutenant Shibley on 22 April 1942.[7]

Davidson's Absence on the Mainland

As the men at O'ahu's pursuit bases pondered their mission and the future, Brig. Gen. Howard C. Davidson was largely unavailable to lead them. In accordance with Headquarters, Hawaiian Department Special Orders No. 256, Davidson, Lt. Col. Carroll A. Powell (department signal officer), and

Maj. Arthur W. Meehan (operations officer for the Hawaiian Air Force) received instructions to observe the maneuvers of the 2nd Interceptor Command in Seattle, Washington, from 28 October through

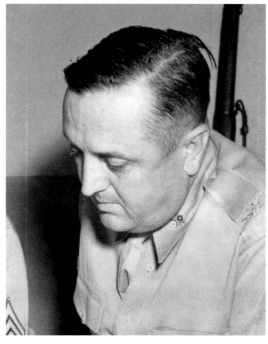

Col. Carroll A. Powell (SC) studies the work of a Signal Corps draftsman, circa August 1942. **NARA II, 111-SC-142172, cropped**

Brig. Gen. Howard C. Davidson, circa December 1942, soon after taking command of the Army Air Force Technical Training Command. Prior to his transfer Davidson led the 7th Fighter Command in Hawai'i. **NARA II, 342-FH-4A-07554, cropped**

Maj. Arthur W. Meehan, circa 1941–42. **IUA, P0067076, cropped**

2 November to study and adapt that command's "set-up for the defense of the Hawaiian Islands."[8]

During Davidson's absence it appears that no one person assumed responsibility for overseeing the 14th Pursuit Wing's day-to-day operations. Prior to his departure, Davidson asked Col. William J. Flood to serve as "acting Executive of the Fighter Command" and to function in an advisory capacity to "help the [pursuit] groups along." Davidson felt that "an old officer ought to be around" to whom the tactical commanders could turn for advice, although Flood, a mere base commander, possessed neither tactical responsibility nor authority. Essentially, Davidson's departure left the two group commanders—Maj. Paul W. Blanchard Jr. and Maj. William R. "Wild Bill" Morgan—on their own.[9]

Davidson, Powell, and Meehan boarded the steamship *Matsonia* in Honolulu Harbor and sailed for San Francisco on 15 October. On arrival the trio reported to Hamilton Field; from there, on 20 October, they flew north to Seattle, making several stops along the way, and arrived at Hamilton, Washington, on 22 October.[10]

The maneuvers of the 2nd Interceptor Command commenced five days later and concluded on 2 November. Unlike the setup on Oʻahu, the warning system on the West Coast apparently did not yet employ radar. Davidson nevertheless described the command's operations, patterned after "methods used in London," as "very successful." Eight thousand civilian ground observers communicated via telephone with a central headquarters where young women marked the progress of the "invaders" on a large plotting board. Davidson declared that "the efficiency of the organization was amazing," although he was probably thankful that Hawaiʻi relied on radar rather than eight thousand civilian volunteers.[11]

Davidson's party left Seattle almost immediately for Wright Field in Ohio, where Davidson was scheduled to meet with Brig. Gen. Henry J. F. Miller, chief of the Air Service Command (ASC), which had been established only sixteen days earlier—two days

after Davidson and company boarded the *Matsonia*. Among his other responsibilities, Brigadier General Miller supervised storage and issue of Air Corps supplies and "overhaul, repair, maintenance and salvage of all Air Corps equipment" outside the scope of local repairs by the squadrons or base engineering units.[12]

The next portion of Davidson's trip took him to Mitchel Field on Long Island, where he dropped off Lieutenant Colonel Powell to visit American Telephone and Telegraph to ascertain whether critical telephone equipment was available for shipment back to Hawaiʻi. Davidson meanwhile likely conferred with Brig. Gen. John C. McDonnell of the 1st Interceptor Command, activated earlier in the summer at Mitchel Field on Long Island. The group flew south to Bolling Field near Washington, D.C., for four days of meetings. With their business almost concluded, Davidson, Powell, and Meehan started home, first visiting Pope Field in North Carolina to observe maneuvers of the air defense system there. After a grueling series of flights, the three officers arrived in San Francisco and boarded the *Lurline* on 27 November for the return voyage to Oʻahu, expecting to arrive on Wednesday, 3 December.[13]

The P-40 Conference

Meanwhile, on 26 November, just before Davidson boarded the *Lurline* in San Francisco, two dispatches from CNO Adm. Harold R. Stark arrived at Adm. Husband E. Kimmel's headquarters in Hawaiʻi.

The first of Stark's messages was probably a reaction to the information that Admiral Kimmel intended to transfer most of the aircraft of Marine Aircraft Group 21 (MAG-21) from the Ewa Mooring Mast Field on Oʻahu to Wake and Midway Islands. The dispatch expressed Stark's preference that the men and equipment of MAG-21 be kept where they were, to be "available for expeditionary use." As an alternative, and with the War Department's approval, Stark proposed using Army pursuit aircraft to reinforce Wake and Midway, with twenty-five planes to be placed on each of the advance bases. The Navy would ferry the Army planes and pilots via aircraft carrier, launch them to their destinations (Wake Island would be first), and land ground personnel and essential supplies by boat. Stark made it clear that the Navy would also be responsible for supplying the two bases, and for all subsequent transport of Army supplies and equipment. The Army men transferred from Hawai'i were to be quartered in tents. Making reference to another hot-button issue, neither the two small provisional fighter groups at Wake and Midway nor their ground echelons were to interfere in any way with the passage of B-17s on their way to the Philippines. The two atolls were small and their infrastructure quite limited. A large number of smaller aircraft restricting access to runways, aprons, and fueling facilities was to be avoided at all costs; additionally, fuel and lubricants might be in short supply, hence Stark's admonition. Stark followed his initial dispatch with another two minutes later, at 1410, that announced the Army's offer of "infantry for reinforcing defense battalions now on station" at Wake and asked for Kimmel's recommendations regarding the number of troops he desired. The Army would not, however, supply additional antiaircraft batteries.[14]

At 0900 the following morning, Kimmel convened his staff and that of Lieutenant General Short to consider Stark's requests. Various other commanders were present at the conference as well, including Vice Adm. William F. Halsey (ComAirBatFor), Rear Adm. Wilson Brown (ComScoFor), Rear Adm. Patrick N. L. Bellinger (ComPatWing 2), Rear Adm. Claude C. Bloch (Com14), Major General Martin of the Hawaiian Air Force, and Lt. Col. James A. Mollison, Martin's chief of staff. It is unfortunate that no one on either of the staffs present at the conference made a *formal* record of the 27 November meeting, which historian Gordon W. Prange later dubbed "the P-40 Conference." Such conferences were frequent and usually took the form of informal conversations without minutes. Still, it is surprising that there is no record of this particular meeting, in that the

somewhat contentious discussion dealt directly with America's most critical advanced bases.[15]

Although buttressed by endorsements from the Navy and War Departments, Stark's proposal raised so many questions that the meeting ran on for two to three hours. Discussion hinged primarily on whether the Army's planes could be used for such a purpose, and if so, which specific type the *Enterprise* should take. Numerous practical and logistical questions arose during the meeting, but, curiously, there is no evidence that anyone on either staff mentioned the *Enterprise*'s transport of Army fighters to Hawai'i in February 1941, which set a precedent for such an operation.[16]

Among the most important points those present did discuss was that once launched from an aircraft carrier, the Army planes (lacking arrestor gear) could not return to the carrier and land. Arrestor gear issues aside, few if any Army pilots had received training in carrier landings. Consequently, any aircraft ferried to Wake and Midway would be stuck there for the duration of the war. Lieutenant Colonel Mollison insisted that such a move "was contrary to our mission, which [is] the defense of Oahu."[17]

That the aircraft would indeed be stuck on Wake or Midway likely prompted debate regarding which pursuit types Short might relinquish. Perhaps looking first to the defense of Hawai'i, Martin proposed that the older P-36As be sent, as "those were the ones we could afford best to lose." Although Kimmel's reaction to that proposal is unknown, it could not have been positive. He depended on Wake Island for future naval operations in the central Pacific. To Short's credit, he conceded that "if we are going up against the Japanese we [want] the best we [have] instead of the worst." Martin's P-40s were the most effective fighters in the Hawaiian Air Force's inventory. In the event of war, the late-model fighters would be better used in the critical defense of far frontiers rather than languishing in the backwaters of O'ahu.[18]

That sentiment reflected just how lightly the staffs regarded the possibility of O'ahu coming under air attack. Well aware that a significant depletion of

Rear Adm. Husband E. Kimmel, Commander Cruisers, Scouting Force (ComCruScoFor), 10 January 1941, shortly before his elevation to Commander in Chief, U.S. Fleet (CinCUS). **HWRD, cropped**

Lt. Gen. Walter C. Short, commanding general, Hawaiian Department, standing in the shade in front of his headquarters, 27 August 1941. **NARA II, 111-SC-125881, cropped**

Martin's frontline fighter strength would weaken Oʻahu's air defenses, Kimmel queried his war plans officer regarding the possibility that Japan would launch a surprise attack on Hawaiʻi. Without hesitation Capt. Charles H. "Soc" McMorris—Kimmel's War Plans Officer—replied, "None." Neither Kimmel nor Bloch expressed any difference of opinion.[19]

Another pair of issues arose when Kimmel questioned the P-40s' operational capabilities: "What may I expect of Army fighters on Wake?" At that juncture, Halsey entered the fray and pointed out that Army pursuit planes did not venture more than fifteen miles offshore due to fears that the pilots could not find their way back to base. Kimmel snorted, "Then they are no damn good to me." Short sidestepped the issue of his aviators' inability to navigate back to Wake and brought up the command issue. If he was to "man these islands," he had to exercise command over them. Kimmel—his blood now up—exclaimed, "Over my dead body! The Army should exercise no command over Navy bases." Short replied, "Mind you, I do not want these islands. I think that they are

better manned by Marines. But if I must put troops and planes on them, then I must command them."[20]

After considerable discussion, the assembled staffs reached an impasse. At least for the time being, reinforcement of Wake and Midway by the Army was a dead issue. Hamstrung by the Army pilots' lack of offshore experience, the limited capabilities of their aircraft, and lack of a unified command who might have forced the issue of base control, the group backed away from Stark's recommendation. Kimmel decided to deploy some of the Marine fighters from Maj. Paul A. Putnam's VMF-211 at the Ewa Mooring Mast Field instead. Although Stark was disappointed in Kimmel's decision, he admitted that the arrangement appeared "to be [the] best that [could] be done under the circumstances." He advised Kimmel, however, that the War Department would instruct Lieutenant General Short "to cooperate with [the] Navy in plans for use of Army pursuit planes."[21]

Despite Kimmel's decision to utilize VMF-211, there is ample evidence that the Army anticipated future transfers of Wheeler's fighters to Wake and

Midway. Two War Department memos pondered information that the Navy would not share its lumber stockpiles on Midway for construction of the twenty-three tent frames the deployed aircrews would require. Every board-foot at Midway had already been allocated to critical construction projects. At Wheeler, Colonel Flood (Davidson had not yet returned) compiled logistical data for potential moves to Wake and Midway, and passed the figures to Major General Martin's staff. Flood reported that the organizational equipment to support operations for 12 aircraft (roughly 1 squadron) required a shipment exceeding 23 tons that would occupy 3,100 cubic feet—the equivalent of 4 small bedrooms packed to the ceilings. That total did not include ammunition. Twenty days of operations with 2 missions per day per plane totaled almost 90 additional tons and another 3 bedrooms—again, packed to the ceilings. The manpower requirements to sustain operations of the same 12 aircraft were similarly prodigious.[22]

In gauging combat readiness, equipment, and level of training, it is almost certain that the authorities at Wheeler had previously earmarked the 6th and 19th Pursuit Squadrons (and possibly the 72nd and 73rd Pursuit Squadrons) for deployment to bases west of Hawai'i. Massive quantities of equipment and ammunition at Wheeler lay crated and stockpiled in Base Engineering and the squadron hangars while

**Personnel Required for Operations
of a Twelve-Plane Squadron**

Personnel Type	Men Req'd
Commissioned Officers	17
Crew Chiefs	12
Armorers	12
Communications Men	6
Engineers	12
Operations Clerks	3
Supply Clerks	3
Headquarters Clerks	3
Total	68

Col. Charles H. MacDonald, commander of the 475th Fighter Group, circa March 1944, at Nadzab Field in Australian New Guinea. As a first lieutenant, MacDonald was one of two pilots who participated in the P-40 test flight from the *Enterprise* on 28 November 1941. He finished the war as the third-ranking Army Air Force fighter ace in the Pacific Theater with twenty-seven air-to-air kills. **Stanaway**

the units awaited word regarding their impending deployment.[23]

Kimmel appeared to keep the Army option open. To that end he instructed Vice Admiral Halsey to hoist two Army P-40 pursuit planes onto the *Enterprise* and launch them at sea "to show the Army that it was possible to fly Army fighter planes off carriers"—again ignoring the fact that the *Enterprise* had done something very similar in February. Against a background of utmost secrecy regarding delivery of VMF-211 to Wake Island, Halsey had less than a day to work out the details of the voyage. He notified the Army that he needed two planes and pilots delivered immediately to Ford Island. The two men selected—1st Lt. Charles H. MacDonald, operations officer with the 19th Pursuit Squadron, and 1st Lt. William J. A. Bowen of the 6th Pursuit Squadron—were obvious choices. Both pilots had amassed just over a thousand hours

F/C William J. A. Bowen on 1 March 1939 during flight training at Randolph Field. With Charles MacDonald, he participated in the P-40 fly-off from the *Enterprise* on 28 November 1941. **NARA II, 18-PU-009-043-4031**

of flying time and were among the P-36A pilots who had launched from the *Enterprise* and flown into Wheeler nine months before. That same day, the pair had executed seven practice takeoffs and landings out of Wheeler. With orders to report to the *Enterprise*, they took off one last time in two P-40Bs and bounced onto the runway at NAS Pearl Harbor in the late afternoon or early evening of 27 November. At that juncture, the *Enterprise* was moored along 1010 Pier across the channel from Ford Island, starboard side to berth B-3. How the two P-40s transferred on board is unclear; they were probably hoisted onto a barge, taken across the main channel, and then brought on board by one of the *Enterprise*'s cranes.[24]

In the predawn darkness of 28 November, with the two planes and their pilots on board, the *Enterprise* commenced lighting boilers at 0445 and got under way at 0733. With the destroyers *Ellet* (DD 398) and *Fanning* (DD 385) on plane guard duty, the *Enterprise* went to flight quarters at 0930. The carrier recovered her own air group along with

eleven VMF-211 Wildcats that morning but did not commence preparations to launch the Army P-40s until midafternoon, when MacDonald and Bowen climbed into their fighters, warmed up the engines, and waited for the *Enterprise* to turn into the wind. Then, reenacting on the same flight deck what had transpired on the ship 280 days ago, MacDonald took off at 1513. Bowen followed suit four minutes later and the P-40s turned toward O'ahu, landing shortly before 1600.[25]

The 27 November War Warning

As the Navy worked to reinforce Wake Island, dramatic events were occurring in the Army as well. On 27 November, Col. Robert H. Dunlop, the Hawaiian Department's adjutant general, was in Lieutenant General Short's office in Building 13 (Headquarters, Hawaiian Department) at Fort Shafter. At about 1430, Col. Walter C. Phillips, Short's chief of staff, brought in "a very important message from General [George C.] Marshall" and handed it to Short. The gist of the 162-word wire from the Army chief of staff was as follows:

▶ Negotiations with Japan had ended, and there was little hope of their being resumed.

▶ While Japan's intent was uncertain, hostile action was possible at any moment.

▶ Although the United States wanted Japan to commit the "first overt act," Short was not to jeopardize Hawai'i's defenses in the meantime. Additionally, he was to undertake reconnaissance and other necessary measures, though taking care neither to alarm the public nor to disclose his intent.

Nowhere did Marshall's message mention any direct threat to the Hawaiian Islands.[26]

Short's thoughts might have turned to the staff conference at CinCPac headquarters the previous day during which Captain McMorris stated flatly that there was no possibility of a surprise attack against Hawai'i. In addition, Short knew "from repeated conversations with the Navy that the

Gen. George C. Marshall's "war warning" message received at Headquarters, Hawaiian Department during the early afternoon of 27 November 1941. **NARA II, RG 80**

Japanese vessels were supposed to be either in their home ports or proceeding to the south. [The Navy] had no information indicating that any Japanese vessels were proceeding east [toward Hawaiʻi]." With no indication of external threats to the islands mentioned in Marshall's dispatch, and worried about Oʻahu's supposed vulnerability to internal threats, the sabotage-conscious Short had heard and read enough. After consulting with Colonel Phillips, he decided Alert No. 1 should take effect for the Hawaiian Department.[27]

Alert No. 2 and Alert No. 3 addressed external threats, No. 2 designed for the nonimminent variety and No. 3 dealing with serious, imminent threats. Alert No. 1 was "a defense against acts of sabotage and uprisings within the island, *with no threat from without*," which fit Short's notion of the situation. Its provisions called for the Hawaiian Air Force to "protect all vital installations on posts on OAHU garrisoned by air forces" and to "assist in defense of air fields on outlying islands by cooperation of local base detachments with District commanders," who

Headquarters, Hawaiian Department (Building 13), Fort Shafter, July 1938. **NARA II, RG 77**

themselves were to defend "against acts of sabotage and maintain order in the civil community."[28]

Alert No. 1 Goes into Effect

Ninety minutes later, at about 1600, Short held a fifteen-minute discussion with his staff regarding the decision to institute Alert No. 1 status before ordering the alert into effect and directing notification of his echelon commanders and Lt. Col. Kendall J. Fielder (G-2 for the Hawaiian Department).[29]

Later that afternoon, Short conferred with Maj. Gen. Frederick L. Martin of the Hawaiian Air Force and Martin's chief of staff, Lt. Col. James A. Mollison. Short did not seek Martin's approval for Alert No. 1—that decision was final—but instead informed him of the reasons for the decision and discussed its implications for the Hawaiian Air Force. Short explained that all available information indicated that the dangers to Oʻahu "lay within the population of the island." Martin concurred, and the discussion turned to training issues within the Hawaiian Air Force. The two generals agreed that the higher alert states would have an adverse impact on training, especially the soon-to-end B-17 transition instruction, and decided

to continue the training as long as possible. Despite the wording in Marshall's message that referred to undertaking "such reconnaissance and other measures as you deem necessary," Martin agreed that they would take only "necessary measures against sabotage."[30]

Not long after his meeting with Short, Martin summoned his tactical and base commanders, described the message outlining "the strained relations between the Japanese and United States," and told them that Short had declared an antisabotage alert in response. The airfields were to gather their planes into "groupments" on the ramps and aprons so that they could be guarded more effectively against sabotage. Colonel Flood, who was still functioning as Brigadier General Davidson's proxy at Wheeler Field, was uneasy about drawing the field's fighters together and asked Major General Martin directly *"if we could continue to disperse."* Martin answered, "Well, Flood, no. The orders are to concentrate your planes." Martin left the dispersal door ajar, however, saying that he would check into the matter. Later—possibly on 28 November—Flood received a teletype message from Hawaiian Department headquarters that reiterated the earlier directive to draw in his planes. It was signed, "Short." Flood concluded that the department expected organized sabotage of which he was unaware. The matter was closed and there would be no dispersal of planes—at least for the time being.[31]

Martin Modifies Alert No. 1's Status

At some critical juncture, however, Major General Martin appears to have changed course regarding Alert No. 1 and allowed Wheeler and Hickam Fields to disperse their aircraft or maintain their dispersed positions, despite the very explicit directive handed down from Lieutenant General Short via Alert No. 1. That such dispersal occured is indisputable, being documented in many oral histories and accounts from both Hickam and Wheeler Fields that describe aircraft remaining in, or moving to, revetments or dispersal points on the perimeters of the respective airfields.[32]

On 2 December—five days into the alert— Martin issued a memo acknowledging that his command was indeed on antisabotage alert status. The memo enlarged upon Alert No. 1's instructions as contained in the Hawaiian Department Standard Operating Procedure (SOP), pending publication of a subordinate SOP for the Hawaiian Air Force. It outlined a brief series of instructions for each of the bombardment and pursuit wings, the three field commands, and the Hawaiian Air Depot.[33]

The second paragraph of the memo included this statement: "Prepared positions for the defense of Air Force installations will be manned at once." The instruction *appeared* to extend beyond the scope of antisabotage alerts and conflict with Short's order. Additionally, Martin's order adopted a wording similar to that of the Hawaiian Department's procedure for Alert No. 3—the highest alert, which required "the occupation of all field positions by all units." Among the few "field positions" at Wheeler were the aircraft revetments south and east of the landing field. True to Martin's discussion with Short, all training was to continue at full tilt. This required

Actions Taken by Major General Martin	Alert Level in Which Action Was Allowed
Aircraft & crews dispersed to revetments	Alerts No. 2 & No. 3
Field positions occupied	Alert No. 3
Aircraft armed [?]	Alert No. 3
Training continues	Alerts No. 1 & No. 2

armorers to maintain an ammunition supply in the revetments. In effect, therefore, all aircraft were either armed or had ammunition containers nearby for quick installation, although it is unclear whether or when Martin gave explicit orders for actual arming to occur. Again, this measure diverged from the provisions of Alert No. 1, which did not specify the arming of aircraft.[34]

Thus, Martin appears to have devised a hybrid alert status incorporating elements of Alert No. 2 and Alert No. 3 but inclining more toward the latter. This action might have confused officers under his command who were still thinking in terms of Alert No. 1 as described in the Hawaiian Department's SOP—hence the *necessity* of issuing his "Alert No. 1" memo. Martin thus ensured that his officers knew what was expected of them, despite the Alert No. 3 taste and feel in and around the revetments.

Questions remain, however. Most important, was Lieutenant General Short aware of Martin's actions? Why did Martin take the actions he did, and what did he expect to accomplish? The first question is impossible to answer. Although Martin addressed the "Alert No. 1" memo to a distribution, that distribution has not survived, so whether Martin notified General Short officially is an open question. The authors have found no admission, document, or hearing testimony to indicate that Flood, Martin, or Short revealed to anyone that aircraft were dispersed in *apparent* violation of Short's specific instructions to draw them in. That there was an informal understanding between Martin and Short cannot be discounted, although there is no evidence that such an understanding existed.

As to why Martin took the actions he did, there are three possible, interrelated reasons. Martin testified later that he "*never* wanted" to concentrate aircraft on the aprons, notwithstanding the difficulty in guarding them when they were dispersed. Second, Short had enjoined Martin to continue his training unabated. Further, subsequent to his meeting with Short, it is possible that Martin decided that for the sake of safety he needed to disperse aircraft in the unlikely event of external threat. Dispersal to the revetments addressed the need for training that simulated field conditions, Martin's reluctance to group all his aerial assets on the aprons, and concerns regarding external threats. With his aircraft in the revetments, the hybrid alert addressed all his concerns. Martin's decisions appear to have been his own. There is no evidence of any external pressure brought to bear on him by or from Lieutenant General Short, or impetus by the Navy to modify the alert further.[35]

Martin's actions addressed the need to react quickly to external threats. As for internal sabotage, the machine guns that faced outward every one hundred feet or so guarding the field constituted a deterrent far more powerful than any diffuse network of sentries toting bolt-action rifles on the parking apron would have done. Aerial training proceeded apace as well, as attested to by a study of the IFRs for pilots in the 19th Pursuit and 42nd Bombardment Squadrons. There was a two- to three-day period from 29 November through 1 December during which flying all but ceased at Wheeler and Hickam. Significantly, however, pilots picked up the pace on 2 December (coincidental with the release of Martin's alert memo), *with the same mission code (presumably training) being noted for practically all flights well before and after the alert went into effect.* Additionally, the dispersed positions of the aircraft put the aircrews in relatively primitive operating conditions—an excellent primer both for bomber crews headed for the Philippines and for fighter pilots supposedly headed for Wake or Midway.

Finally, to deflect hand-wringing in the higher commands regarding the threats from Japanese submarines, the 86th Observation Squadron's O-47Bs flew out of Bellows Field regularly, performing an average of sixteen daily search or patrol sorties close to the shores of Oʻahu (Sundays excluded). Similarly, the PBYs of PatWings 1 and 2 flew dawn patrols over Admiral Kimmel's operating areas where the Pacific Fleet trained. In essence, the O-47/PBY activity freed Martin from the distraction of having to mount patrol and reconnaissance missions that would disrupt training.[36]

Although the authors believe that Martin *authorized* dispersal of Wheeler's fighters to the revetments on 2 December, we do not know which squadrons actually moved and when, and which were already dispersed and declined to "draw in." Except for the 78th Pursuit Squadron, which was already in the revetments, and the 44th and 46th at Bellows and Haleiwa respectively, the location of the remaining six squadrons during the first three to four weeks of November is uncertain. Their morning reports are completely silent with respect to location on base. Going into December, however, it is clear that—apart from the units at Bellows and Haleiwa—at least five of the seven remaining squadrons had deployed to the revetments.[37]

At Haleiwa, the 46th Pursuit Squadron felt the effects of the alert as well. While the pilots engaged in gunnery training, the ground echelon followed suit with orders to set up machine guns around the approximately two-thousand-foot land perimeter of the airstrip and drew the squadron's planes into a line, with portable floodlights (probably trucked in from Wheeler) to illuminate the planes at night. In a departure from the month-long periods of training at Bellows Field, the 46th's stay at Haleiwa ended after eighteen days when orders sent the squadron back to Wheeler and the 47th Pursuit to Haleiwa. As of 27 November, support troops and non–Air Corps men engaged in purely defensive activity, reporting to supply warehouses to draw weapons and ammunition.

Ordnance companies manned defensive positions at Wheeler, Bellows, and Haleiwa. The 741st Ordnance Company occupied a sandbagged position atop the Headquarters Building, a position that had been prepared during previous alerts.[38]

Davidson Returns, 3 December 1941

On Wednesday, 3 December, the *Lurline* arrived off Honolulu boasting the second-largest passenger list in her history. The reporter for the *Honolulu Star-Bulletin* struck a somewhat somber note, though, observing that "the mark of Hawaii defense was plainly seen on the ship." A large proportion of the individuals on board were "defense workers, wives of defense workers joining their husbands here, [and] army and navy wives." Among the more notable arrivals were Brig. Gen. Howard Davidson, Lt. Col. Carroll Powell, and Maj. Arthur Meehan, who had finally concluded their stateside junket. Although "several squadrons of army planes" flew over the ship outside Honolulu Harbor to welcome the trio home, the greeting probably did not put Davidson in

a particularly festive mood. There was too much to be done over the next few days. He had to finish a report for Major General Martin on the trip just completed and confer with the Hawaiian Air Force staff regarding the possible creation of interceptor and maintenance commands in the Hawaiian Department.[39]

The Alert Ends

When no internal threats of sabotage developed, what little tension there was concerning the alert subsided. Many had come to see it as one in a long succession of tiresome, pointless exercises, and Lieutenant General Short's decision to vacate the department-wide alert was a relief to all. Based on testimony from Short and Major General Martin before the Roberts Commission, Short probably intended for the alert to extend until Saturday, 6 December. Martin jumped the gun, however, by ordering his men to stand down on Friday, 5 December, with some units receiving word as early as late Thursday. Martin's reasoning was that moving aircraft from the revetments back to the aprons was complicated and required substantial

The *Lurline* south of the piers off Honolulu Harbor following one of her many voyages to Hawai'i from the West Coast. **Wenger**

time and effort. An early start to that process ensured time for the customary parades and inspections on Saturday so that his men would be free to leave their bases with only the usual number of guards standing watch over the aircraft during the night of 6–7 December.[40]

Movement of aircraft to the pavement fronting the hangar line required substantial preparation. Trucks lumbered across the field transporting men, tools, equipment, and aircraft ammunition from the revetments, and machine guns and ammunition from the dug-in defensive positions in the rear. Evidence suggests that Wheeler's P-40s and P-36s were towed to the apron in stages (limited by the number of ramp tractors), with some squadrons making an early transition. On Thursday, 4 December, the 78th Pursuit Squadron was among the first units to begin the complicated evolution. By Friday the men had returned all equipment to their hangar and were busy washing aircraft in their assigned positions on the apron between Hangars 3 and 4. Crews from other squadrons arranged aircraft "tail section to wing trailing edge of the opposite row. Row after row." The aircraft were still fully fueled after the alert, although armorers had removed the .30- and .50-caliber ammunition from the wings and noses and stowed the relatively fragile .30-caliber containers in the squadrons' hangars.[41]

Other planes were not moved until very late the next day. Pvt. Milroy L. Richardson's crew from the 6th Pursuit Squadron did not receive word to move their P-40 back to the parking apron until 2300 Saturday night. The reason for the lengthy delay is uncertain, although the 6th Pursuit might have served as the wing's ready squadron to provide cover during the earlier movements. Darkness made the task of towing aircraft back to the squadron parking area even more difficult. Crews lined up the fighters in neat rows, filling the gap on the pavement south of Hangar 3 and Tent City. As Richardson's squadron was among the last to be repositioned, he did not get to bed until after 0300 on 7 December.[42]

The men of the 741st Ordnance Company were among the support troops at Wheeler released from alert status on Friday. At about 1700 word came that the alert was off and that the company had orders to "take all machine guns back to the arms room, put them away, and you will be off over the weekend." Similarly, while the pursuit squadron crews were still swatting mosquitos down in the revetments, Wheeler's quartermaster, Lt. Col. Joe C. Rogers (QMC), informed his men that the alert had run its course. A notice on the bulletin board near Pvt. Mannie E. Siegle's office announced the happy news that the men were free to go into town Saturday night.[43]

On Saturday, 6 December, the men received orders to form for a full parade and first-class inspection, and to relieve both the external and interior guards. Having already placed aircraft on the aprons, the men cleared an open area on the pavement directly in front of the hangars, pushing the aircraft into line toward the southern edge of the apron. After the parade and inspection—and for the first time in nearly a month for many—men received passes to leave the base. Anyone who wanted a pass received it. Since there was to be no flying on Sunday to speak of, the planes remained in their positions after the inspection.[44]

The compact squadron formations on Wheeler's parking apron—mostly in two rows for each unit, wingtip to wingtip, facing east—made for more efficient use of the much-reduced number of guards. The order to vacate the alert and draw in the fighters on which O'ahu depended for its defense transformed Wheeler's pursuit assets into gasoline-laden, toothless targets. Ironically, during the alert, the situation at the airfields was 180 degrees out of sync with what Short intended and ordered but was perfectly aligned with what was truly needed to face the coming attack. Now, during the last weekend of peace, the tables turned; unwittingly, the authorities in Hawai'i set in place circumstances in which meaningful resistance to inbound aerial threats would be impossible.

So eager were the men to have done with the alert and get to town that few paid much attention at the inspection, particularly regarding words of wisdom from their commanders. First Lt. Lewis M. Sanders, however, commanding the 46th Pursuit Squadron, "told the men & officers after inspection not to dismiss the warning lightly and be prepared for an alert. Less than 24 hours later we were at war."[45]

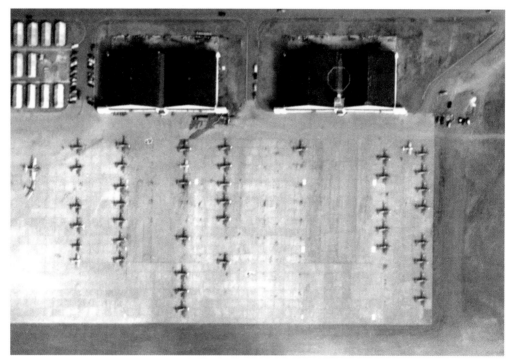

The east end of Wheeler Field's parking apron south of the hangar line, 1 October 1941. This vertical view shows the parking arrangement for the 18th Pursuit Group's squadrons in front of Hangars 3 and 4 two months prior to the attack and illustrates the typical arrangement of aircraft at Wheeler and their segregation by squadron. The most probable arrangement of the units is (*left to right*): (a) group headquarters squadron, probably an OA-9 and AT-6 directly south of the tent city; (b) (6th Pursuit) twelve P-40s and one natural metal P-26 south of Hangar 3's western bay; (c) (44th Pursuit) a similar arrangement below the hangar's eastern aircraft bay; (d) (78th Pursuit) a solitary P-40 below Hangar 4's western side (the balance of the squadron had just deployed for five weeks of training at Bellows Field); (e) (19th Pursuit) five P-40s with the balance of the unit probably flying; (f) one P-26 and eight P-40s at right, at the end of the apron—possibly pulled from existing units for the future 73rd Pursuit Squadron. That squadron formed four days later, on 5 October. On the apron in front of Hangar 4 (*right*), note also the six fueling pit boxes (small white rectangles) extending to the south, three on each side. **NARA II, 80-G-279368, cropped**

Chapter Seven

"THE TOWN WAS JUMPING!"

The Last Hours of Peace

Word that Lieutenant General Short had canceled the November alert was welcome news to the officers and enlisted men of the Hawaiian Department. The Wheelerites had been cooped up for a week—and in some cases for longer than that—and were ready to blow off some steam in town. The merchants and proprietors in Honolulu, Waikīkī, and elsewhere were eager to see the good times roll as well. The lenient issue of passes augured well for burgeoning crowds and extreme congestion in town.

The men were free to leave the base after the customary Saturday inspections and parades. Predictably, having managed to find transport into

The Nu'uanu Pali Road north of the Ko'olau Range weaves atop ridgelines in the lower portion of the photograph toward the Pali Pass at center. View looks southwest toward Honolulu, 19 November 1931. **USMHI**

The Lau Yee Chai restaurant in Waikīkī was a favorite dining spot for servicemen with passes into town. View looking north near the convergence of Kalākaua and Kūhiō Avenues. Second Lt. George Welch and 2nd Lt. Kenneth Taylor ate at the restaurant on the evening of 6–7 December. **Wenger**

Honolulu, Wheeler's airmen also found that the Pacific Fleet was in, and the streets were "rivers of white." Mixed amongst the sailors were soldiers and airmen from other bases across Oʻahu. "The town was jumping!" Like the Wheelerites, the Bellows men were eager to hit the town. Most could hardly wait to cross the Koʻolaus into the city on Saturday afternoon. "Honolulu was wide open, and everybody was drinking and doing their own thing."[1]

Pvt. Fred R. Runce of Wheeler's 696th Ordnance Company had been unable to go into town during the last weekend in November, so he was flush with cash. He stopped at his favorite Chinese restaurant in town to eat his favorite pork dish, then continued east into Waikīkī. Curiously, that locale was not "hopping" sufficiently to suit his expectations. After spending six or seven dollars—a tidy sum in those days—he decided to return to Wheeler. Runce came through the gate shortly before midnight and retired to the new wooden barracks, west of the Cantonment, into which his unit had recently moved. Although he usually did not get up for breakfast on Sunday, he found that the trek to the barracks had sharpened his appetite.

As Runce was deciding in favor of breakfast at Wheeler, Pfc. Ernest A. Brown of the Headquarters Detachment at Bellows Field was sleeping off a long, raucous night in Honolulu that had been punctuated by a brief dustup with the Military Police. It was early Sunday morning before he boarded the bus that transported him and his companions over the Pali Pass to Bellows at about 0200. Exhausted by the good times and the bus ride back to the base, Brown hit the sack and went out like a light.[2]

With all the time in the world but little money in his pockets, Pvt. Byron Kolbert spent the afternoon window shopping in Honolulu and then retreated to the swimming pool at the YMCA. At about 2200 he toyed with the idea of hitching a ride to Hickam Field

Servicemen gather near the front of the Army and Navy YMCA at the corner of Richards and Hotel Streets, circa 1940. **Wenger**

to look up a friend who could put him up for the night but decided against it. He thumbed his way back to Waimānalo and Bellows and went straight to bed. Years later, Kolbert concluded that the exhausting alert and the equally exhausting night of partying in Honolulu that followed had left the men spent and groggy on Sunday.[3]

Among the officers from Bellows seeking a night out was 2nd Lt. Phillip Willis, though with a different motivation than usual. Willis' best friend, 2nd Lt. Millard Shibley, had died in a takeoff accident at Bellows Field on the morning of 17 November, and Shibley's parents had asked Willis to accompany the body of their only child back home. Usually an officer stationed on the West Coast oversaw the delivery of remains to the grieving parents and attended the funeral, but Willis took the parents' request all the way to Lieutenant General Short. To Willis' surprise, Short approved the journey stateside and issued "a half-inch stack of orders" to make the trip. Most of Willis' clothing (except for his tuxedo) was already on a ship in Honolulu Harbor, as was Shibley's body. Willis was to leave on 8 December, travel to Tulsa, and meet his fiancée at the funeral there. The engaged couple planned to fly back to Hawai'i on a Pan American clipper several days later.[4]

On the evening of 6 December, Willis and a few other officers went to Hickam's Officers' Club for a party honoring his departure. Such a gathering was a tradition for officers' prior to *any* absence—short or long term—with every officer present "obligated" to buy the departing officer a drink. With no orders other than to board the ship on Monday, Willis eagerly took advantage of his fellow officers' generosity. He returned to Bellows between 0300 and 0400 on 7 December, shucked off his tuxedo jacket and shoes, and fell into bed.[5]

Although they had been marooned at Haleiwa Field only since 3 December, the 47th Pursuit Squadron's pilots were eager to hit the town as well. Second Lt. Kenneth M. Taylor drove back to Wheeler and rushed to the Officers' Club/BOQ (Building 302), where he and 2nd Lt. George S. Welch had "borrowed" a room from an acquaintance so they would have a convenient place to sleep when the good times were done. Taylor eschewed the customary all-night card game at the club and instead donned his tuxedo and headed into town for a night of carousing with Welch and some other pilots. After a Chinese meal, Taylor and Welch joined in the action at the Royal Hawaiian and the Moana—Waikīkī's main hotels. They returned to Wheeler quite late, having

A 1930s postcard portrays an idyllic view of Waikīkī and its two famous hotels, the Royal Hawaiian at lower center and the Moana at left. **Jerrold J. Staley**

concluded the evening at the Hickam Field and Pearl Harbor Officers' Clubs.[6]

Few of the men in the 46th Pursuit Squadron, exhausted by the rigors of the early December move from Haleiwa to the revetments at Wheeler, were eager to party in Honolulu that night. After stowing their gear and equipment, and repositioning the squadron's aircraft on the parking apron, some simply "sacked out" while others "just sat around and had a couple of beers and 'BS-ed' and went to bed." 2nd Lt. Gordon H. Sterling Jr. and 2nd Lt. Eldon E. Stratton had to put the good times in town on hold pending completion of unusual weekend flight duty. At some point during the day on Saturday they took off in an AT-6 to give the fledgling Stratton some sorely needed flight training. He had received his wings only five weeks earlier and had less than five hours' flying time since his arrival on 22 November. After an hour and ten minutes, the AT-6 landed, and Stratton and Sterling were free to go into town.[7]

Although months later critics would allege drunken brawls on the base that night, the officers and NCOs who stayed on base and went to the service clubs on the evening of 6 December noted no unusually heavy drinking. Second Lt. Stephen G. Saltzman played cards in the 98th Coast Artillery Officers' Club at Schofield Barracks. Most of the other junior officers were drinking that evening, but Saltzman noticed no drunkenness, although he did not leave the general area of the club. Schofield mirrored the clubs across the way at Wheeler Field; there was no drunkenness, only the usual social drinking, dancing, and partying that one might see at any country club or nightclub in the States. "After all, [the base] was just like a small-town community."[8]

Some men looking for a good time off base ventured no farther than nearby Wahiawā. Anticipating the opportunity "to live it up over the weekend," Pvt. John J. Springer of the 25th Material Squadron was in a big rush "to get everything put away and get cleaned up." Despite those frantic preparations, Springer decided to stay on base and relax in Tent City on Friday night. On Saturday, he lounged about, met some friends for a beer in the base canteen, and

The town of Wahiawā, nestled against Wheeler Field, looking northeast, 17 August 1937. The aircraft carrying the photographer was over Wheeler's northeast corner. **USAMHI**

then went bar-hopping in Wahiawā, "a small town [that] had a lot of liquor, and that's all it was—a place to have a good time." After staying a couple of hours, the group returned to Wheeler, played cards, and "just had a ball." At 0200 on Sunday morning Springer "hit the sack and went to sleep on a beautiful Hawaiian night." Pvt. Will Roy Sample also went into Wahiawā to "go find a beer joint and sit and drink" on 6 December, knowing that he was not on duty Sunday and was free to enjoy himself.[9]

The men wishing to venture farther off base but avoid Honolulu had options as well. Cpl. Vladamir "William" M. Shiflette III of the 73rd Pursuit Squadron went with other airmen to nearby Kemoʻo Farms for dinner on Saturday night. The establishment was well known for its steaks, and a man who avoided the expense of transportation into Honolulu could plow the money into a sumptuous T-bone dinner. Shiflette had duty at 0800 Sunday morning, so he started back to Wheeler at about 2130. The situation at the barracks was nothing but routine when he arrived. Pvt. Mannie Siegle likewise decided against going into Honolulu and took in a movie and a boxing match at Schofield Barracks instead. He returned to Wheeler at about 2330. Other airmen crowded theaters in Honolulu and Waikīkī to watch a first-run movie. Pfc. Edmund H. Russell, a butcher assigned to Wheeler's 18th Air Base Group, went to see *Dive Bomber*, a 1941 release starring Errol Flynn and Fred MacMurray.[10]

Many of those who went into Honolulu returned early due to scheduled duties or to avoid the crush of soldiers, sailors, and Marines who overwhelmed the mass transit system when it was time to return to base. Cpl. John P. Munn of the 72nd Pursuit Squadron went into town with some friends on Saturday afternoon but returned to Wheeler at about 1800—hardly a late night of carousing—then talked and played cards late into the evening. That same afternoon Sgt. Henry J. Straub—a mechanic with the 78th Pursuit Squadron—attended the Pineapple Bowl football game between the University of Hawaiʻi and Fresno State Normal School. Straub went for a dinner in

Honolulu afterward but made a relatively early return to Wheeler Field at about 2100 because he had charge of his barracks bay. Straub's quarters were on the top floor of the three-floor 600-Man Barracks. His bunk was in the corner facing east toward the Headquarters Building and south overlooking the airfield.[11]

Some of Wheeler's married couples remained close to home for a quiet evening. Everett and Sunny Stewart and two other couples had received an invitation from Stewart's squadron commander, 1st Lt. John S. Evans, for two-table bridge in Quarters 444-B. The Stewarts played cards and returned to Quarters 448-A at about midnight because Sunny wasn't feeling well.[12]

The pleasures of home and family kept many men in their quarters. Flora and SSgt. Stephen Koran spent the last Saturday night of peace at home with their newborn daughter Ellen, "giving no thought to what was going on outside."[13]

7 December 1941, Early Morning

Some men at Wheeler were up before sunrise on the morning of 7 December, whether they wished to be or not. Pvt. Milroy Richardson had been in bed for only an hour when an unwelcome tap on the shoulder awakened him at 0400. He had completely forgotten that he was working KP for fellow armorer Pvt. Earl T. Post. He dressed and hurried down to the kitchen, where the cook volunteered to fix him a quick breakfast. Richardson put in an order for eggs and fried potatoes but cooked the sausage himself. The noonday meal on Sundays was usually well attended, so Richardson set to work peeling a massive mound of potatoes. Sunup found him still hard at work in the kitchen on the first floor of Barracks No. 1 (Building 68).[14]

Pvt. Charles L. Hendrix of the Headquarters Squadron, 14th Pursuit Wing was up at 0600—early for a Sunday—because he planned to meet some friends in town and attend services at Central Union Church on the corner of Beretania and Punahou Streets. Brigadier General Davidson arose at 0630 and went into the bathroom to shave. Base commander Col. William Flood was up early as well. He walked out to retrieve the Sunday paper and chatted with neighbors in front of his quarters.[15]

Wisconsin native Pfc. Carroll T. Andrews of the Headquarters Squadron, 18th Pursuit Group had just finished breakfast and was getting dressed for church call. He knew it would be a busy day. Andrews played the organ during Catholic masses at Wheeler and had recently been appointed assistant to his priest, Capt. Edward A. Taylor. Andrews lived on the third floor in Barracks No. 1, which housed the 6th Pursuit Squadron and the 18th Pursuit Group's headquarters squadron. The headquarters unit had the top floor, overlooking the Schofield Plain to the south. On a clear day, the visibility was good enough to see Pearl Harbor in the distance.[16]

Pvt. John Springer awoke with guts churning from his revelries in Wahiawā. Thinking that a beer might settle his queasy stomach, he rousted close friend Pvt. Henry Zdanovich from the 674th Ordnance Company. After deciding to walk to an all-hours Japanese bar in Wahiawā, Springer and Zdanovich dressed and ambled east down Santos-Dumont Avenue past the Fire Department/Guard House and hangars.[17]

Pvt. Mannie Siegle had planned to sleep late that Sunday—he usually did—but Pfc. Philip Appici was working in the mess hall (probably Building T-57, west of the 600-Man Barracks) that morning and awakened Siegle with the announcement, "You know, we have pancakes this morning!" When Siegle mumbled, "Don't bother me," Appici persisted. "Come on! Get up and go with me!" There was neither beer nor breakfast for SSgt. Stephen Koran that Sunday morning. He was still in bed in the NCO quarters, though sitting up, with baby Ellen's bassinet alongside.[18]

Japanese Aircraft over O'ahu

The warm yellow dawn spilling through the windows of Staff Sergeant Koran's quarters foretold nothing of what lay only minutes away. With the blessing of Emperor Hirohito, the Japanese Empire had decided to go to war with the United States, Great Britain, and the Netherlands. Under the command of Vice Adm. Nagumo Chūichi, two hundred miles north of O'ahu *Kidō Butai*, or the Carrier Striking Force—composed of six aircraft carriers supported by battleships, cruisers, destroyers, and submarines—was racing south toward Hawai'i. Their mission: immobilize the U.S. Pacific Fleet at Pearl Harbor to eliminate American naval interference during Japan's conquest of the resource-rich "Southern Area."

Nagumo's carriers launched a powerful initial strike of 183 aircraft under Cdr. Fuchida Mitsuo starting at 0600 on 7 December 1941. The winged host that thundered two miles above the cloud-covered Pacific must have presented a majestic sight. Fuchida's force of 49 Nakajima B5N2 Type 97 carrier attack bombers (*kankōs*) occupied center stage at 3,000 meters while Lt. Cdr. Takahashi Kakuichi's 51 Aichi D3A1 Type 99 carrier bombers (*kanbakus*) rode above them at 3,500 meters, stepped back on Fuchida's port quarter. Another force of Type 97 *kankōs*—Lt. Cdr. Murata Shigeharu's 40 torpedo bombers—lay below at 2,800 meters on Fuchida's starboard quarter. Fighters circulated above the force at 3,800 meters in 3 elements— one group each positioned forward, aft, and directly above the main formation—all meandering to and fro to avoid overrunning the slower bombers below. Almost half of the force—40 torpedo bombers and 49 horizontal bombers—was to target American battleships and aircraft carriers. Lt. Cdr. Itaya Shigeru's 43 Mitsubishi A6M2 Type 0 carrier fighters (*kansens*) were to provide top cover and strafe O'ahu's airfields if circumstances allowed.

The fifty-one dive-bombers were to strike American air power at NAS Pearl Harbor and at Hickam and Wheeler Fields. Responsibility for destroying these targets rested on Lieutenant Commander Takahashi, the overall commander of the dive-bomber force from the aircraft carriers *Shōkaku* and *Zuikaku*:

Shōkaku dive-bomber group
Lt. Cdr. Takahashi, 26 aircraft
Target: NAS Pearl Harbor
(Navy patrol bomber base), 9 aircraft
Target: Hickam Field
(Army bomber base), 17 aircraft
Zuikaku dive-bomber group
Lt. Sakamoto Akira, 25 aircraft
Target: Wheeler Field
(Army fighter base)

Selection of the airfields as targets indicated Japanese concern for the safety of their carriers north of O'ahu and of the strike units over the island. While the nine lead aircraft under Takahashi's direct command would attack the PBY patrol bombers at NAS Pearl Harbor, his two subordinate *chūtai*s (units of six to twelve aircraft), under Lt. Yamaguchi Masao, were to strike Hickam Field and destroy its heavy bombardment force of B-17 Flying Fortresses. All three of Lt. Sakamoto Akira's *chūtai*s were to attack Wheeler Field and destroy the Americans' capacity to intercept and interfere with the Japanese formations.[19]

Fuchida sighted land about fifteen miles northeast of Kahuku Point (the northern tip of O'ahu) shortly before 0738. Finding that he was off course to the east, he turned south-southwest in order to align the inbound strike with the intended point of landfall. As the inbound strike force awaited the deployment order, Fuchida had to decide whether a surprise attack was possible. That decision would drive the details of the deployment north of the island. Although cloud cover north of O'ahu prevented visual acquisition of the entire island until the last moment, Fuchida "surveyed the heavens above and around." The absence of both heavy antiaircraft fire and American interceptors in the skies ahead suggested that surprise had been achieved. Satisfied, at 0740 Fuchida instructed FPO1c Mizuki Tokunobu, his radioman, to telegraph the general deployment order—the first radio message sent from the inbound air strike force:

··–·· ·–––· –––
ト-ツ-レ (to-tsu-re), or
"Assume preliminary charge formation."[20]

「リサ乙」抜萃

行動	アマレ	集合セヨ(集合点……高度……百米旋回方向……)
行動	シアラ	集合点ヲ……トス(ニ改ム)
行動	マチ	待合セヨ
行動	ミセ	右旋回(高度…百米)
行動	ヒセ	左旋回(高度…百米)
行動	シケ	進撃セヨ
行動	シツレ	進撃隊形制レ
行動	ノ連送	高度ヲ上ゲ
行動	ヤ連送	高度ヲ下ゲ
行動	ハナ	遠ザカレ
行動	ヨレ	近寄レ
行動	ソノ	速力(計器指度)…節トナセ
行動	ケウ	嚮導セヨ
行動	サキ	先行セヨ
行動	タコ	単独行動セヨ
行動	ブコ	分離行動セヨ
行動	ヨテ	予定ノ如ク行動セヨ
行動	ヨヘ	予定ヲ変更ス
行動	カエ	(…ノタメ)引返セ
行動	カレチ	集合セル中隊毎ニ散レ
行動	カレセ	集合セル小隊毎ニ散レ
行動	イシ	位置知ラセ
行動	ソ連送	位置不明方位測定セヨ
行動	ボミ	母艦ヲ認ム
捜索	ソウ	(….ヲ)捜索セヨ
捜索	ソシ…	捜索針路000度
捜索	カイ…	開度000度
捜索	シシ	進出距離….
捜索	ソテ	側程….
捜索	ソコハ	索敵攻撃配備トナセ
偵察	テサ	(….)ヲ偵察セヨ
敵発見	テキ連送	我敵(…)ヲ認ム(方位000度 距離00)
敵発見	ミ連送	敵戦斗機見ユ
敵情	ン	敵針(000度)
敵情	テキシ	敵ノ基準針路(000度)
敵情	テソ	敵速(….節)
指揮	シコト	指揮官機故障(…ハ)指揮ヲ執レ
指揮	シキケ	(ノ)指揮ヲ承ケ
攻撃	ケカイ	警戒(セヨ)
攻撃	クヨ	空戦用意
攻撃	ク連送	我空戦中
攻撃	トツレ	突撃準備隊形制レ
攻撃	コモ	攻撃目標
攻撃	モヘ	攻撃目標….変更セヨ
攻撃	バヒ	爆撃基準高度….百米トナセ
攻撃	トヨ	距離ヲ縮メ突撃用意
攻撃	ト連送	全軍突撃セヨ(突撃方向00度)
攻撃	ツ連送	突撃セヨ(突撃方向000度)
攻撃	コマ	攻撃待テ
攻撃	コヤ	攻撃止メ(終了)
攻撃	ウテ	(….ヲ)銃撃セヨ
攻撃	ミイ	命中(….弾[本])
攻撃	ヒタ	(敵….方ニ)避退セヨ
攻撃	カチ連送	我敵…ヲ爆撃ス(地点…)
攻撃	ラル連送	我敵…ヲ雷撃ス(地点…)

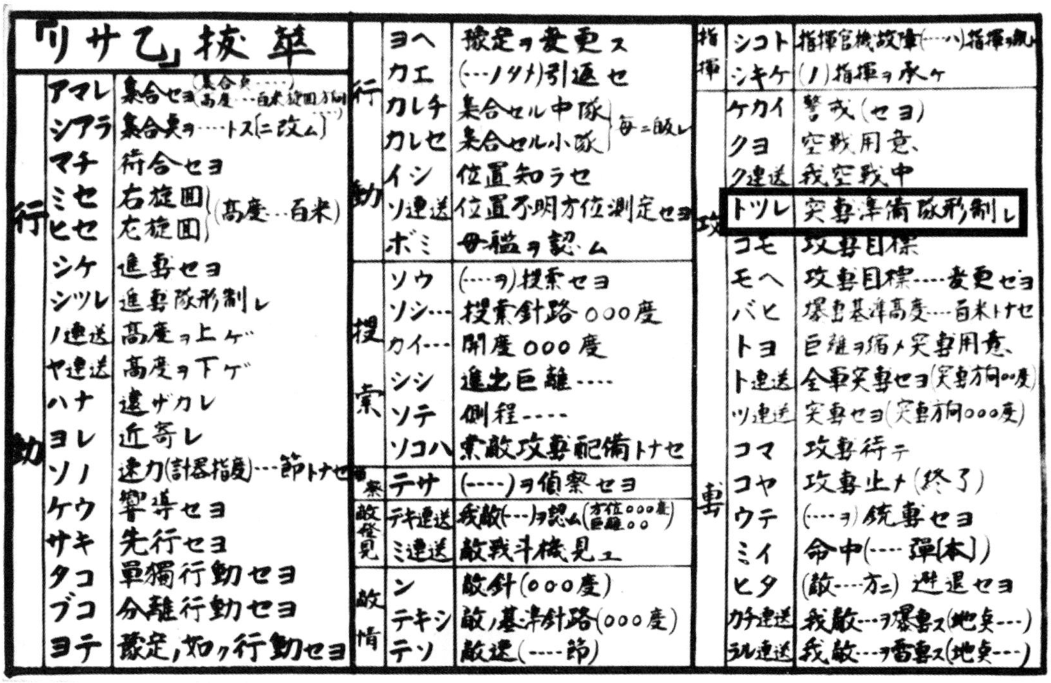

Page of a codebook retrieved from Japanese aircraft wreckage after the attacks on O'ahu. In the box at upper right is the *katakana* code word *to-tsu-re* for the command, "Assume preliminary charge formation." **NARA, RG 80, via Mulligan**

To reinforce that order *and* to signal the method of deployment, Fuchida opened the center canopy of his Nakajima Type 97 to fire a single "Black Dragon" flare to signal that surprise had been achieved. The strike force would employ a "no force" (*kishū* 奇襲) method of attack, and the torpedo bombers would immediately attack the ships in Pearl Harbor. Had the element of surprise been lost, Fuchida would have fired two flares and the formation would have deployed to execute a "force" (*kyōshū* 強襲) attack method, in which the dive bombers and fighters would attack the airfields to suppress resistance in the air before the other units attacked the harbor. Upon receipt of the "no force" signal, Lieutenant Commander Murata's torpedo bombers were to fly directly south and skirt the north end of the Ko'olau Range into the harbor area first; the dive-bombers would follow, and Fuchida's high-level bombers would strike last. Fuchida pointed his flare pistol into the air at 0740 and squeezed the trigger.[21]

On Fuchida's left, Takahashi's southbound formation of fifty-one carrier bombers saw the flare and deployed to attack the island's three largest airfields. Just before making actual landfall over O'ahu, Takahashi led the first-wave dive-bomber force into a sharp, climbing turn to the right to avoid the heavy cloud cover over the Ko'olau Range, passed over the strike force, and ascended to a standby altitude of four thousand meters. From this position northeast of O'ahu Takahashi was to unleash the attacks on Wheeler, NAS Pearl Harbor, and Hickam after the lead elements of Fuchida's bombers attacked the battleships.[22]

The original deployment plan called for the dive-bomber units to leave their standby position and advance straight into their respective target areas from a position upwind and approximately twenty miles northeast of the airfields. At the time Fuchida ordered the deployment, however, Takahashi was already within the general area from which he was to commence bombing attacks, as his ascent to the standby altitude was to have occurred much farther north of O'ahu. His cramped position out to the northeast forced a shift to west of the Ko'olau Range that posed an additional risk of alerting the Americans, all brought on by the heavy cloud cover that hid O'ahu from the north.

Until that juncture, the launch, flight, and approach had gone off without a major hitch, excluding the proximity of Fuchida's deployment to O'ahu. All seemed well at first, with Murata (actually in a moment of indecision) appearing to be leading his torpedo group toward Pearl Harbor. Takahashi banked outside to the west, opening the distance between his unit and the airfields, thereby allowing Murata's torpedo bombers to strike first.[23]

Then, with his strike ready to cross the northern coastline, Fuchida's meticulous plans unraveled before his eyes. After the horizontal bombers changed to their new southwesterly course across northern O'ahu, Fuchida looked toward the harbor, hoping to see Murata charging south; instead, the relatively low-flying torpedo group was about two thousand meters ahead, but *practically parallel* to Fuchida's new southwesterly course. The torpedo units had orders to fly south into Pearl Harbor after receiving Fuchida's signal. What was wrong? Could clouds have prevented Murata from seeing the flare signal to attack? After waiting briefly for Murata's force to separate onto the southerly course toward Pearl Harbor, Fuchida decided to fire a second flare to alert the torpedo group to charge ahead, directly south. Since the short interval for the two-flare "force," or "no surprise," signal had long passed, surely no one would misinterpret the repeated signal intended for Murata alone. Thus, at about 0742, some three miles offshore from the Kahuku Sugar Mill, Fuchida *aimed directly at Murata* and fired a second flare.[24]

The second flare appeared to correct Murata's southwest turn, but it also provoked an unintended response from the dive-bombers. The second Black Dragon probably caught the eye of Takahashi's observer, Lt. (jg) Koizumi Seizō, who brought the flare to his chief's attention. Far above and to the right of Fuchida, Takahashi thought that the second flare signaled, "Force!" Without voice communication and too far away for hand signals, Takahashi believed himself to be acting under orders to strike immediately and deployed his units accordingly. While Fuchida fumed, Takahashi's force raced south at full throttle at about 0743. Approximately four miles northeast of Wheeler, Takahashi rocked his wings, signaling Sakamoto to break away and attack Wheeler Field, which lay practically dead ahead, while Takahashi continued south toward NAS Pearl Harbor and Hickam Field. The dive-bombers' initial approach to Wheeler Field—generally from the northeast—and their subsequent circulation pattern prior to the attack gave rise to the popular but false notion that Lieutenant Sakamoto's bombers attacked out of Kole Kole Pass. Meanwhile, Takahashi continued his approach to NAS Pearl Harbor and Hickam

Field, speeding down the wide valley that separated the Wai'anae and Ko'olau mountain ranges toward the sugar fields on 'Aiea heights just north of Pearl Harbor.[25]

Lieutenant Sakamoto, meanwhile, having been released from the main dive-bomber force, cut west and undertook a flyby and target assessment from the south side of Wheeler's turf runways with his group of three *chūtais* in line astern. After passing by Wheeler he circled north, turned east, and flew over Schofield Barracks' lower expanse, with Wheeler's hangars out to his right. Banking hard to the south, he set his final attack course from out of the north-northeast. As the trailing two *chūtais* under Lt. Ema Tamotsu and Lt. Hayashi Chikahiro descended into Wheeler out of their left- and right-hand spirals, they peered at the target area below. Pair after pair of hangars stretched out to the west,

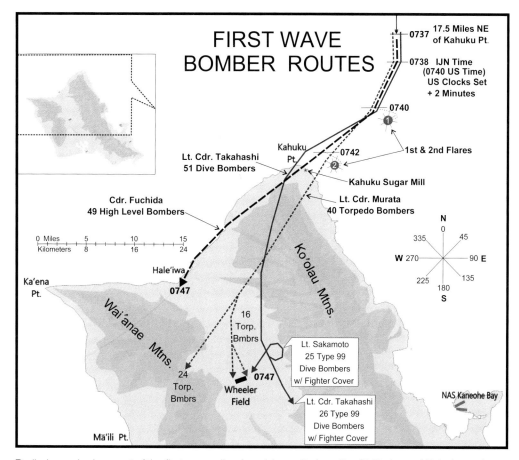

Preliminary deployment of the first-wave dive-bombing units from the *Shōkaku* and *Zuikaku* under the command of Lieutenant Commander Takahashi. The *Zuikaku* unit approaches Wheeler Field while the *Shōkaku* unit continues southeast toward Pearl Harbor and Hickam Field. **Di Virgilio**

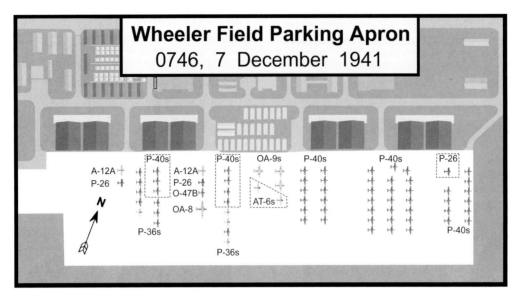

Wheeler Field's aircraft parking apron on the morning of 7 December 1941. Although the field provided a parking diagram (broken down by squadron) to the Roberts Commission, there were substantial departures from the scheme in actual practice, particularly among the squadrons of the 15th Pursuit Group and the utility aircraft of the headquarters squadrons in the 17th Air Base Group and the two pursuit groups. Japanese photographic documentation is similarly ambiguous due to smoke from aircraft burning on the apron. Two Japanese photos—both taken south of the apron looking northeast—provide the best evidence. One (p. 162) shows fighters from the 15th Pursuit Group to best advantage, and the other (p. 163) best documents planes of the 18th Pursuit Group. Although a substantial number of aircraft were in the hangars and in engineering buildings to the west, we show only those in front of the hangars. **Di Virgilio**

and the wide parking apron south of the hangars was crowded with parked American aircraft—all perfectly aligned with the prevailing winds to form almost perfect targets. With impeccable timing, Lieutenant Sakamoto's *Zuikaku* dive bombers had concluded their circular recon of Wheeler Field just as Lieutenant Matsumura's low-flying torpedo units from the carriers *Sōryū* and *Hiryū* were finishing their flyby west and east of the slumbering airfield.[26]

Dive-Bombers and Fighters Approach Wheeler Field

As the pilots of the incoming air strike made visual acquisition of Oʻahu, Lt. Ema Tamotsu—a *chūtai* commander of nine *Zuikaku* carrier bombers—breathed a sigh of relief. Had the thick layer of cumulus clouds below the inbound first wave caused Commander Fuchida to commit a navigation error, the formation might have missed the island altogether. But now, Lieutenant Ema was convinced that the attack would be a success. As Ema's dive-bombers cleared the towering Koʻolau Range, the clouds parted and the skies cleared to reveal "Hoirā Hikōjō" (Wheeler Aerodrome), which "lay nude and bright in the . . . morning sunshine." Ema thought the "quiet, beautiful sight . . . so unreal . . . almost fantastic," and oddly antithetical to the war he was about to start.[27]

The sight of Wheeler Field and the multitude of aircraft gleaming in the early morning light was an enormous relief to FPO2c Hori Kenji piloting the lead aircraft in the *shōtai* (a unit of two to four aircraft) immediately following Ema's. "As we were all ready, we now just awaited the execution order." There was nothing left for Hori to do but plunge into the assault and listen to his plane commander, Lt. (jg) Ōtsuka Reijirō, in the rear seat rattle off the altitude in two-hundred-meter increments during the attack dive.[28]

The twenty-five pilots under Sakamoto's command began their deployment over Wheeler with the knowledge that no Americans would interfere. Japanese carrier fighters flying five thousand to six thousand meters over O'ahu had rushed forward to seize the skies ahead from the American defenders—and saw nothing but empty airspace. Fighter pilot FPO1c Muranaka Kazuo from the *Hiryū* was amazed to find "no enemy at all!" Still, as a precaution, fighter units from the *Sōryū* and *Hiryū* (then providing top cover for the dive-bombers) set up near Wheeler Field, scanned the horizon and airspace below them, and determined that no American fighter opposition was forthcoming. Lt. Suganami Masaji led his eight *Sōryū* carrier fighters down toward Wheeler at 0747 to strafe the base only a minute or so after he saw Sakamoto's carrier bombers go into their attack dives, hoping the bombers would finish their deadly business before the *Sōryū*'s fighters reached attack altitude.[29]

Attack Orders

Each of Lieutenant Sakamoto's dive-bombers carried one No. 25 (250-kg) Type 98 land bomb fused for a one-tenth of a second delay to ensure that bombs would penetrate the hangars' roofs prior to detonation. The bombs were to be released at 650 meters (just over 2,100 feet) to ensure maximum penetration. Although the higher altitude sacrificed accuracy, the targets were stationary.[30]

Strict operational orders restricted target selection at Wheeler to *hangars only*. Strafing would have little effect if most of the aircraft were inside the hangars. Should Sakamoto's men fail to destroy the hangars—and the aircraft presumed to be inside—hordes of American fighters might rise up and doom the success of the inbound second-wave strike. Orders also regulated the timing of the attack on Wheeler. If the Japanese achieved tactical surprise, under no circumstances were Sakamoto's planes to enter their attack dives until Lieutenant Commander Murata's torpedo bombers passed by, or over, Wheeler Field on their way south to the harbor.[31]

Commander Fuchida's original deployment plan called for *all* of the torpedo bombers to stand down the wide plain that separated the Ko'olau and Wai'anae mountain ranges. Heavy clouds over the Ko'olaus caused Murata to veer right with the intent of skirting the western shore of the island. Although committed to his new course, Murata released the torpedo units from the *Sōryū* and *Hiryū* so that they might pass directly south toward targets in the western half of Pearl Harbor. Accordingly, he rocked the wings as a signal to Lt. Matsumura Hirata from the *Hiryū* for sixteen torpedo-laden *kankō*s to separate left and fly south along the rugged inland slopes of the Wai'anae Range.[32]

Sōryū's Torpedo Unit Strafes Wheeler

Just before Matsumura's torpedo bombers bypassed Wheeler to the west, subordinate Lt. Nagai Tsutomu, the impetuous commander of the *Sōryū* torpedo unit, asked Matsumura to release him to attack fleet anchorages in the northwestern part of the harbor. Nagai pulled even with his chief and jabbed his finger at the windscreen. Matsumura rocked his wings and released the *Sōryū* unit then approaching Wheeler Field.[33]

Lt. Nagai Tsutomu, commander, *Sōryū* torpedo-bombing unit, circa 1941–42. **BKS**

WO Mori Jūzō (circa 1944), *Sōryū* torpedo-bombing unit, flew as wingman for Lt. Nagai Tsutomu. Mori's decorations are (*left to right*): Golden Kite, Order of the Sacred Treasure, Order of the Rising Sun, and the China Incident War Medal. **Prange**

Illuminated by the early morning sun, Wheeler attracted unwanted attention from Nagai's crews. In second position behind Nagai was FPO2c Mori Jūzō. Focused on piloting his plane instead of on the landscape below, Mori failed to notice Wheeler Field until he was in the vicinity of Wahiawā and had almost passed east of the base. The young pilot was flabbergasted to see "what appeared to be two hundred fighters in line in front of the hangars" two hundred meters below him—a stark illustration of the enormous gulf between the "have" and "have-not" nations. With the sure knowledge that these American fighters posed a direct threat to his survival ("They'd finish us!"), Mori screamed through the voice tube for his radioman/gunner—FPO2c Hayakawa Junichi—to open fire on the aircraft massed on the concrete hardstand below. Although it is unlikely that his guns did much damage to the parked fighters, Hayakawa could claim that he had fired the Japanese naval air arm's first shots against the United States in the Pacific War. Several other

rear gunners followed suit and opened fire from five hundred meters' range, including FPO2c Wakamiya Hideo, two planes back from Mori, and others from the *Hiryū*—even Matsumura's gunner.[34]

The torpedo bombers did not go unnoticed on the ground. At about 0745, SSgt. Harold J. Moore, a radio electrician with the 19th Pursuit Squadron, had finished breakfast and was enjoying the beautiful morning when he noticed "single engine aircraft flying very low near the far end of the field." He "paid little attention to it for the moment, for the Navy often came in this way and on some occasions would clear their guns in [Kīpapa] Gulch."

Other aircraft to the west seemed to follow that plane's route. Sgt. Christopher Ward of the 46th Pursuit Squadron likewise noticed planes skirting the periphery of the field, from north to south, at very

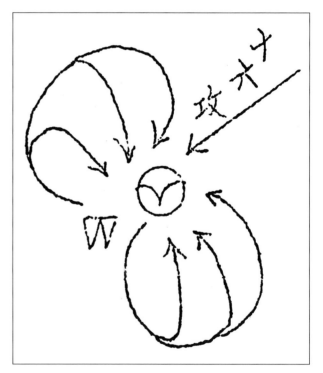

Deployment of the *Zuikaku* dive-bombing unit over Wheeler Field, as diagrammed in the *Shōkaku*'s action report from the Hawaiian Operation. While there is conclusive eyewitness testimony that the 1st *Chūtai* (under Lieutenant Sakamoto's direct command) attacked from upwind, this diagram suggests strongly that most of the bombers attacked across the prevailing winds. These factors underlie the authors' interpretation of the *Zuikaku* unit's deployment and directions of attack. **BKS**

low altitude. Ward and fellow airplane mechanic Cpl. Willard B. Phillips surmised that they were Navy aircraft because they were painted light gray underneath with dark paint above.[35]

Lieutenant Sakamoto Deploys

With Lieutenants Matsumura's and Nagai's torpedo planes having passed Wheeler, Lieutenant Sakamoto considered how to deploy his *Zuikaku* dive-bombing unit of three *chūtai*s totaling twenty-five aircraft

over the American fighter base. Sakamoto had to deliver systematic, thorough bombing and strafing attacks and yet also prevent unnecessary delays and loitering in or near the target area that might invite interception.

Eventually, Sakamoto decided to employ an "anvil" attack, whereby his men would bomb from several directions in rapid succession. Just prior to the unit's commitment to its final attack dives, the aircraft—alternating *by chūtai*—would wheel out in

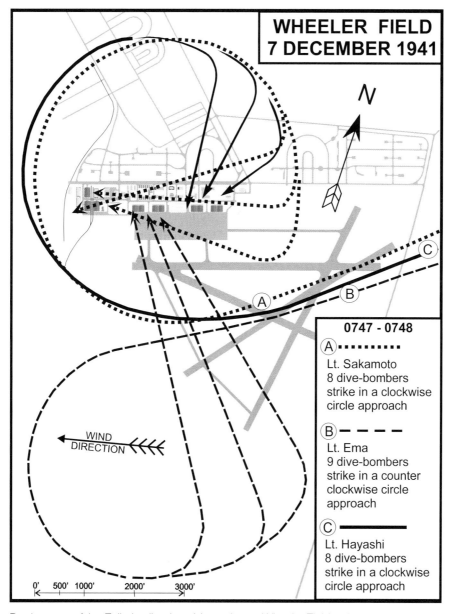

Deployment of the *Zuikaku* dive-bombing unit over Wheeler Field, as interpreted by the authors. **Di Virgilio**

single file to port and to starboard. The 1st Chūtai under Lieutenant Sakamoto would dive into the target from generally northeast along the axis of the flight line. The 2nd Chūtai under Lieutenant Ema was to spin out left and press forward generally from the south. Lieutenant Hayashi's 3rd Chūtai would deploy in a manner similar to Sakamoto's, though circling to the right and attacking generally out of the north.[36]

Thus, most of the bombers would attack across the axis of Wheeler's flight line and have to contend with a brisk crosswind coming in from the east-northeast. Ideally, the first bomb (Sakamoto's) would drop on the large "hangars" (actually, maintenance and engineering buildings) farthest downwind at the western terminus of Wheeler's flight line. The commanders of each *chūtai* were to assign each of their three component *shōtais* to *one of the hangars*. With the *chūtai* leader (*chūtaichō*) anchoring on the westernmost undamaged target, his second *shōtaichō* would select the next hangar upwind, as would the third *shōtaichō* in line. This series of "stepladder" attacks would *progress upwind* and ensure minimum smoke interference with subsequent target selections.[37]

No known document sets forth Sakamoto's rationale for such an unusual and complex deployment, which contrasted sharply with that employed over Hickam Field. Most likely, Sakamoto thought that a single stream of bombers attacking from one direction (with obligatory intervals separating the *chūtais*) would expose his unit to American defenders for longer than necessary. Under this double pinwheel scheme, the bombers would be in and out quickly with a decreased risk of interception while at low altitude, albeit with the hazard of adjacent, parallel columns of aircraft moving in opposite directions. As executed, the Wheeler attacks violated the Imperial Navy's preferred dive-bombing tactics of the day: *attacking with the wind.*[38]

Shortly after Lieutenant Nagai's torpedo bombers passed by on the way to Pearl Harbor, at 0745 Sakamoto's three *chūtais* of dive-bombers passed over, or by, the base from upwind. The three dive-bomber units then reversed course, wheeled about in single file, and attacked by *shōtai*, with Sakamoto's lead unit of eight aircraft plummeting in from the northeast.[39]

As Lt. Ema Tamotsu at the front of the 2nd Chūtai made his last turn to port and entered his attack dive, he glanced upward at Schofield Barracks in the distance. For a brief moment, his thoughts wandered back to 1936, when as a midshipman he had visited Hawai'i and Schofield Barracks. Turning back to the grim business at hand, Ema mused that Wheeler Field "was lined with well parked rows of fighter planes" that presented "an ideal target for the dive-bombers."[40]

At about 0745, Pvt. Charles L. Hendrix of the 17th Air Base Squadron left the 600-Man Barracks on his way to the Central Union Church in Waikīkī. He was almost halfway to the gate when he heard a group of aircraft high overhead and a quick burst of machine-gun fire, as if a pilot were clearing his guns. That was not unusual, though the aircraft did not sound like the planes he normally heard at Wheeler. Hendrix concluded that they were Navy aircraft. Pfc. David B. Stephenson observed "three strange airplanes of the fighter-bomber type with tricycle landing gear" (probably referring to the Type 99 carrier bombers' fixed landing gear) approaching Wheeler from the east as if they intended to buzz the field. Stephenson could not remember seeing that type of aircraft at Wheeler before.[41]

Chapter Eight

"DEAR GOD, WHAT DID WE DO TO DESERVE THIS?"

The First-Wave Attacks at Wheeler

Positioned to deliver a pincer-like attack on the unsuspecting Americans, the Japanese prepared to unleash a storm of 250-kilogram high-explosive bombs on Wheeler Field's hangars and parking apron.

Sakamoto's 1st Chūtai Attacks: Engineering Buildings and Warehouses

Farthest downwind to the southwest, squadron leader Lt. Sakamoto Akira supposedly dropped the first bomb of the Pacific War on (or at least he aimed at) Building 23—the Base Engineering (Machine) Shop—at the western boundary of the flight line. The action over Wheeler Field preceded that over Pearl Harbor by five or more minutes. By any measure of timing, the Japanese rain of ruin on Oʻahu had begun.[1]

In the absence of engineering records from Wheeler documenting the damage or an action report from the *Zuikaku*, it is impossible to determine precisely how Sakamoto's lead *chūtai* selected and hit its targets. Their orders were to attack the hangars, and *only* the hangars. Sakamoto, leading the column, and his wingman, FPO1c Sakamaki Hideaki, were the first to strike. Their bombs fell relatively close to the buildings of the Engineering Department at the western end of the airfield, perhaps due to the stiff tailwind. Sakamoto's bomb probably fell into the temporary buildings or warehouses just beyond the Machine Shop to the west, with the southernmost of the two oblong frame buildings likely catching the first two bombs. The blast (or blasts) obliterated the warehouse; only the framework for the loading dock doors remained. This southernmost strike also ruptured the lines to the field's gasoline station and set the fuel afire. The explosion's fireball and smoke plume set in place the westernmost marker for the stepladder tactics the dive-bomber units would employ and indicated exactly where the next pilot was to drop his payload.[2]

F1c Tanaka Gorō and WO Ujiki Tazuchi, piloting the third and fourth aircraft in line, most likely delivered strikes against the Machine Shop. One of the bombs passed through the building's asbestos-protected, corrugated metal roofing and exploded either just inside the building or on the concrete apron outside after penetrating the structure's west wall. The other bomb detonated in the front half of the building and caused heavy damage, although an interior concrete block wall absorbed much of the blast and

This view looking south of Wheeler Field's engineering buildings in the opening minutes of the raid documents the first bombs dropped against the United States in the Pacific War. Smoke rolls out of the Machine Shop (Engineering Department) (*upper center*), and fires at the base's gasoline station rage out of control (*upper right*). Just below the gasoline fires, a bomb, or bombs, have demolished much of a wood-frame warehouse that was identical to the building seen just below. At the intersection of Foote and Wright Avenues (*lower left center*), a light patch just over the curb marks the location of a crater from an explosion that demolished a small warehouse just to the right. **Satō Collection via PHAM, cropped**

The demolished warehouse shown at right in the above photograph, looking northwest. Wheeler used part of this building as storage for bags of concrete. Airmen on the other side of the base observed a large cloud of white dust mushrooming out of the building when the bomb detonated. Although not readily apparent, this image is a double exposure, with a group of tiny men "standing in front of" the debris at the far left. The double exposure also caused an apparent "two-tone finish" on the rafters from an upended roof section on the right. **NARA II, 111-SC-176604**

A bomb detonation—possibly from Sakamoto's 250-kilogram bomb—opened this crater along the eastern wall of the wood-framed warehouse seen in the previous images. Note the bags of concrete at center and the roof section at the far right. **Aiken, NMPW**

saved the tool room and the machine shop on the other side. The explosion wrecked the electrical shop, paint shop, and sheet metal shop, although most of the machinery survived.[3]

Pfc. Jack Elgart, a sheet metal worker with the 25th Material Squadron who was the hangar guard on the night of 6–7 December, was resting in a bunk set up in the Final Assembly Shop (Building 24) just east of the Machine Shop when the bombs struck.

Elgart went outside, looked up, saw the Japanese aircraft overhead, and ran in the opposite direction. He took refuge at Schofield Barracks until the raid ended. SSgt. Harold C. Hitt, an aircraft mechanic with the 72nd Pursuit Squadron, left his breakfast on the table in the squadron mess and hurried to the Final Assembly Shop to help remove three or four P-36As and P-40s that had been undergoing maintenance during the days preceding the attack.[4]

Debris-strewn area next to the site of the former concrete storage warehouse. Door frames marking the location of a loading dock remain. The ruins of the gasoline station protrude into the picture at the far left. Just discernible in the background at far right are the engineer's cab and tender of an Oahu Railway locomotive. **NARA II, 111-SC-176605**

The Machine Shop, looking north, showing damage inflicted by two bomb hits. One passed through the west wall and detonated just outside the building, demolishing the masonry door pocket on the left, and another detonated in the interior and carried away large sections of the roof and siding from the front gable. The Air Corps Warehouse stands intact immediately behind. **NARA II, 111-SC-128347**

One pilot in Sakamoto's *chūtai* appears to have dropped his bomb at the northwest corner of the intersection of Wright Avenue and Foote Avenue Extension. The bomb failed to strike any building, but the force of the blast destroyed a warehouse (Building T-631) west of the intersection and inflicted relatively light damage on a barracks (Building T-616) across the street to the north and on a quartermaster warehouse (Building T-604)

southwest of the intersection. The balance of the bombs, which included one possible impact near the southwest corner of the parking apron, failed to strike other buildings. The hits on the Machine Shop affected only a few pursuit planes undergoing overhaul in the Final Assembly Shop. The majority of Hawai'i's fighter strength was amassed in the open, on the parking apron to the east. Thus, the opening strike was largely a waste of ordnance.[5]

View looking west at the intersection of Foote and Wright Avenues where a 250-kilogram bomb exploded next to the street, wrecking Building T-631, a small warehouse. Although the force of the blast blew away much of the warehouse's supporting structure, the southwestern half of the building was largely intact. **NARA II, 111-SC-176607**

Looking north from the same intersection, Building T-616 suffered only loosened siding. **NARA II, 111-SC 176608**

Across Wright Avenue looking south, the Quartermaster Warehouse (Building T-604) was protected by its low profile and location on a downslope. The terrain probably deflected the main force of the explosion above the gabled roof. Note on the right the outside-brace boxcar (No. 1567) from the Oahu Railway. **NARA II, 111-SC-176606**

First-Wave Attack on Wheeler Field, Lt. Sakamoto Akira
Zuikaku Dive-Bombing Unit
1st Chūtai, Lt. Sakamoto Akira

	Pilot	Radioman/Rear Gunner
21st Shōtai	Lt. Sakamoto Akira	WO Izuka Yoshio
	FPO1c Sakamaki Hideaki	FPO2c Fujioka Torao
	F1c Tanaka Gorō	F1c Yamaguchi Masaru
22nd Shōtai	WO Ujiki Tazuchi	FPO1c Amemiya Sadao
	FPO1c Saitō Masuichi	FPO2c Negishi Masaaki
23rd Shōtai	FPO1c Nakanishi Yoshio	FPO1c Matsumoto Hikoichi
	FPO2c Katō Kiyotake	F1c Tsuji Shirō
	F1c Kawamura Osamu	F1c Izumi Kiyoshi[6]

Lt. Sakamoto Akira, commander of the *Zuikaku* dive-bomber group, seen during the early months of 1942. Sakamoto left the Yokosuka *Kōkūtai* and joined the new carrier's air group on 24 October 1941. **Prange, cropped**

The Americans on the ground who had dismissed the incoming air strike as a routine overflight by the Navy quickly received a frightful awakening. In Tent City, the sound of machine-gun fire awakened Cpl. Carl W. Shrader, an airplane mechanic with the 72nd Pursuit Squadron. He lifted the tent flap by his bunk and saw an aircraft "swooping diagonally across the field toward a construction project on the opposite side of the base." While Shrader watched this ship (believing it was a Navy plane staging a mock attack), his tentmate Pfc. Merle M. Thayer—an armorer with the 72nd—went to the opening of the tent, looked up, and cried out, "It's the Japs!" Shrader ran outside just in time to see a monoplane with fixed landing gear roar by overhead. More planes "peeled off at various altitudes above the first." As Shrader and Thayer watched in horror, the lead ship released a bomb "which arced down to the refueling area and exploded with a blast which erased any doubts of enemy action."[7]

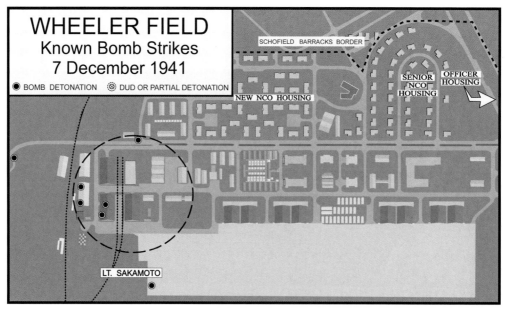

Known bomb strikes for the eight aircraft of Lt. Sakamoto Akira's 1st Chūtai. Only five strikes are accounted for, based on Sakamoto's operational orders that split attacks among his three *chūtai*s on three distinct groups of hangars (or hangar-like buildings). "Ownership" of the crater at far left near Wright Gate is uncertain, but the strike on the lower apron was likely from Sakamoto's unit. The three unaccounted-for bombs might have been duds that left no discernible craters, or perhaps were undocumented impacts on the parking apron. **Di Virgilio**

Seconds after Pvt. Charles Hendrix heard planes high overhead, one of them broke through the cloud layer at about two thousand feet and dove on the west side of the field. Pfc. David Stephenson thought that it dropped "a medium sized trash can," perhaps containing flour as a practice bomb did. The object detonated in the distance as "smoke and dust boiled up from the ground." Other planes appeared in a matter of seconds, coming from every direction, in a perfect Japanese anvil attack.[8]

Pvt. Philip B. Parrigin and fellow mechanic Pvt. Jack M. Spangler had left the 600-Man Barracks and were on the way to eat breakfast at Wheeler's Post Exchange. The two airmen from the 24th Material Squadron had just turned westbound on Wright Avenue when a thunderous explosion far to the west shook the ground and a plume of fire and smoke erupted in the distance. Although he was unaware of it at the time, Spangler had witnessed the first bomb explosion of the Pacific War. Back in the big barracks, SSgt. George V. Biggs—a general clerk with the Headquarters Squadron, 14th Pursuit Wing—grumbled about being roused from his slumber by the Navy "whitehats." He and others nearby "chortled with glee about the court-martial that the Navy pilot would get when he got back to Ford Island." David Stephenson, however, was now certain that the explosion was due to enemy action. He hurried to the enlisted bunk area of the 18th Air Base Group's headquarters squadron and "yelled . . . out that we were being attacked by planes." As everyone dressed and ran for their duty stations, Stephenson exited the rear entrance of the barracks and sprinted north up the slope to Wright Avenue. At that moment, it seemed the bombs were all falling far to the west.[9]

Pfc. Edmund H. Russell—a butcher assigned to the 18th Air Base Group at Wheeler Field—was looking at the next day's menu in the 600-Man Barracks' mess hall when he heard aircraft diving on the field. At first he "thought the Marines or the Navy was out to play war games," but then it sounded as if a plane had crashed. Russell went to the window,

AvnCdt. Edmund H. Russell during flight training, circa 1943. **Russell**

saw smoke in the distance, and then heard another explosion. "This can't be two airplanes that crashed," he thought. A third explosion sent Russell scurrying out the rear of the mess hall toward the "Wahiawa [Leilehua] school where there was a row of eucalyptus trees" where he might take cover.[10]

Sgt. Henry J. Straub—a mechanic with the 78th Pursuit Squadron in Barracks No. 1—was still in bed at about 0750 when he heard aircraft diving over the field and machine-gun fire. "The Navy is out early this morning and it sounds as if they are using live ammo," he said to a man nearby. Straub went out onto the screened veranda and saw a plane diving on the fuel storage area. As the ship banked, Straub spied the "Round Red Meatball" and yelled, "Japs! Hit the deck!" The bomb struck near a long, wood-framed building used to store concrete bags, and a huge cloud of dust billowed up.[11]

Pvt. William J. "Bill" Young and two other acquaintances were outside near Barracks No. 1 when they noticed aircraft circling at about six thousand to eight thousand feet. As the planes peeled away from their formation, one of the men said sarcastically,

"Maybe it's the fucking Japs." The trio's laughter died when the lead airplane dropped an object that detonated at the west end of the field. "Holy mackerel! It *is* the fucking Japs!"[12]

Stephen and Flora Koran were at home in their NCO duplex with newborn daughter Ellen when they heard engine noise and an explosion. When they looked outside and saw bombers attacking the western end of the field, Stephen, knowing his quarters' proximity to the flight line, screamed at Flora, "Let's get out of here! It's the Japs!" Flora grabbed a down comforter, doubled it, and covered the bassinet, fearing that the detonations might rupture the baby's eardrums. A terrifying thought entered her mind as she pulled on her clothes: "What if they poisoned the water?"[13]

At Quarters 120 on Wright Avenue across from Barracks No. 3 and Wheeler's Dispensary, Bess Lalumendier heard what "sounded like dozens" of aircraft engines. Her husband, MSgt. Henry J. Lalumendier, the senior aircraft mechanic for the 73rd Pursuit Squadron and certainly an expert in Army Air Force engine noise, remarked that the Navy must have acquired new aircraft because he didn't recognize the sound of the airplanes. Their curiosity piqued, the couple walked out the front door and peered south through the "barracks quad" toward the hangar line across Wright Avenue. As they left the house, the first plane in line passed over them and dropped a bomb on the western end of the airfield. The Lalumendiers knew that the Japanese were attacking when they saw the insignia on the aircraft.[14]

In Quarters 680, Room 16 (Building T-680) in the new bachelor officer barracks near the east end of Wright Avenue, 2nd Lt. Francis S. Gabreski was in the dumps over a double date gone bad with girlfriend Kay on the previous evening. The other couple—fellow pilot 2nd Lt. John M. Thacker and his girl—had a falling out as well. As he dragged himself to the bathroom to clean up and shave, Gabreski heard the roar of an aircraft passing over and then "explosions and

the rattle of machine gun fire." Hurrying to the window, he soon realized that the base was under attack. He ran the length of the hallway "yelling at the pilots to get out of bed." As black smoke poured out of the buildings and hangars to the west, the pilots pulled on their flight clothing and headed out the door, only to be forced to the ground by gunfire from a passing bomber that strafed the barracks.[15]

At Quarters 435-A, a duplex that fronted Vought Avenue midway between Lilienthal Place and Frutchey Road, 1st Lt. Lewis Sanders "showered, shaved [and] dressed in leisure clothes." As he walked out to pick up the Sunday paper, the sound of many aircraft engines attracted his attention, particularly "an unfamiliar staccato sounding exhaust as the pilots rapidly changed settings." Suspecting the worst, he ran back inside the duplex, looked out a west-facing window, and watched Japanese aircraft bomb buildings to the west. Sanders immediately alerted wife Lillian and their two overnight guests—one of whom was an Air Corps wife recently evacuated from the Philippines—and instructed the three women "to dress in substantial clothing, pack canned goods, blankets, and items to sustain them for a few days and listen for word to move away from the air field." As shell casings clattered down on the rooftop and trash cans behind the quarters, Sanders donned a uniform and flight jacket, intending to make a run for his hangar toward the opposite end of the flight line. Just then, 2nd Lt. John Thacker drove up from the BOQ (where he had quarters in Room 10), screeched to a halt in front of the duplex, and ran inside his commanding officer's front door. Sanders said a quick goodbye to Lillian, then yelled, "Let's go!" and the two men sped toward the hangar.[16]

Far to the east in the senior officer housing on Curtis Loop, Col. William Flood—Wheeler's base commander—heard a thunderous *wang!* in the distance and scanned the horizon past the hangar line, thinking that some military maneuver had gone awry. After the second *wang!* Flood ran inside to get his hat, suspecting the worst. As he emerged from his quarters he saw Japanese aircraft "with the Rising Sun clearly evident" overhead. They were flying so low after their dives that "you could almost hit them with a rock if you had it." Flood's first reaction was burning anger at "all those bastards bombing and strafing the base." In his quarters nearby, Brig. Gen. Howard Davidson—head of the 14th Pursuit Wing—attributed the engine noises to "those damn Navy pilots jazzing the base!" On hearing the explosions, Davidson ran outside to see enemy planes "dive-bombing Wheeler like a bunch of Apaches at a massacre." Events were moving forward so quickly "that one scarcely had time to think." In addition to his command, Davidson was concerned for the safety of his four children, the two youngest of whom were ten-year-old twin girls. When spent shell casings began raining down on Davidson's Quarters 366 at the top of Curtis Loop, "bouncing along like grasshoppers on the prairie," the twins—Julie and Frances—raced out onto the front lawn and began collecting them as if they were Easter eggs.[17]

Capt. Donald D. "Don" Flickinger (MC), medical officer of the day for 7 December, walked outside Quarters 309 on the southeast corner of Vought Avenue and East Sperry Loop to drive to the Dispensary for morning sick call and saw the attack unfolding to the west. Disbelieving what his eyes and ears were telling him, Flickinger went back inside his quarters to compose himself. After his knees stopped shaking, he got into his car and drove the three blocks to the Dispensary in the barracks quad, seeing practically no one on the way. The attack was a total and complete surprise.[18]

Dive-Bombers and Fighters Strafe Wheeler

Smoke obscured visibility over the target area even before Sakamoto's *chūtai* finished its work. Rather than waiting for the bombers in the two other *chūtais* to complete their runs, Sakamoto's pilots commenced strafing the field. The pilots in the trailing units that were circling Wheeler joined them and set up "strafing attacks against planes and installations." The attacks were a wild free-for-all, with some pilots making as many as four or five passes, speeding over Wheeler Field at all angles at what seemed an insanely low altitude. FPO2c Hori and a few other pilots dove low and opened fire on the "outside barracks" (the Tent City). Although they noted that soldiers on the ground were now returning fire, they nevertheless delivered their attack against minimal opposition. To Lieutenant Ema's knowledge (save for one hit on Hori's plane), none of his attacking aircraft suffered any damage.[19]

First-Wave Attacks on Wheeler Field
Lt. Suganami Masaji, *Sōryū* Fighter Unit

1st Shōtai	2nd Shōtai	3rd Shōtai
Lt. Suganami Masaji	WO Tanaka Hitoshi	FPO1c Noda Mitsuomi
FPO1c Mita Iwao	FPO3c Hagino Kyōichirō	FPO2c Yoshimatsu Kaname
FPO3c Suzuki Shinichi	F1c Doikawa Isao	

Lt. Okajima Kiyokuma, *Hiryū* Fighter Unit

16th Shōtai	17th Shōtai
Lt. Okajima Kiyokuma	FPO1c Noguchi Kijirō
FPO1c Muranaka Kazuo	FPO3c Harada Toshiaki
FPO2c Tahara Isao	F1c Sento Tetsuo

Lt. Suganami Masaji circa 1941, commander of the *Sōryū* fighter unit. **Prange**

Lt. Okajima Kiyokuma, commander of the *Hiryū* fighter unit during the Hawaiian Operation, seen here on board the *Zuikaku* in early 1942. Okajima had a great deal of carrier experience, having served on the *Sōryū*, *Hiryū*, and *Kaga* prior to reporting to the *Zuikaku* on 5 January 1942. **Prange, cropped**

The strafing attacks by the dive-bombers overlapped by ten minutes with those of Lt. Suganami Masaji's fighters from the *Sōryū*, which commenced their runs at 0755. Lt. Okajima Kiyokuma and his *Hiryū* fighters circled Wheeler while Sakamoto's pilots were still in their bombing runs and Lieutenant Suganami's fighters had joined the fray. The attacks had moved forward "as scheduled inflicting heavy damage to the enemy." The attacks mesmerized FPO1c Muranaka Kazuo, Okajima's no. 1 wingman, who later recalled seeing "flashes of fire caused by hits on hangars. . . . Looking back [toward] following comrade planes I could see them grinning with sharp eyes hungry for good games. Making a single row formation we went down though breaks of clouds. The Wheeler airbase was already a sea of fire." After Okajima ordered his fighters to deploy and descend, he aborted the attacks because the airspace over Wheeler was "so crowded with our planes." Okajima's pilots turned left, spiraled up and outward, and headed south toward an alternative objective: the Marine Corps' Ewa Mooring Mast Field.[20]

WO Muranaka Kazuo, wingman to Lieutenant Okajima while serving in the *Hiryū* fighter unit during the Hawaiian Operation. Seen here circa 1944. Muranaka's decorations are (*left to right*): Golden Kite, Order of the Rising Sun, and the China Incident War Medal. **Prange**

The immediate reactions of the airmen and their dependents at Wheeler ran the gamut from deep anger to sheer panic. The thoughts of many doubtless mirrored those of radio operator Sgt. Charles D. "Smiley" Boyer of the 72nd Pursuit Squadron at the moment he realized that an attack was under way: "Dear God, what did we do to deserve this?" No one escaped the bedlam and confusion. After pulling on his clothing, Pfc. William F. Winzenburg—an airplane mechanic with the 45th Pursuit Squadron—rushed out of his wooden barracks. Across Wright Avenue in the NCO housing, screaming women and children were pouring out of their homes. The men also found it difficult to control their fear. Pvt. Ray E. Hadwick, who was in Wheeler's Control Tower at the beginning of the attack, abandoned his post and took cover in a ditch adjacent to the hangar line.[21]

Pvt. Kenneth E. Krepps and the other men from the 46th Pursuit Squadron burst out of their mess hall when the attack began, but the instinct for survival and the desire to reach cover proved overpowering. Squadron mechanic Sgt. John F. Plassio sprinted out of the mess hall and turned north toward the NCO quarters. When a bomb landed uncomfortably close and the strafing began, Plassio spied an open manhole and dove in. SSgt. James B. Young—the squadron's mess sergeant—was about twenty feet ahead of everyone else when a bomb explosion tossed him fifteen feet into the air. Krepps thought that the sergeant "was a goner" but heard later that Young survived the ordeal with a broken shoulder. General clerk Pfc. Donald D. Plant was not so fortunate. He died from wounds sustained just as the bombing attack began "while assisting, voluntarily, in the removal of injured of another organization." Reportedly, Plant had run ahead to secure a stretcher for a comrade. Krepps remembered Plant—who had the bunk next to his—as "a brave boy."[22]

In Barracks No. 1, Pfc. Carroll T. Andrews heard planes zooming over the hangar line across the street and then felt concussions from the bomb explosions shake the building. Tracers streaked into the barracks and tore through several bunks, showering the men with glass and wood splinters. Still disbelieving, Andrews looked out the window and saw the dark red markings on the attacking planes. "It seemed . . . absolutely impossible, but smoke and exploding hangar buildings across the street sort of convinced us." During the early phase of the attack, Andrews and the other men "could not understand why the Navy planes were not up in the air," although they did notice "a wide, very black cloud of smoke from Hickam–Pearl Harbor rising in the sky."[23]

Pvt. Ronald F. Norton—an armorer with the 6th Pursuit Squadron—joined the frantic stampede exiting the barracks to the north, away from the attacks, but when he reached the front lawn wondered, "Where do I go now?" Two bombers approaching with machine guns blazing forced Norton to take shelter under the building's overhang, pinning him against the exterior wall. After checking on another airman hit by gunfire, whom he presumed was beyond help, Norton raced back inside the barracks and darted up to the second floor where he had started, went out on the squad room's veranda, and watched the debacle unfolding below. Wheeler's fighters disappeared in sheets of flame, "burning furiously" in a scene of utter pandemonium as men ran in every direction. Realizing the folly of remaining exposed on the veranda, Norton again descended the stairs and joined a group of airmen at the barracks' entrance. All concluded that going to the flight line was suicidal. Japanese pilots were machine-gunning men on both sides of the building. Dead and wounded men littered the lawn and the streets.[24]

The front of the older, permanent barracks faced north, away from the flight line, so men hoping to get out and run toward their hangars rushed the rear entrances. In Barracks No. 1, however, they were unable to exit because an iron gate locked by the charge-of-quarters to detain latecomers blocked the way. Using a steel bar, airmen finally forced open the gate. Back inside, a supply sergeant opened up shop and distributed rifles and bandoliers of ammunition to all comers.[25]

Pvt. Gordon F. Smith, quartered in the 600-Man Barracks with the 17th Air Base Squadron, ran down three flights of stairs to a hallway where he encountered his squadron CO, Capt. Sherwood E. Buckland, and requested orders. "He was pretty shook up, and couldn't give me one," Smith recalled. "I finally said, 'Good God man, give me an order!'" Buckland blurted out, "Go to the Fire Station!" Smith ran the whole distance, prodded along by strafers. On his way he saw a young airman who had lost both legs while trying to help another man to the Dispensary. Horrified but anxious to help, Smith stopped, but medics picked up the mangled airman and bore him away.[26]

Back in the NCO Quarters, now aware of the dangers outside, Henry and Bess Lalumendier raced to their car in back of their home and scooted underneath. From that comparative safety they watched the dive-bombers deploying for their anvil attacks and setting up strafing runs on the aircraft parking apron and buildings near the flight line. As the planes opened fire in their vicinity, the couple "prayed hard" while bullets ricocheted off the paved tennis courts one hundred yards away to the west. Still underneath the car, Bess watched an elderly soldier, clearly still inebriated from the night before, staggering unsteadily down Wright Avenue. She held

her breath as the old soldier weaved from side to side down the avenue, untouched, and wondered whether the zigzagging might be saving his life because he presented a moving target with locomotion perpendicular to the strafers' line of attack.[27]

SSgt. Mobley L. Hall—an airplane mechanic and crew chief with the Headquarters Squadron, 18th Pursuit Group—was among those at Wheeler who lived off the base, though in his case only across the boundary that separated Wheeler from Schofield Barracks. He was at home in Quarters 724 on Duncan Street when he heard the first bomb explode at Wheeler. Afraid that something was amiss, he got in his car and hurried toward Hangar 3, his duty station. The dive-bombing attack was in full swing when he arrived, with many Japanese planes overhead.[28]

Across the street from the 19th Pursuit Squadron's Barracks No. 4, Wheeler's Tent City housed—among other units—the cadre for a new squadron in the 18th Pursuit Group. Incendiary ammunition fired by Japanese aircraft killed many of the tents' still-sleeping occupants. The 72nd Pursuit Squadron suffered more casualties—eleven men killed and fifteen wounded—than any other unit at Wheeler Field. Highest ranking among the dead was 1st Sgt. Edward J. Burns of Pittsfield, Massachusetts, shot through his chest.[29]

Wheeler Field's Photographic Laboratory (Building 28). View looks northwest in July 1934, nine months after the lab's completion. The Utilities Shops (Building 62) are to the left. **NARA II, RG 77**

Documenting events on film began almost immediately. Pvt. Morton Kamm, who had just concluded his training at Wheeler's photography school, sprinted down Wright Avenue to the Photo Lab (Building 28) for a camera and film but found the door locked. Photographer SSgt. Joe K. Harding and wife Frances were reading the morning paper in bed when the attack began. Harding dashed to the Photo Lab to retrieve his Speed Graphic camera, possibly meeting up with Private Kamm in front of the locked door. The two men broke down the door and grabbed two Speed Graphics and film. Kamm raced out to the flight line and "took as many pictures of the action that time and film would permit." After his last exposure, Kamm returned to the lab, left the exposed film, and went out again. Harding likewise recorded all but the first few minutes of the attack. With Pvt. Morley J. Bishop of the 17th Air Base Squadron tagging along with a huge bag of film, Harding took dozens of photos before returning the exposed film to the lab. He was later dismayed to learn that almost all the film (including motion picture footage) from early in the attack disappeared in the chaotic days that followed.[30]

Pilots Depart for Haleiwa

Suffering the aftereffects of a night of hard partying, 2nd Lt. George Welch and 2nd Lt. Kenneth Taylor of the 47th Pursuit Squadron tried to ignore the sound of aircraft engines that woke them in their borrowed room in the Officers' Club/BOQ. Thinking the initial explosion on the western end of the flight line was an accident, Taylor remarked foggily, "By God, George, that's one Navy pilot who won't disturb our Sunday morning sleep any more!" Alarmed at additional explosions and machine-gun fire, both men stumbled out of bed. Taylor struggled with a pair of basketball warm-up trunks, then pulled on the tuxedo trousers he had worn the night before.[31]

Along with four or five other officers, Taylor and Welch ran out the club's front door and onto Wright Avenue. For what Welch estimated was at least five minutes, the shocked officers gaped in amazement at the unfolding attack. Eventually, they ran back inside and sounded the alarm to the officers whose rooms opened off the inner courtyard of the Club/BOQ. Then, remembering their aircraft at Haleiwa Field, Taylor went to the telephone in the hallway and called the squadron at Haleiwa to let the field know that they were on their way. The next task was to reach Taylor's Buick sedan parked in front of the club—no task for the faint hearted as the Japanese were already strafing the base. While Taylor struggled to decide when to race for the car, Welch joked, "Well, let's wait 'til we hear the burst of machine gun [fire] and then we'll run. The bullets are already behind us." To Taylor, "it seemed years instead of minutes" before they were in his car and on their way to Haleiwa.[32]

Second Lt. Harry W. Brown and his best friend 2nd Lt. John L. "Johnny" Dains, both of the 47th Pursuit Squadron, had not yet gone to bed after an all-night party in town celebrating the completion of their aerial gunnery qualifications out at Haleiwa Field. They had finally returned to Wheeler, undressed, and were having a nightcap on the first floor of their quarters when bomb explosions drew them outside. They ran out the door to find "the sky alive with Japanese airplanes working over Wheeler." In the frantic rush to dress, Dains could find no socks. The pair ran out to the parking lot behind the barracks, jumped into Brown's blue Ford Tudor coupe, and raced toward the married officer quarters area on Lilienthal Place to pick up 1st Lt. Robert J. "Bob" Rogers, the squadron's temporary commander while Capt. Gordon H. Austin was away on a deer-hunting trip to Maui. Dodging machine-gun fire from a strafing dive-bomber, Brown detoured south toward the flight line and then back north to Rogers' quarters. When they had collected Rogers, the three fighter pilots set off for Haleiwa at about 0810, close on the heels of Taylor and Welch.[33]

Haleiwa was not an option for the pilots whose aircraft lay burning on Wheeler's apron. Knowing that dead aviators would be of no use, some of the

F/C Everett W. Stewart, 1 March 1939, during flight training at Kelly Field. **NARA II, 18-PU-039-440-4153**

F/C John S. Evans, 31 October 1938, during flight training at Kelly Field. **NARA II, 18-PU-027-127-3901**

Katharine Stewart lived with her older brother, 1st Lt. Everett Stewart, and sister-in-law in Quarters 448-A and was a civilian employee at Wheeler's Air Corps Supply Station. **Stewart Etherington**

men took shelter in quarters until the immediate danger passed. Their instinct to report to the flight line, however, remained strong. First Lt. Everett W. Stewart's first impulse was to leave wife Sunny and sister Katharine, rush to the apron, get airborne, and go after the bombers. Remembering that having seen—even at a distance—all his squadron's aircraft burned, however, he concluded a moment later, "Hell, I don't have an airplane, so what can I do?" He picked up the telephone and dialed 467 to consult with his squadron commander. When 1st Lt. John S. Evans answered, Stewart asked, "What are you going to do?" Evans replied, "I'm going to stay right here until they quit attacking us." Stewart confirmed that he would do the same. Even inside their quarters, however, the pilots and their families were not entirely safe. In the ten-unit apartments in Building 372 on Lilienthal Place, Japanese gunfire struck the unit occupied by 2nd Lt. Richard A. "Dick" Toole of the 46th Pursuit Squadron and his wife. Lucille was in the bathroom when a round penetrated the wall, ricocheted, and barely missed her.[34]

F/C Richard A. Toole, 17 March 1941, during flight training at Brooks Field. **NARA II, 18-PU-093-464-7645**

MEN ON THE GROUND MOUNT A DEFENSE

Airmen worked desperately to extinguish the flames among the fighters burning on the apron. SSgt. Paul R. Cipriano—an armorer from the 19th Pursuit Squadron—retrieved ammunition and containers from the burning aircraft. Despite well-founded concern for their own safety, airmen flocked to the hangar line to save planes and guns and as much ammunition as possible. Pvt. James R. Piggott of the 44th Pursuit Squadron, an airplane mechanic, recalled: "Several of us worked our way down to the flight line through several fires set ablaze by the deadly accurate bombing [and strafing]. Our intent was to help with trying to move the parked P-40 and P-36 fighter aircraft in front of the hangars. We were able to move a few but the fires became so intensely hot that we soon had to give this up."[35]

As the attack was still unfolding, SSgt. Melvin L. Miller and the other men from the 19th Pursuit went to find guns and ammunition to fight back, but the weapons were locked away. They quickly located someone to open the lockers in Hangar 3. Men of the 72nd Pursuit from the adjacent tents just to the west attempted to draw rifles and ammunition as well, but the armorers initially refused to deviate from the normal routine of issuing them. As the gravity of the events unfolding on the outside sank in, however, the pace quickened dramatically, and those now armed rushed outside to mount a defense against the Japanese.[36]

A gun crew atop Wheeler's Fire House (Building 64) drew praise from the airmen on the ground. Pvt. Raeburn D. Drenner rushed into the building's dormitory and informed the men what was transpiring outside their doors. One group—Drenner included—attempted to carry a .50-caliber machine gun to the roof, but strafing drove them back. "Everyone," he later admitted, "was scared silly and confused." Summoning their resolve, however, the guards mounted the roof for another try.[37]

It was Wheeler's Guard Section—supervised by SSgt. Kraig L. Van Noy of the 18th Air Base Group's headquarters company—that finally set up the .50-caliber Browning on the roof. Pvt. Ralph C. Riddle of the 17th Air Base Squadron volunteered to man the weapon. With "utter disregard for his own safety, Private Riddle cleared a jam, reloaded the gun, and fired continuously at enemy planes until all Japanese aircraft had dispersed," actions for which he was awarded the Silver Star. Although few at the base ever learned of Riddle's heroism, his valor was a source of great encouragement for those who did. Riddle received assistance from Cpl. George J. Van Gieri of the Headquarters Squadron, 18th Air Base Group, and Pvt. Raymond J. Guerin of the Headquarters Squadron, 15th Pursuit Group, who had been a prisoner in the Guard House when the attack started.[38]

Staff Sergeant Van Noy did more than supervise the machine gun on the roof. With no officer present, he assumed command of the Guard Section and "dispatch[ed] fire fighting equipment to points where they were most needed." After Sgt. Milton J. Dunn broke into the storeroom, Van Noy directed

Wheeler Field Fire Station/Guard House, looking northwest, 12 November 1941, twenty-five days prior to the attack.
NARA II, 342-FH-3B-48701

issue of arms and ammunition, coordinated activities of the sentries at Wheeler's gates, and supervised the release of prisoners from their cells at the rear of the building. Wheeler's Guard House held at least seven prisoners at the time of the attack. Procedures called for all prisoners to be released in such circumstances, and six of the seven airmen were restored to duty on 7 December or the day after; only one was returned to his cell after the raid. After helping to man the machine gun on the roof, Corporal Van Gieri stood watch over the telephones of the Guard Section, relayed messages, and "by his action, contributed materially in keeping casualties to a minimum."[39]

After one of the guards released Pvt. Henry C. Brown—incarcerated for his attempted P-36 joyride on 9 September—he and several other men ran outside. Some felt that they had jumped out of the frying pan and into the fire. Brown took cover in a bomb crater nearby and kept an eye on the dive-bombers as he tried to dig deeper. "Every one dropped a bomb, [and] that darned bomb . . . looked like it was coming right for you." The panicked Brown figured, "God, I got this hole, but everybody's after me!"[40]

A moment like something out of a Buster Keaton silent comedy provided Brown with a brief diversion.

He watched an airman run from a nearby building and dive under a truck for protection, only to have another man jump in the truck and drive it away, leaving the man prone and exposed in the middle of the street. Brown and the other occupants of the crater quickly snapped back to the horror of the moment as they saw a large bomb detonate in the distance, sending a white-hot splinter into the stomach of a man running for cover. The airman clasped his abdomen, took several steps forward, and fell dead, cut down "in full stride." Two soldiers attempted to move him to cover but put him back on the ground as soon as they saw that he was beyond help.[41]

Wheeler's new 600-Man Barracks became a focal point of determined efforts to set up defenses. First, however, the barracks had to be evacuated. One of the obvious places to begin was the mess hall. Pfc. Daniel A. Mahoney was among those present when the first bomb exploded. As soon as he identified the airplanes outside as hostile, Mahoney warned everyone to clear the room. Bruce Harlow and Gottlieb J. Kaercher, the 1st sergeants of the 24th and 25th Material Squadrons, evacuated the barracks' top two floors as a precaution against bomb strikes and, in the absence of officers to direct them, sent the men "to protected areas and to locations where their combat services could be best utilized." Kaercher dispatched men to the Fire Department and Dispensary. Harlow gathered and supervised the noncommissioned officers in efforts to keep order and reduce confusion.[42]

Ema's 2nd Chūtai Attacks
HANGARS 1 AND 2

After spiraling out to the left during its deployment over Wheeler, the *chūtai* of nine *kanbaku*s under Lt. Ema Tamotsu aligned their sights on a pair of double hangars—Hangars 1 and 2—home to the squadrons of the 15th Pursuit Group. As Ema commanded the unit immediately behind Sakamoto's, he was in a superb position to view his chief's attack. He watched "Sakamoto's planes unload their bombs with direct hits and flames. . . . Debris broke loose through the air in a flash." Ema detected no activity whatsoever on the ground and saw no American planes taking off. He also noted that his men had received poor intelligence regarding the base's air strength; although the Japanese believed that 250 aircraft were based at the field, Ema saw no more than half that number on the ground. Incredibly, there was still no opposition as Ema dove in, although two machine guns finally opened up from "the tower on the air field" (possibly the sandbagged position that had been left intact atop the Administration Building after the recent alert).[43]

Lieutenant Ema reported leading his men into their dives from about 3,500 meters and, after releasing bombs, pulling out at about 350 meters. He and his two wingmen—FPO3c Nohara Tadaaki and F1c Egusa Shigeki—scored three hits on or near Hangar 1. Sgt. Christopher Ward was in front of Hangar 1 when the attacking aircraft loosed their bombs.

> It seemed like everything then went into slow motion for me. I remember flattening out on my knees and elbows, stomach off the ground, fingers in my ears and yelling to keep my mouth open. . . . I managed to get up and run out from the hangar about 100 yards where I used up three clips from my 45 cal. pistol trying to hit the rear gunner[s] in the dive bombers as they pulled up from their dive. . . . [I] marveled at having all my appendages still attached. I really had to feel each arm and leg to believe they were there. I lost two of my guard detail to the bombs & strafing.[44]

View looking southeast from the intersection of Santos-Dumont Avenue and the entryway in front of the Fire Station, toward the back of Hangar 1. The western half of the hangar sustained major damage from fires and explosions, but the eastern half is more or less intact thanks to the actions of Wheeler's firefighters. Note that the hangar's doors were blown inward by the detonation of a near miss just outside the rear of the building. **NARA II, 111-SC-128350**

Details of damage to the rear of Hangar 1, looking southeast. The crater visible in the pavement at the lower left center demonstrates that the bomb exploded with a low order of detonation, although strong enough to blow in the hangar doors and cause significant blast and fragmentation damage. **Aiken, NMPW**

Hangar 1 viewed from the front, looking northwest. Pvt. Stanley J. Jaroszek forced open the hangar's doors with his tow truck to allow Wheeler's firefighters to enter. Jaroszek may have resorted to ramming the doors, causing at least three sections to collapse inward. The proximity of the Fire Station in the background at center shows that the firemen did not have far to travel. Fire and blast damage destroyed at least four aircraft in the hangar (*left to right*): a P-26 with a partial aircraft number visible, P-40B "156" flown by 2nd Lt. George Welch on 24 November, another P-26 in the far background, and a P-36A. It is not known whether Fort Shafter or Wheeler Field photographers took this photo, although its composition is almost identical to 111-SC-128352 at NARA II. **TLM, P.000,385**

The specific targets that each of Lieutenant Ema's remaining pilots selected are uncertain. Hangar 2 escaped completely except for strafing damage. Although the crews were under strict orders to limit bombing attacks to hangars, two of them seem to have found the aircraft on the apron too tempting a target to pass up. The resulting conflagration sent a gargantuan smoke plume boiling up from the apron in front of the hangars, partially obscuring the undamaged Hangar 2 and making the bombers' secondary assignment—systematic strafing of the western end of the apron—almost impossible. The black billows hiding Hangar 2 probably diverted the attention of Ema's other crews to large buildings behind the flight line as well, in particular Barracks No. 1 (Building 69) and Barracks No. 4 (Building 71) on the north side of Santos-Dumont Avenue.[45]

BARRACKS NO. 1, BARRACKS NO. 4, PX

Prior to the attack on the barracks, other explosions nearby had prompted the men in Cpl. Bertram E. Swarthout's squad room to head down to the ground floor. Many men from the 6th Pursuit Squadron were attempting to exit the building at the same moment, and the stairs were jammed. As Swarthout arrived on the ground floor, one of the 250-kilogram bombs dropped by Ema's subordinates struck the southeast corner of Barracks No. 1 after careening through a second-floor window, and crashed through the ceiling into the mess hall. The detonation damaged the kitchen, the second floor, and the dining room; destroyed the mess sergeant's room; and killed or wounded many airmen. David L. Crabtree of the 6th Pursuit had just rushed inside the barracks hall when the thunderous explosion occurred, and the concussion threw him back out the front door.[46]

After the blast, Sgt. Francis A. White, an airplane mechanic, "crawled through the smoke and rubble to the front porch where I could see that our hangar and most of our . . . brand new P-40s were all ablaze." White needed help from Pfc. James E. Whit, one of the cooks, to move the orderly room door, which had been blasted off its hinges. The burly White had a terrible gash at his temple, an injury "that would have floored the average man." At a spot nearby, a group of men had followed the instructions

The bomb hit on Barracks No. 1 (Building 69). The bomb reportedly entered through a second-floor window, penetrated into the mess hall below, and detonated. The blast ejected debris outward thirty to forty feet from the building. **NARA II, 111-SC-127020**

The interior of the mess hall inside Barracks No. 1, showing damage to the second floor's support columns. The bomb blast displaced the pillar at left a foot or more at its upper end. **Aiken, NMPW**

of a technical sergeant to go into the hall and remain there. The bomb explosion killed many of them in the passageway. The survivors exited the building onto the rear porch, facing the hangars, where Pfc. Glen F. Heller rendered first aid to the wounded. Heller's clothing was bloody "from head to foot." He later related of the experience, "The whole thing was a bad sight."[47]

Having just received his issue of arms and ammunition, Pvt. Ronald F. Norton was about to exit the rear entrance when the explosion occurred at the opposite end of the building. Norton heard later that not one of the seventeen men in the vicinity survived. On impulse, he ran upstairs, retrieved his camera, and took photographs. "To this day I don't know what prompted me to do this."[48]

Damage to the eastern end of the PX complex, looking west, from among the array of four concrete barracks. A bomb explosion opened the crater along the curbing at lower center and carried away the outer wall, wrecking the interiors of the tailor shop and barbershop. At right, the sales room also sustained significant—though less catastrophic—damage. **Aiken, NMPW**

Demolition of the partially destroyed PX has begun in this February 1942 view looking northwest. Wrecking crews are clearing the shop building, with the sales room probably not far behind. Evidently, the large building to the rear that housed the restaurant, lunchroom, and beer garden was not destroyed in the raid as Hickam's beloved "Snake Ranch" was. **Cressman**

Outside, Pvt. Winston S. Jones was on the north side of Santos-Dumont Avenue when the blast knocked him unconscious. When he came to, Jones was on the other side of the street. Even airmen in Barracks No. 2 to the north felt the concussion from the bomb detonation. As Pvt. Joseph T. Pawlowski of the 44th Pursuit Squadron attempted to exit via one of the stairways, the barracks shook from the explosion. Pawlowski lost his footing and tumbled down the remaining steps.[49]

One of the last bombs dropped by Ema's *chūtai* came down in the street between Barracks No. 4 and the Post Exchange complex (Building T-70) near the center of the barracks quad. The wood-framed PX sustained considerable damage from the blast, particularly to the tailor and shoe shops,

The bomb crater at left very nearly compromised the structural integrity of the building forming Wright Gate at Wheeler's western terminus. It is possible that the bomb came from the Type 99 carrier bomber flown by F1c Tanioku Shu. **NARA II, 111-SC-128339**

First-Wave Attack on Wheeler Field, *Zuikaku* Dive-Bombing Unit
2nd Chūtai, Lt. Ema Tamotsu

	Pilot	Radioman/Rear Gunner
24th Shōtai	Lt. Ema Tamotsu	WO Azuma Tōichi
	FPO3c Nohara Tadaaki	FPO2c Sugimoto Tetsuji
	F1c Egusa Shigeki	FPO3c Kawazoe Masayoshi
25th Shōtai	FPO2c Hori Kenji	Lt. (jg) Ōtsuka Reijirō
	FPO3c Taketani Takeshi	FPO1c Fukukaidō Sanetomi
	F1c Tanioku Shu	F1c Iwatanaga Isami
26th Shōtai	WO Fukunaga Masato	FPO1c Ishikawa Shigekazu
	FPO1c Igata Sakuo	FPO2c Shirakura Kōta
	FPO3c Amachika Susumu	F1c Hirokane Goichi

although the concrete barracks suffered only super-ficial damage.[50]

The Japanese did not have it all their way. F1c Tanioku Shu, one of Ema's crews, experienced mechanical difficulties after his bombing run. FPO2c Hori, who was piloting the 25th Shōtai's lead air-craft, looked back and saw that Tanioku's *kanbaku* "was very slow in ascending." Probably alerted to

the situation by his plane commander/observer, Lt. (jg) Ōtsuka Reijirō, Hori circled back and saw that the 250-kilogram bomb was still slung underneath Tanioku's aircraft. After making a hand signal that he would attempt another run, Tanioku descended in an apparent attempt to release his bomb. Although the results of his efforts to shake the ordnance loose are unknown, it is possible that his bomb was one of

Lt. Ema Tamotsu, commander of the 2nd Chūtai, *Zuikaku* dive-bombing unit, in early 1942 on board the *Zuikaku*. Ema accrued critical carrier training on the *Akagi* from November 1939 into August 1940. **Prange, cropped**

WO Hori Kenji, *Zuikaku* dive-bombing unit, seen later in the war. Over Wheeler Field, he piloted the number four aircraft in Lieutenant Ema's 2nd Chūtai. Of his unit, only he and Lieutenant Ema survived the war. **Hori**

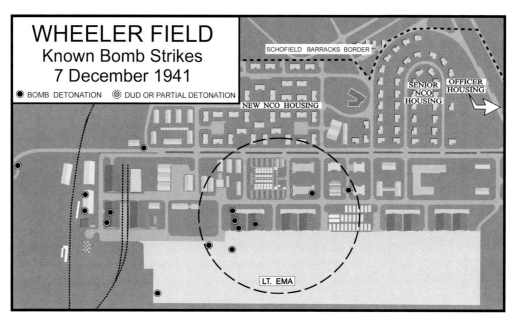

Known bomb strikes for the nine aircraft of Lt. Ema Tamotsu's 2nd Chūtai. It is obvious that discipline had broken by this stage in the attack, because four bombs landed on the apron and barracks rather than the hangars. It is thought that the bomb hit at the far left, near Wright Gate, was due to a hung bomb on an aircraft in Lieutenant Ema's *chūtai*. **Di Virgilio**

those that struck far behind the hangar line, possibly at Wright Gate well to the west of the field proper. Meanwhile, seemingly unaware of Tanioku's problem, Lieutenant Ema pulled back on the stick to gain altitude, not so much to view the carnage below as to satisfy his curiosity regarding damage being done to Pearl Harbor far to the south.[51]

FIREFIGHTING, HANGAR 1

Blast damage, fires, and concussion from bomb detonations had jammed the front doors of Hangar 1, and try as they might, the men were unable to open them manually. Pvt. Stanley J. Jaroszek, still manning a tow truck with orders to remove a refueling tanker, used his vehicle to pull the doors open so that three pieces of firefighting equipment from Wheeler's Fire Department could get inside. The firefighters quickly began extinguishing the blaze, which was threatening to envelop both hangar bays. SSgt. Charles A. Fay—an aircraft mechanic with the 72nd Pursuit, twice wounded in the strafing—taxied one aircraft after another from the intact side of the hangar to safety. For "his initiative, presence of mind, coolness

under fire, and determined action [that] contributed to a large extent toward driving off [the] sudden, unexpected enemy air attack," Fay was awarded the Silver Star.[52]

Meanwhile, a group of men from the 46th Pursuit Squadron had approached the western side of Hangar 1 to remove machine guns and ammunition from the armaments room, but the fire raging in the building made that impossible. Much of the hangar's roof had caved in, and the intense heat had melted the roofing tar in the "intact" portion. The molten liquid "was falling down just like rain inside" while exploding gasoline and ammunition hurled debris into the air.[53]

When they finally gained access to the hangar, the Fire House crews had their work cut out for them. Taking charge of the large fire truck, Pfc. Vernon C. Rider entered the west bay of Hangar 1, which was enveloped in flames. With the assistance of Pfc. Ethelbert E. Lovell (Rider's crewman), Pfc. John J. Ostrum in charge of a small chemical truck, and Pfc. Ford E. Dodd with the crash truck, Rider moved various vehicles (including a large oil tanker) away from the flames. Only then, as gasoline tanks exploded around them, did Rider and his crew tackle the fires in the hangar. Their heroic efforts prevented the blaze from reaching the adjoining bay, "thus preserving valuable government property." Dodd's crash truck expended all its chemical fire suppressants in the process. The intelligent and determined efforts of the three crews saved the eastern bay of Hangar 1; the blast from explosions had either burned or blown out the siding on the front gable.[54]

Another firefighting crew attacked Hangar 1's fires from the rear. Pvt. Raeburn Drenner and Pfc. Adrian S. Black of the 24th Material Squadron drove a fire truck (and at least one other vehicle) to a fire hydrant across Santos-Dumont Avenue. Their movements caught the attention of pilots from the *Zuikaku*, who strafed the area and seemed to concentrate on the men and their truck. But it was the planes' observers with their "swivel action" machine

guns that gave the firefighters the most difficulty. As the "cat and mouse game with the strafing planes went on," the men on Drenner's truck managed to attach their fire hose to a hydrant. One plane came in at barracks level and sprayed the men directly behind Hangar 1 with gunfire, damaging the hydrant and holing the hose in several places.[55]

As with Hickam Field, Wheeler Field had a civilian fire chief. Oregon native Ross I. Ewing possessed twenty years of firefighting experience in California and had served thirteen years as captain of the Los Angeles Fire Department. Ewing had arrived in Hawai'i on 26 March 1941 and took over as Wheeler's fire chief on 13 August. The Ewings—wife Esther had arrived on 10 July—set up housekeeping in Quarters 146-A in a duplex facing west on Elleman Road not quite two blocks away from the Fire House. Ewing realized that he "faced his toughest assignment . . . when a large part of Wheeler field was left in flames."

View of the area behind the flight line just behind Hangar 1. Circled are (*right*) Wheeler's Fire Station and the Guard House behind it and (*left*) the duplex in which civilian fire chief Ross Ewing lived with wife Esther. The couple lived in the left-hand unit, 146-A, only a short walk from the station. **NARA II, 342-FH-3B-48707, cropped**

Wheeler's firemen were not caught napping on 7 December. Ewing said in 1946: "The Japanese tried to do a thorough strafing job on the air strip while fires were breaking out simultaneously all over the field. We had a hard time in the usual army sense of the term while we brought all our prior experience and knowhow to minimize fire damage that day."[56]

FIGHTING BACK

Pfc. Arthur W. Fusco—a radio electrician with the 45th Pursuit Squadron—was on guard duty in Hangar 2 when the attack began. Immediately concluding that his rifle was useless against the dive-bombers, he tried to break into the armament shack for something bigger but was unable to gain access. He "could hear the dive bombers dropping their bombs right up the line [and] blowing up the hangars. I was counting them and knew—the next one was meant for the [hangar] I was in." Fusco ducked into an office underneath a metal stairway, which seemed the only safe place to be. The next bomb struck Barracks No. 1 outside to the north. Bullets pinged against the metal steps sheltering Fusco, making a curious ringing sound. During a brief break in the action, Fusco heard the telephone ring on a nearby desk. Thinking the call might be important, he left his shelter and answered it. A captain's wife on the other end complained that the noise had awakened the baby and asked if her husband would please put a stop to it. Even years later Fusco still wondered who the woman was and whether she had heard—before or since—the kind of language he used just before slamming down the receiver.[57]

Other men were a bit better at maintaining their composure. Under heavy fire, 2nd Lt. Edward I. Pratt Jr., adjutant for the 18th Air Base Group, twice drove his car though the main area of the attack "transporting officers from the Bachelor Officer Quarters area, to their respective organization hangars." On the second trip, gunfire disabled Pratt's vehicle and forced him to retreat on foot to his headquarters in the 600-Man Barracks. For this action and for moving

Maj. Wallace Bloom, circa 1943. In December 1941 Bloom, assistant personnel officer for the base, commanded Wheeler's Provisional Ground Defense Company. **Bloom**

vehicles endangered by fires started by a bomb strike near the PX Warehouse west of the barracks Pratt received the Silver Star.[58]

Fearful that panic-stricken locals might impede access to the base, the guards at the gates called for reinforcements. First Lt. Wallace Bloom—Wheeler's assistant personnel officer and commander of the Provisional Ground Defense Company—was among those who answered the call. As spent shell casings rolled down his tile roof outside Quarters 451-B east of Lilienthal Place, Bloom placed wife Oralia and four-month-old daughter Winifred on a mattress in the windowless inner hallway of their duplex before leaving. His car damaged by machine-gun fire, Bloom cut a zigzag path afoot—west by southwest from building to building—until he reached the 600-Man Barracks, where he and other airmen used a rifle butt to splinter the locked supply room door. He assembled about twenty men on the spot, armed them with rifles, and led the detachment away to guard the Wahiawā gate.[59]

Meanwhile, back at the 600-Man Barracks, men from the 24th and 25th Material Squadrons converged on what was probably the barracks' main supply room to draw weapons. They ran into an unexpected roadblock when an NCO refused to release any weapons without authorization from the squadron commanders. Despite the men's urgent pleas, the NCO stood firm. "He got his authorization," one airman later recounted, "in the form of a punch in the mouth." Pvt. Charles A. Zelonis Jr. and two other men from the 24th overpowered the sergeant, rushed into the room, and started breaking out .30- and .50-caliber machine guns.[60]

Other airmen found ways to distribute arms and ammunition as well. Cpl. Edward R. Young of the 14th Pursuit Wing, with no more authority than his two stripes, broke off the lock on the headquarters squadron's gun room door. Assisted by fellow clerk Pfc. Robert E. Kincaid, Young dispersed machine guns to everyone who came by. It so happened that among the arms there were two .45-caliber pistols—one tagged to Brigadier General Davidson. Young delivered the sidearm to Davidson personally as soon as he reported to wing headquarters in the Administration Building. Elsewhere, after clearing the 600-Man Barracks' mess hall, Pfc. Daniel A. Mahoney took personal charge

of a .30-caliber machine gun that he liberated from one of the storerooms. TSgt. William L. Bayham and SSgt. John T. Benton did much the same, although they set up their .50-caliber machine gun just outside the supply room door, with Bayham firing and Benton feeding the belted ammunition.[61]

Maj. Hilmer C. Nelson, circa early 1942. At the time of the attack, Nelson commanded Headquarters Squadron, 18th Air Base Group under Col. William J. Flood. **Nelson, cropped**

Wheeler's 600-Man Barracks (Building 72) on 9 June 1941, looking west. The side and rear elevations show the open verandas where men from the 18th Air Base Group and its component squadrons set up machine-gun positions, most of them probably on the top floor to gain a better field of fire toward the flight line to the left. Men erected strongpoints on the adjoining grounds as well. Note the moderately steep slope of the terrain, running from the front of the building (not visible here) at right, down to the flight line one block away to the left. **NARA II, RG 77**

Hence, when Maj. Hilmer C. Nelson (commander of the 18th Air Base Group's headquarters squadron) arrived only minutes after the raid began, noncommissioned officers had the situation in hand. Taking the reins from his capable first sergeants, the major "directed and coordinated the establishment of eight .50 caliber and three .30 caliber machine guns on the rear porches and adjoining grounds." Assisted by 2nd Lt. Carl M. Sidenblad and First Sergeant Kaercher, Major Nelson "supervis[ed] the action of the various gun crews" to gain maximum fire power.[62]

Since the Browning machine guns were water-cooled, Pvt. Gerald L. Suprise ran relays with two water cans between the gunners and water spigots so that the guns' water jackets would not go dry. When the supply of ammunition ran low, TSgt. Anthony A. Albino commandeered an officer's personal car and secured additional ammunition for the gunners on the barracks' porches. He twice drove to Wheeler's Ordnance Warehouse "to enable the machine gunners to continue the operation of their guns and to throw up a heavy curtain of fire." For his bravery, Albino received the Silver Star.[63]

Two airmen man a water-cooled .50-caliber Browning M2 machine gun from a tripod mount on Wheeler's parking apron, looking south from the hangar line. Note the two hoses that carried coolant water to the water jacket that enclosed the barrel. Although the gun could be operated without the coolant water, its accuracy diminished as the barrel heated, and the pattern of the shots became more widely dispersed. **NARA II, 111-SC-127004, cropped**

A Type 0 carrier fighter (*circled at center*), probably from the *Sōryū*, passes on a westerly track over Wheeler's senior officer housing on Curtis and Sperry Loops.
Satō Collection via PHAM, cropped

RETREATS FROM THE CENTER OF ACTION

After failing to draw a weapon at the 600-Man Barracks and with no means to defend himself, Pfc. Leonard T. Egan of the 73rd Pursuit Squadron ran all the way to the officers' housing area and took cover on a front porch. Just as Egan was entering the housing area, an officer dashed out from one of the houses carrying flight gear, followed by his wife holding a little boy in her arms. "Look at what the little yellow bastards are doing to us!" she shrieked. "Look and remember!" Egan took newfound courage from the woman's fierce anger. Whenever he needed to summon the will to stay the course in the war years that followed, he would close his eyes and think of that fearless young mother.[64]

While some airmen chose to evacuate on their own, others actually received instructions to do so. When a master sergeant ordered the men gathered about Pfc. Carroll Andrews to move as quickly as possible to Schofield Barracks, the frightened airmen unhesitatingly obeyed. Andrews was well known for his connection with the Catholic music program at Wheeler. On the way to Schofield, one of the men running with him admitted that he had not been to Mass or Confession in years and sought Andrews' help with an Act of Contrition to "make an emergency Peace." As they continued to Schofield, Andrews encountered a Filipina woman running with a baby. Recognizing him from Mass, the frantic woman beseeched Andrews to baptize her child. The pair entered an NCO's residence, found a bottle of water (the faucets were not working), and baptized the infant. Both Andrews and the mother broke down in tears and wept before they separated.[65]

Cpl. Carroll T. Andrews, 18th Air Base Group, circa early 1942. Andrews served as a general clerk in the group's headquarters squadron and also assisted Fr. Edward A. Taylor as an organist and music director. **Ford**

Leilehua High School (*center right*) was a safe haven for dependents and airmen who sought shelter from strafing aircraft during the raid. **NARA II, 80-G-30555, cropped**

The NCOs' garage (Building 198) where Pfc. David Stephenson encountered a lost child. **NARA II, RG 77**

Retreating toward the shelter of Leilehua High School, Pfc. David B. Stephenson passed the flagpole and reached Building 198, an open-air NCO parking shelter with a corrugated iron roof supported by a framework of four-inch boiler tubes. Inside the shelter he discovered a small child wandering about. With the help of another airman, Stephenson restored the child to its mother, "who was in a state of shock and hysterical."[66]

Pvt. Mannie Siegle and Pfc. Philip Appici likewise headed toward Leilehua High School, intending to take shelter on the school grounds. Upon scaling a four-foot fence that blocked their way, they were astonished to find a crowd of terrified women and children from the adjacent NCO bungalows on Langley Loop—all in various stages of undress and some even naked. The wife of one master sergeant had been so terrified by the attack that she left her child behind. "Go get my child! Go get my child!" she screamed repeatedly. The people around her had a difficult time holding her back.[67]

TSgt. James W. McAdams—a chief clerk with the Headquarters Squadron, 18th Pursuit Group—ran out of his barracks and crawled beneath a wooden platform supporting a pyramidal tent, losing a shoe in the process. When he tried to recover the shoe, machine-gun fire struck him in the lower leg. He was taken to Schofield and treated by "a small middle-aged Army nurse" who stood on the hospital steps in a dress stained with the blood of the men she had tended. The nurse shook her fist at the low-flying aircraft coming from the direction of Wheeler, screaming, "You dirty SOBs!" at the top of her lungs.[68]

Hayashi's 3rd Chūtai Attacks
HANGAR 3 AND APRON
One last unit of carrier bombers had yet to attack Wheeler's hangars. The 3rd Chūtai of eight aircraft under Lt. Hayashi Chikahiro charged in as Lieutenant Ema's aircraft were leaving, nearly running into them head-on. The smoke rising from American aircraft burning on the apron and the relative inexperience of the *Zuikaku* crews increased the odds that the attacks would be disjointed and chaotic.[69]

Lieutenant Hayashi had drawn the assignment of destroying Hangars 3 and 4. Pvt. Leigh Hildebrant of the 674th Ordnance Company was running east toward the Headquarters Building when he witnessed the attack of Hayashi's lead *shōtai* and thought that he saw three bombs falling at once. Hayashi's attack

In about 2006, the son of Lt. (jg) Satō Zenichi of the *Zuikaku*'s horizontal bombing unit visited the Pearl Harbor Air Museum with fourteen of his father's photographs from the Hawaiian Operation. Although the museum failed to scan the photographs at truly high definition, the resolution is sufficient for publication. The authors were able to place three of them in chronological sequence by using the status of the first five rows of aircraft on the east end of the parking apron. The first image of the series, seen here looking northeast, is the only such photograph in which the aircraft of the 15th Pursuit Group (toward the western end of the apron) are visible. To the east, a substantial number of the P-40s (and a few P-26s) remain intact, though strafing attacks are under way. **Satō Collection via PHAM**

From the opposite direction, looking southwest, the fifth row of American fighters is fully enveloped in flames, with additional aircraft igniting on the fourth row. **Satō Collection via PHAM/NARA II, 80-G-30555**

More aircraft on the fourth row have ignited, placing this photograph third chronologically. Perhaps more significant, however, are the four Type 99 carrier bombers visible in the image. Two are at the center right at low altitude, probably pulling out of strafing runs on the apron. Two other aircraft at much higher altitude cross in the opposite direction, toward the photographer. The bombing of the field is not yet complete. The PX Warehouse west of the 600-Man Barracks is still intact, as is the door pocket on the east side of Hangar 3. The white plume of smoke superimposed on the NCO Quarters "loop" might be the strike on Quarters 121. The morning colors ceremony appears not to have taken place, as the flagpole north of the Administration Building at right center is bare. **Satō Collection via PHAM**

This Satō photo looking south from behind the flight line just north of Wheeler's boundary with Schofield Barracks shows the full effect of the smoke plumes on visibility over the target area. Of particular interest is the smoke drifting west from the rear of Barracks No. 1 (*upper left*) following the bomb hit in the mess hall. The west aircraft bay of Hangar 1 burns a short distance to the right. **Satō Collection via PHAM**

Fires burn in both sides of Hangar 3 in this photograph, looking south, taken during the attack by men from the Wheeler Photo Lab. The few surviving photos taken during the attack itself are the work of the Wheeler Lab. The Signal Corps' photographers from Fort Shafter were not present during the raid. Although their photographs all "date" from 7 December 1941, weather conditions and the status of the apron and hangars make it likely that the Fort Shafter photographers exposed some of their negatives the day after the attack. **Aiken, NMPW**

started out well. At least two bombs scored hits on Hangar 3, setting fire to both bays, blowing out the west wall, and wrecking the southeast corner.[70]

Just as the units under Sakamoto and Ema had done, Hayashi's pilots strayed from their orders, which mandated attacks on hangars only, and targeted the parking apron and buildings behind the hangar line. As a result, Hangar 4 sustained only minor damage from machine-gun fire and debris from the easternmost strike on Hangar 3. At least

four bombs impacted the parking apron in front of the latter structure. Although one of the four (near the east end of the hangar) landed close enough to the hangar to be regarded as a miss, the other three were sufficiently far away to be classified as deliberate strikes against aircraft on the apron.[71]

PX WAREHOUSE

Two poorly aimed bombs intended for the 600-Man Barracks missed the mark. One bomb landed

Hangar 3 looking northeast. Damage from bombs that carried away two-thirds of the west wall and caused major damage to the roof is consistent with two direct hits on the western bay of the hangar. Bulldozer tracks on the pavement in the foreground indicate that cleanup of the base is well under way.
NARA II, 111-SC-128353

Hangar 3, looking northwest. One bomb—which probably detonated just inside the hangar's southeastern corner—blew apart the building's door pocket at right center, revealing the layer of stucco applied to the exterior of the cinderblock masonry. The destroyed door pocket supported the steel lintel that spanned the front. Clearing of the hangar's interior has not begun, and the remains of at least three P-40s are still inside. **NARA II, 111-SC-127025**

Wreckage from P-40s of the 18th Pursuit Group at the far eastern end of the parking apron at Wheeler Field. Note the fire-extinguishing equipment in front of the P-40 burning in the foreground. View looks southeast, probably during the lull between the two attack waves. **Aiken, NMPW**

in an open area, possibly east of the barracks, and did little damage; the other fell about two hundred feet west of the barracks and struck near the nearby PX Warehouse, which burned to the ground. Pfc. David Stephenson was sprinting west down Wright Avenue and had just reached the intersection with West Langley Loop when the second bomb landed. The blast threw the young private halfway across

Wright Avenue. He "felt numb all over" after hitting the ground but struggled to his feet, determined to move away from the vicinity as quickly as possible.[72]

Far to the east, having long since abandoned hope of attending Central Union Church in Honolulu, Pvt. Charles Hendrix turned and ran west down Wright Avenue toward the barracks to change out of his civilian clothing, but the Japanese bombers and fighters

The wreckage of the PX Warehouse smolders southwest of the 600-Man Barracks in the distance. Nothing was left of the temporary wooden structure after the raid except charred debris between the scorched concrete support piers. One (unconfirmed) tale explaining the building's rapid and complete demise was that a large quantity of vehicle tires had been stored inside it. The burned-out van (*right center*) was apparently one of the vehicles that 2nd Lt. Edward I. Pratt Jr. was unable to move and save from the flames. Note the east wing of Building T-57 at the far right, one of Wheeler's temporary mess halls. **NARA II, 111-SC-176609**

strafing the field impeded his progress. Hearing bullets thud against the ground, he headed for the nearest doorway—the front entrance to the Officers' Club—just as Capt. Philip S. Robbins, material officer for the 18th Air Base Group, burst through the door. When Robbins asked Hendrix to go with him to the 600-Man Barracks, the young private followed obediently, though reluctantly, because he "could see bombs falling all around it and a big cloud of smoke—I was sure that the barracks was on fire." The smoke was probably

from the poorly aimed bomb strikes east and west of the barracks, because Robbins and Hendrix found the barracks untouched except for "broken windows and screens knocked off by the concussion."[73]

With Hayashi's dive-bombers delivering their payloads in rapid succession, "it was all over in just a few minutes." Cpl. John P. Munn recalled only six to eight bombers attacking in his area. Munn also remembered, quite distinctly, the dull thuds of explosions far off to the south reverberating up

First-Wave Attack on Wheeler Field, *Zuikaku* Dive-Bombing Unit
3rd Chūtai, Lt. Hayashi Chikahiro

	Pilot	Radioman/Rear Gunner
27th Shōtai	FPO1c Andō Gorō	Lt. Hayashi Chikahiro
	FPO2c Tanimura Shōji	FPO1c Fukae Kakuichi
	F1c Tanaka Tadaji	F1c Fukumoto Takeshi
28th Shōtai	Lt. (jg) Kazuhara Takashi	FPO1c Kawase Kōji
	FPO2c Iwamoto Shigeru	FPO3c Hagiwara Michiharu
	FPO2c Sugazaki Masanari	F1c Uwa Kazuo
29th Shōtai	FPO1c Inagaki Fujio	WO Koyama Shigeru
	F1c Matsumoto Yoshiichirō	FPO2c Uetani Mutsuo

Lt. Hayashi Chikahiro, commander, 3rd Chūtai, *Zuikaku* dive-bombing unit, in early 1944 as air group commander of the Tsingtao (China) Kōkūtai. He reported to the carrier on 10 September 1941 and was promoted to lieutenant seven weeks later. After he left the *Zuikaku* on 5 January 1942, Hayashi joined the Suzuka (Japan) Kōkūtai, where he served for more than a year. **Yoshino, cropped**

the "pineapple plain" from the direction of Pearl Harbor.[74]

One of Hayashi's first four bombs (possibly intended for Hangar 3) may have drifted west into Tent City, where the 72nd Pursuit Squadron was under canvas on the "city's" eastern end, although there is no known photographic or textual evidence of any bomb strike or crater among the tents. Flying bullets as well as bomb splinters from hits on Hangar 3 certainly shredded some canvas and inflicted casualties among the tents' inhabitants. At some point prior to the raid, a gasoline tanker truck had been parked adjacent to, and just south of, the "city" of nineteen-man tents. During the dive-bombing attacks, an aircraft skimmed low over Pfc. Donald M. Arras—a mechanic with the 72nd Pursuit Squadron—and opened fire on the gasoline tanker. Pvt. George Seibel and another truck driver from the 18th Pursuit Group's headquarters squadron had just left the area when the tanker exploded. Flames and flying debris set at least eight of the tents on fire. Providentially, a fire engine from Schofield Barracks arrived on the scene to extinguish the blaze.[75]

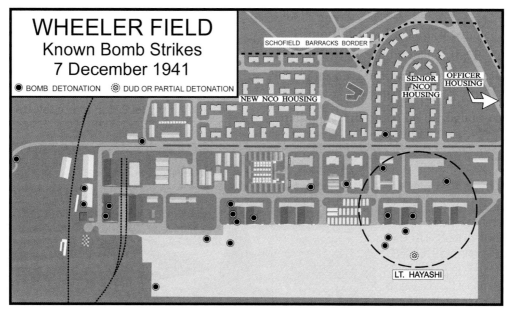

Known bomb strikes for the eight aircraft of Lieutenant Hayashi's 3rd Chūtai, with all eight impacts accounted for. Previous comments regarding duds, impacts on the parking apron, and breakdown in discipline apply here. Note the strike in the senior NCO housing above the circled cluster of craters, perhaps due to a premature release in Sakamoto's 1st Chūtai. **Di Virgilio**

Burned ruins of the canvas barracks at the east end of Tent City, looking northeast toward the battered Hangar 3. Of special interest is the burned-out and ruptured gasoline tanker parked curbside next to the tents, with Hangar 3 just beyond. Close examination of the tanker reveals a large rupture and the presence of a tractor in front. Also, Hangar 3's window frames nearest the tanker are bent *inward*, evidence that the gasoline explosion might have preceded the bomb detonation inside (which would have blown the windows outward). Other intriguing details in the image are the contents of the last two tent frames at right center—one being used to store racks (bed frames), and the other for stacks of M1917 helmets. Note also the .50-caliber water-cooled machine gun on the roof of the 600-Man Barracks. **NARA II, 111-SC-134875**

The charred remains of a tent at the far eastern end of Tent City, adjacent to Hangar 3, looking northwest. Photographs taken after the raid of the vicinity show it unlikely that a bomb detonation *within the site* was the cause of the fires. In the background, note Barracks No. 4 on the left, and the 600-Man Barracks on the right. **NARA II, 111-SC-127034**

Armorer Pvt. George Tillett was still in the 72nd's section of Tent City when what he thought was a bomb exploded near his tent and sent a piece of steel tearing into his left shoulder. The concussion lifted him out of the tent and threw him to the ground, breaking his leg. Unable to get up, he crawled under a nearby vehicle and watched Japanese planes roar past, strafing the base at treetop level. Two airmen from his squadron put him into a pickup truck (with flat tires) and drove him to the Dispensary, where doctors found wounds to Tillett's left foot, left shoulder, both legs, and a hit to his right arm that partially severed the nerve to his hand. Tillett did not learn until later that a strafer's bullets, not a bomb, had set off the explosion of the gas tanker.[76]

QUARTERS 121

Pvt. Jack Spangler watched as a *kanbaku* appeared to dive on the 600-Man Barracks to drop its bomb and then pulled up and jinked right to avoid the blast. Instead of the barracks, however, the bomb landed on the opposite side of Wright Avenue between NCO Quarters 121 and 122. Spangler, briefly knocked unconscious by the blast, came to and crawled away on hands and knees with "red lava dirt embedded in every inch of [his] body." Quarters 121—the Langley Loop residence of MSgt. Fletcher S. Randall, wife Ruth, and their three children—took the brunt of the explosion, although it was not a direct hit. The Randalls were not present when the bomb struck, having fled Quarters 121 in the opening moments of the raid. Although one of the crews from Ema or Hayashi could have been responsible, the residence was directly in line with Sakamoto's approach from upwind, so an inadvertent release cannot be ruled out.[77]

Airmen Struggle to Report for Duty

Even before the attacks began to taper off, armorers and mechanics from all parts of the base were trying to reach the flight line. Pvt. Donovan S. Ginn, an armorer with the 78th Pursuit Squadron, was one of them, but "there was just too many bombs."

Looking west at Quarters 121 at the center—the residence of MSgt. Fletcher S. Randall at the intersection of Wright Avenue and Eastman Road. The 250-kilogram bomb fell about fifteen feet from the large window that faces toward the lower right corner of the photograph. **NARA II, 342-FH-3B-21435, cropped**

In addition to the bombs and strafing, the many thousands of rounds of machine-gun ammunition in Hangar 3 had begun to "cook off." Ginn retreated west back to the bomb-damaged Barracks No. 1 and summoned the will to run across Santos-Dumont Avenue to the hangars, but strafing Japanese aircraft drove him back to the southern, rear porch of the barracks. Ginn's squadronmate SSgt. Ernest W. Owen, a fellow armorer, remarked that the helter-skelter confusion reminded him of Election Day back in Harlan County, Kentucky.[78]

As officers converged on the flight line, some proceeded to the apron and hangars straightaway while others prudently decided to wait until the attacks abated. It would be difficult to find an officer who arrived on the scene with greater celerity than did 1st Lt. Teuvo A. "Gus" Ahola, technical supply officer for the 19th Pursuit Squadron. After he eluded strafers by sheltering behind an embankment, Ahola finally gained the hangar line to find that some of the 19th's aircraft at the east end of the apron were intact. He jumped into the cockpit of the nearest fighter, started the engine, and unlocked the controls, freeing

1st Lt. Teuvo A. "Gus" Ahola with the 47th Pursuit Squadron at Bellows Field during the summer of 1942. **Stevens, cropped**

the stick and rudder pedals from their restraining cables. While taxiing away from the fire area, Ahola saw a Japanese dive-bomber heading straight for his slow-moving P-40. Determined to "ram the son-of-a-bitch," Ahola pushed the throttle forward, expecting the plane to lift as it gained speed. When that did not happen, a glance aft revealed why: the fabric on the elevators had burned away. Having escaped from the *Zuikaku* dive-bomber, Ahola continued across the landing mat toward the revetments along the south edge of the field with a repairable aircraft, fortunate to be alive.[79]

Second Lt. Francis Gabreski decided to go from his apartment to the flight line on foot, but then accepted a ride in a car filled with pilots for the short distance remaining to Hangar 1. Seeing that no one was in charge and issuing orders, the pilots "pitched in where it looked like [they] could be most useful," which was saving the undamaged fighters. Gabreski turned to, pulling chocks from the wheels and pushing aircraft a safe distance away from the fires, even though "the heat and smoke were terrible." Ammunition exploding in the hangar and refueling trucks parked in the vicinity added to the danger. No one could move the trucks because no one had the keys. "It was chaos," Gabreski remembered. "We just had to leave the fuel trucks where they were."[80]

As the last bombs fell on Wheeler, 2nd Lt. Henry W. Lawrence Jr. of the 45th Pursuit Squadron ran next door to the quarters of 1st Lt. Woodrow B. "Woody" Wilmot in Quarters 446-A off Fenander Avenue to catch a ride to the hangars; the pair got into Wilmot's car and headed for the flight line. Just as the car passed the 15th Pursuit Group's headquarters, squadron commander Capt. Aaron Tyer—who had sprinted down to one of the east-west thoroughfares that spanned the base—flagged down Wilmot and jumped in. When they reached the apron in front of the hangars, the men defied the fires and strafing aircraft and "automatically began doing the same thing: taxiing the P-36s and P-40s that hadn't been destroyed out to the partially completed revetments and then racing back to [the] hangar." The airmen and officers used every means of conveyance possible—military and civilian—to transport machine guns and ammunition to the revetments.[81]

Base commander Colonel Flood rushed to the flight line while the attack was still under way. The hangars had taken "an awful beating" by the time he arrived. Nevertheless, he detected little or no panic among the officers and men, all of whom were fighting back determinedly. The Japanese attackers seemed to hover directly over the airmen who were frantically trying to move aircraft away from the fires, and strafing cut down a number of those men. At a time when a commander might be expected to inspire courage in his subordinates, Flood found that it was *he* who drew strength from the endurance and bravery of men who fought to save their aircraft and carried machine guns to the tops of buildings to return fire against their tormentors. General Davidson rushed down to the parking apron as well and at the very height of the strafing attacks helped his officers and men to disperse the surviving aircraft. Although the various squadrons were segregated, the planes within each squadron were packed close together, and the fires and tangled wreckage complicated the efforts to save the surviving aircraft. While Davidson's presence undoubtedly inspired the men on the apron, his absence from the Headquarters Building disconcerted 1st Lt. Charles G. "Turk" Teschner, the 14th Pursuit Wing's officer of the day. Teschner took a "recon wagon" to the flight line, where he found the wing commander pushing aircraft out on the apron. Following his chief's example, Teschner pitched in as well.[82]

Flood testified several years later that he suspected that the Japanese aircraft had employed incendiary ammunition, because the American fighters, still sitting on the apron fully fueled to avoid the lengthy process of fueling on Monday, "went up right away." There was so much smoke that the men had difficulty seeing anything in front of the hangars. Flood described the scene as "a pitiful, unholy mess. . . . It was like the day of doom."[83]

F/C Charles G. "Turk" Teschner, 5 June 1940, during flight training at Kelly Field. **NARA II, 18-PU-92-456-5393**

When SSgt. Mobley L. Hall arrived on the flight line following his drive from Schofield, he checked the aircraft status for the 18th Air Base Group's headquarters squadron. The unit had only three aircraft: a pair of North American AT-6 trainers and one Grumman OA-9 twin-engine amphibian. Hall's AT-6 (probably A.C. Ser. No. 40-2097) was in commission but was still in Hangar 3 after having a new engine installed. Unfortunately, the aircraft burned inside the bombed hangar. The squadron's other AT-6 and the OA-9 were out on the apron, and Hall got in the cockpit of the AT-6 (probably A.C. Ser. No. 40-2099), hoping to move it out of harm's way. Although the plane had a severed oil line, Hall managed to start the engine and taxi the plane away from the fires on the apron.[84]

Bombers Return to the *Zuikaku*

Following twenty-five minutes of bombing and strafing, Lieutenant Sakamoto reformed his unit, and at about 0815 began the flight back to the *Zuikaku*. Two of the group's crews—including that of pilot FPO1c Inagaki Fujio and observer/plane

Type 99 carrier bomber EII-203 during its return flight to the *Zuikaku* in the late-morning hours of 7 December 1941. **Yoshino Yasutaka**

WO Koyama Shigeru, commander of the 29th Shōtai in Lieutenant Hayashi's 3rd Chūtai, *Zuikaku* dive-bombing unit. **BKS**

FPO1c Inagaki Fujio, pilot for WO Koyama Shigeru, 29th Shōtai, 3rd Chūtai, *Zuikaku* dive-bombing unit. **BKS**

commander WO Koyama Shigeru of Hayashi's *chūtai*—had descended so low during the strafing that the carrier's maintenance men found telephone wire wrapped around their wheels. Inagaki and Koyama were well aware of the wire ensnared on their tail wheel as they approached their carrier. They circled the *Zuikaku* several times until crewmen on the flight deck signaled that it was safe for them to land.[85]

Wheeler's Chaplains Set to Work

Capt. Emil W. Geitner (Presbyterian), Capt. Alvin A. Katt (Lutheran), and Capt. Edward A. Taylor (Roman Catholic)—Wheeler's three chaplains, all assigned to the 18th Air Base Group's headquarters squadron—immediately set to work comforting the wounded and the dying. Captain Katt "had admired the pink and gold sunrise" from Quarters 353 on Sperry Loop early that morning. Upon hearing explosions and blasts in the distance, however, he turned his attention southwest toward the flight line and "saw P-40s melt[ing] like wax" on the parking apron. Katt had just taken possession of the new "cantonment type chapel" that opened in October 1941, one of the first structures of its kind in the Pacific. Early in the raid, when Japanese aircraft crossed the field spraying machine-gun fire at the Americans, Maj. William R. "Wild Bill" Morgan (commander, 18th Pursuit Group) and group staff officer Capt. William S. Steele dove under the new chapel for cover. Although raked by incendiary bullets, the chapel did not catch fire, which Katt termed "a miracle."[86]

Initially, Katt reported to Wheeler's Dispensary; from there he moved to the hospital at Schofield, where he encountered Jewish chaplain Capt. Harry P. Richmond, who had rushed to the hospital after hearing of the attack over the radio. The two men helped to identify the dead airmen in the morgue—a grim and difficult task due to lack of identity disks and the dismembered corpses. Captain Katt came upon the body of a boy who would have sung in his choir that morning. The young man's mother had written to him about her son only a few days before the attack, and Katt wondered what he would write to her now. Reflecting on the suffering he had witnessed that day, Chaplain Richmond wrote: "Observing patients; some on stretchers on the floor, others on white sheets in beds, you knew that war, with all its unspeakable horror and terror was here. . . . It was time for action, for ministration, for help to those who were first in service and sacrifice for God and country."[87]

Opinions on Japanese Tactics

During the attacks and after, the men took a keen interest in the Japanese tactics; some even offered grudging admiration. Second Lt. William J. Feiler, the 72nd Pursuit's assistant engineering officer, had been returning to his bachelor apartment from Mass when engine noises attracted his attention. Looking up, he "located the formation about 10,000–12,000

F/C William J. Feiler, 4 June 1941, during flight training at Kelly Field. **NARA II, 18-PU-028-131-8775**

feet directly over Wheeler. They peeled off and came down in string formation and dive bombed our hangars and ramp." First Sgt. John E. Quasnovsky thought he had seen the attacking aircraft form a "Lufbery Circle"—perhaps his interpretation of the very loose figure-eight formation that Pfc. John P. Young thought the dive-bomber pilots employed to maintain a systematic flow of their aircraft over the field during the bombing and strafing attacks.[88]

Pvt. Charles D. Boyd of the 18th Air Base Group observed that some of the dive-bombers made a sharp, 90-degree turn to the south after releasing their bombs, and then turned east to set up strafing runs on the parking aprons from upwind. Pfc. Horace G. Moran noticed that the dive-bombers split into two components after dropping their 250-kilogram bombs; one formation strafed from the north and another from the south. The efficiency with which the Japanese pressed home their attacks on Wheeler awed 2nd Lt. Danforth P. "Danny" Miller Jr. of the 6th Pursuit Squadron: "[The] Japanese knew their gunnery (wasted no ammo; did not o[ver]heat barrels), [and] efficiently executed their plan. Never in my Army Air Corps experience did we emulate their cost-effectiveness. . . . Did we ever plan, rehearse, *and* execute any mission involving over 100 aircraft as well as the Japanese did theirs?"[89]

Damage Assessment

Lieutenant Sakamoto reported that the first wave of attackers had set six aircraft hangars afire, though he mentioned none of the other buildings bombed. Assuming that the Japanese counted not only the twin pursuit hangars but the Machine Shop and the wood-framed warehouse just to the west as well, their count was fairly accurate, as those structures were either completely destroyed or very heavily damaged. Other buildings not included in the Japanese tally suffered as well, notably the PX Warehouse (burned to the ground) west of the 600-Man Barracks, Barracks No. 1, and Quarters 121 in the NCO residential area. In addition, cheated of targets along the flight line, strafers targeted many structures, particularly in the base's residential sections.[90]

Japanese damage estimates from the strafing are difficult to evaluate because the units' results were combined. Sakamoto's dive-bombers claimed to have accounted for nineteen aircraft; Suganami's carrier fighters claimed seventeen more, for a total of thirty-six American aircraft set afire during the strafing. Taking into account the additional sixty aircraft destroyed in the "six hangars set on fire," the Japanese claimed a total of ninety-six aircraft destroyed. According to Air Force documents furnished to the Roberts Commission in late December, the Americans reported that 106 pursuit planes were unusable after the raids. Thus, the Japanese error in their estimate of damage at Wheeler was only 9 percent.[91]

The Japanese pilots' lack of discipline in target selection denied them a more orderly, systematic progression of attacks, although they achieved results comparable to those at Hickam Field nevertheless. As catastrophic as the damage and loss of life caused by the bombing and strafing were, the material

damage to Wheeler Field could have been decidedly worse had the attackers exercised greater restraint. The Japanese could have badly damaged Hangars 2 and 4 with relative ease. In particular, the decision to drop bombs onto the parking aprons hampered bombing effectiveness to a remarkable degree. The resulting clouds of smoke rolled skyward to obscure the pilots' view of the hangar line, particularly from the south, and significantly interfered with the strafing attacks.

It is difficult today to appreciate the crushing weight of responsibility that pressed down on Wheeler's commanders when stillness descended over the field. At some point, Colonel Flood looked south from Wheeler's elevated vantage point on the plain between the Koʻolau and Waiʻanae ranges and saw the smoke boiling up from the direction of Pearl Harbor. That view foretold the magnitude of the morning's disaster—a debacle that encompassed all of Oʻahu. Similarly, the smoke rising from Wheeler could be clearly seen from Pearl Harbor.[92]

By the time that Cpl. Franklin Hibel—a clerk with the 14th Pursuit Wing's headquarters—had dressed on Sunday morning, Japanese aircraft

Sgt. Franklin Hibel, circa 1942. **Hibel**

were zooming past his windows on the second floor of the 600-Man Barracks. Hibel rushed to Brigadier General Davidson's headquarters in the Administration Building, a long half-block east, and found the "general and his staff directing counter measures against the enemy." Within earshot of the young clerk, Davidson shared a piece of disturbing intelligence: a "Japanese invasion via troopships was due shortly and . . . the enemy had us 'cold.'"[93]

Davidson knew that the American forces still functioning after the attack could not retaliate effectively; hence, the burning desire to strike and lash out had to be tempered by an overarching need to conserve what resources remained for searches and patrols to deal with subsequent incoming aerial assaults. And the men at Wheeler, Bellows, and Haleiwa knew with certainty that more challenges lay ahead.[94]

Chapter Nine

"DISPERSE ALL YOUR PLANES AND FLY FULLY LOADED WITH AMMUNITION"

The First-Wave Attacks at Haleiwa and Bellows

At Haleiwa Field along O'ahu's leeward shore, Pfc. Adalbert B. Olack—one of ten radio operators in the 47th Pursuit Squadron—woke up at 0600 on Sunday even though the unit had closed down its switchboard and radios. After finishing breakfast, Olack chatted outside the mess tent with the squadron's mess sergeant, Sgt. Ross Olson. Sometime before 0800, Olack and Olson looked up and counted seventy-two aircraft flying at high altitude toward Honolulu.[1]

Cpl. Earl Boone had just finished breakfast when he "heard terrific noise from above." He looked up and began to count the aircraft flying two miles overhead. Thinking that the Navy was on maneuvers, he quit counting at forty-six. Boone had indeed seen aircraft on maneuvers, but they were from the wrong navy. He was among the first servicemen on O'ahu to see Cdr. Fuchida Mitsuo's forty-nine high-level bombers headed for Pearl Harbor.[2]

Shortly before 0800, Olack felt "rumbling noises," looked to the south-southeast, and saw black smoke on the horizon in the direction of Pearl Harbor.

Realizing that something unusual had transpired, he opened the switchboard and checked the line for Schofield Barracks. It was "buzzing" with activity

F/C Karl F. Harris, n.d., during flight training. Harris was the officer of the day at Haleiwa Field on 7 December 1941. **NARA II, 18-PU-039-181-10366**

F/C Charles E. Kneen, n.d., during flight training.
NARA II, 18-PU-051-237-10390

regarding attacks in progress on the island. After learning of the attacks, 2nd Lt. Karl F. Harris—Haleiwa's officer of the day—shrieked at the men that "Japanese planes were bombing and strafing." He turned to his friend (and the only other officer present), 2nd Lt. Charles E. Kneen, and asked Kneen "to help him cope."[3]

Second Lieutenant Kneen, the technical supply officer for the 47th Pursuit Squadron, had only a bit more than two and one-half hours in AT-6s and P-26s, but his lack of post–flight school experience did not prevent him from taking the steps to ensure that his squadron was ready for battle. He had awakened earlier to the sound of heavy-caliber gunfire in the far distance and knew that enemy air action was under way. Kneen "surveyed the situation," gathered the enlisted men, and related the sobering news "that a state of war existed." At about that same time, Corporal Boone remembered that the guns had been removed from all the aircraft for a thorough cleaning and were in "cold storage" in an armaments tent. Boone sprang into action, "grabbed everyone available[,] and got gun[s] in aircraft that were

flyable." The armorers began loading the guns with ammunition. Aware that purposeful activity served as an antidote to fear, Kneen ordered sidearms and ammunition to be distributed, and told the men to break out two .30-caliber machine guns for antiaircraft defense. He ordered the mechanics to preflight all available aircraft and told the armorers to ensure that machine guns and ammunition were on board those planes—and to *charge the guns.* Crews topped off the planes' fuel tanks and warmed up the engines to prepare for immediate takeoff as soon as pilots arrived from Wheeler.[4]

As the men at Haleiwa readied planes for the pilots then en route, 2nd Lieutenant Taylor and 2nd Lieutenant Welch fought a battle of their own on the ten-mile road that connected Wheeler with Haleiwa. Between the strafers overhead and the numerous "dead-man curves," particularly over streams in the second portion that ran to Waialua, the road was a treacherous stretch. Although the local police were known to patrol the road for speeders, the two lieutenants saw not a one this morning. In any case, Kenneth Taylor later said, "if the cops would [have tried] to stop us . . . we would have just run over them." Although Taylor later maintained that he sped along at one hundred miles per hour, he also estimated that the trip took ten minutes or more, so a more reasonable average speed was sixty or even less given the curves and need to pass near, or through, the towns of Waialua and Hale'iwa.[5]

Not far behind Taylor and Welch on the road to Haleiwa, Second Lt. Harry Brown and his carpoolers experienced somewhat greater difficulty en route with strafing aircraft. As Brown's car careened up "the narrow winding road at breakneck speed" shortly before 0820, a Japanese carrier bomber appeared and opened fire but missed. The enemy plane banked and turned, forcing the rear gunner to cut loose at full deflection and fire along a line perpendicular to the car's path. The Japanese missed once again as Brown swerved to avoid the tracers. First Lt. Bob Rogers screamed at Brown to pull off into an adjoining cane

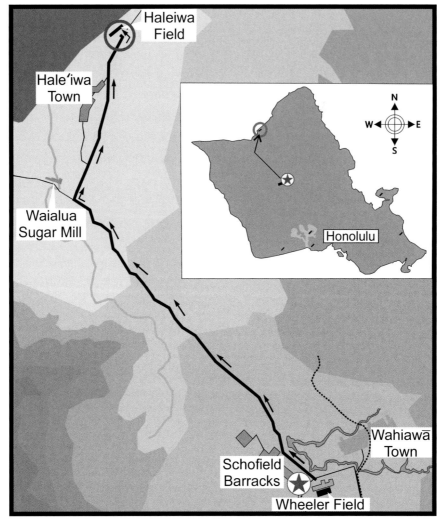

The route northwest from Wheeler to Haleiwa Field taken by Taylor, Welch, Brown, Dains, and Rogers on the morning of 7 December 1941. **Di Virgilio**

field for cover while 2nd Lt. Johnny Dains laughed maniacally "at the Mack Sennett–like chase scene." Brown refused to let up on the accelerator and "bore down on Haleiwa."[6]

Haleiwa: Unexpected B-17s Land

Tension and excitement reigned at Haleiwa as it became obvious that the Japanese were making a surprise attack on Oʻahu. Another surprise that morning was the pair of B-17s that appeared at the tiny airfield. The two were elements of an inbound flight of twelve B-17Cs and B-17Es that had left Hamilton Field, California, in the early evening of 6 December. The flight into Oʻahu was only the first of six legs intended to take the bombers through Midway and

Wake Islands, Port Moresby in New Guinea, Port Darwin in Australia, and finally to Manila. There, the planes and crews were to reenforce a massive heavy bombardment force assembling in the Philippines under Gen. Douglas MacArthur to deter Japanese aggression in the Far East.

The twelve tired B-17 crews had expected to land at Hickam Field and enjoy a day of rest in Waikīkī, but instead they flew into an unanticipated war and scrambled to find safe landing spots. Eventually, they set down at different locations: Hickam, Bellows, Wheeler, and the emergency field at Kahuku Village. First Lt. Harold N. "Newt" Chaffin and Capt. Richard H. Carmichael decided to set down their B-17Es at Haleiwa.[7]

Haleiwa Field, looking east, on 4 September 1941. The pilots driving from Wheeler to Haleiwa would have come up the road at right and turned left into the field along the narrow lane at right center. Supposedly, ground crews pulled aircraft back into the tree line or scrub just below the lane. Reaching the optimal position for takeoff required taxiing aircraft toward the bottom edge of the bright patch at lower center. Oil stains mark the customary parking area at center. **NARA II, 80-G-279358**

Earlier that morning, as Captain Carmichael's bomber closed in on Hickam Field, he and his crew could see huge fires both at the field and inside Pearl Harbor to the northwest. Carmichael called the tower and established contact with his friend Maj. Gordon A. Blake, who told him that an attack was under way. Carmichael decided to have done with Hickam and turned north toward Bellows Field, using the fringe of the clouds spilling over the Koʻolau Range to shake an attacking Japanese fighter.[8]

B-17 Flight, 6–7 December 1941
88th Reconnaissance Squadron
Crew No. 2, B-17E (A.C. Ser. No. 41-2430)

1st Lt. Harold N. Chaffin	O-22469	Pilot
2nd Lt. Mabry Simmons	O-413549	CoPlt.
2nd Lt. Walter H. Johnson	O-425372	Comm.
AvnCdt. Hubert S. Mobley	14044084	Nav.
TSgt. Russell E. Mackey	6529581	Eng.
SSgt. Lucius W. Weeks	6559337	Eng.
Sgt. Irving W. McMichael	6580398	Rad.
Pfc. Robert K. Barnard	6934107	Rad.[9]

Just behind Carmichael, 1st Lieutenant Chaffin also attempted to contact Hickam's tower for landing instructions. Following three aborted landings, Chaffin "swung away from the scene of conflict, carefully observing the air for other planes and

F/C Harold N. Chaffin, 13 October 1938, during flight training at Kelly Field. **NARA II, 18-PU-015-072-3885**

scanning the ground for a possible landing place." His engineer, TSgt. Russell E. Mackey, had served previously in Hawai'i and suggested Haleiwa on O'ahu's leeward shore, halfway up the coast. Short on fuel and reluctant to waste time with even a partial circumnavigation of the island, Chaffin climbed over the Wai'anae Range—a tricky maneuver given the air currents tumbling off the mountains—and reached Haleiwa at about 0820. After a successful landing, the crew disembarked and moved the plane off the runway.[10]

As Chaffin was landing at Haleiwa, Carmichael arrived east of Wheeler Field and judged conditions there to be worse than at Hickam. With only forty-five minutes of fuel remaining, he proceeded around the western end of the Ko'olau Range, turned east, and followed the North Shore toward "our old gunnery camp on windward Oahu, Waimanalo" (Bellows Field). Seeing NAS Kaneohe Bay on fire, he turned north again to the emergency field near the Kahuku Sugar Mill and golf course, but then he remembered Haleiwa, where he had operated fighters earlier in his career. The tiny strip was only 1,200 feet long, but at least it might not be under fire. Carmichael landed at about 0825—though not without difficulty—and found that Chaffin had come in before

Lt. Col. Richard H. Carmichael, circa October 1942. **NARA II, 342-FH-4A-07089, cropped**

him. Carmichael taxied up to a clump of trees, and the crew clambered out of the B-17 "in a high state of confusion and excitement" and started concealing the big Boeing with tree branches.[11]

Shortly after Carmichael cut his engines, he heard the screech of tires from two cars making the left-hand turn onto the base from present-day Route 83. Taylor and Welch were in the first car, and Brown, Dains, and Rogers were right behind. The 47th Pursuit's designated "parking apron" was a patch of oil-stained turf just north of the entry into the field. Ground crews had either taxied the base's fighters to the trees and brush south of the strip for safekeeping and turned them into the wind or were already preparing the planes there.[13]

Taylor and Welch found that their crew chiefs, Sgt. George W. Wilson (Taylor) and SSgt. Cecil H. Goodroe (Welch), had almost finished readying their P-40s for action. Unfortunately, mechanics and armorers had been unable to address one key aspect of preparedness: neither P-40 had use of its nose guns—two .50-calibers that fired through the propeller arc. During gunnery training at Haleiwa

B-17 Flight, 6–7 December 1941
88th Reconnaissance Squadron
Crew No. 1, B-17E (A.C. Ser. No. 41-2429)

Capt. Richard H. Carmichael	O-20203	Pilot
2nd Lt. Donald O. Tower	O-375039	CoPlt.
2nd Lt. Kermit E. Meyers	O-430057	Nav.
AvnCdt. Theodore I. Pascoe	16003996	Bomb.
TSgt. Wallace A. Carter	114199	Eng.
SSgt. Jack R. Tribble	6887454	Eng.
SSgt. Sam Tower	6557672	Rad.
SSgt. Harold D. Boyer	6565343	Photo.
Capt. James W. Twaddell Jr.	O-20254	Weather Off.[12]

A B-17E rests on what the authors believe to be the turf landing field at Haleiwa. The authors are unaware of B-17 flights to or from that location except for those that occurred on 7–8 December 1941, or at least prior to the field's extension to the south and incorporation of Marston Mats. If these assumptions are correct, the aircraft is probably that of Maj. Richard H. Carmichael, who delayed flying his bomber to Hickam until 8 December on order to first strip it of unnecessary weight and receive a ground shipment of aviation fuel. Such a delayed departure would have allowed for this photograph to have been taken. **Aiken, NMPW**

in the months prior to the attack, pilots practiced using only their .30-caliber guns, so .50-caliber ammunition was neither needed nor available at the field.[14]

Bellows Field
A SLOW START

Life at Bellows Field had begun as a typical Sunday morning in paradise; no blizzard of enemy aircraft had yet descended. A few men were on duty this Sunday as if it were any other day of the week. SSgt. Snowden Steuart, a clerk with the Headquarters Detachment, arrived at the Bellows Field Sub-Depot and opened the Supply Warehouse at about 0730. A great many men, though, chose to sleep off the effects of the previous night's hard partying in Honolulu. Pvt. Richard A. Mergenthaler of the 86th Observation Squadron had gotten up early to finish a letter to Lorraine Mae Beebe, his sweetheart, and was ready to drop it into the mail.[15]

2nd Lt. Samuel W. Bishop, circa 1 October 1940, shortly after his arrival at Wheeler Field on 26 September. **Stevens, cropped**

First Lt. Samuel W. Bishop of the 44th Pursuit Squadron was relaxing in bed with the morning newspaper, enjoying life "at the end of the vine in the most peaceful part of the world"—until one of the squadron's sergeants entered the tent and said, "There's something funny going on." Bishop put aside his paper and stepped outside, where "he could hear low flying planes" several miles to the north "and see smoke billowing skyward" from NAS Kaneohe Bay. Wondering what on earth the Navy was up to on this Sunday morning, he began to dress with increasing uneasiness.[16]

As their clocks ticked past 0800, Bellows' airmen on the windward shore were still oblivious to the disaster unfolding at points north and west. The series of jolts that would rock them to their senses was only minutes away. At 0810, Hickam Field called the headquarters at Bellows and requested the services of a fire truck because the base was on fire. When a subsequent call disclosed that Hickam was actually under air attack, Bellows dispatched its fire truck and the base's fire chief. Pvt. Earl Bigelow of the 86th

Observation Squadron had just finished breakfast when he "heard fire truck sirens leaving" and rumors of a fire at Pearl Harbor.[17]

Men who tuned in to Honolulu's commercial radio stations heard more hints of trouble. Second Lt. Wayne H. Rathbun lived in Kailua three miles north of Bellows Field with three other pilots from the 86th Observation Squadron. Having no duty scheduled for Sunday, Rathbun was just starting a late breakfast when he turned on the radio and heard reports of attacks on Pearl Harbor and Hickam Field. After he "rousted [his] buddies out of the sack," they pulled on their uniforms and headed for Bellows. Back on base, Sgt. John E. Ireland of the 86th Observation Squadron was primed for a morning of sport flying at John Rodgers Airport. When he reached the main gate, however, the guard on duty advised him to turn back. Ireland turned on the radio and heard confusing messages regarding an enemy attack on Oʻahu.[18]

With word passing up the chain of command, at 0827 Bellows Field finally went on alert. It was probably at about this time that word went out to disperse

Maj. Edmund C. Sliney, circa 1935, during prior duty in the Hawaiian Department as chaplain with the Hawaiian Division at Schofield Barracks, seen in his 1934 Chrysler four-door sedan with "best friend" Lobo. Though difficult to discern, Sliney has pins for Hawaiian Division Headquarters on his hat and shoulder straps. Note also the "SCHO 694 BKS" tag atop the Hawaiian license plate. **Spinney**

the aircraft and turn out the men. Pvt. Elmer J. Steffan, one of twenty-six other soldiers from the Quartermaster Corps who served with the base's headquarters, was shaving in preparation for church when a message came over the radio that "Oahu was under bombing attack by the Japanese." Neither Steffan nor any of the men nearby took the report seriously until their "regular Army Sergeant" burst into the room "blaring to get a move on and report to [their] various stations for duty." The men rushed out of the barracks, but incredibly, no one sounded, or heard, a general alarm.[19]

Sunday Mass at Bellows proceeded on schedule. Fr. (Lt. Col.) Edmund C. Sliney celebrated 0630 Mass at Hickam Field, where he was head chaplain. Afterward, he and his sisters Minnie and Sadie, who were visiting from Massachusetts, piled into an Army vehicle driven by Pvt. John Coveney for the quick drive to Bellows to set up for the 0830 Mass in the theater at the Barracks Loop. After hearing confessions and setting up the altar, Father Sliney vested and prepared for Mass, though he anticipated light attendance because the men were either sleeping late or overnighting in town.[20]

THE ATTACK

As the drama was beginning to unfold at Bellows, about five miles to the northwest a pitched battle was already under way on the Mōkapu Peninsula. Eleven Japanese carrier fighters from the *Shōkaku* and *Zuikaku* strafed the patrol bomber base at NAS Kaneohe Bay shortly before 0800 to destroy the Navy's long-distance aerial search assets. Although the enemy fighters did not eliminate the base's capabilities, the attacks thoroughly stunned the aviators, sailors, and Marines there. With the attackers' ammunition nearly exhausted, Lt. Kaneko Tadashi— overall commander of the two fighter units—broke off the engagement. After assessing the damage done to the target, Kaneko flew southeast alone, following O'ahu's coastline, to reconnoiter what was thought to be a fighter base at *Berōsu Hikōjō*—Bellows

Lt. Kaneko Tadashi, commander of the *Shōkaku* fighter unit, circa 6 December 1941. *Maru*

Field—his unit's secondary target. Not content with a high-altitude reconnaissance, at 0840 Kaneko spiraled down for a low-level firing pass from seaward, perhaps to obtain a better estimate of the base's aircraft strength.[21]

Shortly before 0800, while Lieutenant Kaneko's fighters were attacking NAS Kaneohe Bay, Pvt. Ronald J. Nash reported for guard duty and took up his post in the warehouse area downslope from Bellows' Barracks Loop. The only incident of note was a single airplane that "came in from the ocean and made a pass over the air strip." The plane's presence did not seem out of line to Nash, however, as it was not at all unusual for Navy aircraft to buzz the base.[22]

Other men were not so blasé. After finishing his breakfast, Cpl. Arnold J. Trempler—an aircraft mechanic from the 44th Pursuit—was strolling across the road toward Bellows Beach when he heard and then saw a silver single-engine fighter with a black cowling approaching the field. As soon as the plane opened fire, Trempler recognized Lieutenant Kaneko's descent toward the field for what it was,

The Dispensary (Building T-38) at Bellows Field, looking southwest, circa 1935. The tents beyond the trees at right are remnants of the old Air Corps Range Camp. **NARA II, RG 77**

broke into a run, and dove into a depression at the end of the runway. Aiming for the field "directly from the sea," Kaneko set his sights on the two rows of aircraft—eleven P-40s, five O-47Bs (with one additional undergoing maintenance), and two silver O-49s—and opened fire. The proximity of these targets to the Dispensary and rows of tents from the old Air Corps Range Camp almost guaranteed that Kaneko's gunfire would strike the latter locations as well. After his only burst at "the airfield, planes and tents," which might have used the last of his *kansen*'s ammunition, Kaneko circled the field, turned west, and banked over the adjacent plantation village, "revealing unbelievably" to those on the ground the Rising Sun insignia on his wings. Corporal Trempler scrambled to his feet and hurried to locate Capt. Arthur R. Kingham, his squadron commander, for orders. Damage to the base from the strafing proved minimal, with some tents and the Dispensary holed in places. The only casualty was Pfc. James A. Brown, a clerk with Bellows' Medical Detachment, who suffered a leg wound while in his tent. Kaneko, having seen an estimated thirty-five two-seat airplanes at the field, opened his radio and requested an attack on Bellows.[23]

Kaneko's strafing attack seems to have raised comparatively few eyebrows at Bellows. Units and individuals took such independent and varied actions that it is difficult to place events in their proper sequence. Among the first to react decisively, sans orders or official notification, were airplane mechanics Cpl. Donald H. Halferty and SSgt. Edward J. "Ed" Covelesky of the 44th Pursuit, who were basking on Bellows Beach when Kaneko made his strafing pass. Halferty and Covelesky sprinted to the P-40 parking area and began dispersing the aircraft from their position in a straight line south of the runway, although other men probably jumpstarted that evolution (due to the alert some fifteen minutes earlier) and had begun the process of arming the planes by unzipping the cowlings to load .50-caliber ammunition. The armorers would finish the job.[24]

Arming the P-40s, however, was no simple matter. Per standard procedure, the machine guns had been removed from the airplanes for a thorough cleaning following the previous week of gunnery practice, and they had yet to be reinstalled. The armorers who had accompanied the squadron to Bellows were responsible for these tasks, and for loading the installed guns. In the absence of manpower to transport the machine guns and ammunition from the squadron's temporary armament tents to the aircraft, airplane mechanics stepped up to help. MSgt. Paul F. Postovit, the 44th Pursuit Squadron's line chief, arrived and instructed SSgt. Cosmo R. Mannino "to preflight and combat load all aircraft." Despite Mannino's best efforts, however, the shorthanded ground crews were able to ready only three fighters.[25]

Adding to the confusion, between 0845 and 0900 a Boeing B-17C Flying Fortress was spotted coming in from the east, trailing smoke and clearly intending to land from upwind. When Staff Sergeant Steuart peered out of the Supply Warehouse and saw the B-17 attempting to land *against the red light in the tower*, he knew trouble was brewing.[26]

The bomber (A.C. Ser. No. 40-2049) was also part of the inbound flight of twelve B-17s from the West Coast. Flown by 1st Lt. Robert H. Richards, with copilot 2nd Lt. Leonard S. Humiston, the plane had

B-17 Flight, 6–7 December 1941
38th Reconnaissance Squadron
Crew No. 7, B-17C (A.C. Ser. No. 40-2049)

1st Lt. Robert H. Richards	O-395292	Pilot
2nd Lt. Leonard S. Humiston	O-398703	CoPlt.
AvnCdt. William F. B. Morris	18001246	Nav.
AvnCdt. George E. Gammans	14034719	Bomb.
SSgt. Joseph S. Angelini	6853524	Eng.
SSgt. Erwin B. Casebolt	6561339	Eng.
SSgt. Melvin D. Zajic	6859921	Rad.
Pvt. Vernon D. Tomlinson	19030242	Rad.
SSgt. Lawrence B. Velarde	6555988	Arm.[28]

F/C Robert H. Richards, 28 March 1940, during flight training at Kelly Field. **NARA II, 18PU-077-375-5181**

been attacked by Japanese fighters just as it rounded Diamond Head. Two crewmen were wounded in the attack, and the number-one engine was damaged. Giving up on landing at Hickam, Richards turned toward Bellows, hoping to make an emergency landing there.[27]

Unfortunately, Richards attempted to land just as Cpl. Earl E. Sutton, one of the P-40 mechanics, taxied his aircraft toward the dispersal area on the opposite side of Bellows' runway. Distracted by the landing hazard posed by the fighter crossing from

1st Lt. Robert Richards' B-17C, "49" (A.C. Ser. No. 40-2049), at Bellows Field after skidding off the southwest end of the narrow runway on 7 December 1941. **NARA II, 111-SC-127752**

left to right, Richards either overshot or misaligned with the runway and circled around for a second try. At that point, men on the ground could see that *two* of the Boeing's engines trailed smoke. On that second pass, the B-17C touched the pavement halfway down the runway. Although Richards set his brakes immediately, the Fortress "sailed across the end of the strip[,] across [an] irrigation ditch and into [a] pineapple field." The base's ambulance roared up and screeched to a halt at the end of the strip, and the wounded members of the crew were loaded on board.[29]

The 44th Pursuit Squadron's slow and confused start at Bellows was the result of chain-of-command and procedural issues at headquarters. When radio electrician Pfc. Dean P. Parker came into the tent of parachute mechanic Sgt. George Lawrence and squadron clerk Cpl. Keith A. Schilling and said that "a plane just flew over and straffed [*sic*] the field," Schilling volunteered to go to the squadron's operations tent and call Wheeler Field to report it. Calling Wheeler from Bellows was a time-consuming task. It required a long-distance call to Honolulu and

requests to be connected first with Schofield Barracks and then with Wheeler. When someone in the 18th Pursuit Group operations office finally picked up the telephone, Schilling asked, "What's going on?" The voice on the other end commanded, "Disperse all your planes and fly fully loaded with ammunition." At that juncture, 2nd Lt. John B. Farrar Jr., assistant operations officer, and 1st Lt. Maurice C. Phillips joined Schilling in the tent. Phillips was the senior officer present. Although Phillips passed on the (by now) almost superfluous order to disperse and arm the fighters, he instructed Schilling to call Wheeler back for confirmation. Schilling had just initiated that byzantine process once again when someone from the 86th Observation Squadron burst in and breathlessly instructed them to "get all planes loaded with ammo, to take off, and call fighter control when they were high enough to get through."[30]

Meanwhile, with Mass under way at the base theater, Private Coveney—Father Sliney's driver—heard about the crash-landing of the B-17, approached the priest, and advised him that some sort of an attack was under way. Sliney—still facing the altar—promptly

F/C John B. Farrar Jr., 18 March 1941, during flight training at Kelly Field. **NARA II, 18-PU-027-129-7802**

F/C Maurice C. Phillips, 16 May 1940, during flight training at Kelly Field. **NARA II, 18-PU-073-349-5363**

interrupted the liturgy, wheeled about, and announced that the island was under attack and the men should report to their stations. Pfc. Raymond F. McBriarty, a gunner in the 86th Observation Squadron, hurried from the theater toward the squadron's armament shack as 1st Sgt. Francis E. Clark blew his whistle and screamed at the men to "get to the line!" After reaching the shack, McBriarty drew two .30-caliber machine guns and two hundred rounds of ammunition. He tossed the "flexible" gun into the rear seat of his assigned O-47B (aircraft 1/86O) and then installed the "fixed" gun in the right wing with one hundred rounds of ammunition stowed by the landing gear; then he installed the flexible gun and its ammunition in the rear cockpit.[31]

Meanwhile, Sgt. Arthur H. Cochran of the Bellows Headquarters Detachment ran to the wrecked B-17C at the end of the runway to assess the situation. He rushed to Bellows' Headquarters Building to report the incident and was surprised to find a chaplain acting as base commander. First Lt. John P. Joyce, an infantry officer assigned to the Headquarters Detachment as officer of the day, had directed 1st Lt. Ernest J. Blackford, Bellows' new Protestant chaplain, who had been serving there for only two weeks, to take temporary command of the field. His new status as base commander notwithstanding, Blackford ordered the loudspeaker system at the field opened and advised all men to report to their respective orderly rooms immediately.[32]

Thus, after fits and starts, the ground crews of the 44th Pursuit Squadron received official instructions from higher authority—though now moot—to disperse their fighters. Bellows' headquarters then received a teletype message from the 14th Pursuit Wing at Wheeler stating that Wheeler was under attack by many aircraft, and Bellows needed to get its fighters into the air as soon as possible. Chaplain

Ernest J. Blackford as a junior at Union University in Jackson, Tennessee. *Lest We Forget,* 1936

Blackford tapped Sergeant Cochran as a messenger to deliver the message to the Control Tower, which in turn relayed the order to flight operations.[33]

Strangely, there were still men who had *just* awakened. After seeing the dramatic landing of the B-17, Pvt. Harry E. Cornelius of the 86th Observation Squadron burst into the tent of fellow truck driver Pvt. John M. Neuhauser, shook him awake, and announced: "A B-17 just landed downwind and crashed into the gully, the guys inside are all shot up, a plane fired shots into our Dispensary, and [a] cab driver just drove in from Honolulu and said the Japs are dropping bombs on Pearl Harbor!" Neuhauser, still groggy with sleep, seemed unable to grasp the news until Cornelius slapped him and said, "I'm not kidding! Get the hell out of bed!" Neuhauser got dressed, and the two men drove up to the top of the hill and saw the damaged bomber sitting off the end of the runway.[34]

Chapter Ten

"IT WAS AN AWFUL LOOKING SITUATION"

Haleiwa and Wheeler Launch Their Fighters

Around 0830 at Haleiwa, 2nd Lt. Kenneth Taylor and 2nd Lt. George Welch, wearing life jackets and flight helmets, were awaiting instructions and the release of their planes when Maj. Lorry N. Tindal arrived at the Interceptor Command's Information Center at Fort Shafter and took over duties as chief controller. It was probably Tindal who contacted Haleiwa with the request that the pilots "take any pursuit [they] had and take off and proceed to 'Easy' [Barber's Point] at 8,000 feet." Without tactical orders at the squadron level, Taylor and Welch took off on their own initiative after 0840, just as the second-wave strike units deployed northeast of O'ahu for their attacks on the Pacific Fleet in Pearl Harbor far to the southwest.[1]

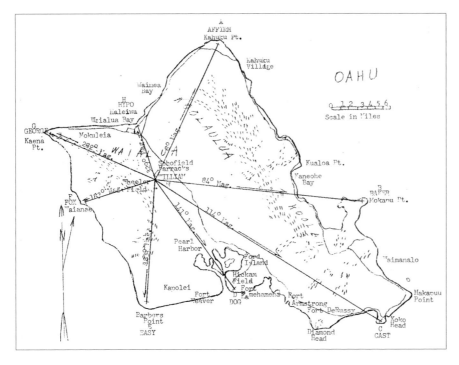

Map from the *Tentative Manual of Interceptor Command*, October 1941, showing the geographical points along O'ahu's coastline to which fighter aircraft would be directed by the controller in the Information Center at Fort Shafter. Easy (Barbers Point) at the lower left center was Taylor and Welch's first objective. **AFHRA**

With Taylor and Welch having taken two of the three available P-40s, 2nd Lieutenant Dains reportedly jumped out of 2nd Lt. Harry Brown's car and into the remaining P-40 and prepared for takeoff. Although 1st Lt. Robert Rogers was acting squadron commander and could have claimed that P-40 for himself, he chose instead to ensure that all was in order at the airfield before taking to the air. As none of the remaining aircraft (all P-36As) were yet available, he and Brown would have to wait.[2]

In the interim, a Japanese dive-bomber executed several strafing passes on the field. Only later did it occur to Brown and Rogers that while driving from Wheeler they might have led a Japanese aircraft—perhaps the same one that had strafed them on the road—straight to Haleiwa. Although the timing of the strafing attack is uncertain, it most likely occurred within the narrow span of time between the first-wave and second-wave attacks, after the departure of Taylor and Welch but prior to that of Dains. The Japanese pilot "sprayed the field" while Brown and others took cover under the wings of some P-36s. Brown, feeling 100-octane fuel dripping onto his neck, "decided that wasn't much of a hiding place" and ran south of where the fighters were

parked. "[I] got behind a tree and my imprint may still be on it," he later said dryly. At the north end of the field, the B-17 crews attempting to camouflage their planes with tree branches heard someone shout that the field was about to be strafed. Capt. Richard Carmichael and his weather officer, Capt. James Twaddell, sprinted to the beach and lay prone behind a large rock. While they were hiding, a huge wave crashed over them, soaking them and ruining their wristwatches. TSgt. Wallace A. Carter, a crew chief, and SSgt. Sam Tower, a radio operator, reportedly unpacked one of the .30-caliber machine guns and opened fire on the attacking aircraft, which left the scene and set the stage for Dains to take off.[3]

Wheeler Field

While the men at Haleiwa were the first to send fighters aloft that morning and battled a single *kanbaku*, the airmen at Wheeler Field struggled to cope with the consequences of the dive-bombing and strafing attacks they had just endured. Fortunately, reinforcements for those efforts arrived as airmen returned to the base for duty. After Mass in town was cut short, SSgt. Charles H. Leyshock of the 18th Pursuit Group's headquarters squadron got in his car

Schofield Barracks Hospital, 17 September 1940. Seriously wounded casualties evacuated from Wheeler Field's Dispensary were taken here. View looks north. **NARA II, 342-FH-3B-48299, cropped**

and raced toward Wheeler, coaxed along by an occasional strafer. Leyshock needed no map back to the base; the tower of smoke drifting southwest from the airfield was a clear marker. Upon arrival, he fought fires on the apron and in the hangars and tended to the wounded. The more seriously wounded airmen and those already dead were taken from Wheeler's Dispensary to the large hospital at Schofield one and a half miles away to the northwest.[4]

Equally important tasks included strengthening Wheeler's defenses. Accompanied by an officer and several other men, Pvt. Jack Spangler set up machine guns—one .50-caliber gun on the roof of the 600-Man Barracks facing south toward the hangars, and another gun on the northeast corner of the barracks' roof. Airmen hung mattresses over the railings on the balconies as shields not only against Japanese gunfire but, of more immediate concern, against the ammunition cooking off in Hangar 3 to the southwest. Other defenders acted alone. Having been emancipated from his cell in the Guard House, Pvt. Henry Brown was determined to find a weapon—any weapon. He ran back to the Guard House armory and received a riot gun with five rounds. More effective weapons carried by other men outside—Springfield bolt-action rifles and Browning Automatic Rifles—underscored the utter uselessness of Brown's riot gun, but he stood ready to take on the Japanese when they returned.[5]

With Wheeler now an armed camp and more attacks expected, it was imperative that evacuations get under way. The terrified dependents needed little prompting. As soon as SSgt. Homer R. Baskin of the 6th Pursuit Squadron and his wife in Quarters 256-A got dressed, they began evacuating dependents from married NCO quarters to Wahiawā. As the first attacks ended, chief clerk TSgt. Herbert C. Ward left the shelter of Quarters 253-A and reported to headquarters, 15th Pursuit Group while his wife and three other women left the base for shelter in Wahiawā as well.[6]

Despite the men's determination to fight back, optimism was in short supply. As the Japanese

dive-bombers and fighters disappeared over the horizon, Cpl. John P. Munn of the 72nd Pursuit made a quick visual survey of the parking apron and saw burning aircraft along the apron's entire length. A few planes looked intact, but most were burned to cinders. "It was an awful looking situation," he recalled. That grim outlook fed frustration. The attack was an intense ordeal for Pvt. David C. Cameron—a radio electrician from Bellows Field who had just completed Wheeler's radio school—and every attempt he made to cope with the disaster ended in failure. He labored with other airmen to extinguish the flames that consumed the Post Exchange Warehouse, and later to assemble a .50-caliber water-cooled machine gun on the back porch of the 600-Man Barracks. Both attempts were unsuccessful.[7]

Nonetheless, there were bright spots—and in the most unexpected places. The mood on the flight line was measured and professional, and there seemed to be little panic. "Well here's what we've got left," men were saying. "What are we going to do with it?" The men made quick, informed decisions regarding the fate of each aircraft. Any plane that appeared repairable was taken immediately to the revetments.[8]

The crews fighting fires on the parking apron choked with smoke and aircraft wreckage made slow but steady progress, although an additional distraction drew their attention away from the work at hand. Perhaps due to Wheeler's relative isolation and the men's preoccupation with recovering from the first-wave attack, there is no evidence that anyone there was expecting the incoming flight of B-17s from the West Coast. Eventually, one of the twelve planes—a B-17C (A.C. Ser. No. 40-2054) piloted by 1st Lt. Earl J. Cooper—set down at Wheeler Field.[9]

It is unknown whether Cooper attempted to contact Wheeler by radio before landing, although the fires and the columns of dense black smoke should have signaled the absence of a welcoming committee. The ground crews racing to tow intact aircraft across the landing mat to the protection of the revetments further complicated Cooper's attempt to land. Pvt.

Tom Hutchinson and 1st Lt. Malcolm A. "Mike" Moore, one of the 46th Pursuit Squadron's flight commanders, had tied "a solid looking P-40" to the rear of Hutchinson's truck, and the latter drove with Moore in the Tomahawk's cockpit to steer. Just as Hutchinson stepped on the gas, Cooper's B-17 appeared on a downwind landing approach. Hutchinson weaved from side to side, uncertain where the bomber would land, while Moore shouted for Hutchinson to stop. The B-17 cleared the truck-Tomahawk tandem with room to spare but plowed a long furrow in the turf before Cooper managed to brake it to a standstill.[10]

As if interference from Lieutenant Moore's P-40 was not enough, Cooper faced fire from the ground when the .50-caliber machine gun on the northeast corner of the 600-Man Barracks opened up. Pvt. Jack Spangler, who was at the other roof gun, claimed years later that he saw the crew in the bomber trying to wave off the gun crews. The .50-caliber gun, perfectly positioned to take on the "enemy bomber," sprayed a stream of bullets toward the B-17 until an officer arrived and threatened to shoot the gunner unless he allowed the B-17 to land.[11]

After landing at about 0920 Cooper reported to base commander Col. William J. Flood, who was well known locally for his practical jokes. Cooper, of course, knew nothing about that and was astonished

F/C Earl J. Cooper, 29 March 1940, during flight training at Kelly Field. **NARA II, 18-PU-018-088-5100**

when Flood told him to rearm and refuel his aircraft and take off in pursuit of the Japanese carriers. When the forlorn Cooper explained that he had just flown twelve hours from the West Coast and was exhausted, Flood answered, "I know, son, but there's a war on." Cooper responded that he would comply, requesting only a cup of coffee before leaving. Unable to continue with the charade, Colonel Flood told the young pilot to get some rest, adding that he *would* be called upon to fly the next day. Flood said later that Cooper's willingness to go off in pursuit of the Japanese carriers "show[ed] the splendid type of young men we had in the Pacific." Following Cooper's unorthodox landing and reception by Colonel Flood, the crewmen of the B-17C "had wild tales to tell of their ordeal while under attack by Japanese aircraft."[12]

Meanwhile, many of the fighters from the 18th Pursuit Group—and many of Wheeler's P-40s—lay in ashes on the east end of the parking apron. On the apron's west end, however, the inadvertent smokescreen laid by Lieutenant Sakamoto's dive-bombers had hidden many of the 15th Pursuit Group's planes. Thus, it fell upon the 15th to send up fighters late in

B-17 Flight, 6–7 December 1941
38th Reconnaissance Squadron
Crew No. 5, B-17C (A.C. Ser. No. 40-2054)

1st Lt. Earl J. Cooper	O-395120	Pilot
2nd Lt. Richard J. Eberenz	O-386381	CoPlt.
2nd Lt. John A. Crockett	O-430053	Nav.
AvnCdt. Jim B. Buchanan	14042600	Bomb.
TSgt. Jesse R. Broyles	6761221	Eng.
Sgt. Lee W. Best	6581083	Eng.
Cpl. Elmer G. Lippold	6290981	Eng.
Sgt. Joseph J. Bruce	6910319	Rad.
Pvt. Don C. McCord Jr.	19051852	?[13]

the attack and afterward. In the 15th Pursuit Group's headquarters, Sgt. Frederick T. Bowen remained at his post throughout the bombing and strafing and "maintained telephone connections with tactical squadrons of his group. As a result of this action, one squadron [the 46th Pursuit Squadron] was able to get their planes into combat. Sergeant Bowen displayed calm and cool judgment, disregard for his own personal safety and commendable devotion to duty." Bowen's dedication cleared the way for Wheeler's aerial response to the Japanese second-wave strike.[14]

Readying the fighters, however, took more than mere communication. Along with other mechanics in his unit, Pvt. Guy Messacar Jr. of the 46th Pursuit Squadron worked feverishly to get airplanes ready for action. Most of the "surviving" aircraft had sustained damage of some sort, but by "taking parts from the damaged planes and doing a lot of patching up," mechanics had four P-36As ready for flight soon after the first attack wave had departed. Patching the battered P-36s was only part of the battle, however, because the aircraft were unarmed, and

at least some had had their machine guns removed. Squadron commander 1st Lt. Lewis M. Sanders authorized requisitioning guns, and Pfc. Wilbur S. Carr and others from the group headquarters staff drove a car heaped with machine-gun ammunition east to the revetments where the 46th's P-36s lay. SSgt. Robert S. Turk Jr., armament chief for the 46th Pursuit Squadron, ably assisted by mechanic SSgt. William R. "Willie" Wright and armorer Pfc. Marion B. "Pappy" Leesch, supervised the loading of ammunition in the four P-36As being readied for flight. Sanders later described the scene: "Pilots & crew chiefs taxied the P-36s to the revetments on the east boundry [sic] of the landing field, armorers followed with belted ammunition[.] Radio, parachute and oxygen carriers were waiting at the revetments. The .50 cal. guns were loaded, oxygen turned on [and] radios checked."[15]

Guy Messacar Jr., former airplane mechanic with the 46th Pursuit Squadron, seen here after the war, circa 1950. **Robinson**

Pvt. Robert S. Turk Jr. at Hickam Field, circa 1940, posing behind RE/102, a B-18 from the 5th Reconnaissance Squadron. Note the wind gust lock that secures the rudder to the vertical stabilizer. **Turk, cropped**

A portion of Wheeler Field's revetments looking east-northeast on 10 October 1941. Kamehameha Highway runs north–south (*left to right*) along the top of the photograph, with Wright Avenue along the left margin. Revetments of the conventional U-shaped design are nestled against the highway. Aircraft taxied into the revetments (*upper left*) through parallel earthen berms. Two new apartment buildings for bachelor officers are in the upper left corner. Most junior officers and pilots lived there.
NARA II, 80-G-279373, cropped

Sanders selected three men—all "superior pilots, well-disciplined and trained"—to join him in the four-man flight. Second Lt. Philip M. Rasmussen, the squadron's adjutant, flew as Sanders' wingman. Second Lt. John M. Thacker, the unit's supply officer, would lead the second element with 2nd Lt. Othniel Norris, the 46th's communications officer, as his wingman. Before taking off, Sanders briefed the pilots, ground officers, and airmen, stressing the desperate situation before them and the need for "careful reaction to enemy attacks and incursions." He insisted on strict compliance with his orders, though tempered with "free use of initiative." Already impressed by the men's courage, bravery, and resourcefulness, Sanders felt no call to mention the need for "unflinching response and resistance."[16]

There were more 46th Pursuit Squadron pilots on hand in the revetments than there were aircraft ready to fly. Among those pilots was 2nd Lt. Gordon H. Sterling Jr., who watched quietly as Sanders and the three pilots he selected for the mission prepared

for takeoff. As the squadron's assistant engineering officer, Sterling had followed the airplanes from the apron to the revetments where armorers installed the guns and loaded ammunition. As the ground crews assisted the pilots into the P-36s, Othniel Norris suddenly clambered out of the cockpit and announced that the parachute harness was too large for him. While Norris sprinted to the nearby parachute truck to select a better-fitting harness, Sterling exercised the "free use of initiative" that his commander enjoined earlier and blurted out, "Hell, I'm going to fly. Here's my chance." With the plane ready, engine running, and cockpit unoccupied, Sterling bolted for Norris' aircraft, "determined to fight to the finish." Before climbing into the cockpit Sterling removed his wristwatch and handed it to SSgt. Hugh Turner, the crew chief, shouting over the engine noise, "Give this to my mother! I'm not coming back!"[17]

Sterling was not the only pilot with an eye on Norris' plane—the 45th Pursuit Squadron's last surviving P-36A. Second Lt. Henry W. Lawrence Jr.

also intended to claim the fighter. He had helped to prepare this P-36 for flight back in the revetments, assisting with machine-gun installation and loading ammunition, and considered it his. When all was in readiness, Lawrence walked down the line of revetments to inform Capt. Aaron Tyer—his squadron commander—that he and the plane were ready to depart and asked for orders. Captain Tyer replied, "Go down to Hickam and see if there are any bombers to escort."[18]

While Lawrence and Norris sought orders and parachute harnesses, Sanders, Rasmussen, Thacker, and Sterling advanced their throttles and cleared the area that fronted the revetments. Rather than taxiing to the far end of the field to take off into the wind, the four took off straight from the revetments east of the hangar line. When 2nd Lieutenant Lawrence ended his conversation with Captain Tyer, he ran back to find an empty revetment where "his" P-36 had been warming up. Just then, Sanders' flight roared overhead, cleared the field in advance of 0930, and "entered the overcast at 2000 [feet] headed southeast." When Lawrence complained to Staff Sergeant Turner, the crew chief replied, "Sir, Lieutenant Sterling took it! . . . What could I do?"[19]

Desperate to get in the air, Lawrence "soon found another P-36A that was ready to go" and, without asking Tyer for orders this time, took off intending to join up with Sanders' flight, which was by then several minutes out. Lawrence soared over Wheeler, "zigzagging frantically and looking for any other airplane, friend or foe." Finally leveling out at about ten thousand feet, he located two aircraft far below. His blood up, Lawrence charged his .30- and .50-caliber machine guns and dove to the attack— only to see that they were friendlies, supposedly a P-40 and a P-36A piloted by squadronmates 1st Lt. Woodrow B. "Woody" Wilmot and wingman 2nd Lt. William F. Haning Jr., who had taken off several minutes after Lawrence. Wilmot signaled Lawrence to form on his left wing, and the three sped south toward Hickam Field. As the trio of Americans

F/C Henry W. Lawrence Jr., circa 1940–41, during flight training at Maxwell Field. **NARA II, 18-PU-054-249-7497**

F/C Woodrow B. Wilmot, 13 October 1938, during flight training at Kelly Field. **NARA II, 18-PU-100-504-4011**

drew close to Pearl Harbor, antiaircraft fire from trigger-happy sailors and Marines on board the ships below grew heavier. Since there seemed to be no airworthy bombers at Hickam to escort and

F/C William F. Haning Jr., circa 1941. **NARA II, 18-PU-38-178-9743**

F/C Fred B. Shifflet, circa 1940–41, during flight training at Maxwell Field. **NARA II, 18-PU-084-410-7147**

antiaircraft fire was making closer examination of Hickam extremely dangerous, Wilmot and company "circled around the island" in search of the enemy elsewhere but found none. With no orders coming over the radio and fuel low, the frustrated Americans turned back toward Wheeler.[20]

After he landed, Lawrence "saw a well shot up P-40 on the field" brought back to base by 2nd Lt. Fred B. Shifflet, who had also attempted a sortie to Hickam Field. When the ground fire started, Shifflet came in at low altitude to show that he was friendly. The nervous gunners on the ground wanted none of it, however, and increased their volume of fire. Lucky not to have been killed, "Crazy Shifflet" landed with two flat tires.[21]

At least two other pilots from the 46th Pursuit Squadron took off not long after Sanders and Wilmot. First Lt. Malcolm Moore had earned the opportunity to sortie that day, quite apart from the ordeal of dodging Cooper's Flying Fortress. Early in the attack, he had driven his automobile to the hangar line and assisted with the firefighting at Hangar 1, helping to save aircraft and ammunition nearby. Although the

P-40 that he and Private Hutchinson had towed to the revetments was not usable, Moore secured P-36A 91/15P (probably readied by SSgt. Robert Turk) and took off at about the same time as his squadronmate Othniel Norris in another P-36A. The pair shaped independent courses for Kaʻena Point, where they hoped to engage the enemy. Neither pilot had waited for hard intelligence regarding the composition and location of the attacking Japanese forces, although Moore received a garbled radio message in which he recognized the words "Kaʻena Point."

In the meantime, the 47th Pursuit Squadron's pilots were still trying to reach Haleiwa. Early in the attack on Wheeler, 1st Lt. John J. Webster had obtained a rifle and laid down fire continuously until the Japanese departed, at about 0815. Then he proceeded by automobile to Haleiwa, intent on taking to the air against the enemy.[22] For the time being, the engineers, mechanics, and armorers at Wheeler and Haleiwa Fields had done everything possible to gather pilots, prepare aircraft for flight, and send them aloft. Additional efforts would have to await available aircraft.

Chapter Eleven

"DISPERSE THE FLYABLE AIRCRAFT AND PREPARE THEM FOR LAUNCH"

Fighter Action over Oʻahu

Shortly before 0900, with Japanese aircraft of the second wave already in their attack runs elsewhere over Oʻahu, the dispersal area at Bellows Field was a beehive of activity. At least three of the 44th Pursuit Squadron's P-40s were all but ready, prompted by Lt. Kaneko Tadashi's brief attack one-half hour before. Three young lieutenants stood ready to take to the air. Samuel W. Bishop, the senior of the three, was communications officer for the 44th and had been appointed a 1st lieutenant only thirty-seven days earlier. Second Lt. George A. Whiteman, the squadron's assistant personnel officer, was one of the very few Army aviators who could boast that he had taken off from an aircraft carrier (the *Enterprise* on 21 February). Rounding out the threesome was 2nd Lt. Hans C. Christiansen, the unit's assistant engineering officer.

Whiteman's usual crew chief—SSgt. Edward J. "Ed" Covelesky—was not present, so SSgt. Homer Garcia stood in to oversee and complete the preparations. Fortuitously, the .30-caliber ammunition had been loaded the day before. A truck arrived with belts of .50-caliber ammunition, and the armorers standing by completed loading the nose guns on Whiteman's P-40, which was certainly "no sitting duck due to ammo."[1]

F/C Oscar B. Myers Jr., 18 March 1941, during flight training at Kelly Field. **NARA II, 18-PU-066-317-7918**

A different pilot reported to that aircraft, however. After picking up his parachute and life jacket, 2nd Lt. Oscar B. Myers Jr. ran to the plane he had been sharing with Whiteman during the previous week's training. Myers was a relatively junior lieutenant with only eighty-five hours in fighters after flight school. Just after Myers had settled into the seat and armorers had finished loading the .50-caliber ammunition, Whiteman appeared and told him to leave the cockpit. Though still a 2nd lieutenant, Whiteman had more than 450 total flying hours and had certainly qualified in gunnery, whereas Myers probably had not. In any case, the "youngster" climbed out of the cockpit, and Garcia helped the far more experienced Whiteman get in.[2]

The Second-Wave Attack at Bellows Field

The men at the Barracks Loop on the eastern end of the base had heard about the earlier "attack" by Lt. Kaneko Tadashi, but not all were aware of the general alarm. The single Japanese fighter had, however, prompted a sobering discussion by the field's Headquarters Detachment. Although the men had received no orders or direction, they concluded that it would be wise to leave the barracks and arm themselves. Pvt. Byron Kolbert and half a dozen men jumped into an old woodie station wagon and headed downhill toward the Armament Shack. They had just started down the slope from the Barracks Loop when they saw a formation of aircraft in what appeared to be groups of three approaching Bellows from over the Ko'olau Range. When the men were fifty yards from the Operations Building, the planes deployed for what obviously was an attack. The driver set the woodie's brakes, and the occupants tumbled out near the flight line and scurried for cover. Kolbert slithered under a gasoline tanker truck near the runway but thought better of it and scrambled behind the Operations Building. The men back at the Headquarters Detachment's barracks, lacking weapons to offer resistance, dove for cover, some in the kneeholes of their desks. Those brave enough to peer out the windows saw attackers who seemed to appear from all directions at once amid the hammering of machine-gun and cannon fire.[3]

JAPANESE TACTICS

What the American airmen had seen above them was the second-wave fighter unit as it deployed at 0930 to strafe Bellows Field. Lt. Nōno Sumio from

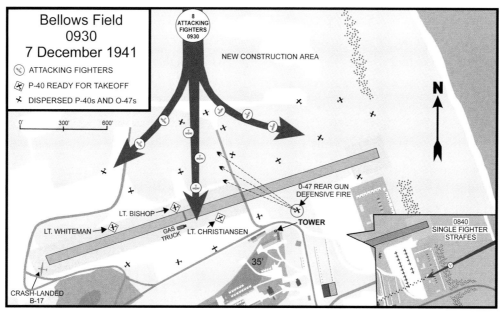

Deployment of the *Hiryū* fighter unit over Bellows Field. The positions of Christiansen, Whiteman, and Bishop are approximate. **Di Virgilio**

the *Hiryū* led the eight carrier fighters (of the nine original planes in the unit, the trailing pilot, F1c Chiyoshima Yutaka, had aborted due to mechanical problems shortly after takeoff).[4]

Although the *Hiryū*'s air group report is silent regarding Nōno's tactics, it is possible that the short-handed trailing *shōtai* under FPO1c Matsuyama Tsugio had instructions to suppress all takeoffs by the Americans, thus freeing the balance of the unit to strafe stationary targets at will. The initial Japanese deployment suggests such a division of labor; as Lieutenant Nōno led his fighters into the vicinity of Bellows from the north-northwest, his own lead *shōtai* continued south over the runway. Upon approaching the runway, the 2nd Shōtai under Lt. (jg) Shigematsu Yasuhiro broke left toward the ocean. The 3rd Shōtai under Matsuyama broke right and presumably set up attacks on the leeward end of the runway where any American pilot would have to taxi prior to takeoff. Assigned to stationary targets of opportunity, the remaining six aircraft formed—as described by one U.S. observer—a Lufbery Circle with three rounded corners. One side of the circle roughly paralleled the runway, and the other two served as routes in and out of the airfield. Scissoring back and forth over the core of the base, the two formations caught many targets in a crossfire that fueled the Americans' perception that the Japanese were coming in from all directions and there was no place to hide.[5]

With the overall objective of eliminating Bellows' fighters as a threat to bombardment units over other airfields and Pearl Harbor, the Japanese harried the men and machines on the ground with a vengeance. Fortunately, orders to disperse and arm all aircraft—including the P-40B/Cs of the 44th Pursuit Squadron—had followed the brief strafing of the first wave, and the six strafing carrier fighters had a difficult time locating suitable targets. One potential target stood out, however: a lone P-40 from the 44th sat fueled, armed, and ready to go near the runway in front of the Operations Building. Moments earlier, 2nd Lt. Hans Christiansen had been in the cockpit

2nd Lt. Hans C. Christiansen, probably while assigned to the 44th Pursuit Squadron in Hawai'i, in a lighter moment, perhaps at a picnic or lū'au. **Lambert via Stevens**

with mechanic Pvt. Elmer L. Rund perched next to him on the wing. As Christiansen looked northwest toward the mountains he saw a group of airplanes that appeared to be coming in from Wheeler Field. Rund slid off the wing, and Christiansen left the cockpit and followed him, perhaps intending to confer with the pilots after they landed. When the two men heard shouts that the inbound aircraft were attacking, the Japanese fighters were already over the base, firing as they came. Christiansen tried to reenter the cockpit, but gunfire struck him down. With blood spewing all over his Mae West, Christiansen fell backward off the wing and tumbled to the ground at the feet of his horrified mechanic. It appeared to Rund that his pilot had died almost instantly.[6]

Seconds before Christiansen met his end, George Whiteman settled into the cockpit of his P-40 on the opposite side of the runway with Homer Garcia in attendance. Someone nearby pointed up at what appeared to be a dozen aircraft approaching roughly from the direction of NAS Kaneohe Bay. Realizing that the field was about to come under attack, Garcia

Pvt. Elmer L. Rund at Wheeler Field, circa 1941. **Stevens**

shouted over the engine noise, "Here they come!" Whiteman yelled, "Yeah!" and gunned the engine. Garcia jumped off the wing and dove for cover under the bed of a two-and-a-half-ton truck, perhaps forgetting that the truck was loaded with crates of .50-caliber ammunition. With the enemy aircraft near and closing fast, he perceived only a space that offered refuge. First Lt. Sam Bishop was also in one of the dispersed positions to the north where mechanics and armorers were warming up the squadron's P-40s and installing guns and ammunition. When the *Hiryū* carrier fighters appeared, Bishop cut the arming process short, even though only the .30-caliber machine guns in one wing had been armed, and joined Whiteman in the frantic race to get into the air.[7]

Back near the Operations Shack, Private Rund was pinned down by the Zeroes' intense gunfire and forced to dodge from one side of the airplane's engine to the other, at one point even taking cover behind the wheels. Mechanic Sgt. Joseph Ra, who had been nearby when Christiansen fell, sheltered under the P-40's tail section. Amid the gunfire, both men

looked up and noticed a lone P-40 taxiing toward the land end of the runway. Second Lieutenant Whiteman had pushed the throttle forward as far as he dared to get to the end of the runway so he could take off.[8]

As Whiteman bravely taxied west, one of the Japanese fighter pilots—probably FPO1c Matsuyama or FPO1c Makinoda Toshio of the 3rd Shōtai—opened fire, and "clearly visible" tracers stabbed through the air toward Whiteman, who nevertheless managed to get airborne. After the P-40 took off, Garcia scooted to the other side of the truck bed "and saw Whiteman in an almost vertical left bank and turn, headed for the ground." The terrain blocked Garcia's view, so he did not see Whiteman's plane impact the ground. Braving machine-gun fire, men from Whiteman's crew ran toward the beach with a fifty-pound fire extinguisher in a vain attempt to douse the flames and save their pilot's life.[9]

SSgt. Ed Covelesky, Whiteman's assigned crew chief, had been standing atop one of Bellows' many sand dunes and *did* see the crash. As Whiteman lifted the nose of his P-40 away from the runway, he

F/C George A. Whiteman, 5 September 1940, during flight training at Kelly Field. **NARA II, 18-PU-099-497-6047**

presented a clear target to Matsuyama and Makinoda barreling in from behind. Tracers slammed into the top of the canopy. Almost immediately, the aircraft snapped its right wing almost straight up and arched into the dunes left of the runway. A black smoke plume typical of a high-octane gasoline explosion marked Whiteman's funeral pyre.[10]

Sam Bishop, still back on the runway, had more than enough problems of his own, and it is uncertain whether he knew that Whiteman had crashed. His anger was directed at the enemy and at the situation in general. Later, he remembered thinking at that moment, "This is a hell of a mess." Two carrier fighters—probably throttling back and/or scissoring

to avoid overtaking Bishop's slow-moving P-40—overshot him, and he fired at them as they passed by, "holding the trigger down all of the time because the planes were all around me." Finally off the runway and relieved when he could retract his landing gear and reduce drag, Bishop "hugged the water" on a flat trajectory, attempted to increase his speed, and turned north. Although Bishop's reasoning for the turn is unclear, he might have thought it better to be forced down in shallow water, or he may have been encouraging the Japanese to stay in their circulation pattern over Bellows, where they had bigger fish to fry than a solitary damaged fighter. The Japanese pilots—probably Matsuyama and Makinoda—stuck

1st Lt. Samuel W. Bishop, circa mid-1942, in the cockpit of another Pearl Harbor survivor, P-40B, A.C. Serial No. 41-13308, nominally assigned to the 19th Pursuit Squadron on 7 December 1941, though out of service in first-echelon maintenance at the time of the attack. The aircraft was in the second batch of P-40Bs that arrived in Hawai'i on the *Enterprise* in April 1941.
NARA II, 342-FH-3A-40712

to his tail, however, hurling a blizzard of bullets and cannon shells that repeatedly found their target. The Curtiss lost way and crashed into Kailua Bay about one-half mile offshore. Although he was almost knocked senseless by the crash, Bishop extricated himself before the fighter sank and commenced swimming ashore with (according to one account) a wound behind one knee. Because the Japanese continued to strafe the wreckage, it is unclear whether Bishop suffered the wound while airborne or after he crashed. He went into the water off Lanikai, just short of Nā Mokulua (the Twin Islands: Moku Nui and Moku Iki). Exhausted and in pain from a grazed arm (according to yet another account) and a wrenched back from the water landing, Bishop finally hobbled onto the beach. Local media on Oʻahu reported that a woman at Lanikai helped him ashore, administered first aid, and transported him to NAS Kaneohe Bay for treatment. Bishop returned to flight duty on 17 December.[11]

The courage exhibited by Christiansen, Whiteman, and Bishop inspired those who witnessed it on the ground and typified the behavior of Oʻahu's airmen. Despite such valor, however, the Japanese successfully suppressed all opposition by the Army pilots within minutes, leaving airmen on the ground with no option but to defend themselves, stay alive, and carry the fight to the enemy another day.

The previous incursion by Lieutenant Kaneko was a pinprick compared with this new, far heavier, and more sustained assault. Few of the men could offer more than token opposition to the enemy fighters above. Pvt. Earl Bigelow of the 86th Observation Squadron stood in front of his barracks and squeezed off twelve rounds at the attackers from his 1903 Springfield. When he heard someone yell, "Take cover!" he realized the recklessness of maintaining such an exposed position. "I ran to the nearest utility pole and hugged it. Adrenalin faded and my knees turned to rubber at that point."[12]

Other men were only now tumbling from their beds. Wrung out from partying at Hickam the previous evening, 2nd Lt. Phillip Willis slept though the initial strafing attack on Bellows. He knew something was wrong only when he heard machine-gun fire and bullets began penetrating the roof of his quarters. The dire situation became clear when he looked out the window and saw one of the base's fuel trucks afire on the flight line and Whiteman's P-40 burning in the dunes north of the runway. Thinking, "Us Texans like to die with our boots on," and still wearing his tuxedo trousers and shirt, he pulled his cowboy boots from his footlocker, donned his flight jacket and helmet, and ran outside to see carrier fighters from the *Hiryū* strafing the base against little or no opposition.[13]

Private Kolbert described Lieutenant Nōno's attacks as a systematic assault that made it impossible to emerge from cover: "We couldn't dare budge." Two men, however, took great risks in attempting to set up a .50-caliber Browning water-cooled machine gun outside the Armament Shack while the Japanese "spray[ed] the be-Jesus out of that area." As soon as one aircraft completed a pass, another was behind it seeking out targets. The enemy pilots even appeared to throttle back to make their ground-level runs at extremely slow speed. Kolbert stated later that it was like seeing a Piper Cub pull up. The attacks lasted for about fifteen minutes. Interestingly, there was no panic among the men; a generous helping of confusion—"you couldn't avoid confusion"—but no panic.[14]

Pfc. Raymond F. McBriarty had just loaded the flexible .30-caliber Browning in the rear cockpit of Maj. Charles B. Stewart's O-47B (1/86OS) near the parking area when Japanese planes appeared from the northwest and a *shōtai* of carrier fighters took the O-47 under fire. McBriarty jumped out of the cockpit and into the sand, then "tried to dig a hole with [his] hands, elbows and knees." Realizing that there was no place nearby that would offer protection, he reentered the O-47's rear cockpit and turned the .30-caliber Browning on the attackers. The ammunition he had just finished loading dated back to the early 1900s—ball only, no tracer, no armor-piercing,

Bellows Field, looking northeast, 1 October 1941, showing a portion of the runway and aircraft parking areas. One oral history indicates that, at night, crews usually drew the aircraft together between the runway (*left*) and the original tent cantonment of the Air Corps Range Camp (*upper right*). Note that a P-26 and O-47B are in that parking area rather than the area at lower left, where aircraft engaged in operations were parked during the day. The area at the top of the photo is where Pfc. Raymond McBriarty's O-47B sat when he opened fire on Japanese fighters from the *Hiryū*. **NARA II, 80-G-279366, cropped**

no incendiary. Wondering all the while what damage he was inflicting, McBriarty held his ground until the end of the attack, having fired about 450 rounds. He thought that he might have landed hits on the fuselage of one aircraft and on the engine of another. Pvt. William B. Burt—who had earlier helped McBriarty retrieve a generous supply of .30-caliber ammunition—mounted the rear cockpit of another O-47 and maintained fire throughout the strafing attack

as well, even though he had no previous gunnery training. Burt and McBriarty each received the Silver Star for their extraordinary bravery.[15]

The cumulative amount of damage the defenders inflicted on the *Hiryū* carrier fighters is unknown because the unit's air group report failed to specify the number of hits sustained by each aircraft. The report sent to Lt. Col. Edward M. Raley—intelligence officer for the Hawaiian Air Force—regarding

Second-Wave Attack on Bellows Field and NAS Kaneohe Bay
Hiryū Fighter Unit
Lt. Nōno Sumio

11th Shōtai	12th Shōtai	13th Shōtai
Lt. Nōno Sumio	Lt. (jg) Shigematsu Yasuhiro	FPO1c Matsuyama Tsugio
FPO1c Higashinaka Tatsuo	FPO1c Nishikaichi Shigenori	FPO1c Makinoda Toshio
FPO3c Nitta Haruo	FPO2c Todaka Noboru	F1c Chiyoshima Yutaka (abort)

Ens. Nōno Sumio, graduate of the 61st class at Etajima, during training with the 27th pilot class, circa 1935. At the time of the Hawaiian Operation, Nōno was a relative latecomer to carrier aviation, having been posted to the *Hiryū* on 1 November 1940. **Prange**

F1c Nishikaichi Shigenori during flight training, circa 1938. **USAR**

the events at Bellows stated that "one plane leaving was seen to be streaming gas from the belly tank." That aircraft was probably carrier fighter BII-120, piloted by FPO1c Nishikaichi Shigenori, who later crash-landed on Ni'ihau after failing to rendezvous with the submarine I-74. The skipper, Cdr. Ikezawa Masayuki, had taken station south of the island to rescue aircrews unable to return to their carriers.[16]

After Lieutenant Nōno's eight *Hiryū* pilots expended their ammunition and withdrew to the east, Staff Sergeant Covelesky ran to Lieutenant Whiteman's crash site. The P-40 had impacted at a rather flat angle, and very little remained of the plane but smoldering ashes. The "largest piece of wreckage could fit into a 50 gal[lon] drum." Covelesky located the P-40's instrument panel and found that a Japanese bullet had penetrated the center of the turn-and-bank indicator. Whiteman's charred remains were still strapped in the pilot's seat, the intense heat having burned away his extremities and exposed flesh. Covelesky helped the ambulance crew

lift the pilot's seat out of the plane and place it into the ambulance. The memory of the grotesque scene stayed with Covelesky for the rest of his life.[17]

SSgt. Cosmo R. Mannino of the 44th Pursuit Squadron wrote fifty years later that men on the ground at Bellows owed their lives to the bravery and sacrifice of Christiansen, Whiteman, and Bishop for diverting the Japanese away from the field. Some forty-three years after the attacks, Homer Garcia, Whiteman's stand-in crew chief, wrote: "Knowing the enemy was overhead and he had only one runway to use, Whiteman demonstrated [a] tremendous amount of courage in attempting to take off under those conditions. I will remember Whiteman if I live another 200 years."[18]

Action over Barbers Point and Ewa

Equally tense and dramatic events unfolded over the alluvial plain of southern O'ahu that separated Pearl Harbor and Barbers Point. Around 0900, dive-bombing units under the overall command of

Lt. Cdr. Egusa Takashige commenced their attacks on the Pacific Fleet in Pearl Harbor. Afterward they were to gather in two preliminary assembly areas prior to flying to the primary rendezvous area north of Ka'ena Point. The preliminary assembly for the *Akagi* and *Kaga* carrier bombers was ten nautical miles due west of Barbers Point; the units from the *Sōryū* and *Hiryū* were to assemble ten nautical miles north of NAS Kaneohe Bay. The pilots did not adhere strictly to these provisions, however. A number of the *Hiryū*'s kanbakus withdrew west rather than north and mixed with the bombers from the 1st Carrier Division. Along their flight path from Pearl Harbor toward Barbers Point lay the Ewa Mooring Mast Field, where Japanese intelligence indicated that the U.S. Navy based about eighty carrier-borne aircraft. The Marines' field at Ewa was too tempting a target for the withdrawing carrier bombers to pass up.[19]

The order in which the dive-bomber units arrived over Ewa is uncertain. By the time the second-wave aircraft drew off to the west, formation discipline had broken down. The chaos over the harbor and the effects of target selection fractured air organization even down to the shōtai level; the rendezvous off Barbers Point would provide ample opportunity to reset the formations. Hence, it is likely that the dive-bombers proceeded toward Ewa in small groups rather than reorganizing by chūtai prior to their arrival. Presumably the *Akagi*'s unit arrived first and *Hiryū*'s shortly thereafter, interleaving with the *Akagi* bombers. Those unfortunate enough to take up position in the rear soon found themselves in the gunsights of 2nd Lt. Kenneth Taylor and 2nd Lt. George Welch.[20]

After Taylor and Welch took off from Haleiwa in accordance with instructions from Fort Shafter, they climbed through a broken overcast at three thousand feet and vectored south toward Easy (Barbers Point) on O'ahu's southwest coast. They patrolled that area at eight thousand feet but "didn't see anything except a fire at Pearl Harbor." At that altitude and in the hazy conditions, details of Pearl Harbor ten miles distant—not to mention approaching enemy aircraft at low altitude—would have been difficult to discern.[21]

The dive-bombers that had attacked Pearl Harbor did not withdraw to the west and commence strafing runs over the Mooring Mast Field until 0905 or 0910 at the earliest. How long Taylor and Welch tarried at Barbers Point is uncertain. Assuming a takeoff time from Haleiwa of around 0840, it seems reasonable that they patrolled near Barbers Point from around 0845 until they "noticed twenty or thirty aircraft in a traffic pattern at Ewa, the Marine Landing field." They turned east as much to determine the nature of the aircraft as anything else. On the way to Ewa they saw a large, camouflaged bomber in the distance. Recollecting that the B-18s and B-17s at Hickam Field were in natural metal finish, they concluded that the aircraft was Japanese "and started after it." After pulling alongside the plane (possibly the B-17E of 1st Lt. Karl T. Barthelmess), they realized from the markings that it was friendly and returned their attention to the aircraft orbiting Ewa. "Our first thought was that the Marines were taking off to help us," Taylor later recalled. "But as we came close, we knew that these were Nips who . . . were strafing the field." The aircraft in the traffic pattern were Type 99 carrier bombers, fresh from their attacks on Pearl Harbor. Taylor and Welch roared in to intercept them.[22]

With Welch in the lead and Taylor six hundred feet back and to one side, the two Americans dove on a string of Japanese planes (which they now estimated to be a dozen aircraft) and wheeled around onto the end of the string. Taylor, perhaps on the inside of the turn, had practically pulled even with Welch when the pair attacked two trailing bombers from Lt. Nakagawa Shun's *Hiryū* unit. Welch targeted the trailing kanbaku piloted by F1c Fuchigami Kazuo with F1c Mizuno Yasuhiko in the observer's seat. Mizuno was so busy firing at the ground that he failed to detect the P-40B closing in behind. Welch sent a five-second burst into the Type 99, which he

View looking west down O'ahu's southern shore from Pearl Harbor, past the Ewa Mooring Mast Field at right center toward Barbers Point in the distance, 1 July 1941. It was in this airspace that 2nd Lt. Kenneth M. Taylor and 2nd Lt. George S. Welch intercepted Type 99 carrier bombers from the *Akagi*, *Kaga*, and *Hiryū*.
NARA II, 71-CA-171B-ENCL-C, cropped

later claimed "burned up right away"; in fact, the bomber had sustained only a punctured fuel tank. The *Hiryū*'s air group report indicates that Fuchigami nursed his stricken *kanbaku* back to the carrier with its fuel tank leaking like a sieve. Meanwhile, Taylor opened fire on a second *Hiryū* bomber thought to be crewed by pilot FPO2c Toyama Tsunayoshi and observer F1c Murao Hajime. "I let him have a short burst," Taylor reported. "I don't think I let him have more than fifteen rounds—and as he flamed he went into the most perfect slow roll I've ever seen" and impacted "the surf, right there on the beach."[23]

Interleaved with the *Hiryū* bombers were those of the *Akagi*'s under Lt. Chihaya Takehiko. George Welch quickly latched onto a carrier bomber in Lt. Abe Zenji's heretofore unscathed *chūtai*, that of pilot FPO2c Gotō Hajime and observer/rear-gunner FPO2c Utsuki Michiji. Utsuki unleashed a torrent of 7.7-millimeter bullets toward the P-40B charging in from behind. Welch gave the Japanese crew full credit: The "rear gunner was shooting at me. One bullet put a hole through my cooling radiator, and I got one in my prop and one in the nose"; an incendiary round passed "through the baggage compartment just in rear of [the] seat." With smoke pouring

from his engine, Welch pulled up above the clouds to assess the damage to his plane. The disappearance of Welch's smoking plane led the Japanese to conclude that Utsuki had scored a victory over his pursuer.[24]

Welch considered bailing out, but finding that his rudder still worked, and thinking that the Japanese might strafe him during his descent, he returned to the fight. By that time, however, the Japanese aircraft over Ewa "had scattered in all directions." Taylor, having lost track of Welch, now engaged Utsuki (who was still firing from the rear cockpit) and incapacitated him with his first burst of fire. Gotō took his smoking dive-bomber out over the water, and Taylor concluded that he could not bring it down (although in fact the aircraft *did* go down). Low on fuel and out of ammunition, Taylor elected to fly back to Wheeler, angry at himself for exhausting his .30-caliber ammunition at such an inopportune time. "With more ammunition, or more judicious use earlier, I could have destroyed several more of them," he later said. Intent on renewing the fight, Taylor continued to Wheeler to have his plane serviced, as did Welch.[25]

At least three other Japanese aircraft reported damage from the American fighters over Ewa. Lt. (jg) Ōbuchi Keizō, leading the 2nd Shōtai in Lieutenant

FPO2c Gotō Hajime, pilot, *Akagi* dive-bomber unit, Kagoshima Air Base, circa May 1941. **USAR 1673, cropped**

FPO2c Utsuki Michiji, observer, *Akagi* dive-bomber unit, Kagoshima Air Base, circa May 1941. **USAR 1673, cropped**

Abe's unit, conducted three strafing runs before he ran afoul of Taylor and Welch. Ōbuchi's Type 99 sustained multiple hits, including one that shattered the Plexiglas canopy directly over his head. Checking on the other crews in his *shōtai*, he noticed that FPO3c Iizuka Tokuji's aircraft was leaking fuel and ordered him to proceed back to the *Akagi* immediately. Lt. Ibuki Shōichi, leader of the *Kaga*'s 3rd Chūtai of carrier bombers, was headed toward the preliminary assembly area west of Barbers Point when he decided to attack Ewa. Suddenly, his observer, FPO1c Uchikawa Yūsuke, shouted through the voice tube, "Hit on the auxiliary electrical box!" Then, "Enemy fighter, port quarter, below!" Uchikawa fired at the attacker and instructed Ibuki to evade the enemy fire by turning right, but the American retreated as suddenly as he appeared. Lieutenant Ibuki again turned his attention to the airfield below, making two firing passes prior to turning west toward the primary rendezvous off Ka'ena Point.[26]

The saga of the air battle over Ewa had not yet played out for the crew of the stricken Type 99—brought down by Taylor—that crashed into the water just off Barbers Point. FPO2c Gotō, the pilot, survived the landing, but it is unclear whether FPO2c Utsuki did. In any case, Gotō escaped the wreckage and extracted Utsuki, who had done everything possible to protect his plane and pilot. After Gotō gained the beach, he buried his comrade, who was probably dead by the time Gotō got him ashore, in a shallow grave on the beach—so shallow that Utsuki's feet protruded from the sand. Gotō then went inland where observers on the ground conjectured that he wandered aimlessly among the kiawe trees near Barbers Point until soldiers from the 55th Coast Artillery Regiment confronted and killed him on 9 December.[27]

Combat over Ka'a'awa

Reinforcements for Taylor and Welch—though regrettably few in number—were on the way. Among the first to arrive was 2nd Lt. John L. "Johnny" Dains, who took off from Haleiwa shortly after Taylor and Welch did, sometime after 0840. Apart from fragmentary details gleaned from individuals at Haleiwa and Wheeler Fields and an incomplete

7 December entry on his December IFR, very little is known of Dains' activities once he was in the air. That lack of concrete information has fueled debate for decades concerning the specifics of Dains' actions that day.

The most likely scenario is that, after takeoff, Dains attempted to chase a *Zuikaku* dive-bomber that had strafed Haleiwa. With the *kanbaku* accelerating away from the field, Dains would have given up hope of pursuit almost immediately. Assuming that he had his radio on, Dains might well have heard chatter regarding Bellows Field (also heard later by 2nd Lt. Harry Brown) and flew generally toward Bellows and Pearl Harbor. Dains arrived in time to see and pursue a carrier bomber from the 2nd Carrier Division just as the plane exited the harbor after the second-wave attack. He shot down the bomber off Ka'a'awa on the windward shore. Quite likely the

bomber was headed toward the preliminary rendezvous point for the *Sōryū* and *Hiryū* carrier bombers approximately ten miles north of NAS Kaneohe Bay. Dains had sufficient time for the air combat near Ka'a'awa and a quick flight into Wheeler to replenish fuel and/or ammunition prior to the 0930 arrival of carrier bombers from the *Kaga*.[28]

Among the few surviving details regarding Dains' activity is the account of then-Pvt. Philippe A. Michaud. In the predawn hours at Ka'a'awa on O'ahu's windward shore, men from the SCAWH (Signal Company, Aircraft Warning, Hawaii) were operating station 7CU, one of the mobile SCR-270 radar units on O'ahu. Their radar was to cover a pie-shaped area extending roughly north and east. The schedule at the site called for the men to operate their equipment only from 0400 to 0700. Lack of manpower was not the sole reason for the short

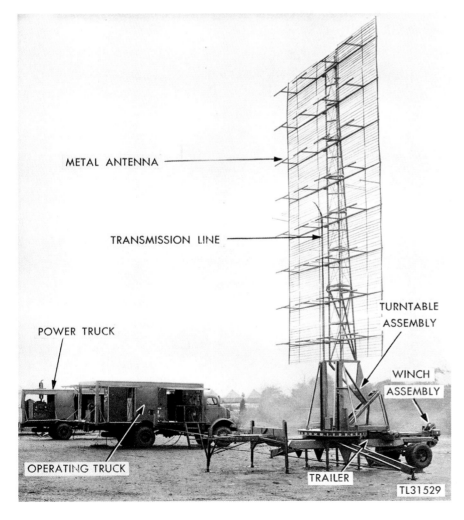

METAL ANTENNA

TRANSMISSION LINE

POWER TRUCK

TURNTABLE ASSEMBLY

WINCH ASSEMBLY

OPERATING TRUCK

TRAILER

TL31529

SCR-270 mobile radar unit, circa 1941. Although the unit was indeed "mobile," transporting and erecting it, particularly in rough terrain, posed challenges. Note the azimuth indicator at the base of the radar's "bedspring" antenna. To change the direction of the 20-degree swath the radar was viewing, the antenna had to be rotated manually to the new azimuth. Thus, tracking targets was a cumbersome process, particularly if the target was moving perpendicular to the antenna's azimuth. "Sweep" radars providing a 360-degree view were not yet available. **Wenger**

operating hours. Power for the station came from an onsite generator that required daily maintenance, and the Hawaiian Department had curtailed the hours of use for fear that major components might fail. Replacement parts would have to be shipped all the way from Fort Monmouth, New Jersey.[29]

After the men at Ka'a'awa shut down their radar set for the day at 0700 on 7 December, they reported to their mess tent for breakfast. Later, the sound of "planes maneuvering as in a dog fight overhead" attracted their attention. They concluded that a couple of pilots were out having fun on a Sunday morning but nevertheless went outside for a look. The glare of the early morning sun made locating the planes difficult. The aerial maneuvering gradually moved seaward, with one aircraft clearly chasing the other. When the air action had moved perhaps a mile or so offshore, Private Michaud and the others heard bursts of machine-gun fire. "One of the men remarked, 'Boy, those guys are really not fooling around.'" At that juncture "the plane being chased threw out a puff of smoke and went downward, crashing into the sea, perhaps 3/4 of a mile beyond the reef." As soon as the plane went down, its pursuer "hightailed it westward over the [Ko'olau] Range." The pursuer was Dains, and his victim may have been a Type 99 carrier bomber from the *Sōryū* crewed by pilot FPO3c Maruyama Kenji and observer/plane commander FPO2c Kuwabara Hideyasu.

The sergeant in charge of the radar station decided that the incident warranted a report to the Information Center at Fort Shafter and went off to make the call. Just before the sergeant returned, the phone rang in the radar unit's operating truck. The voice on the other end shouted, "Get back on the air! Pearl Harbor is under attack!" While the men scurried back to their posts, Johnny Dains headed back over the mountains to have his P-40B serviced at Wheeler Field.[30]

Back across the island at Haleiwa Field, meanwhile, the mechanics and armorers of the 47th Pursuit Squadron labored feverishly to ready

additional aircraft for flight. Second Lt. Harry Brown was in line for the next available plane, 1st Lt. Bob Rogers—as acting squadron commander—having decided to stay on the ground temporarily to take charge of the field. First Lt. John J. Webster arrived sometime after 0830 and was also ready to take off. While details regarding the order and times of take-off are unclear, the probable sequence was Brown (P-36A), Webster (P-40B), and Rogers (P-36A), with each pilot taking off separately subsequent to 0900 as soon as his fighter was ready to go.[31]

Meanwhile, the first three pilots airborne from Haleiwa, all flying P-40Bs, sought fuel and ammunition at Wheeler Field, which was by all accounts "a complete wreck." Dains, likely the first to arrive, informed one of the armorers that he had been in combat, and the armorer noted damage to the P-40. Whether Dains took on fuel in addition to ammunition is unclear. Dains took off on his second sortie of the day just as 2nd Lt. George Welch landed. Welch's plane had taken battle damage as well, though more serious than Dains'. Accounts disagree as to whether Welch received a new aircraft because the radiator in his old one was damaged. SSgt. William G. "Bill" Temple Jr., a mechanic with the 19th Pursuit, later maintained that there was another P-40 available—serviced, fueled, and armed—and that Welch switched aircraft. Another narrative states that after Welch landed, a member of the ground crew asked him what he needed; he indicated ammunition only and received instructions to taxi down the apron—probably to Hangar 3 or 4—to have his ammunition replenished.[32]

By that time, Taylor had also landed. After fueling from Wheeler's Aqua system, he taxied his P-40B alongside Welch's to get ammunition, then jumped out of the cockpit and retrieved a set of coveralls. While Welch took a cigarette break, SSgt. Augustine Malachoski, Pfc. Stuart W. Sweeney, and SSgt. Paul R. Cipriano—all armorers from the 19th Pursuit Squadron—armed Welch's P-40 with .50-caliber belts retrieved from Hangar 3. Other mechanics whose planes had been destroyed by the Japanese were using "every means possible to disperse flyable aircraft and prepare them for launch," but they also pitched in to prepare the two fighters just landed.[33]

Sources disagree regarding the type of ammunition the armorers loaded into the two P-40s. Pvt. Harry P. Kilpatrick, a munitions worker with the 741st Ordnance Company, maintained that he rearmed the aircraft just in from Haleiwa with .30-caliber ammunition only, and that no .50-caliber ammunition was available. SSgt. Bill Temple insisted that the reverse was true. Taylor himself later said that he had only one .30-caliber gun firing because the armorers had installed only one of the boxes of .30-caliber underneath the wings. While the root cause of the ordnance problems is uncertain, confusion, time constraints, and shortage of armorers, ammunition, and boxes could all have played a part.[34]

Wheeler Field
TAYLOR AND WELCH BATTLE
KAGA'S CARRIER BOMBERS

As Dains, Taylor, and Welch were being fueled and armed at Wheeler, SSgt. David I. Walsh, a clerk with the 19th Pursuit Squadron, arrived on the base, having convinced his brother-in-law (employed at the Pearl Harbor Navy Yard) to drop him off on the way to work. Walsh's brother-in-law virtually pushed him out the door before racing on to Pearl Harbor. Dumped unceremoniously at Wheeler's gate, Walsh found that the field was under strafing attack.[35]

At about 0930 or shortly thereafter, an unknown number of *kanbaku*s from the *Kaga*'s dive-bombing unit under Lt. Makino Saburō appeared south of Wheeler and commenced strafing the field, coming in from Pearl Harbor, south to north. As the ground crews shouted, "The Japs are coming back again!" both Taylor and Welch sat tensely in their P-40s, ready to take off as soon as crews completed arming them. Welch was the first to get back into the air. An east or west takeoff would have put him at a nearly

fatal disadvantage, as the Japanese needed only to have turned right or left to pull onto his tail. Hence, Welch took off south, *directly into the Japanese aircraft*. He went into a "full throttle climb for about three minutes in a low turn to the left." A Japanese bomber cut in behind Welch, who could see tracers whizzing by, but he managed to shake off the attack and outclimb the enemy.

Armorers from the 19th Pursuit Squadron—including SSgt. John L. Palinkas—had just started loading .30-caliber ammunition into Taylor's P-40B when the Japanese appeared. Palinkas was still crouching atop one of the wings arming a machine gun when Taylor opened the throttle. Palinkas tumbled backward off the wing and landed on his head, knocked unconscious. In the rush to get airborne, Taylor collided with the ammunition dolly in front of the aircraft, slightly damaging his right wing. Following Welch's lead, he took off directly into the oncoming Japanese.[36]

Struggling to get airborne, Taylor opened fire on the approaching string of *kanbaku*s even before his tail was off from the ground; fortunately for him, the Japanese could not depress the noses of their planes sufficiently to get off shots without crashing into the ground. After lifting away from the landing mat, Taylor pulled up into a chandelle and reversed course to come in behind what he *thought* was "the last airplane in the string." Taylor opened fire and discovered that only one of his six machine guns—a .30-caliber wing gun—was firing, but pressed home his attack nonetheless. The Japanese pilot banked into a series of wrenching turns before further "evasive action and pull[ing] up in a steep climb." At almost that instant, Lt. Makino Saburō—who was either the last pilot in the string or had come to the aid of his subordinate—pulled in behind Taylor and opened fire with his forward-firing 7.7-millimeter machine guns. "One bullet came through the canopy," Taylor remembered later, "through my left arm and shattered on the stabilizer control putting several fragments in my leg."[37]

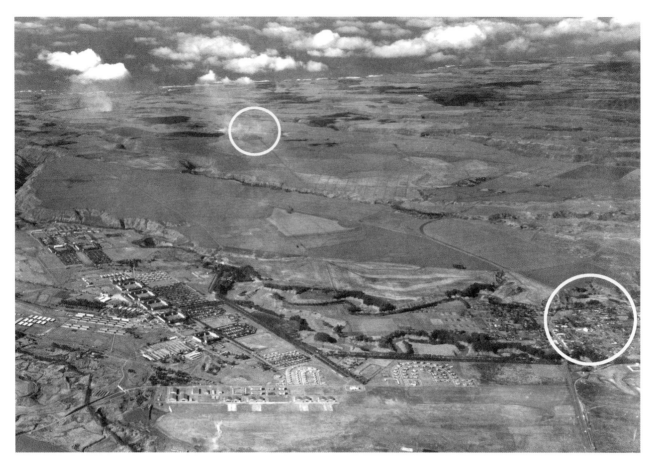

View from eight thousand feet on 23 January 1936, looking north-northwest across Wheeler Field in the foreground, Schofield Barracks at the center left, and the Pacific Ocean in the distance. It was in this airspace that Taylor and Welch intercepted Type 99 carrier bombers from the *Kaga*. The town of Wahiawā (*circled*) is at far lower right. The location of Brodie Camp No. 4 (*left circled area*) is more difficult to pinpoint. If one looks above the center of Wheeler Field's flight line toward the top of the image, the light patch just right of two cloud shadows is Brodie Camp No. 4, matching the location shown in Army and census maps of the time. **NARA II, 342-FH-3B-21437, cropped**

George Welch's climbing turn to the left had brought Taylor into view. From his position behind and about one thousand feet above, Welch could see that his squadronmate was in serious trouble and dove to the attack. He closed on Makino so rapidly that he had to lower his flaps to avoid overshooting him. It seemed to Welch that Makino's rear gunner (WO Sukida Sueo) "was obviously taking movies" and was completely oblivious to the American fighter charging in from above and behind. Once alerted to the danger, Sukida switched from camera to machine gun, opened fire, and sent bullets into Welch's engine, cowling, and propeller. Welch returned fire, and Makino's dive-bomber burst into flames and crashed in the vicinity of 717 Neal Avenue in Wahiawā, near

the town's power substation and adjacent CCC camp. Now free to concentrate on the carrier bomber ahead, Taylor gave chase and with a single working machine gun sent the Type 99 careening down north of Schofield Barracks into Brodie Camp No. 4, about five miles northwest of Wahiawā. Then, bleeding from his wounds, he pulled up into the overcast for safety, disgusted with himself for having focused too intently on the target ahead and becoming a target himself.[38]

Welch would later acknowledge that Lieutenant Makino's bomber might have sustained damage while the observer was filming over Wheeler ("three or four hundred men were shooting at him"), so it is plausible that Welch administered only the coup de grâce. Other men in the vicinity of Wahiawā

Lt. Makino Saburō, circa 1941. **Makino**

unquestionably played a role in the destruction of Makino's bomber. Earlier in the attack, Sgt. Lowell V. Klatt of the Headquarters Battery, 98th Coastal Artillery Regiment had left Schofield Barracks with a convoy of trucks to set up the regiment's command post in the CCC camp just south of Wahiawā. While the men prepared their position, Lt. Stephen G.

Saltzman arrived and related news of the attack and said that it was "the real thing, boys."[39]

While Sergeant Klatt's detail set up a switchboard, telephones, and other equipment, two aircraft pulled out of a dive "right over Kam Highway so that they headed directly into us to strafe us." Saltzman seized a Browning Automatic Rifle (BAR) from one of the enlisted men, and Klatt did the same. With a high-tension line to their backs, the two Americans knelt and prepared to open fire on the approaching *kanbaku*s. The two pilots peeled away in opposite directions—the leading plane to the right and the trailing aircraft to the left. Saltzman and Klatt were unable to fire at the first aircraft, but when the second plane pulled left and "swung right around broadside," the pair "cut loose with the Browning automatics." A few seconds later the men below heard the impact of the plane striking the ground and then a loud explosion, though they did not see the bomber crash because a building behind them obstructed their view. With no other enemy aircraft in evidence, the men ran around the building and saw wreckage and burning aviation fuel spread over a wide area. The intense heat precluded any close examination of the wreck until the fire burned itself out.[40]

2nd Lt. Stephen G. Saltzman (*left*) and SSgt. Lowell V. Klatt (*right*) after receiving Silver Stars from Brig. Gen. Harold F. Nichols at Schofield Barracks, 12 March 1942. **Borozny**

The lot near 717 Neal Avenue where Lt. Makino Saburō's Type 99 carrier bomber crashed after it was shot down by Welch, Saltzman, and Klatt. View looking west from the south side of Neal Avenue. The burned framework of at least one structure is visible in the background at center, and the burned-out wreck of an automobile (probably a 1937 Chevrolet four-door sedan) is on the left. The aircraft's engine is on the right, and the charred remains of one of the crew lie at the lower right center. The railroad crossing sign in the distance and the residence (still extant) at the far right with its distinctive exterior siding are key to interpreting this photo. **AFHRA**

The engine of Lieutenant Makino's aircraft at 717 Neal Avenue, view looking southwest. **AFHRA**

Wreckage thought to be from the Type 99 carrier bomber shot down by 2nd Lieutenant Taylor over Brodie Camp No. 4, five miles northwest of Wahiawā. Note the subcomponent data plate with the Aichi airframe serial number 3133, which may have been mounted to the exposed connection point of one of the two horizontal stabilizers. The proposed association with the Brodie Camp crash is because the artifact shows no signs of fire damage, whereas the wreckage from 717 Neal Avenue showed extensive fire damage. **AFHRA**

The frantic aerial action near Wheeler Field led Taylor and Welch in different directions, though they would reunite later in the day. Taylor landed at Wheeler to have his guns checked and ask for a full load of ammunition. He taxied onto the apron, where 1st Lt. Everett Stewart had been directing salvage efforts. Seeing that Taylor was wounded, Stewart asked him to get out of the plane. Taylor refused: "I'm going to stay in here because if I get out of here, you'll take my aircraft." Stewart forthrightly replied, "You're absolutely right! That's what I want!" Stewart intended to tell Taylor he should go to the Dispensary but never had the opportunity, for Maj. William R. "Wild Bill" Morgan, commander of the 18th Pursuit Group, leapt onto Taylor's wing and ordered him to go after the Japanese who were withdrawing from the center of action. Despite the pain of his bloodied arm and thigh, Taylor obeyed, leaving 1st Lieutenant Stewart standing on the sidelines.[41]

After takeoff, Taylor ventured northwest and came across another *kanbaku* from the *Kaga* (probably en route to the primary rendezvous area) approximately five miles off Oʻahu's leeward shore, north-northwest of Haleiwa Field. Taylor's machine-gun fire damaged the Japanese craft so

badly that there could be little doubt it went down, with the crew probably choosing *jibaku* (self-destruction) as an alternative to simply running out of fuel and ditching or succumbing to mechanical failure. Unable to bring the *kanbaku* down and not

2nd Lt. Kenneth M. Taylor, 47th Pursuit Squadron, at Wheeler Field, probably soon after his arrival on 3 June 1941. **Cressman**

2nd Lt. George S. Welch, 47th Pursuit Squadron, at Wheeler Field on 6 March 1941, thirteen days after he flew his aircraft off the *Enterprise* on 21 February.
Cressman

wishing to press his luck once again, Taylor returned to O'ahu and claimed a probable kill. He closed out his aerial action over O'ahu by returning to Haleiwa late in the morning. When he came in to land and saw "two enormous bombers sitting on our landing strip," he thought that the Japanese had landed and taken control of the field. But he soon discovered that they were B-17s (Chaffin's and Carmichael's B-17Es) that had sought refuge from the attacks at Hickam and elsewhere. Welch, meanwhile, with fuel and ammunition to spare, flew south from Wheeler toward the Ewa Mooring Mast Field and Barbers Point, where he found another Japanese aircraft. He pursued the enemy plane and shot it down five miles off the coast. After patrolling for fifteen to twenty minutes, Welch returned to Haleiwa Field. Both pilots received the Distinguished Service Cross.[42]

Kāne'ohe Bay

On the windward side of O'ahu, four other Army pilots from the 46th Pursuit Squadron would engage the enemy under daunting circumstances.

THE 46TH PURSUIT SQUADRON ENGAGES THE ENEMY

At approximately 0900, the *Sōryū* fighter unit of nine *kansens* under Lt. Iida Fusata arrived over O'ahu and set the stage for the upcoming air battle. Patrols over the eastern portion of the island at about six thousand meters ensured that bombing attacks on NAS Kaneohe Bay by eighteen Type 97 attack bombers from the *Shōkaku* would proceed unhindered by American interceptors. Lieutenant Iida was unable to get his fighters into action over Kaneohe until after 0915 because he was waiting for the bombers (delayed by an aborted run) to clear the area. The smoke boiling out of the naval air station proved such an impediment that, when he did get the strafing attacks under way, after only two runs Iida summoned his fighters, signaled them to form, and led them down the coast to Bellows Field. After two quick firing passes with no results (perhaps only watching the *Hiryū* fighters still engaged over Bellows), Iida formed his men for the flight to the rendezvous point. In the earlier action over NAS Kaneohe Bay, however, defensive fire had holed Lieutenant (jg) Fujita Iyozō's left wing and damaged two of the three aircraft in the trailing 3rd Shōtai. While passing north toward Kaneohe, Fujita noticed thin white lines of aviation fuel trailing behind two fighters from the lead *shōtai* as well—those of FPO1c Atsumi Takashi and Lieutenant Iida. Subsequent to 0930, with the squadron fortunate to have all its pilots alive, Iida directed his group toward Kāne'ohe Bay and commenced climbing, intent on leading his men up to two thousand meters.[43]

During the return flight to Kāne'ohe Bay, however, Lieutenant Iida realized that American ground fire had punctured what was likely his main fuel tank. With his plane venting its precious fuel to the rear, and knowing that a return to his carrier was impossible, Iida doubtless remembered a vow he made back on board the *Sōryū*: were he disabled and unable to return, he would self-destruct by crashing his aircraft into some suitable ground target. Drawing close to his concerned comrades, Iida communicated via hand signals—a finger pointing to his mouth (meaning "fuel") and a wave of his hand in front of his face that indicated his fuel was nearly exhausted. Iida pointed to himself and then the ground—an unmistakable signal that he intended to die attacking the target area—then executed a half roll and dove determinedly straight for the station while his subordinates watched in horror. With hot tears coursing down his cheeks, Fujita watched the friend and shipmate whom he "loved like a brother" dive toward Kaneohe. Iida's comrades "felt weak and helpless," knowing they could do nothing to dissuade him from his chosen fate.[44]

On the ground, meanwhile, sailors at the Armory at NAS Kaneohe Bay noticed a lone fighter coming back over the station. Seeing that the diving aircraft was venting fuel in a manner similar to one that had departed minutes before, one of the sailors seized a BAR from another man, opened fire, and emptied the magazine at the incoming carrier fighter, which was "in a constantly descending line of flight" as if the pilot intended to crash-dive into the Armory from

the south, firing as he came. The fighter ceased firing as it passed over the Armory, inverted, and continued in a gradual descent until it struck the ground.[45]

After 0940, meanwhile, a shaken and saddened Fujita gathered a portion of the splintered command he had inherited from Lieutenant Iida. In the formation that coalesced at about two thousand meters off NAS Kaneohe Bay, Fujita fronted a new lead *shōtai*, with his original wingmen FPO1c Takahashi Sōzaburō and FPO2c Okamoto Takashi behind and to the left and right, respectively. Lieutenant Iida's orphans—FPO1c Atsumi Takashi (still venting fuel) and FPO2c Ishii Saburō—formed a two-plane *shōtai* in echelon left to the rear of Takahashi. The 3rd Shōtai with its damaged aircraft was nowhere in sight, though perhaps struggling to assemble at a lower altitude some distance away. With the final drama in the skies over Kāneʻohe Bay about to unfold, the men at the naval air station below failed to recognize the coming air battle for what it was—the largest fighter-versus-fighter engagement over Oʻahu on that day of infamy.[46]

Lt. Iida Fusata, commander of the *Sōryū* second-wave fighter unit, circa 1940. **Lansdale**

Lt. Fujita Iyozō, probably around the time of his promotion and assignment to the air group on board the aircraft carrier *Hiyō*, circa July 1942. **Fujita**

The Americans Rise to Intercept

Earlier, somewhat before 0930, after executing a downwind takeoff from Wheeler Field, 1st Lt. Lewis Sanders' four P-36As reversed course with a left-hand turn, headed east-southeast, and clawed for altitude. Although there is no known indication that Sanders received any instructions regarding his objective, pillars of smoke rolling skyward from the vicinity of Pearl Harbor drew the flight in that general direction. Sanders probably kept the fighters on a course to position them north of the harbor but far enough away to allow them to use the clouds spilling over the Koʻolau Range as cover.[47]

Sanders then radioed the Information Center at Fort Shafter for orders. The controller, Maj. Lorry N. Tindal, reported "many bogeys over Bellows heading north." Although contemporary doctrine would have led Sanders to venture toward one of the eight well-defined points along Oʻahu's coastline as set forth in the department's *Interceptor Command Manual*, Sanders instead shaped a course toward Bellows Field, bearing 100 degrees, magnetic, converging with the clouds over the Koʻolau Range north of Honolulu. At two thousand feet, Sanders climbed into a layer of broken overcast and closed his intervals to maintain visual contact in the clouds. About a mile east of Bellows Field the fighters "[broke] out of ragged clouds at 8,500 feet"—clouds that probably

1st Lt. Lewis M. Sanders, commander of the 46th Pursuit Squadron, on a visit to Mount Haleakalā, circa late 1941. **Stevens, cropped**

prevented the pilots from seeing the last action over that location during their passage from the west. Seeing no enemy in the vicinity, Sanders remembered Major Tindal's advisory that the bogeys were heading north from that location. Probably unwilling to trade altitude to get a better look at Bellows below the overcast, Sanders led the flight of four P-36As into a climb "at near full throttle." From east

Interception over Kāneʻohe Bay
Sōryū Fighter Unit
Lt. Iida Fusata

1st Shōtai	2nd Shōtai	3rd Shōtai
Lt. Iida Fusata	Lt. (jg) Fujita Iyozō	FPO1c Oda Kiichi
FPO1c Atsumi Takashi	FPO1c Takahashi Sōzaburō	FPO2c Tanaka Jirō
FPO2c Ishii Saburō	FPO2c Okamoto Takashi	FPO3c Takashima Takeo

Hiryū Fighter Unit

13th Shōtai
FPO1c Matsuyama Tsugio
FPO1c Makinoda Toshio

2nd Lt. Gordon H. Sterling Jr., 46th Pursuit Squadron, on a visit to Mount Haleakalā, circa late 1941. **Stevens**

2nd Lt. John M. Thacker, 46th Pursuit Squadron, after receiving the Silver Star at Wheeler Field, 25 March 1942. **Aiken, NMPW, cropped**

of Bellows the four Americans continued generally northwest toward NAS Kaneohe Bay and leveled out at 11,000 feet.[48]

Sanders and company had probably charged their guns either shortly after takeoff or upon emerging from the clouds near Bellows Field to prepare for instant action. Second Lieutenant Rasmussen ran into difficulties when he pulled back the right-hand charging handle for the .30-caliber machine gun to load the first round. When he attempted to fire, the gun was jammed. Repeating the process failed to clear the jam, and he concluded that he "had a dead gun." Frustrated, Rasmussen pivoted to the left handle for the .50-caliber machine gun, drew it out, and released it, whereupon the gun began to fire on its own. He was carrying only two hundred rounds for the left-hand .50-caliber, so he quickly drew the charging handle back to its locked position to stop the runaway Browning from firing.[49]

Very soon after leveling out after crossing the Koʻolaus on his approach to NAS Kaneohe Bay, Sanders saw "eleven enemy planes climbing several

thousand feet below." When 2nd Lt. John Thacker put down the nose of his fighter and leveled out, he too glimpsed Lieutenant (jg) Fujita's planes near the naval air station. They were positioned (except for their high altitude) "like they were on a base leg for the airfield." Providentially, the four Americans were interposed between the sun and Fujita's climbing Zeroes. Sanders seized that opportunity and used it to maximum advantage, maneuvering to maintain his relative position and preserve the element of surprise.[50]

The time had come for Sanders to order the attack. Reluctant to use his radio near the Japanese planes, Sanders rocked his wings, signaling his men

Wheeler Field
46th Pursuit Squadron

1st Lt. Lewis M. Sanders

2nd Lt. Gordon H. Sterling Jr. (vice Norris)

2nd Lt. John M. Thacker

2nd Lt. Philip M. Rasmussen

---

to pull in close. As the formation tightened, Sanders was shocked to see that 2nd Lt. Gordon Sterling, "an inexperienced newly assigned youngster," had taken the place of the seasoned and well-qualified Othniel Norris as 2nd Lieutenant Thacker's wingman. Norris had logged 166 hours in P-36s and 52 in P-40s while Sterling had only 98 and 28 hours respectively in those aircraft; further, Sterling had failed to progress as rapidly as the other new pilots in formation flying and—more important—gunnery. "I couldn't imagine why he was there instead of Norris," Sanders later said.[51]

It is unclear when Sanders reshuffled his formation and ordered Sterling to switch places with Rasmussen, but the least experienced pilot always flew as the flight leader's wingman. Under the circumstances Sanders could do no more; the flight was committed to the attack. When John Thacker pulled alongside to the left, Sanders pointed down to indicate that the left element was to attack the two Japanese aircraft (numbers three and four) left of the

2nd Lt. Philip M. Rasmussen, 46th Pursuit Squadron, 17 December 1941. Cropped from a larger image showing Sanders, Rasmussen, Taylor, Welch, and Brown before the general orders from 5 January 1942 (Taylor and Welch), 18 March 1942 (Rasmussen), and 30 March 1942 (Sanders and Brown) that awarded each pilot with the Distinguished Service Cross or Silver Star. **HWRD, cropped**

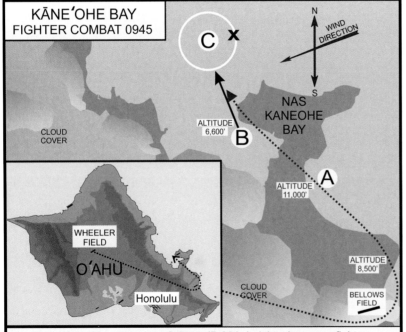

KĀNE'OHE BAY
FIGHTER COMBAT 0945

WIND DIRECTION

N

S

C X

NAS KANEOHE BAY

ALTITUDE 6,600'

B

A

ALTITUDE 11,000'

CLOUD COVER

WHEELER FIELD

O'AHU

Honolulu

CLOUD COVER

ALTITUDE 8,500'

BELLOWS FIELD

A. Formation of four American fighters (P-36As) sights Japanese fighters
B. Formation of six Japanese fighters (Type 0 carrier fighters)
C. Area of aerial dogfight
X. Crash site of 2nd Lt. Gordon Sterling

1st Lt. Lewis M. Sanders' route from Wheeler Field and approach to Kāne'ohe Bay. Sanders was unaware that the *Sōryū*'s 3rd Shōtai was attempting to join Fujita—possibly approaching from a position over the water south of NAS Kaneohe Bay. **Di Virgilio**

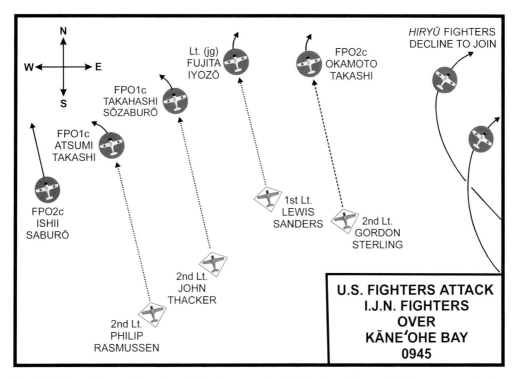

The initial disposition and targeting of the two opposing fighter formations—P-36As commanded by 1st Lieutenant Sanders and Type 0 carrier fighters commanded by Lieutenant (jg) Fujita. Note that the two fighters from the *Hiryū* turned away just before joining, and that FPO2c Ishii played no known role in the action. **Aiken, adapted by Di Virgilio**

leader. Thacker pulled away to the left to confirm the targeting, then closed back in and nodded that he understood. Leaving Thacker to pass instructions to his new wingman Philip Rasmussen, Sanders turned to Sterling on his right, pointed down, held up one finger, and pointed at himself to indicate that he would attack the leader, and that Sterling was to take on the number two Japanese aircraft on the right. The Americans were in position for a textbook attack, blindsiding Fujita out of the sun from above and behind. Roaring toward the Japanese fighters, the P-36s closed rapidly on the enemy formation "from about level flight," entered a shallow dive at nearly maximum throttle, and picked up speed as they closed on Fujita's planes.[52]

Sanders observed sudden movement among the Japanese planes and suspected the enemy pilots had detected his approach. More likely, Fujita had changed course to accommodate what he thought was the late arrival of FPO1c Oda Kiichi's 3rd Shōtai.

The aircraft approaching Fujita's formation, however, were from the *Hiryū*'s trailing *shōtai*—FPO1c Matsuyama and wingman FPO1c Makinoda, who in turn probably expected that they had found carrier fighters from the *Hiryū*. Just before joining Fujita in echelon right on the formation's right side, they saw the single blue fuselage band on an adjacent aircraft and realized that the fighters were from the *Sōryū*. Matsuyama and Makinoda quickly parted company to hunt for their remaining *Hiryū* comrades while Lew Sanders' flight charged down out of the sun.[53]

INTERCEPTION!

As the engagement opened, Rasmussen said more than sixty years later, "We just exploded into dogfighting." The Japanese formation disintegrated, as did that of the Americans, with Sanders, Sterling, Thacker, and Rasmussen pursuing their assigned targets in diverging directions. Maps and information that Thacker provided to David Aiken in 1986 indicate that, initially, the engagement seems to have developed in two areas—a turning dogfight to the west, almost bordering the shore of Oʻahu (Thacker and Rasmussen), and a twisting, diving pursuit farther east, completely over the water (Sanders and Sterling).[54]

FPO2c Ishii Saburō—presumably with a badly damaged fighter—did not participate in the fight; he retired and continued toward the rendezvous. Sanders and Sterling probably scored hits on their first passes, because they had clean shots from dead astern against "non-maneuvering aircraft." Sanders opened fire on Fujita, scoring hits on his fuselage. With smoke drifting aft from his engine compartment and left side, the startled Fujita held steady momentarily and then pulled his staggering fighter up and to the right, perhaps hoping that the American would overshoot. Sanders misinterpreted that movement as a stall and pulled up. At that instant, Thacker and Rasmussen roared underneath Fujita's decelerating *kansen* in pursuit of Takahashi and Atsumi. Sanders, having extended past the enemy formation, leveled off quickly and careened into a tight 270-degree turn to the left to clear his tail. Meanwhile, Sterling chased FPO2c Okamoto, who broke right. After separating to the east farther out over the water, Okamoto entered a nearly vertical dive to evade his pursuer. Having begun his attack out of a shallow but accelerating dive, Sterling's speed probably matched Okamoto's, and the Japanese was unable to shake the American firing from above and behind. Seconds later Fujita—having eluded Sanders' initial attack—did a wingover to the right and saw his wingman Okamoto with a P-36 in hot pursuit. Fujita gave chase to rescue his squadronmate and pulled in behind Gordon Sterling.[55]

Out to the west, Sanders' left element (Thacker and Rasmussen) entered a futile turning battle with Fujita's trailing *shōtai*. Thacker's guns jammed before he was able to score hits on FPO1c Takahashi. He attempted repeatedly to clear the jams while "recharging [the guns] continuously as [he] faked it

and went around with the Japs" in a toothless subterfuge destined to fail. As for Rasmussen, although the degree to which he could truly pursue FPO1c Atsumi is uncertain, it is probable that he discharged only an initial burst of fire before following the Japanese fighters into a wrenching left turn. Rasmussen could open fire only by releasing the locked charging handle of his .50-caliber machine gun. With little more than fifteen seconds of firing time remaining after his gun's initial runaway discharge, he drew back and locked the charging handle to conserve ammunition. The Japanese fighters were outturning the Americans, and Thacker and Rasmussen began to lose ground as all four planes lost energy in the tight turns. The two enemy pilots added to their lead during each of the three to four circuits they all made over Kāneʻohe Bay. It is uncertain how aggressively the two Americans attempted to press their position, but with three inoperable machine guns and one runaway between them they doubtless realized the futility of the pursuit.[56]

Elsewhere, after clearing his tail, Sanders peered east and saw a friendly ship (Sterling) in a near-vertical dive in hot pursuit of a Mitsubishi (FPO2c Okamoto) that was trailing smoke, with Fujita on the pursuer's tail. Sanders dove in pursuit of Fujita, firing as he went, in a desperate effort to save the unidentified friendly, but he was too far behind to drive off Fujita in time. "Just as I closed in, he [Fujita] got a burst at Sterling, whose plane burst into flames . . . ablaze with yellow flames coming from the engine compartment [and] cockpit." Fujita's fighter was trailing white smoke from Sanders' hits as Sterling's P-36 spiraled down out of control. From their position west looking to the east over the Pacific Ocean, both Thacker and Rasmussen saw "one of our P-36's going straight down, on fire, trailing black smoke and a Zero close behind him" at an altitude of three to four thousand feet. Rasmussen surmised that three aircraft "plunge[d] into the waters off the coast" in that engagement.[57]

As all four planes—Okamoto, Sterling, Fujita, and Sanders—plummeted into the offshore overcast,

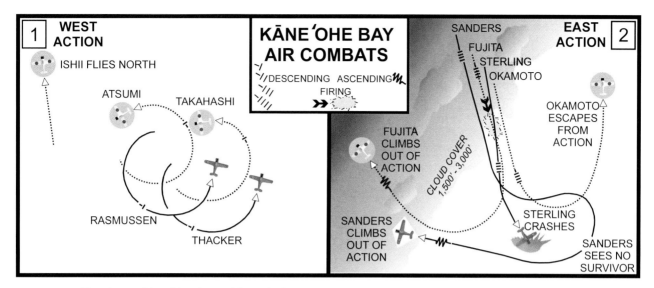

First phase of the air battle over Kāne'ohe Bay between the 46th Pursuit Squadron and the *Sōryū* fighter unit. On the left (*viewed from overhead*), Thacker and Rasmussen engage in the western turning battle with Takahashi and Atsumi, with the two Japanese steadily gaining lead on the Americans. All four aircraft probably lost altitude as their speed decreased in the tight turns. On the right is the twisting, near-vertical pursuit that involved Okamoto, Sterling, Fujita, and Sanders. Fujita climbed out of the action immediately, whereas Sanders spent a brief time searching for signs of an impact in the bay. Note that the planes entered the cloud layer after Sterling caught fire and then emerged while pulling out of their dives. Both Sanders and Fujita almost surely circled while climbing out of the action. **Di Virgilio**

Sanders began his pullout at 1,500 feet, leveled out close to the water, and climbed in a steep 360-degree turn to clear his tail, trading speed for altitude. Seeing no trace of the other three aircraft, Sanders reasoned that "the way they had been going, they couldn't have pulled out, so it was obvious that all three went into the sea. . . . I continued to search for a parachute, life vest or life raft or some evidence of a crash. Finding none I climbed and headed south." Only Sterling had gone down, however. Emerging from the combat with Sterling and Sanders, Fujita and Okamoto had pulled out of their dives upon entering the cloud bank. With no way to determine whether Okamoto had survived, Fujita saw no need to tarry close to the water and immediately climbed to rejoin and assist his men who were battling the P-36s above him.[58]

While Sanders and Fujita struggled for altitude, the *Sōryū* fighter unit's 3rd Shōtai under FPO1c Oda Kiichi arrived on the scene, climbing toward the engagement from the south. It is uncertain whether the three pilots perceived that an engagement was

under way, or even whether they were aware of Lieutenant Iida's demise. Subsequent events indicate that Oda's two wingmen—FPO2c Tanaka and FPO3c Takashima (flying damaged aircraft)—followed at extended intervals. Hence, communications and coordinated actions among them were almost impossible. While Oda squinted to discern whether the *Sōryū* fighters lay to the north, ahead of him—but some distance left—Thacker and Rasmussen were still engaged in the fruitless counterclockwise turning battle, unable to fire at their adversaries. Both Americans had their attention focused ahead and to their left, straining to pull lead on Atsumi and Takahashi. Apparently, Rasmussen was aft of Thacker and on the inside of the curving fight, and both of them were unaware of the threat approaching from the south. Strangely, it seems that neither Oda's brood nor the Americans ahead were aware of each other's presence.[59]

Oblivious to the Americans ahead and to the left, and with his attention drawn elsewhere, Oda flew past Thacker and Rasmussen. Following behind, however, FPO2c Tanaka Jirō spied Thacker. Despite damage to his own fighter, Tanaka continued straight ahead, converged on Thacker's right beam, and set up a quick 90-degree hit-and-run deflection shot, still unaware of Rasmussen trailing still farther out to the left. Almost at the very moment Thacker saw Sterling's natural metal P-36 going down in flames at three thousand feet out to the left, Tanaka opened fire and peppered the American with 7.7-millimeter and/or 20-millimeter fire. Seconds later, Thacker smelled fluid in the cockpit from a severed tail wheel hydraulic line and rightly suspected that he had been hit. He subsequently reported, "I looked behind for fire or smoke, saw none, but knowing I had been damaged, flew inland toward the clouds to escape." Except for Lieutenant (jg) Fujita, Tanaka was the only Japanese pilot in the Sōryū's fighter unit to claim a kill. As Thacker's fighter disappeared into the overcast, Tanaka believed he had scored but was still unaware of an enemy fighter converging from the left.[60]

Rasmussen first caught sight of Tanaka out of the corner of his right eye. The Japanese pilot charging past him from right to left presented a perfect target, though at a high angle of deflection. Leading the enemy aircraft by several lengths, Rasmussen reached for the left-hand .50-caliber charging handle, unlocked it, and let it slide in, and the .50-caliber Browning hammered away. Rasmussen simply held steady and watched Tanaka's kansen fly though his tracers, taking strikes along the length of the fuselage. The carrier fighter was emitting smoke as it pulled away, leading Rasmussen to mistakenly conclude that he had shot it down. The extended burst of .50-caliber proved insufficient to take down Tanaka, however; he returned to the Sōryū with his plane holed in nine spots, though some of the damage might have occurred while he was strafing NAS Kaneohe Bay.[61]

Rasmussen's futile turning battle with FPO1c Atsumi and then the one-sided dustup with FPO2c

Tanaka gave Fujita just enough time to climb back into the fray. Fujita was probably still climbing—and almost to altitude—after the twisting, spiraling fight with Sterling and Sanders. Immediately after Rasmussen watched Tanaka plow through his tracers, he was startled to see Fujita bearing down from dead ahead. "Another Zero came head on to me and almost rammed me," he later said. Fujita, at the opposite end of the encounter, stated ten years later (mistakenly) that Rasmussen came at him with "all guns blazing away" and thought that the American was trying to ram him. Too late for evasive action, the determined and gritty Japanese continued on course, fully intending to crash into his adversary.[62]

At the very last moment, Rasmussen "pulled up violently to the right to avoid being rammed." Evaluation of the damage sustained by his P-36A indicates that Rasmussen did indeed pull up sharply, exposing his underside, and then banked steeply to the right, exposing his wings (topside) and his right fuselage to Fujita's machine-gun fire. With a nearly perfect setup, Fujita opened fire as the American pulled up and then poured a devastating barrage into Rasmussen's wings and fuselage as he rolled right, "scor[ing] many hits." In none of his correspondence, speeches, and interviews did Rasmussen ever claim that he returned fire. Fujita, however, was under the impression that Rasmussen had scored likewise on his aircraft, damaging the engine so badly that he was unsure whether he could make it back to the Sōryū. It is more likely, however, that the accumulated damage to Fujita's engine had finally taken its toll. Neither pilot sought to reengage the other.[63]

Rasmussen felt Fujita's shells strike his aircraft. One 20-millimeter round might have carried away the tail wheel, and at least two other rounds struck the fuselage on the left side. One of those hits exploded in the radio compartment immediately behind Rasmussen's head, blew the canopy apart, and "blew up the radio . . . with a deafening explosion." The interior of the fuselage was showered with fragments, a great many of which dented

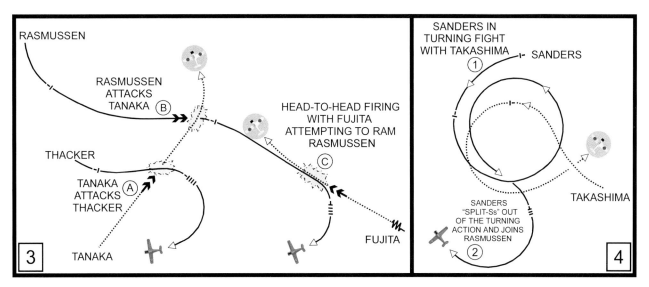

Second phase of the air battle over Kāne'ohe Bay, viewed from overhead. On the left is the action precipitated by the arrival of the 3rd Shōtai, in which Tanaka attacked Thacker at a high angle of deflection and then came under fire from Rasmussen, who in turn took heavy fire from Fujita. On the right is the final turning battle between Sanders and Takashima, during which Sanders split-Sed out of the fight after realizing that Takashima was gaining lead. **Di Virgilio**

and perforated the opposite, right side. A torrent of 7.7-millimeter machine-gun fire at extremely close range scored numerous hits that "laced [the] catwalk on both wings." After a likely evasive turn to the left, Rasmussen's P-36 shuddered under the blows and "tumbled into the clouds below." When he regained a semblance of control, Rasmussen found that his rudder was inoperable (due to severed control cables), although he still had elevator and aileron control. Improvising frantically, he kept the P-36 relatively stable by pushing the "stick to the right corner and add[ing] maximum trim" to counter the rudder, now jammed slightly to the left.[64]

"I was sure that the top of my head had been shot off," Rasmussen later said. "I could feel a mass up there and felt sure it was my brains." There was no blood in the cockpit, though—only shattered Plexiglas, some of which was mixed into his hair. Rasmussen was unhurt, but the ordeal of guiding his battered fighter back to Wheeler Field still lay ahead. He followed Thacker's example and weaved through the clouds while struggling to maintain control of the aircraft. Although coordinated turns (those that employed ailerons *and* rudder) were impossible, Rasmussen

could still make broad, uncoordinated turns using his ailerons only, a task that would require all the flying skill he could muster.[65]

Meanwhile, as Sanders climbed from his initial encounters with Fujita and shaped a course south in the direction of Bellows Field, an unidentified aircraft appeared ahead, slightly higher and closing rapidly. Glimpsing the plane's red *hinomaru* insignia as it flew past, Sanders commenced a steep climbing turn at full throttle, straining to pull in behind it. The Japanese pilot saw Sanders' move and countered with a turn of his own, precipitating yet another turning fight. Sanders found it impossible to get off a shot; even pushing the nose of his P-36 inside the turning circle by "walking the rudder" while pulling back on the stick failed to produce the required lead for a firing solution. Moreover, he thought the *kansen* "was gaining altitude and lead in every turn"; in fact, Sanders was probably losing altitude with every turn, as both fighters bled energy. Sanders analyzed the situation and "realized that if the pilot had any ability, sooner or later he would be able to use his superior performance and altitude advantage to maneuver behind me for a shot. It also occurred to me that he had to be low on gas and probably would turn back north if I succeeded in breaking off."[66]

Sanders' opponent was probably FPO3c Takashima Takeo of the 3rd Shōtai, trapped into the engagement but reluctant to press his position owing either to damage sustained over NAS Kaneohe Bay or lack of ammunition. Bewildered by the Zero's performance and recognizing the suicidal futility of further pursuit, Sanders disengaged with a split-S maneuver and once again dove away south toward Bellows, hoping that the enemy pilot (low on fuel, ammunition, or nerve) would retreat north. Whatever the nature of his adversary's deficit, the maneuver worked. Sanders again found himself alone.[67]

Action over Kahuku and Ka'ena Points

At roughly the same time that Sanders' flight ventured from Wheeler Field east-southeast toward Bellows, 2nd Lt. Harry Brown was flying from Haleiwa in the same direction, having heard radio chatter mentioning Bellows Field. He flew for some time toward Bellows, but seeing "no reason" to continue, reversed course and eventually turned northward toward Kahuku Point, though perhaps toward the coastline between Kahuku and Waimea Bay farther down the coast. As he neared that area, he spotted an unidentified plane and prepared "to pounce" on the supposed enemy but hesitated. The pair circled each other warily, gradually drawing closer, until Brown and 1st Lt. Bob Rogers recognized one another.[68]

Brown moved into position as Rogers' wingman, and Rogers pointed down at three to four Japanese aircraft heading out to sea, almost surely toward the 3rd Assembly Area. The Americans dove and closed on their intended quarry, but it seemed that neither side wished to commit the "first overt act." Brown recalled, "We looked at the Japs and [they] looked back." The Americans broke the ice, with Brown pulling behind one of the Japanese, but it was Rogers who fired first. He cut loose "a sharp burst" and used "a screaming chandelle" to climb out of the action in the direction of Haleiwa and Ka'ena Point.

The enemy plane "disappear[ed] into a cloud bank streaming black smoke," and that was the last Rogers saw of it. Brown selected another target, and the pair "went all over the sky for quite a long time." Pursued in a vertical dive, the Japanese pilot "chopped his throttle [and] dumped his flaps," and Brown flew past him "like an express train," nearly plunging into the whitecaps below. "[I] realized quickly that I was in trouble. . . . I must have almost bent the stick because I pulled so many G's that I blacked out." He rolled out into a cloud bank "in a kind of sloppy [Immelmann] turn" but lost sight of the Japanese, thus ending the action.[69]

It is unclear whether Brown and Rogers were immediately aware of what each did after they separated near Kahuku Point. Having quit the action, they may have decided independently to venture generally southwest toward the vicinity of Haleiwa Field and Ka'ena Point. Rogers was over the peninsula first and again became embroiled in a dogfight, possibly with two or three carrier bombers. Brown could hear Rogers shouting frantically over the radio; he could not understand him but rushed to the rescue. The Japanese pilots scissored back and forth, giving Rogers the fight of his life, with one of them "hard on his tail shooting the hell out of him." While Rogers attempted to shake his pursuers, Brown feinted toward the higher of the Japanese, causing him to break away from Rogers, who dove out of the combat and took his crippled P-36 back to Haleiwa. The other Japanese pilot who had been pursuing Rogers tried to turn away but instead flew into Brown's line of fire and fell toward the sea—Brown's first of eight aerial victories in the Pacific War. Trailing the Japanese plane by only forty to fifty feet, there was no way that Brown could have missed. He was so close that he saw "the rear gunner crumple and the left wing begin to burn." The carrier bomber—possibly from the Sōryū, crewed by pilot FPO3c Kawasaki Satoru and observer/plane commander FPO1c Takahashi Ryōichi—crashed vertically into the water off Ka'ena Point.[70]

2nd Lt. Harry W. Brown seated in the camouflaged Curtiss P-36A fighter (A.C. Serial No. 38-2) he flew on 7 December. The aircraft's radio call number (or "buzz number") is unknown. **Aiken, NMPW, cropped**

1st Lt. Robert J. Rogers, 47th Pursuit Squadron, upon receiving the Silver Star at Wheeler Field on 25 March 1942. **USAMHI, cropped**

After that victory, Brown pulled back on the stick, ascended, and ran head-on into "a covey of thirteen to fourteen planes" outbound toward the Japanese rendezvous. With both sides surprised and at a high rate of closure, no one got off any shots immediately, although that situation changed quickly. The Japanese "fell all over themselves trying to get at me," Brown reported, "all shooting." Brown sped away, however, and the Japanese failed to score any hits.[71]

1st Lt. Malcolm Moore arrived in the vicinity of Kaʻena Point from Wheeler Field in time to witness Brown's combat: "Proceeded to [Kaʻena] Point and saw 3 planes, widely separated. As I watched, two of them seemed to engage in combat. 3rd disappeared. Two planes in combat broke away and one approached me. It was a P-36." Brown had turned back toward base and saw a lone aircraft interposed between his P-36A and safe haven in Haleiwa. Upon closing, he discovered that it was "Mike" Moore of the 46th Pursuit Squadron. He joined Moore as wingman,

then indicated the presence of another enemy plane below at about three thousand feet. Acting as the new element leader, Moore attacked and discovered what he thought to be a dive-bomber. To evade defensive fire, he "dove behind it and came up from below, firing both guns." The pilot turned sharply, and the two aircraft disappeared into the clouds. Moore fired six bursts into the aircraft, then ran out of ammunition and lost the enemy in the clouds. Brown took over and executed a quick firing pass in which he expended his remaining ammunition but failed to bring down the enemy. When Brown and Moore last saw the aircraft, however, it was "in evident distress . . . headed from [Kaʻena] Pt. toward [Kauaʻi] with a cloud of smoke behind him and losing altitude fast." Brown had no doubt that it went down, commenting sarcastically forty-five years later, "He was in 'distress' alright—he was burning and leaving a trail of black smoke." Brown (and Moore's) victim was possibly one of Lieutenant Iida's orphans from over NAS Kaneohe Bay—FPO1c Atsumi Takashi—whom

1st Lt. Malcolm A. Moore, 46th Pursuit Squadron, upon receiving the Silver Star at Wheeler Field on 25 March 1942. **Aiken, NMPW, cropped**

1st Lt. John. J. Webster, 47th Pursuit Squadron, upon receiving the Silver Star at Wheeler Field on 25 March 1942. **USAMHI, cropped**

Lt. (jg) Fujita Iyozō reported seeing ablaze and then going down in a dogfight off the North Shore somewhere between Kahuku and Kaʻena Point. Fujita surmised, perhaps mistakenly, that Atsumi's engine fire was due to a backfire caused by closing the throttle too quickly.[72]

One of the last pilots from the 47th Pursuit Squadron to get into the air from Haleiwa during the attack was 1st Lt. John J. Webster in a P-40B. After patrolling over Haleiwa, he headed west and jumped into a scrum with Japanese aircraft assembling off Kaʻena Point. Though outnumbered and with only three .30-caliber Brownings working, Webster went on the offensive. He dove on the planes from eight thousand feet, overshot, pulled up, gained altitude, and dove on them again. Two of the Japanese aircraft turned into him, and well-aimed bursts punched into Webster's P-40, partially severing his rudder cable. Another round disintegrated upon entering the cockpit and sent splinters into his left leg. Webster broke off the action and returned safely to Haleiwa.[73]

THE COMBATANTS RETIRE TO WHEELER AND *SŌRYŪ*

On Oʻahu's opposite shore, meanwhile, Phil Rasmussen regained control of his fighter in time to spy yet another aircraft drawing close. To his great relief, it was Lew Sanders' olive drab P-36A. After abandoning his frustrating turning fight with FPO3c Takashima of the 3rd Shōtai, Sanders leveled off, made a wide, flat turn to the east, and spotted Rasmussen heading in the opposite direction with smoke coming from the top of his engine cowling. He circled in close on the left rear of the Curtiss for a better look and was appalled by what he saw. Despite Rasmussen's toothy grin, Sanders could only wonder how he was keeping the P-36 in the air with its sagging undercarriage, shattered canopy, missing tail wheel, and severed antenna wires flapping in the slipstream. Hundreds of holes perforated the wings and fuselage (544 by later count). The aircraft looked like it had been attacked with a fire ax.[74]

Rasmussen was indeed having great difficulty controlling his aircraft, so Sanders wasted no time and escorted him back to Wheeler. Fortunately, the Japanese were en route to the rendezvous off Ka'ena Point, and no one in the air contested the pair's homeward movement. It was a different matter on the ground, however. Defenders at Schofield Barracks "had gotten themselves pretty well organized" and opened fire as Rasmussen and Sanders passed over at reduced speed and low altitude in preparation for landing. Fortunately, the intense barrage failed to land hits on Rasmussen, though it underscored the need to get on the ground *quickly*.[75]

As Rasmussen turned into the base leg and attempted to lower his landing gear, the indicator in his cockpit showed that the wheels failed to lower properly. Concluding that the "hydraulic line had been all shot up," Rasmussen was "pumping madly" with his emergency pump. As he flared just prior to touching

down, the gear locked into place. With no "rudder control, brakes, or tail wheel," the P-36 skidded back and forth so badly that Rasmussen simply cut his power. After ground-looping several times, the aircraft finally lurched to a stop. The young pilot recorded later:

As ground crews rushed to my plane to see if was OK, I sat benumbed in the cockpit for moments, unable to take in the rush of events—the attack, my close brush with death, destruction and fire surrounding me. I glanced around—the hangars still burning, the planes sitting in smoldering rows with their backs broken, engines pointing to the sky. Only then did fear enter the equation— the adrenaline had worn down. I looked at my watch—fifty minutes since take off.

Ground crews in front of Hangar 2 service a P-36A purported to be that of 1st Lt. Lewis Sanders late in the morning of 7 December as smoke rises from the tent area and Hangar 3 in the background to the far right. The pilot appears to be speaking with the armorer, who has removed the panel covering the breeches of the .30- and .50-caliber machine guns. Crews have jacked up the left side of the aircraft to examine the landing gear or to change the tire. This photograph also offers one of the best contemporary views of the entry into the central office core that separated the two aircraft bays. **Aiken, NMPW**

A pair of P-36As in front of Hangar 1 on Wheeler's parking apron during the afternoon of 7 December. These two aircraft document efforts to transition the 15th Pursuit Group's aircraft to a camouflage paint scheme in the days just prior to the attack. The plane closest to the camera has no "buzz" numbers, but olive drab paint on the upper wing surfaces has obliterated the roundel at right. The P-36 beyond is still in natural metal finish, with roundels on both wings. Note the P-40 behind it. **NARA II, 111-SC-128351, cropped**

2nd Lt. Philip M. Rasmussen crosses his fingers for continued good luck alongside the P-36A (48/15P) he flew into action over Kāne'ohe Bay. Note the loose antenna wire, the 20-millimeter shell holes in the fuselage, and the missing tail wheel. Rasmussen's rudder is jammed to the left, which explains the extraordinary measures required to stabilize his aircraft. **Rasmussen**

The left side of 48/15P showing fragmentation damage to the aircraft's skin after two 20-millimeter shells detonated inside the fuselage. Note that some of the fragments merely dimpled the skin outward.
Rasmussen

Radio coil sets (components in the tuning apparatus) in the radio compartment of Rasmussen's P-36A, aft of the cockpit, which is just out of the picture to the left. The detonation of a 20-millimeter shell inside this compartment destroyed the plane's radio and almost deafened Rasmussen. The two coils at right are Signal Corps C-216 coil sets manufactured by the Aircraft Radio Corporation in Boonton, New Jersey. The black-and-white placards on the case provided calibration data required for dialing the desired frequency.
Rasmussen

2nd Lieutenant Rasmussen holds up the end of his severed rudder cables inside the open baggage compartment on the left side of the aircraft. **Rasmussen**

Sanders landed without incident and with comparatively minor damage: holes "above [the] fuselage tank and in [the] oil expansion tank." Incredibly, both Americans had emerged from the ordeal unhurt.[76]

Lewis Sanders was enormously proud of the men of his flight. They had acquitted themselves well, having employed—however accidentally—the highside, hit-and-run, diving tactics countless American fighter pilots would use against the vaunted Mitsubishi Zero-sen. But Sanders and his men also made the error of engaging the Zeros in a turning battle, a tactic recognized later as almost suicidal. It was apparent that Oʻahu's pursuit pilots had little or no intelligence on Japanese aircraft in general and the Mitsubishi Type 0 carrier fighter specifically. In their brief "fill in the blanks" combat reports, all three of the surviving Americans from the engagement over Kāneʻohe Bay testified that the aircraft they engaged were "Light Bomber[s], retractible landing gear, rear gunner." Two generations later, Sanders spoke pointedly regarding the strengths of the Type 0 carrier fighter: "I had logged several hundred hours in the P-36 and was getting the most out of it. But my plane was simply outclassed by the Japanese fighter. Our

intelligence later advised that the enemy had no such aircraft, but I knew better."[77]

On the Japanese side, Fujita's Zero had sustained serious engine damage. As disturbing as that damage to his own aircraft was, however, Fujita was more distressed at what had happened to the group entrusted to his command for the first time. He could only conjecture regarding the fate of his missing men. Of his eight squadronmates, only his two original wingmen—Takahashi and Okamoto—formed on their leader following the engagement.[78]

As Fujita led his bruised and diminished flock away from the action over the bay, he shaped a course for the appointed rendezvous in hope of finding Lt. Chihaya Takehiko's *Akagi* dive-bomber unit, which was to shepherd them back to Vice Admiral Nagumo's Carrier Striking Force. The preliminary assembly point for the fighters, designated Point W, was ten kilometers due west of Kaʻena Point, altitude two thousand meters. After reaching this preliminary assembly area, they were to proceed a bit east of north to a position 340 degrees and 20 kilometers from Kaʻena Point—the 3rd Assembly Area—from which all aircraft were to return to *Kidō Butai*. Given the severe damage to Fujita's engine, he probably "cut the corner" and set a more northwesterly course toward the primary rendezvous that lay about thirty kilometers west of Kahuku Point (the northern tip of Oʻahu), where he might pick up the *Akagi* dive-bombers and follow them back to the *Sōryū*.[79]

Reaching the rendezvous northwest of the island, Fujita's fighters met three carrier bombers, formed on the right side of the *kanbaku*s, and followed them toward the carriers. Fujita's engine "sputt[ered] and spit all the way back to the *Soryu*." He was "worried sick" that he would not make it back alive, "a hell of a way to die . . . after surviving the attack and the bitter dog fight above Oahu." At the behest of his squadron commander, Lt. Suganami Masaji, Fujita had calculated a course back to *Sōryū* and *Kidō Butai* based on the carrier's position prior to his takeoff and the wind speed and direction determined from a balloon release. He deferred now to the *kanbaku* crews, each of which carried a navigator in the rear seat. As time passed during the return flight, however, Fujita noticed a *ten-degree* difference between his calculations and the course set by the carrier bombers, which were diverging left. Fearing that his engine would seize at any moment, Fujita decided to take his unit to the right, in conformance with his own course calculation, and was greatly relieved to see the fleet near the anticipated time about 30 degrees out to the right. Fujita's oil pressure gauge read 0 as he took position to land. After he touched down, a portion of one of his engine's fourteen cylinders parted and clattered down in the engine cowling. Fujita knew how lucky he was to return. His maintenance crews agreed, shaking their heads in wonder that their chief had made it back.[80]

EPILOGUE: JOHN DAINS

Although the last flight mentioned here is perhaps better suited to a description of the attack's aftermath, it is a fitting capstone to the inspiring story of the Army Air Force's pursuit pilots in action against

Col. Gordon H. Austin, circa 1944, possibly when stationed at Bolling Field or while in one of various billets near Washington, D.C. **Stevens, cropped**

F/C John C. Wretschko, 1 June 1940, during flight training at Kelly Field. **NARA II, 18-PU-102-513-5417**

F/C John L. Dains climbing into the front cockpit of his trainer at Randolph Field during the spring of 1941, about three to five months prior to his transfer to the Hawaiian Department on 16 August. The aircraft appears to be a North American BT-14, although the squared-off windscreen is atypical. Note the rear-view mirror in the right portion of the windscreen, a hallmark of North American's trainers of the period. Dains logged just over seventy flying hours in BTs at Randolph Field.
Aiken, NMPW, cropped

the Japanese. When 2nd Lt. John Dains landed his P-40B at Haleiwa after his second flight of the morning, the aircraft was so badly damaged that the mechanics took it out of service for repairs. At some point during midmorning, the 47th Pursuit Squadron's commander, Capt. Gordon H. Austin, returned from his deer-hunting junket to Maui and relieved 1st Lieutenant Rogers of command. During the course of the morning, according to one account, Austin received orders to search the Kaua'i Straits, west-northwest of O'ahu. Although the complete makeup of the flight is uncertain, Austin gathered Haleiwa's available aircraft and ordered up a group of pilots, four of whose names are known: 1st Lt. John

C. Wretschko, P-40B; 2nd Lt. John L. Dains, P-36A "149"; 2nd Lt. George S. Welch, P-40B; and 2nd Lt. Irwin W. Henze Jr., plane type unknown. Takeoff was scheduled for 1100.[81]

The details of the flight are murky. The actual number of pilots, takeoff time, and mission are in question. Assuming that the probe of the Kaua'i Straits moved forward, flight leader Wretschko probably did not venture far to "confirm" that the strait was empty, as prior to 7 December fighters did not fly more than fifteen miles offshore. Soon the pilots turned back to O'ahu. Accounts are contradictory regarding subsequent events as well. One narrative says nothing regarding Kaua'i but has the flight

2nd Lt. George S. Welch, 47th Pursuit Squadron, 17 December 1941. **HWRD, cropped**

F/C Irwin W. Henze Jr., 4 June 1941, during flight training at Kelly Field. **NARA II, 18-PU-041-190-8811**

patrolling over Pearl Harbor and Honolulu at 19,000 feet for thirty minutes.[82]

Eventually, however, the flight proceeded toward Wheeler, where the pilots anticipated loading the .50-caliber ammunition that was unavailable at Haleiwa. As the planes neared the landing approach off the western end of Wheeler's landing mat, guns began firing from Schofield Barracks. Dains, on the right side of a two-plane element, took the brunt of the barrage, possibly shielding Wretschko from most of the fire, although the latter recorded in his logbook that he "received a shrapnel hole in [his] left wing." Dains' P-36A staggered earthward, plunged into the ground near Schofield, and burst into flames at 1143.[83]

The aviation fuel on board incinerated the aircraft, leaving very little to recover. Some men hurried to the crash site, including George Welch, but Dains' best friend, Harry Brown, could not bring himself to approach. "I couldn't face it." Chaplain Terence P. Finnegan went to the crash site later that afternoon to extract the broken body of the pilot and administer last rites. Only one arm and a parachute remained, but the pilot could not have been anyone other than Johnny Dains.[84]

Chapter Twelve

"LOOKS LIKE WE'VE HAD IT FOR NOW"
The Aftermath

Visual impressions of the damage Wheeler Field sustained from the attacks depended very much on one's vantage point within the base. Were an airman to walk along Wright Avenue, avoid looking south, and ignore the columns of smoke boiling up from the hangars and aircraft parking aprons, the damage did not appear to be terribly great. If he descended south along the slope toward the flight line, however, the level of destruction was extraordinarily severe and readily apparent. Aircraft wreckage—left to burn itself out—stretched from one end of the apron to the other. Although not all the hangars suffered severe damage, "the airplanes were just so much junk." Since the operational aircraft had

Five P-40s of the 73rd Pursuit Squadron lie in ashes on the eastern terminus of Wheeler's parking apron, view looking southeast around midday on 7 December. Little could be salvaged from the wrecks, even from the engines. Note smoke rising from Pearl Harbor in the distance on the right. **NARA II, 111-SC-134883**

A second view of the end of Wheeler's apron, looking east past the remains of a P-40 of the 73rd Pursuit Squadron. Note the camouflaged P-26 at right and the natural metal Peashooter in the far distance at left. The grandstand of Wheeler's baseball field is in the distance at the far left center; the recently constructed bachelor officer barracks are at the far left. **Aiken, NMPW**

P-40s of the 18th Pursuit Group on the apron in front of the ruined twin bays of Hangar 3, view looking northwest. Hangar 3 and the tent area to the left are still smoldering. **Aiken, NMPW**

been relocated to the revetments during the morning and afternoon hours, the burned wreckage that remained made the level of devastation appear even worse than it was. At ground level from the flight line, it looked to SSgt. Melvin L. Miller as though "every plane and building on our field had been damaged."

Even after engineers from Schofield Barracks arrived, bulldozed wreckage on the parking apron into piles, and disposed of the debris, the extensive damage to the hangars on the flight line remained well into the summer of 1942 as a gruesome reminder of the day's events. The horrific loss among Wheeler's airmen

The burned-out hulk of a Grumman OA-9 rests on Wheeler's apron between Hangars 2 and 3 shortly after the raid. Generally, utility aircraft sat in the space between the parking areas of the two pursuit groups—the 15th to the west and the 18th to the east. Bulldozing and clearing of wreckage probably have not yet started. **Aiken, NMPW**

View looking north into Hangar 3's eastern bay. Concussion from detonations has blown out most of the windows and knocked fascia off the hangar's front and rear gables. Note the P-40 (340?) inside on the left. Debris is still strewn about the apron. **Aiken, NMPW**

compounded the devastation. Until after the raid, the men killed in Tent City between Hangars 2 and 3 lay where they had been cut down. Understandably, the wounded had to be moved first. As 1st Lt. Everett Stewart surveyed the loss in men and matériel, the thought passed through his mind, "Well, it looks like we've had it for now. . . . They got us."[1]

Airmen at Bellows Field on Oʻahu's windward shore, on the other hand, were astonished at how little damage they saw after the severe strafing there. Pvt. Byron Kolbert expected far more damage and casualties. He credited the energetic ground crews for dispersing so many planes to safety. Of the two units stationed at the field—the 86th Observation

A Type F-2 two-thousand-gallon-capacity gasoline tractor-trailer lies burned out along the south side of the runway at Bellows Field on 9 December. Just behind it is a second tanker rig, intact, and apparently camouflaged with palm fronds. Several aircraft are in the far background: to the left of the truck, a surviving P-40; another badly damaged P-40 on one gear, visible just right of the truck, that was wrecked in the predawn darkness of 8 December by 2nd Lt. John A. Moore, who taxied into the P-40C (A.C. Serial No. 41-13337); and one of the 86th Observation Squadron's three O-49s. View looking northwest toward the Koʻolau Range. **NARA II, 111-SC-127015**

1st Lt. Robert Richards' B-17C (A.C. Ser. No. 40-2049), at Bellows Field, is being cannibalized for spare parts for bombers awaiting repairs at Hickam. Items missing include the Plexiglas nose assembly, a wingtip, at least two engines, an aileron, and the plane commander's observation bubble behind the pilots' seats. **Cleveland**

Squadron and the 44th Pursuit Squadron—the latter fared worse, losing the two P-40s piloted by Lieutenant Whiteman and Lieutenant Bishop. As for damage to the base, one Type F-2, two-thousand-gallon-capacity gasoline truck exploded after it was struck by Japanese machine-gun fire, but other damage to the station was superficial. The men seemed somewhat surprised that the theater (the largest building on the base) and the array of new barracks—seemingly obvious targets—sustained no damage. Casualties, though keenly felt, were extraordinarily light. Removal of the bodies of 2nd Lt. Hans C. Christiansen and 2nd Lt. George A. Whiteman had to await the end of the attacks.[2]

Postattack Searches and Patrols

Perhaps owing to the light damage at Bellows, the 86th Observation Squadron took the lead in sending out searches for the attackers. Ironically, one of Bellows' Pregnant Pigeons was the first Army aircraft to search for the Japanese fleet. The O-47B's availability was due in part to the efforts of crew chief SSgt. Harry E. Fitzgibbon, who had been warming up the aircraft assigned to Maj. Charles B. Stewart when fighters from the *Hiryū* struck. Fitzgibbon took cover temporarily in a nearby ditch but returned as soon as he could, and the airplane was sufficiently warmed up for immediate takeoff when Stewart arrived.[3]

Major Stewart commenced preparations for takeoff as soon as the Japanese fighters left the airspace over Bellows Field. Before running through the preflight checks for 1/86O and ensuring that Pfc. Raymond McBriarty had a full supply of ammunition, Stewart instructed McBriarty to secure a radio operator (Pvt. Alfred D. Buonomo) and draw a parachute. McBriarty's assigned 'chute was being packed, so it was necessary to secure a loaner. Only after he had climbed into the rear cockpit did he discover that the harness was far too large for him. Stewart taxied out very rapidly. McBriarty estimated that the O-47 was "doing 55" by the time Stewart positioned the plane at the leeward end of the runway for takeoff. The

Capt. Charles B. Stewart, CO of the 86th Observation Squadron, in the cockpit of an O-47B at Bellows Field, circa 1941. Stewart had served in the squadron since its days at Wheeler Field in 1940. **AFHRA**

ungainly plane lifted off at 0950, with Major Stewart determined to locate the Japanese carrier force. He stayed low and hugged the water off Waimānalo in order to pick up speed, heading "north—a bit east of Kaneohe," the direction the departing Japanese had taken. Sighting nothing but empty seas, he turned west but stayed north of the Koʻolau Range until he reached the Pali Pass. After passing through to the south, Stewart turned toward Wheeler and saw that the base was ablaze. He reversed course and returned to Bellows after an elapsed time of only thirty-five minutes. Because Stewart's sortie had a passing chance of locating the Japanese fleet, it is possible that the flight's brevity was due to engine or mechanical trouble.[4]

It is unclear whether Stewart attempted to brief his other crews before his hasty takeoff or left that task to the operations staff. All the pilots were told to patrol separately over different portions of the island. Initially, that part of the instructions probably

2nd Lt. James H. Robinson of the 86th Observation Squadron at Bellows Field, circa late 1941. Robinson and the other three 2nd lieutenants (Sullivan, Rathbun, and Ring) who flew patrols on 7 December were recent flight school graduates who arrived in Hawai'i on 13 September. **AFHRA**

2nd Lt. Raymond T. Sullivan of the 86th Observation Squadron at Bellows Field, circa late 1941. **AFHRA**

did not apply to Stewart, who planned to follow the departing Japanese aircraft and uncover the invading fleet's location. Crews were not to use their radios unless they spotted enemy aircraft, in which case they would report all information on the enemy immediately. The probable intent of the flights was more to gather intelligence on an approaching third wave of attackers. If the O-47s located the enemy, they were *not* to engage, only to report.[5]

Five minutes after Major Stewart returned, 2nd Lt. James H. Robinson took off at 1030 in 4/86O with observer Sgt. Ellsworth F. Forrest and rear gunner Pfc. Howard P. Glass. After a flight of two and one-half hours, they returned to Bellows with a negative report: no sightings. Similarly, 2nd Lt. Raymond T. Sullivan took off at 1045 with crewmen Pvt. Robert E. Henry and Pvt. Michael Cerillo. Private Henry, in the rear gunner's seat, estimated the flight time as about an hour and a half (actually it was two hours and fifteen minutes) and thought the experience

"kind of exciting for a 21-year-old farm boy from Indiana." Sullivan's crew also found no Japanese.[6]

With Major Stewart's aircraft redlined, only Robinson's (4/86O) and Sullivan's (6/86O) aircraft were still in service. After they landed at about 1300, two hours elapsed before the mechanics checked over the pair of O-47Bs, setting up two additional midafternoon sorties with fresh crews. Captain Stewart approached 2nd Lt. Wayne H. Rathbun and said, "Rathbun, get your parachute. I want you to fly a mission just as soon as we get a plane loaded with fuel and ammunition." Rathbun's first thought was, "How the hell am I going to shoot down a Jap?" At 1500, Rathbun took off in aircraft 6/86O for the squadron's fourth sortie of the day, and the aircraft's second. His crew consisted of two privates, first class—Ralph E. Redburn as observer and Raymond F. McBriarty making his second sortie as a rear gunner. Rathbun steered a course to the northeast straight out over the ocean and test-fired his fixed

2nd Lt. Wayne H. Rathbun of the 86th Observation Squadron at Bellows Field, circa late 1941. **AFHRA**

Pearl Harbor (presumably just south of Ka'ena Point and the Wai'anae Range) and saw "a sickening sight." Maintaining a prudent distance to avoid nervous gunners in the harbor, Rathbun reversed course, lumbered northeast, and then flew clockwise around the island searching for signs of enemy activity. After an elapsed time of two hours and fifteen minutes, Rathbun brought his crew back safely, grateful that the Japanese had not sent in another attack wave, "because the O-47 was certainly not a fighter plane."[7]

Second Lt. Harold K. Ring took off in 4/86O at 1500 with observer Pvt. Henry W. Taxis and rear gunner Pvt. Alfred P. Gardner. Although Ring also extended his flight for more than two hours, he likewise returned to Bellows with nothing to report. The men of the 86th Observation Squadron displayed admirable courage in going out in planes so outmatched by their Japanese counterparts. Had they made contact with the Japanese they would have had little hope of escape.[8]

The pursuit squadrons on O'ahu were also active after the raid. The lack of concrete information regarding the fighter patrols mounted after the attack, however, particularly from Wheeler Field, is frustrating for historians. Even the microfilmed IFRs released by the National Archives in St. Louis do little to document specific flights and missions, although

forward-firing gun, instructing McBriarty to do the same from the rear cockpit. Although McBriarty was an experienced gunner and had fired from the rear seat of Major Stewart's plane (*from the ground*) during the second-wave attack, Rathbun had never live-fired a machine gun. Rathbun headed around the northwest side of O'ahu at about ten thousand feet to a location from which the crew could view

Morning and Afternoon Searches of the 86th Observation Squadron, Bellows Field

Pilot	Observer	Rear Gunner	T/O & Duration	
Aircraft 1/86O				
Maj. Charles B. Stewart	Pvt. Alfred D. Buonomo	Pfc. Raymond F. McBriarty	0950	0:35
Aircraft 4/86O				
2nd Lt. James H. Robinson	Sgt. Ellsworth F. Forrest	Pfc. Howard P. Glass	1030	2:30
Aircraft 6/86O				
2nd Lt. Raymond T. Sullivan	Pvt. Robert E. Henry	Pvt. Michael Cerillo	1045	2:15
Aircraft 6/86O				
2nd Lt. Wayne H. Rathbun	Pfc. Ralph E. Redburn	Pfc. Raymond F. McBriarty	1500	2:15
Aircraft 4/86O				
2nd Lt. Harold K. Ring	Pvt. Henry W. Taxis	Pvt. Alfred P. Gardner	1500	2:30

2nd Lt. Harold K. Ring of the 86th Observation Squadron at Bellows Field, circa late 1941. **AFHRA**

those records have dramatically expanded the list of pilots known to have flown on 7 December. With the notable exceptions of 1st Lt. Lewis Sanders and 1st Lt. Malcolm Moore of the 46th Pursuit Squadron, no mission-specific reports survive. For all the heroism and earnest efforts of the pilots and their support crews on the ground, the postattack flights present a muddled image of chaos, disorganization, and ad hoc operations. In fairness, the men at Wheeler felt that further attacks by the Japanese—including invasion—were imminent, and the disrupted communications and exigencies of the day were hardly conducive to effective recordkeeping. The efforts of these pilots—not to mention those of the ground crews who kept them flying—number among the great untold stories of 7 December 1941. Apart from the fourteen men who engaged in actual combat with the Japanese, no fewer than forty-nine pursuit pilots took to the air that day. Sadly, with exceptions, their stories will likely remain untold.[9]

A notable exception to the lack of pilot rosters is the second mission of three P-36As led by 1st Lt. Lewis Sanders, with subordinates 1st Lt. Malcolm Moore and 2nd Lt. John Thacker. Taking off at 1115 in company with a flight from the 45th Pursuit Squadron, the pilots flew south and posted near Hickam Field at 2,500 feet, presumably to provide escort or cover the takeoffs of two flights of bombers sent out to search for the Japanese—a flight of five A-20As from the 58th Bombardment Squadron that took off at 1127, and another of two B-17Ds at 1140. It is unknown whether Sanders' P-36s and Hickam's bombers ever saw one another because gunners at Hickam drove off the "third-wave attack" flying in from the north, and Sanders and company were forced to circle over Pearl Harbor instead. They received no better welcome there. Remembering that *kanbaku*s of the second wave had circled similarly before entering their attack dives, the shipboard gun crews threw up a heavy barrage of antiaircraft fire at the relatively low-flying fighters. Bullets or shrapnel pierced holes in Sanders' wings and carried away the tire from Moore's tail wheel. Having had their fill over Pearl Harbor, the trio fled and ascended to 24,000 feet, although even with that Olympian view Thacker reported, "No enemy craft sighted." After just under an hour, Sanders led the flight back to Wheeler and landed at 1210.[10]

At Bellows Field, most of the dispersed P-40s of the 44th Pursuit Squadron had survived the attacks. Although the flight records of the pilots are incomplete and somewhat vague, surviving flight information indicates that two distinct patrols went up on the afternoon of 7 December—one of five P-40s at 1245 and another of six P-40s at 1549. SSgt. Homer Garcia remembered being surprised that the squadron had that many aircraft fit to fly. In what was probably the earlier group, pilots under 1st Lt. Cecil J. Looke Jr. embarked on a lengthy patrol lasting approximately one and a half hours. The later group under squadron commander Capt. Arthur R. Kingham most likely had their patrols cut short by deteriorating weather.[11]

At least one other pilot at Haleiwa apart from those already noted took off that morning in search of the enemy: 2nd Lt. Besby F. "Frank" Holmes

2nd Lt. Arthur R. Kingham, circa early 1930s. **NARA II, 18-PU-051-234-1960B**

2nd Lt. Besby F. "Frank" Holmes, circa 1942. Note that he wears a life preserver assigned to "Lt.[?] Martin." **Frank Holmes/Ken Cooke**

F/C John D. Voss, circa August 1941, during flight training at Kelly Field. **NARA II, 18-PU-096-479-9818**

of the 47th Pursuit Squadron. Holmes had gone into Honolulu Saturday evening with Haleiwa tent mate and fellow flight school graduate (Class 41-E) 2nd Lt. John D. Voss. The two were the fresh faces in the squadron, having reported to Wheeler from flight school only twenty-four days earlier. Following ground training, the pair went through a week of flying in AT-6s with the 15th Pursuit Group's Headquarters Squadron and took their first flights in a high-performance fighter—a P-36A—on 21 November. Even accounting for the semi-rigorous training regimen at Haleiwa, each man had fewer than twenty-five hours' total experience in fighters.[12]

After a night of partying downtown, Holmes went to Sunday Mass near the Royal Hawaiian, leaving Voss behind at the hotel. He was surprised when the tempo of the Mass picked up suddenly—so much so that he was unable to follow along in his missal. At the end of the service, Holmes went outside and saw a column of military trucks roaring down the street. Upon reaching the suite at the hotel he learned from an excited John Voss that Hawai'i was under attack.

The two ran outside and flagged down a civilian car to take them back to Wheeler. Finding the base a shambles, they continued on with the civilian driver ten miles to Haleiwa and found a P-36A serviced and ready to go.[13]

Eager to fight but showing his inexperience, Holmes entered the cockpit but could not get the engine started. He used up five of the six available cartridges for the "8-gauge shotgun shell" compression starter before giving up and coaxing MSgt. Elmer T. Lund, the squadron's line chief, into the cockpit to start it for him. Holmes was so inexperienced that he did not know how to charge the guns or turn on the gunsight, and again he turned to Lund for assistance. Armed with one .30-caliber Browning machine gun, Holmes took off and flew southeast toward Pearl Harbor, where "the only people who shot at [him] were the people on the ground." That was enough. He turned tail for Haleiwa and thumped onto the turf after his first "war patrol." The fifteen-minute flight—the shortest of all the flights that day except for those of his ill-fated Bellows brethren—was long enough to initiate him into the exclusive club of fighter pilots who took to the air on 7 December 1941 to do battle with the Japanese.[14]

Aftermath at Bellows

After the attacks ended, O'ahu's pursuit bases immediately looked to heighten their security and undertake recovery and repairs. Men from the base took over half of the local post office to coordinate the efforts, and a small radio group set up shop near Waimānalo just outside the military reservation. Pfc. Ernest A. Brown worked in a group that confiscated all the amateur radios on the island. Telephone employees probably came under the authority of the military as well, using the Waimānalo post office as a command post. While Brown was at the post office late one night, a telephone repairman arrived to perform maintenance on a line. When the man turned on his headlamp to illuminate his work area, shots rang out almost at once, and the lineman came off

the pole "about as fast as I've ever seen anybody come down."[15]

The military shut off public access to the bases almost entirely, with restrictions extending to the adjoining road net. Several airmen without specific duty stations, including Pvt. Byron Kolbert, went to Bellows' Main Gate south of the airfield to secure the entrance and challenge civilian vehicles on the highway in front of the gate. They stayed on duty all day and during the night of 7–8 December. The impromptu guard detail took great satisfaction in challenging the snooty civilians who had looked down "their long, expensive noses at the lowly servicemen. . . . I don't care who you are! Stop! Get out of that car!"[16]

During moments when traffic was light, Kolbert's thoughts turned to the possibility of Japanese invasion. Like many others he was certain that invasion was imminent, probably that very night, because "they've got us now!" Although soldiers strung barbed wire and set up machine-gun emplacements, they knew they lacked the heavier-caliber weapons needed to turn away an invasion force. There seemed even less cause for optimism back inside the base, among both the enlisted men and their officers. About forty minutes after the strafing attack by fighters from the *Hiryū* ended, the commander of Bellows' subdepot appeared for duty at the warehouse and issued an order that probably sent a shiver down SSgt. Snowden Steuart's spine. If invasion was imminent, *everything* was to be destroyed. Later in the day, due to the very exposed position of the airfield's headquarters atop the big hill, field commander Lt. Col. Leonard D. Weddington and his staff evacuated the stone headquarters building and retreated to the plantation headquarters in Waimānalo.[17]

Officers and enlisted men alike patrolled the coast for signs of the invasion force that seemed certain to come. Officers in the 86th Observation Squadron were issued rifles, pistols, and all the ammunition they could carry. "You are on your own," they were advised. "If you don't have [a car], team up with somebody and put your bedrolls in the trunk because we don't know what's going to happen. But there's one damn thing we're certain of. We've got to patrol the beaches." The men roamed the beach all night looking for anything suspicious. Pvt. Richard A. Mergenthaler stood guard in the company of Pvt. Michael Cerillo, an armorer with the 86th Observation Squadron. He could not have been paired with a better squadron-mate. Earlier in the day, Cerillo had flown on patrol in one of the O-47s. Somehow the two airmen acquired a twin .50-caliber machine gun mount from 1st Lt. Richards' ground-looped B-17C, which was still sitting off the end of the runway opposite the beach. The two privates strapped the "twin-fifties" to two-by-four posts and stood by, ready to use them. Years later Mergenthaler reflected that it was fortunate that they had not fired the guns, because the recoil would surely have torn the guns clear.[18]

On the afternoon of 7 December, MSgt. Malcolm W. Pettet—the recently promoted line chief for the 86th Observation Squadron at Bellows—was told that the field might be receiving aircraft from the

MSgt. Malcolm W. Pettet, line chief for the 86th Observation Squadron at Bellows Field, circa late 1941.
AFHRA

Enterprise. Accordingly, Pettet saw to it that portable runway lights were put in place and set up a small floodlight at the land end of the runway.[19]

Repairs: Aircraft and Aprons

Over at Wheeler Field, the paramount task was to repair damaged aircraft and prepare them for flight. As soon as the Japanese attacks subsided, mechanics began scrounging for spare parts among the wrecked fighters on the parking apron. SSgt. David I. Walsh left his refuge in Barracks No. 1 and reported to the flight line, where he doused fires and cannibalized wreckage for parts and .50-caliber machine guns. It was not until about 1300 that his unit—the 19th Pursuit Squadron—was able to launch one of their P-40s into the air. The salvaged material allowed upgrades for Wheeler's P-36As, which as config-ured—for cost reasons—carried one .30-caliber and one .50-caliber machine gun mounted in the nose. As the mounting brackets and hardware allowed guns of either caliber to be mounted, however, the crews installed salvaged .50-calibers along with pilot armor in all the surviving aircraft.[20]

Maintenance crews worked through the after-noon and into the night of 7 December without sleep or breaks, and without food until a truck finally arrived the next morning with sandwiches and cof-fee. Mechanics managed to put fourteen aircraft back in service for the evening patrol on 7 December—an incredible accomplishment. The marathon efforts of mechanics in the 19th Pursuit readied eleven addi-tional fighters for flight operations by 8 December. The importance of Wheeler's sheet metal shop, which had survived the raids, is difficult to overstate. The men there performed work that in ordinary times would have been reserved for the Hawaiian Air Depot at Hickam. Their skills gave Wheeler a leg up in the repairs required to put damaged aircraft back in ser-vice until replacement aircraft could arrive from the West Coast.[21]

Repairs to Wheeler's facilities started almost immediately as well. When the initial raid concluded,

A P-40B, most likely from the 78th Pursuit Squadron, lies in ruins on the pavement in front of Hangar 4; view looking north. An airman atop the left wing is perhaps puzzling over how to remove the two .50-caliber machine guns and blast tubes mounted above the engine. Four other men gathered near a stepladder/platform are salvaging engine components. The propeller as well as the .30-caliber machine guns have already been removed. Note the Control Tower atop the hangar's central office core. **NARA II, 111-SC-134896**

Bulldozed engines from P-40s of the 18th Pursuit Group litter the eastern half of the parking apron at Wheeler Field, probably during the afternoon of 7 December. The two engines in the foreground (with white propeller spinners) are from the 44th Pursuit Squadron; the three in the background (probably with darker spinners) are from the 6th Pursuit Squadron. Note that salvaging is under way on the aircraft in the background. **Aiken, NMPW**

The fuselage of P-36A 3/15P (A.C. Ser. No. 38-36), with aircraft buzz number "3" lies outside the northeast face of Wheeler's Final Assembly Shop at the western end of the hangar line on 7 December. The plane had been in a taxiing accident on 13 November 1941 at Haleiwa Field. Second Lt. Charles M. Parrett had just parked the aircraft after leading a formation training flight with two students when 2nd Lt. Irvin W. Henze Jr. collided with Parrett's parked plane. The third pilot in the flight was 2nd Lt. William A. Waldman in P-36A (38-73). The wings from Parrett's P-36A were removed for transport back to Wheeler for possible repair. According to its aircraft history card, however, the aircraft was "awaiting survey" as of 28 December, and thus by the end of the year had become a candidate for cannibalization and scrapping. **NARA II, 111-SC-128348, cropped**

Bulldozed wreckage of aircraft from the 18th Pursuit Group has been pushed into a pile by the 804th Engineer Battalion (Avn), Company A ; view looking west in the early afternoon hours of 7 December. The wreckage includes a P-26 at right; P-40s at the center; and the right pontoon, wing, and engine of a Grumman OA-9 amphibian. Beyond the wreckage are the smoldering remains of Tent City, set afire during the bombing and strafing attacks by bombers from the *Zuikaku*. At the far right is the south corner of the 100-Man Barracks No. 4, with 200-Man Barracks Nos. 1 and 2 just visible through the smoke at center. Hanger 2 is at the far left—still intact after escaping the bombing and fires of the first attack wave.
NARA II, 111-SC-134886

elements of the 804th Engineer Battalion (Avn) arrived "to repair and protect the field." Less a rear guard left behind, Company A departed Schofield Barracks at 0805 under the command of 1st Lt. Alfred O. Jones (CE) and had its heavy equipment in place at Wheeler by 0838. The immediate requirement was to clear and dispose of aircraft wreckage from the parking aprons and to fill bomb craters so that equipment could gain access to the damaged hangars and institute repairs. By 8 December the company had completed clearing the aprons and could proceed with construction of ground defenses at the field, activity that continued through the end of the month.[22]

Preparations for Invasion

During the later morning and afternoon hours of 7 December, the airmen at Wheeler shouldered tasks for which they had neither training nor expertise. Pvt. William H. Roach Jr. of the 45th Pursuit Squadron drew dangerous duty indeed for a general clerk, being assigned to a crew that was to draw aviation fuel from Wheeler's Aqua system for transport out to Haleiwa Field, which had no independent fuel supply of its own. Alarm sirens sounded at about ten-minute intervals as the men were filling the tanker trucks, forcing everyone to rush for cover and leave the vulnerable vehicles sitting out in the open. Roach and company continued with the highly hazardous activity throughout the nerve-wracking night of 7–8 December.[23]

Back at the 18th Pursuit Group's barracks, at about noon Pfc. Edmund H. Russell was issued a full field pack; unfortunately, it was in pieces. He had never had to assemble such a contraption because he had been trained as a butcher, not an infantryman, but he was fortunate that infantrymen were present to assist. Although Russell also received a rifle, a .45-caliber automatic pistol, a helmet, and a gas mask, he had never fired a gun during his time in the Army and had no training in weapons.[24]

Men accustomed to peacetime Army routines cast aside time-honored procedures in the interest of

setting up the base's defenses. To its credit, Wheeler's Quartermaster Detachment abandoned all use of forms, requisitions, and procedures. If someone needed anything, he asked for it and received it—no questions asked. Pvt. Mannie Siegle received a .45-caliber pistol and counted himself fortunate because he knew how to fire it; not many other men in the Quartermaster Detachment did. Improvisation was among the rules of the day. At about 1600, airplane mechanic Pvt. Jack Spangler received orders to "take two working .50-caliber machine guns with M-2 mounts and seven men to the west end of the field." The "red dirt trench" he and the men in his charge dug during the late afternoon hours was their home for the next three days. Lacking supplies, they drank rainwater they captured in their canteen cups and scavenged guavas to eat. Almost sixty years later he reflected, "Many men lost their lives that day. We were just happy to be alive." Spangler and others received standing orders to respond to each of three alert notifications as follows:

▷ (Whiskey alert!) "Shoot down anything!"
▷ (Wine alert!) "If you can identify your target as Japanese, shoot it!"
▷ (Water alert!) "Hold your fire!"[25]

Some men volunteered for any duty with no thought to what it might entail. With the raid concluded, Pvt. James R. Piggott of the 44th Pursuit Squadron and others reported to the Dispensary, having heard of the "dire need of volunteers to help with [the] wounded." The men from the 44th Pursuit Squadron were "orphans" because almost all their NCOs and officers were fighting at Bellows Field. Piggott described the ghastly duty delegated to him: "Unfortunately I was assigned with a medic to recover and remove dead bodies. I was just barely able to handle this until we had to deal with a torso which I recognized as the remains of a close friend. I then asked for and received orders to serve as a sentry outside the infirmary." Inside the Dispensary, meanwhile, after tumbling from the wing of 2nd Lieutenant Taylor's P-40 and landing on his head, SSgt. John L. Palinkas came under the care of a physician who determined that Palinkas had suffered a seizure. Concluding that he was able to function, Palinkas rose, returned to the line, and spent the night removing ammunition from Hangar 4.[26]

The Long Night of 7–8 December

As if the men were not dispirited enough, by late morning a solid overcast set in over O'ahu, and after midday it began to rain. At some undetermined time later in the day mess hall trucks began the herculean task of distributing coffee and sandwiches to the dispersed men. Anyone who asked for a second sandwich received bad news: food rationing had been instituted at Wheeler. Runners sent to pick up food for their entire unit met with disappointment when the mess personnel refused to hand over more than the one man's fair share. Other individuals went hungry when they could not locate the food distribution points. Pvt. Henry C. Brown remembered that the sight of cut green beans had always made him sick to his stomach, but when the food truck arrived that night, "the thing that tasted the best to me was the damned green beans."[27]

The night of 7–8 December found Pvt. Charles L. Hendrix atop the 600-Man Barracks as part of a .50-caliber machine-gun crew. The rain never let up. Shivering in his wet clothing, Hendrix realized that this was the first time he had been cold during his time in Hawai'i. The men finally received something to eat that night, which helped to break the chill. Hendrix had only a sandwich, but the events of the morning were so unsettling that he had trouble keeping down even that meager meal.[28]

The authorities set in place strict communication procedures in the hours after the attack. Each squadron commander had his command post on the flight line near the aircraft, and the pilots remained close to their airplanes, which by now were all out in the revetments. All communication from the unit commanders to their men had to pass through the orderly rooms (or tents). Cpl. Clarence W. Kindl and the other clerks in the 46th Pursuit Squadron received devices for decoding messages—an activity that was tedious but relatively easy in daylight. After sundown, effective communication became exceedingly difficult and even dangerous. Work in the orderly rooms was particularly frustrating because clerks had to use shaded lights with doubled tent flaps for security. In order to pass orders and messages up and down the chain of command, Corporal Kindl had to walk perhaps half a mile in the inky darkness, from sentry to sentry, all the while praying that the password had not been changed in the interim.[29]

Kindl was right to be frightened. Wheeler Field was an exceedingly dangerous place to be at night. There were "gas" alerts and "any number of short gun bursts" at the least provocation. The airmen were on edge for three nights before they settled down. By some miracle, there were no friendly Army Air Force casualties, but Pvt. Milroy L. Richardson noted that "we shot four water buffaloes and killed a pineapple train."[30]

Just after dark, antiaircraft crews around the field went to Whiskey alert (shoot everything down). That order and the men's general edginess set the stage for tragedy. Pvt. Jack Spangler and numerous others heard an aircraft approaching in the murk, albeit with landing lights on. Although no one knew at the time, it was a Navy Grumman F4F-3A fighter (BuNo 3906) flown by Lt. (jg) Francis F. "Fritz" Hebel from the *Enterprise*. Minutes earlier, Hebel and five other Navy pilots had attempted to land in the dark at NAS Pearl Harbor on Ford Island. The harbor exploded with antiaircraft fire. Two pilots were killed, and Hebel fled north toward an alternate landing at Wheeler Field. Spangler's antiaircraft crew (along with many others) assumed that the fighter's landing lights were a ruse, and as soon as Hebel's stubby Wildcat was in range the men let fly. It was not until about half an hour later that they received the Water alert order (to hold their fire). Yet another

The grave marker for Lt. (jg) Francis F. "Fritz" Hebel, grave no. 575, section C, National Memorial Cemetery of the Pacific. **NARA, St. Louis**

thirty minutes passed before a party of medics was sent out to assist the pilot, were he still alive. Spangler and the others heard the medics going out, and it seemed that sentries challenged them every fifty feet. Grief-stricken over his error (and that of others), he told his crew that if they challenged the medics, he would shoot them.[31]

Spangler heard later that their guns did indeed bring down an American in Kīpapa Gulch near Wheeler, but that the Navy pilot had survived and told the medics that he had been injured in an air battle with the Japanese out to sea. Whatever the source of the report, and whatever relief it might have provided to Spangler and other gunners at Wheeler Field, the story was false. Fritz Hebel died at the hands of his countrymen. Medics pulled him from 6-F-1, critically injured and barely alive, and he was taken to the General Hospital at Schofield Barracks. According to hospital records, Lieutenant Hebel died in the early morning hours of 8 December.[32]

Optimism, Pessimism, and Rumors

It is difficult to gauge or describe an average mood and mindset of the servicemen on Oʻahu in the wake of the Japanese attacks, because no one frame of mind predominated. It is indisputable that the servicemen on the island were afraid. Overlaying their fear, however, was a complex array of other emotions unique to each man. To a greater or lesser degree, they were able to manage their fear and execute their duties.

The men at Wheeler had no doubt that soon "we would have Japanese troops on the island, and that would be it." Most of them expected that they would need to abandon the base and fight from the hills. Resigned to that eventuality, Pvt. Henry Brown secured a rifle and ammunition and prepared himself for what might come. Rumors circulated that the Japanese had landed their ferocious Imperial Marines and had dropped paratroopers onto the island. Pvt. Kenneth E. Krepps was defiant, though not optimistic regarding the island's prospects. He "was sure they had us, but [we] were going to let them know that the 'Pineapple Army' wasn't any pushover."[33]

Rumors were as thick as Oʻahu's pesky mosquitos, reflecting the men's anxiety and fear. Isolation in their dispersed positions around the base and the lack of authoritative information made the situation worse. Ironically, airmen themselves kick-started the rumor mill earlier in the day when men from the 73rd Pursuit Squadron—supposedly in a defensive position on the baseball diamond—received "news" via a battery-powered shortwave radio that picked up the very worst of the rumors. Of course, as the information had come via radio, it had to be true.[34]

Men heard that Japanese troops had come ashore at Kahuku Point. Japanese paratroopers had landed as well, clad in blue coveralls. Although Pfc. Edmund Russell was wearing his khakis, many men close by were in blue work coveralls. An advisory came that, after a certain time, anyone in a blue uniform would be shot. "Well, it was a quick change to get out of those blue uniforms that we were in." Word was passed that the invaders deployed some sort of death ray that they used against Wheeler's guards, thus reviving the terror of Orson Welles' *War of the Worlds* broadcast of 1938. During that terror-ridden evening following the attack, men were ready to believe almost anything.[35]

Disturbing "news" said that the native Japanese living on Oʻahu had collaborated with the invading troops. Such resonated with SSgt. Charles H. Leyshock and many others and confirmed their long-held suspicions and assumptions. Although Leyshock attributed the success of the Japanese attack to superior planning and coordination, he believed that they received aid from fifth-column activities. Stories circulated that Japanese in Hawaiʻi had burned directional markers in sugarcane fields by day and lit gasoline fires by night. Pvt. Robert B. Williams, a general clerk with the 45th Pursuit Squadron, heard that military police had entered Japanese homes in Wahiawā and found radio transmitters and receivers. Elsewhere on the island, it was said, the Japanese population banded together, broke into an arsenal, and killed the people on the spot. Another rumor circulated that the authorities picked up the manager of Kemoʻo Farms—Joseph R. Itagaki—allegedly in a Japanese uniform boasting, "I surrender as a spy." Ironically, Itagaki was as fierce an American patriot as any man on Oʻahu. He later served with great distinction with the 442nd Regimental Combat Team in Europe.[36]

Even enlisted men were aware that the Army depended on the U.S. Pacific Fleet to protect its installations on Oʻahu. Among the most debilitating rumors was that the fleet was lost, defeated at sea, and enemy troopships were streaming into Pearl Harbor. The towering columns of smoke rising from the harbor seemed to provide necessary physical evidence. One of Hawaiʻi's two infantry divisions had been

wiped out in desperate fighting, one rumor said. All ships between Hawaiʻi and the mainland had been torpedoed and San Francisco was being invaded, said another.[37]

Bellows Field had its own rumors, intensified by the field's isolation and lack of prepared defenses. Its bordering beach seemed tailor-made for an amphibious assault. The prospect of Japanese invasion on the night of 7–8 December had everyone upset and jumpy. Although Bellows' formal wartime defenses would take days to establish, machine-gun positions and entrenchments went up quickly along the beach, manned by airmen divided into defensive squads. Pfc. Ernest A. Brown received an appointment as squad leader and a spot promotion to sergeant from Colonel Weddington. "I never did get to be a corporal," he later said. In the event of trouble, his squad was to rush with rifles out to their assigned trench and repel the hordes.[38]

Among the officers of the 86th Observation Squadron, 2nd Lt. Phillip Willis assumed that a paratrooper landing would set up Oʻahu for a full-scale invasion. Willis believed that the island's mountain ranges were honeycombed with ammunition dumps. "I didn't know how much. I was just hoping we had enough." Lacking direct knowledge of how the rest of the island had fared in the morning's attacks, men assumed the very worst. And with no Navy or Air Force behind them, the defenders could not possibly turn back an invasion. While wandering the beach in the darkness, Willis mused, "This thing could last four or five years before we get home, or they might capture us before tomorrow's over."[39]

Patrols: Haleiwa and Bellows

With the prospect of invasion on everyone's mind, it was critical that Bellows and Haleiwa Fields on the east and west shores of Oʻahu, with their relatively intact complements of P-36s and P-40s, be prepared to watch for Japanese invasion attempts, whether by air or by sea. The pilots of the 47th Pursuit Squadron at Haleiwa had furnished the lion's share of the

Afternoon Patrol, Haleiwa Field, 7 December 1941
73rd Pursuit Squadron

Aircraft	Pilot	Duration
P-40B	1st Lt. John S. Evans	1:15
P-40B	1st Lt. Everett W. Stewart	1:10
P-40B	1st Lt. Charles E. Taylor	1:05
P-36A	2nd Lt. Floyd E. Lambert	0:20
P-40B	2nd Lt. John L. McGinn	1:00

aerial resistance that morning and had conducted postattack patrols as well. Since the Japanese had destroyed all the aircraft assigned to Wheeler's 73rd Pursuit, that squadron's pilots packed up and rode out to Haleiwa in the afternoon drizzle to relieve the beleaguered 47th.[40]

The 73rd Pursuit pilots flew five sorties during the late afternoon of 7 December, after which the drizzle transitioned over to general rain. And that night, "it *really* started raining." Unfortunately, no one had thought to provide accommodations for the relief pilots. Lacking even tents, the pilots laid their

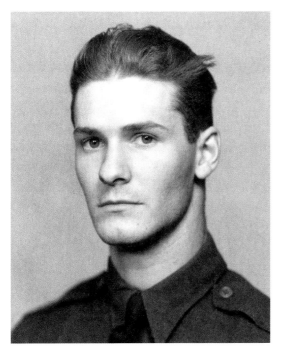

F/C Raymond K. "Skeets" Gallagher, 14 February 1940, during flight training at Kelly Field. **NARA II, 18-PU-032-148-4830**

minimal bedding on the sodden ground and pulled tarpaulins over themselves to keep out the rain. First Lt. Everett W. Stewart and 1st Lt. Raymond K. "Skeets" Gallagher fought a nightlong battle for a tarp that was big enough for only one man. As at Wheeler, the men at Haleiwa fired at "invaders" all night long, blasting away at any noise they heard in the dark, so sleep was impossible. When Stewart drew his rations the next morning, he received a candy bar and a bottle of beer.[41]

Haleiwa slated the 73rd Pursuit Squadron for flight operations early on the morning of 8 December as well. Sometime before daylight, six pilots were sitting in their aircraft warming up on the grass landing strip—which was short even for experienced pilots—when a voice cut sharply through the murk: "Take off! The Japs are coming in!" 1st Lieutenant Stewart, in the second flight element, had to taxi around one of the six planes that had nosed over in the soft ground, shortening the available runway length even more. "It was pitch dark—no lights, no nothing, with a slight bit of daylight just ready to come over the top." The five remaining pilots pushed their throttles to the stop and just made it over the trees on the northeast end of the strip, then shaped a course for Pearl Harbor. The pilots did not know their exact position owing to the darkness; they just headed in the general direction of Pearl Harbor. When they arrived over the harbor, "all the ships that were left let loose, and it was just like fireworks coming up through the clouds." The five fighters skedaddled up above the clouds and encountered strong northeast

Dawn Patrol, Haleiwa Field, 8 December 1941,
73rd Pursuit Squadron

Aircraft	Pilot
P-36A	1st Lt. Floyd D. Colley
P-40B	1st Lt. John S. Evans
P-40B	1st Lt. Raymond K. Gallagher
P-40B	1st Lt. Everett W. Stewart
P-40B	1st Lt. Charles E. Taylor

winds that blew them off course. Once again unsure of their exact location, the Wheelerites finally landed safely at the Ewa Mooring Mast Field. Following a brief interlude as guests of the Marine Corps, all five aircraft took off again and flew to Wheeler—likely to pick up .50-caliber ammunition, which probably was still not available at Haleiwa.[42]

Meanwhile, the dawn patrol out of Bellows on the opposite shore was under way as well, although according to the 8 December diary entry of Cpl. Victor H. Peterson, operations that morning began poorly. As the 44th Pursuit Squadron, with eight P-40s in commission, taxied for takeoff in the predawn darkness, one of the fighters ran into P-40C "337" (A.C. Ser. No. 41-13337). Although the details are vague, it appears that 2nd Lt. John A. Moore approached the P-40C (probably from behind) and struck its tail with his right wing. Either the force of the impact or

2nd Lt. John A. Moore's P-40 lies collapsed on one gear alongside the runway at Bellows Field on 9 December after Moore collided with a P-40C on the taxiway in the predawn darkness of 8 December. Note the shredded left wingtip with evidence of the impact extending halfway to the open gun ports. Crews have removed the damaged propeller and the machine guns. The four open access doors under the wing indicate that armorers removed the .30-caliber ammunition boxes as well. **NARA II, 111-SC-127000**

P-40C "337" (A.C. Ser. No. 41-13337) on 9 December following the collision with Moore's P-40 the previous morning. The gun ports on the leading edge of the right wing are still open after the machine guns were removed. **NARA II, 111-SC-127012**

F/C John A. Moore, 18 March 1941, during flight training at Kelly Field. **NARA II, 18-PU-065-308-7911**

Moore's braking spun his plane counterclockwise and collapsed his right landing gear. The now-higher wing tore through 337's fuselage aft of the cockpit, and Moore's propeller chewed its wingtip, damaging 337 so severely that it was written off as a total loss. It seemed that the plane was "born for hard luck," having been wrecked twice within six months. Second Lt. George Whiteman—who had lost his life the day before—wrecked it [as aircraft 18P/105] at Wheeler on 22 July 1941, although it was subsequently repaired. Corporal Peterson attributed Moore's mishap to "a case of nerves and I think everyone was tired, also it was dark and no lights." The pilots were reluctant to use their lights because gunfire from jumpy guards "could mean death." Interestingly, pilots were in such high demand that Moore nevertheless took part in a patrol later that day.[43]

Prisoner of War Number One

Closer to first light on 8 December, a soldier at Bellows Field saw what he thought to be aircraft wreckage floating offshore. He reported the sighting to Capt. Edward

F. Kent, recently detached from the Headquarters Company, 21st Infantry Regiment to serve as Bellows' ground defense officer. Captain Kent contacted the Control Tower at Bellows, and the airman on duty there spotted the object offshore as well.[44]

Second Lt. Jean K. Lambert, one of the 86th Observation Squadron's combat observers, had spent most of the night "in the operations shack . . . listening to the radio." Between 0600 and 0700 Lambert and others were preparing for the first reconnaissance flight of the day when a call from the control tower advised that a suspicious object was "in the water, out by the reef, off the beach end of the runway." Maj. Charles Stewart, commanding the 86th Observation Squadron, instructed 1st Lt. James T. Lewis to take off, with Lambert as an observer, to investigate the sighting.[45]

The flight was not a long one, approximately fifteen minutes. While Lewis circled the area where the object was supposed to be, Lambert crawled

2nd Lt. James T. Lewis of the 86th Observation Squadron in the cockpit of an O-47B at Bellows Field, circa 1941. Lewis investigated the sighting of Ensign Sakamaki's submarine that beached near Bellows. Salvage crews soon discovered that the boat was a two-man "midget" submarine, although still a vessel of some size. **AFHRA**

2nd Lt. Jean K. Lambert of the 86th Observation Squadron at Bellows Field, circa late 1941. Lambert was 1st Lieutenant Lewis' observer during the flight of 8 December. **Lambert**

2nd Lt. Paul C. Plybon, 298th Infantry Regiment, Company G, captor of Ens. Sakamaki Kazuo on 8 December 1941. **Plybon**

down into the Plexiglas enclosure in the O-47's lower fuselage. Although there was insufficient light to use the plane's aerial camera, the nature of the object was quite obvious: a submarine had grounded on the reef. Lambert saw no signs of life through the waves crashing over the boat. He raised Major Stewart on the radio, described the boat, and promised to make a sketch of it when he returned. After ten minutes or so of circling at low altitude, Lewis turned back toward Bellows. He "briefed [Stewart], who then called Department Headquarters to report the situation."[46]

As the morning grew brighter, the submarine came to the attention of troops on the beach. Second Lt. Paul C. Plybon was second in command of Company G, 298th Infantry Regiment—a Hawaii National Guard unit called up into federal service fourteen months earlier. Elements of the 298th had bivouacked for weeks at the beach near the end of Bellows' runway.[47]

With "less than 200 men and 10 miles of beach to defend," 1st Lt. Clarence R. Johnson (the commander of Company G) had assigned Plybon the beachfront

near Bellows Field. Having been advised to expect the invasion around 0400 on Monday morning, Plybon instructed his men to dig trenches and set out barbed wire and telephone cable. By nightfall he and his men "were functioning like a well greased machine." Well greased or not, Plybon was greatly relieved that "the witching hour had arrived [with] no attack." He nevertheless made one last trip up and down the beach that morning, double-checking communications and general readiness.[48]

When Plybon climbed atop a sand dune with his binoculars to scan the beach, surf, and ocean beyond, he discovered what appeared to be a stake in the water a considerable distance out from the beach. He turned to Cpl. David M. Akui—who had stayed with him all night as a runner—and asked if he remembered seeing a stake that far out from shore. "No sir—no stake out there," Akui answered. Plybon handed his binoculars to Akui and told him to take a look. Akui "became very excited" when he focused on the "stake" and indicated that there was indeed something there. Retrieving the glasses, Plybon saw

Cpl. David M. Akui, 298th Infantry Regiment, Company G, captor of Ens. Sakamaki Kazuo on 8 December 1941. **NGEF**

Ens. Sakamaki Kazuo in captivity, probably in late December 1941. **NARA II, RG 80**

a wave breaking over a submarine conning tower. "I knew even in the dim light that it was [a] sub fouled on the reef." Continuing to watch, Plybon noticed "a flash of white in the water." Again he passed Akui the binoculars and asked him what it was. After Akui guessed that the object was a turtle, Plybon grabbed the glasses and saw that it was a man who appeared to be trying to ride the waves to shore. The two soldiers walked down the beach and placed themselves at the spot where the swimmer would most likely land. When a huge comber picked up the man and threw him down into the surf, Plybon and Akui waded into the water "and pulled out a man—Japanese and obviously an officer. He was clad only in the tight, white, Japanese battle suit of underwear into which was sewn the traditional good luck & religious symbols." The man was so exhausted that Plybon and Akui had to assist him to their weapons carrier for transport back to headquarters at Bellows. The as-yet-unidentified Japanese man captured at 0540 that morning was Ens. Sakamaki Kazuo of the Imperial Japanese Navy.[49]

Plybon and Akui transported Sakamaki to the Operations Shack (see illustration on page 34), where Major Stewart, 1st Lieutenant Lewis, 2nd Lieutenant Lambert, Sgt. Fred F. Dean, several enlisted men, and infantry officer 1st Lt. Ernest S. Groneweg were waiting. Plybon entered with Akui and Sakamaki and announced that the Japanese man was an officer from the submarine that was aground on the reef. Plybon asked Stewart to (1) detail a squad to get the Japanese officer to Fort Shafter and G-2 *fast*; (2) call the submarine base at Pearl Harbor and tell them that there was a Japanese submarine on the reef; and (3) call NAS Kaneohe Bay to see if they had aircraft available to fly over the sub and drop a small bomb to free it from the reef.[50]

Stewart placed the calls as Plybon requested, but before the squad arrived from Fort Shafter some of the enlisted men wanted to rough up Sakamaki. Plybon reminded all present that Sakamaki was a prisoner of war and had to be treated as such, and he convinced Major Stewart to order the enlisted men out of the building. Then Plybon asked for a blanket and some food for the prisoner. One of the men produced a boiled egg. Confident that the situation was in hand, Plybon returned to his men on the beach.[51]

The remaining Americans who stayed in the shack with Sakamaki for about an hour were not in a hospitable mood. Tempers flared when Sakamaki refused to speak. Apparently, 1st Lieutenant Groneweg took charge of the situation and attempted to interrogate Sakamaki, although the "interrogation" seems to have consisted of not-so-veiled physical threats, as the American officer "wanted to shoot Sakamaki right then and there." Perhaps an hour into the prisoner's captivity at the Operations Shack, 2nd Lt. Lee E. Metcalfe and someone from "the military intelligence staff" arrived and whisked the Japanese officer away, not a moment too soon. Little had gone right at Bellows during the last twenty-four hours, and the capture of such a valuable prisoner was a feather in everyone's hat.[52]

Personnel Issues and Logistics

Meanwhile, formal evacuation of dependents to the comparative safety of Honolulu and other communities moved forward, although some residents chose not to wait for Army trucks to bear them away. Bess Lalumendier left Quarters 120 in her husband's car and spent three nights in Haleʻiwa, listening to her car radio for news. After a few nights there she decided to return closer to Wheeler and stayed with friends in Wahiawā. She was able to get word of her whereabouts to her husband, who came to see her on Wednesday, 10 December, and gave her his helmet and gas mask. She cherished those mementos of her husband's love and thoughtfulness the rest of her life.[53]

Once the dependents had been taken to safer places, the military organizations on Oʻahu coped with logistical and personnel issues brought on by Hawaiʻi's isolation and its vulnerable supply lines. Although no concrete information was in hand regarding the Imperial Navy's submarines and their ability to disrupt delivery of critical shipments from the West Coast, one had to assume the worst. The Hawaiian Air Force needed reinforcements, weapons, ammunition, replacement aircraft, and fuel. The limited food supply on Oʻahu was of immediate concern as well. Very quickly, strict rationing measures took effect. In anticipation of coming food shortages, Wheeler cut back to serving two meals a day. Despite that draconian measure, there was some improvement in messing arrangements as men now rotated in from their defensive positions to take meals in the mess halls. The return to "normal" messing enhanced morale and also relieved considerable pressure on the mess personnel, who no longer had to deliver meals to widely dispersed men. The men were far from normal, however. "It was so quiet you could hear a pin drop—no one said a word and everyone had a blank expression on their face. Every time a plane flew over low we would drop our food and run."[54]

Despite the other shortages on Oʻahu in the near term, pursuit pilots were plentiful. The real issue was experience. Recent arrivals from flight school were quickly declared to be fully qualified fighter pilots, regardless of their shortcomings in gunnery, formation flying, and flight time in high-performance aircraft. The 47th Pursuit Squadron—still operating out of Haleiwa—was typical. Charles E. Kneen, Karl F. Harris, and Joseph Oblak, all second lieutenants, had arrived in Hawaiʻi on 19 November. In the seventeen days prior to the attack each had accumulated a paltry two hours of touch-and-go landings in AT-6s and one solo flight in a P-26B. One week after the attacks they were flying P-40s—something that would have been unthinkable only a month before.[55]

Aircraft Replacement and Base Refurbishment

The surplus of pilots contrasted sharply with the severe shortage of aircraft. Issues of Oʻahu's defense aside, without aircraft to replace those lost on 7 December, comprehensive training and the acquisition of combat skills by newer pilots would be almost

Pursuit Aircraft Availability at Wheeler Field

Type	On Hand before Raid	Under Maintenance before Raid	On Hand after Raid	Unusable after Raid	Usable after Raid
P-40C	12	3	7	10	2
P-40B	87	32	50	63	25
P-36A	39	19	35	23	16
P-26A	8	1	3	6	2
P-26B	6	3	5	4	2
TOTALS	152	58	100	106	47

Note: The figures in this table are as they appear in the Roberts Commission exhibit.

impossible. The table above puts the aircraft situation into perspective.[56]

The table shows that more than one-third of Wheeler's pursuit assets were out of service at the time of the attack, although the vast majority of those were in first-echelon maintenance—minor repairs that did not necessarily require presence in the hangars. Only eleven P-40s were in second- and third-echelon maintenance, which usually did require hangar facilities. The figure for aircraft destroyed represented half of the available aircraft *in service*, but only a third of the *total on hand*. Although the potential thus existed to put about one hundred aircraft back into service, aircraft that were cannibalized or simply written off reduced that figure. Compared to the fifty-seven P-40s and thirty-five P-36s on hand after the raids, as of 17 December there were forty-three and twenty-seven, respectively, either available or under maintenance—testimony to the dogged perseverance of Wheeler's mechanics.[57]

The authorities on Oʻahu were expecting material assistance from the West Coast to arrive about one week after the attack. The earliest fighter aircraft arrivals appeared at Hickam Field's wharf, on the island's south shore, about mid-December, an indication that the aircraft were already disassembled and crated on 8 December and were shipped to Oʻahu the next day. Thus, three fighter types—P-39Ds and P-40D/Es—probably began arriving on or around 15 December. The aircraft arrived crated and disassembled, with the Hawaiian Air Depot at Hickam Field tasked with their reassembly. "This job was not easy," the depot's historian noted. The mechanics were not familiar with these new planes—especially the Bell P-39D—and neither spare parts nor technical information was included with the crates. No records detail precisely how long aircraft assembly took, but evidence suggests that the process consumed no more than about twenty-four hours, with six to eight aircraft arriving each day.[58]

Assembly was only one phase of the work required before the planes could be delivered to units in the field. Flight-testing of the assembled airframes followed and proceeded at "terrible risk to the lives of the pilots," who forged ahead with their work for weeks on end. Lt. Col. William L. Boyd and Maj. Kingston E. Tibbetts were among the four senior pilots who shouldered this responsibility. Pilots from Wheeler's pursuit groups—mostly senior first lieutenants—performed what were probably the final test flights at Hickam Field, each about fifteen to thirty minutes' duration. At some point, these same pilots delivered the fighters to Wheeler or other locations. Most of the testing and delivery moved forward during the last week in December, although there were isolated tests and/or deliveries to Wheeler Field as early as 16 December. Availability of the P-39Ds first shows up in the Hawaiian Air Force War Diary as of 26 December, along with a large quantity of new model P-40s and additional P-39s appearing on the following day.[59]

Lt. Col. William L. Boyd, test pilot for reassembled pursuit aircraft shipped to Oʻahu in the latter weeks of December 1941. Seen here at Hickam Field circa March 1941 shortly after his promotion to lieutenant colonel while assigned to Headquarters, 18th Bombardment Wing. **AFHRA**

In the final days of 1941 the Army worked hard to erase the vestiges of the Japanese attacks. The transformation took place remarkably quickly, particularly in light of the destruction at Wheeler Field on the afternoon of 7 December. The seven craters punched through the aircraft apron had been filled in, with only the variation in tone of the concrete patches and the fragmentation damage radiating from the center point of the craters suggesting their former presence. Burning aircraft and aviation fuel had scarred the apron as well, almost exclusively on its eastern end under the wreckage of the 18th Pursuit Group's P-40s, but this damage was hardly discernible.[60]

Damage to Hangars 1 and 3 and to the Machine Shop (Building 23) was far more serious and took much longer to repair, but the wreckage had been cleared and refurbishment started. By 28 December 1941 the roof of Hangar 1 was in place, and the mangled roof, siding, and masonry of Hangar 3 had

been removed to make way for permanent repairs. The process of reconstructing the framework of Hangar 3 was still under way during a Silver Star/Purple Heart award ceremony in front of Hangar 3 on 3 July 1942.[61]

Grudges, Conspiracies, and Retrospective

Through the succeeding years and generations, survivors of the Japanese attacks pondered supposed failures by military commanders and leaders in Washington that many felt were responsible for the disaster on Oʻahu. Everyone from privates to general officers held opinions on the subject. Among that latter group was Brig. Gen. Howard Davidson. Although Davidson was somewhat hostile to Washington after the attack, he was not among those who believed that President Roosevelt withheld knowledge of a coming Japanese attack on the islands to force America into the war. He believed that Roosevelt had not "the foggiest notion that [the Japanese] would hit Pearl Harbor." Davidson did note, with some irony, that Japan probably did the United States a favor by bringing America into the war when it did. Although certainly not discounting the loss of life at Pearl Harbor in any way, the Japanese sank "old battleships" that would have been of relatively little value later in the war and initiated the design and construction of far more useful ships. Davidson also felt that it was fortunate that the Japanese attacked Hawaiʻi rather than the Panama Canal, which would have inflicted a far more crippling blow to America and its ability to fight.[62]

Others held far harsher opinions of the leaders in Washington and ascribed the worst possible motives to them. In an oral history interview with the University of North Texas in 1978, Byron Kolbert admitted to harboring deep resentment toward President Roosevelt and other leaders who allowed the Pearl Harbor disaster to occur even though Japanese codes had been broken and Japan's intentions were well known. Washington "had it down almost to the day when it would happen before it happened. They knew where it was going to happen, and that was Oahu." Kolbert believed that Roosevelt was under pressure from Winston Churchill to bring America into the war against Germany. "I just felt like I'd been taken."[63]

Everett Stewart also numbered among those who believed that Roosevelt "allow[ed] us to be attacked out there." In ironic contrast, however, he reasoned that in allowing the attack, Roosevelt unified America and made Japan's defeat inevitable. "But," Stewart added, "it was the last good thing he ever did."[64]

Others, such as Fred Runce, admitted that they lacked a complete picture but still felt that indecision at the command level led to failures that increased Oʻahu's vulnerability. Raeburn Drenner concluded that the complete surprise with which the Japanese delivered the attack could only have been achieved with outside help. That notion reflected a continued underestimation of Japanese capabilities that would feed conspiracy theories for generations.[65]

Many veterans could not find it within themselves ever again to trust a Japanese person. Kolbert admitted to being uneasy in the presence of anyone he knew to be Japanese, regardless of how well dressed and educated the person might be. He had great respect for their industry and hard work after the war, and admitted, "They're wonderful people. But I guess that knife that was put in my back along with many others, and all of the months that followed, and the hardships that we had to go through because of what they did . . . I just don't feel like a completely trusting person around them anymore."[66]

When asked, virtually all servicemen agreed that the Japanese missed a golden opportunity to take out Hawaiʻi on the opening day of the war. Brigadier General Davidson concluded in retrospect that the best time for another major attack would have been during the afternoon of 7 December, because the Americans had barely started to regain their balance and sort out operable aircraft. But the Americans had missed opportunities of their own. Davidson maintained that full use of the revetments (which were *not*

occupied on the morning of 7 December) would have made it far more difficult for the Japanese to destroy his fighters in substantial numbers. He was certain that a larger proportion of the 14th Pursuit Wing's fighters would have emerged unscathed from the worst of the bombing and strafing.[67]

One surprising aspect of the attacks was their "short" duration—less than two hours—and limited scope. After transferring from Bellows Field to the 72nd Bombardment Squadron at Hickam, Pfc. Ernest A. Brown often flew over the Navy Yard and saw the arrays of aboveground fuel-storage tanks. "Why on earth didn't the Japanese bomb those oil tanks?" he wondered. Taking the time to deprive the fleet of that fuel "would have put the Navy out of business."[68]

Most felt that the Japanese should have followed up the raids with an immediate invasion. Having heard the same rumors regarding landings and paratroopers as everyone else, John Munn and many acquaintances wondered why the Japanese did not seize Hawaiʻi, as "they could have easily done it." Thirty years later, Everett Stewart agreed wholeheartedly. The element of surprise was *the* underlying reason for Japan's spectacular success, he thought, buttressed by the high level of planning and preparation. Not mounting a follow-up invasion was Japan's greatest failure. "They could have walked across the island on the first day."[69]

First Lt. Everett W. Stewart never divulged when or whether thoughts of becoming a fighter ace entered his mind in the days following the attacks on Wheeler Field. He passed the required five aerial kill threshold on 29 March 1944 and finished the war with eight air-to-air victories, albeit gained against the German Luftwaffe over Europe rather than against the Japanese. Eleven other Wheeler survivors reached or surpassed the mark as well, some by a substantial margin. It is likely that ace status was an aspiration of many American fighter pilots present on Oʻahu on 7 December 1941—a desire to mete out retribution to those who invaded the skies over Wheeler Field.[70]

Letters and Memories

As the war dragged on, servicemen and their families clung to cherished memories kept alive by mementos, snapshots, and, invariably, letters. Pvt. Richard A. Mergenthaler of the 86th Observation Squadron had an unusual souvenir from that dreadful day on Oʻahu: the letter that he never mailed on 7 December from Bellows Field to his sweetheart, Lorraine. Mergenthaler carried the letter with him for nearly three years until he returned home in November 1944, married Lorraine, and delivered the letter in person.[71]

Letters written after the death of a serviceman took on added meaning, particularly as remains could not be shipped back to the United States while the war lasted. The letters sent to the family of 2nd Lt. John L. Dains constitute a particularly memorable correspondence. Johnny's father, Roy L. Dains, wrote from Mount Olive, Illinois, to his son's group commander. After a few words regarding the disposition of his son's personal effects Roy Dains came to his central concerns: the location of his son's grave and the circumstances surrounding his death. "Can you tell me how my son was killed? Was he killed before he had a chance to get any of those yellow rats?" Ten days after the letter arrived, Capt. Emil W. Geitner, Wheeler's Presbyterian chaplain, wrote to Mr. Dains that he was taking care of Johnny's effects and would forward the balance from his checking account. Regarding Dains' manner of death, he wrote, "I wish to tell you that your son died while in combat with the enemy and gave very good account of himself before he was brought down. We mourn with you and yours the loss of this promising young officer." Geitner went on to add that Dains was buried with full military honors at Schofield Barracks Cemetery.[72]

John Dains' best friend, 2nd Lt. Harry W. Brown, also wrote to his friend's parents, prodded in part by the fact that he had been "appointed to 'Close the books' on Johnny" and gather his effects for Chaplain Geitner.

I know that at this hour no word can assuage the infinite sorrow and sense of bereavement that you are suffering. Still, I know too some word other than the terse official notification that you received might do something towards lightening the heavy load that now lies on your hearts—perhaps in some manner help dispel the penumbra of pain. I write as one who, I'm more than proud, yes, even grateful, to state, Johnny considered as his best friend. I write as one who loved him even as you.

Brown related details about the wild car ride from Wheeler to Haleiwa, although he was careful not to mention the base names. He provided the number of the aircraft ("149") in which Dains took off on his final mission and assured the Dains that their son died a hero's death and that "there could have been no pain in it for it was instantaneous." Remembering his friend as a happy man who refused to find fault in anyone, Brown closed by saying, "Heaven is a better place for his being there."[73]

Dains himself had written one last letter to Bea, his onetime sweetheart, which opened with a morose pronouncement.

If and when you ever receive this letter, I will have been shipped home in a basket. . . . [M]y only regret is not to have snatched you up and married you, while I had the chance. I can truthfully say I liked you more than any one person I've ever known. I am wishing you all the joy & happiness possible. I remain yours forever.

With all my love, John[74]

Base leaders also wrote letters of condolence. Wheeler commander Col. William J. Flood sent such a letter to 623 West 24th Street in Sedalia, Missouri. John C. Whiteman—father of 2nd Lt. George A. Whiteman—probably received the letter shortly after a telegram from the War Department announced his son's death. It is unknown whether Flood was acquainted with the young pilot who perished in a fiery crash on Bellows Beach, but the letter's deeply personal quality led Whiteman's descendants to retain it as a cherished memento of their loved one. Colonel Flood wrote:

> You have lost a son; Freedom has gained a martyr; and you may be proud through your tears, in the knowledge that millions of souls in the world bow with me in homage to your son for the supreme sacrifice made by him, the giving of his life for his country. I salute your son, and I honor you.
>
> Wm. J. Flood
> Colonel, Air Corps,
> Commanding[75]

If one considers only the higher death toll at Hickam Field and the vast number of the dead and wounded at Pearl Harbor, it would be tempting to minimize the human toll of the 14th Pursuit Wing and the three airfields at which its component commands resided—thirty-seven killed and eighty-one

wounded. Although casualty figures can be useful, one must always take care not to trivialize the magnitude of any suffering. The death of each man carried a unique horror that changed every individual who witnessed it and survived to tell of it.[76]

A great many survivors of the horrific experiences at Wheeler, Bellows, and Haleiwa Fields—perhaps the majority—spoke of the day's events only with great reluctance. Even fifty years after the attack, Lawrence Gross—an airplane mechanic with the 45th Pursuit Squadron—found his memories too difficult and painful to process. On a sheet attached to his 18 March 1991 application to the Pearl Harbor Survivors Association, he wrote: "I have tried over the past 49 years *not* to remember the actual attack on Pearl Harbor, particularly at Wheeler Field where I witnessed too many dead and mutilated bodies." Men experienced a varied mixture of emotions when thinking about O'ahu and 7 December 1941—pleasant memories of the days before merging with unpleasant ones of the attacks and their aftermath. In October 1986, while reflecting on his affection for the base and its men, Edward White of Wheeler's 24th Material Squadron wrote: "I have a lot of fond memories

The site where 2nd Lt. George A. Whiteman crashed in the sand dunes at Bellows Beach and was reportedly buried. At least one witness at the crash site maintained that an ambulance took Whiteman's body away soon after the crash, presumably to the Dispensary. Whiteman's remains were taken to Schofield Barracks Cemetery for a 9 December 1941 burial in Plot 4, row F, grave no. 30. The sign to the rear of the cross reads, "This area is the final resting place of our comrade Lt. George A. Whiteman who was killed in action 7 December 1941. Please do not trespass." Later in 1942 (perhaps in April) there was an installation ceremony at the site for the newly formed VFW Post 94 (the Christiansen-Whiteman Post).
Gayle Kent

of Wheeler Field, and had many friends there . . . some of whom are still there in the Punchbowl."[77]

The stark reality of the day burned its imprint into the minds of many veterans, who were able to recall in astonishing detail the names of friends and acquaintances with whom they shared the common experience of war and who retained vivid memories of the day until advancing age or death claimed their consciousness. For some, memories of 7 December 1941, the day that changed their lives and those of their countrymen, took on an illusory quality. Pfc. Vernon C. Rubenking wrote to Walter Lord while the latter was gathering material for his book *Day of Infamy* in 1956: "You know, Mr. Lord, it's going on fifteen years since that day—December 7, 1941. Since that day and the many weeks and years to follow, I get to thinking about it sometimes, and it sort of seems like a dream. There are things that happened to me during those war years that I'll *never* forget, though."[78]

What of America's memory of 7 December 1941 as a nation? Will Americans allow our collective and institutional memory to become clouded by deep-seated biases against anyone and anything that does not speak to our self-interest and self-absorption? Unfortunately, there will always be those who identify with that sordid sentiment. If Americans are to move forward as a nation, however, it remains for us to recognize the value, and the goodness, of America's past sacrifices and to enshrine these men of 7 December 1941 so that their value and their goodness are never forgotten.

NOTES

CHAPTER 1. "SITUATED ON THE ELEVATED PLAINS OF MAGNIFICENT OAHU"

1. *History, Wheeler Field, T.H. 1922–1944* (hereinafter *Wheeler Field History*), Air Force History Support Office, Bolling AFB (hereinafter AFHSO), reel A0086, file AAFLD-Wheeler (1922–1944), 2; Steven E. Clay, *US Army Order of Battle 1919–1941*, vol. 3: *The Services: Air Service, Engineers, and Special Troops, 1919–41* (Fort Leavenworth, Kans.: Combat Studies Institute Press, 2010), 1371; "Hqrs. 5th Group (Obs.) Luke Field, H.T. [*sic*], Jan. 14," *Air Service News Letter* 6, no. 5 (9 March 1922): 20, Air Force History Research Agency, Maxwell AFB (hereinafter AFHRA); photograph 342-FH-3B-21798, Still Picture Branch, NARA II.

2. "Free Ballooning over Texas," *Air Service News Letter* 7, no. 13 (22 March 1920): 20, AFHRA.

3. *Wheeler Field History*, 2; photograph 342-FH-3B-21797, Still Picture Branch, NARA II; interpretation of photography in record groups 80-G and 342-FH, Still Picture Branch, NARA II; "Greetings from Wheeler Field, H.T." [*sic*] (hereinafter "Greetings from Wheeler Field"), *Air Service News Letter* 7, no. 5 (5 March 1923): 7. Based on aircraft history cards and documents at AFHRA, the first aircraft assigned to the airdrome at Schofield Barracks were almost certainly DH-4As, prior to the modernization program undertaken by the Boeing Aircraft Company to refurbish the planes with welded, steel tube fuselages. See Peter M. Bowers, *Boeing Aircraft since 1916* (Annapolis: Naval Institute Press, 1968), 66–67.

4 "Greetings from Wheeler Field," 7.

5. *Wheeler Field History*, 3; Leatrice R. Arakaki and John R. Kuborn, *7 December 1941: The Air Force Story* (Washington, D.C.: GPO, 1991), 38; "Major Sheldon Harley Wheeler," Hawaii Aviation, https://aviation.hawaii.gov/airfields-airports/oahu/wheeler-field/major-sheldon-harley-wheeler (hereinafter Wheeler bio), accessed 2 July 2019; "Death of Major Sheldon H. Wheeler, Air Service," *Air Service News Letter* 5, no. 28 (28 July 1921): 3.

6. "Death of Major Sheldon H. Wheeler," 3; Wheeler bio.

7. Constructing Quartermaster, Wheeler Field, "Completion Report on Construction of Six Steel Hangars" (hereinafter "Completion Report on Six Steel Hangars"), 10 September 1923, 1–2, Records of the Chief of Engineers, entry 391, box 328, binder 1, RG 77, NARA II.

8. "Completion Report on Six Steel Hangars," 2–3.

9. "Completion Report on Six Steel Hangars," 4.

10. "Completion Report on Six Steel Hangars," 5; "Changes in Air Service Organizations in Hawaii," *Air Service News Letter* 7, no. 19 (12 October 1923): 3.

11. Analysis of photography in "Completion Report on Six Steel Hangars," and in RG 342-FH in the Still

Picture Branch, NARA II; *Wheeler Field History*, 4; War Department, QMC Form 117, "A.C. Bomb Storage Warehouse," Records of the Chief of Engineers, entry E393, box 280, folder 2, RG 77, NARA II; Post Utilities Officer, Wheeler Field, "Completion Report on Construction at Wheeler Field at Schofield Barracks, T.H.," n.d., 1, Records of the Chief of Engineers, entry 391, box 328, binder 1, RG 77, NARA II; photograph 342-FH-3B-21831, Still Picture Branch, NARA II.

12. Constructing Quartermaster, Hickam Field [*sic*], "Report on Construction Activities at Wheeler Field, Territory of Hawaii, Covering the Period 1935–January 6, 1941," 24 February 1941 (hereinafter "Construction Activities at Wheeler"), 1–2, Records of the Chief of Engineers, entry 391, box 328, binder 2, RG 77, NARA II; *Congressional Record: Proceedings and Debates of the First Session of the Seventieth Congress of the United States of America* (hereinafter *Congressional Record*), vol. 69, pt. 9, 19 May to 25 May 1928 (Washington, D.C.: GPO, 1928), 9732–9733; selected completion reports for construction at Wheeler Field, entry 391, box 328, RG 77, NARA II.

13. "Construction Activities at Wheeler," 2; Headquarters, Hawaiian Department, "Completion Report on 4 Air Corps Double Hangars, 1 Air Corps Machine Shop, 1 Air Corps Assembly Shop, 1 Air Corps Warehouse" (hereinafter "Completion Report on Hangars and Shops"), n.d., 1, Records of the Chief of Engineers, entry 391, box 328, binder 1, RG 77, NARA II; photograph of Barracks 303 at Albrook Field, 26 October 1931, authors' files; Headquarters, Hawaiian Department, "Completion Report on Four Air Corps Barrack Buildings Together with Certain Roads, Walks and Other Utilities Therefor at Wheeler Field, Schofield Barracks, T.H." (hereinafter "Completion Report on Barracks"), n.d., 1, Records of the Chief of Engineers, entry 391, box 328, binder 1, RG 77, NARA II.

14. "Construction Activities at Wheeler," 2; Headquarters, Hawaiian Department, "Completion Report on Construction of Forty-Two (42) Sets of Married N.C.O. Quarters, One Building for Bachelor N.C.O.s, Together with Roads, Walks and Other Utilities Therefor at Wheeler Field, Schofield Barracks, T.H." n.d. (hereinafter "Completion Report, Construction of NCO Quarters"), 1–5, Records of the Chief of Engineers,

entry 391, box 328, binder 1, RG 77, NARA II; telephone conversation, JMW and Jessie Higa, 29 August 2019; photograph 342-FH-3B-21827, Still Picture Branch, NARA II.

15. Analysis by architectural historian Mark R. Wenger. See photograph 80-G-279373, NARA II, Still Photo Branch, for evidence of the new roof design. True adobe (rather than stucco over concrete) would have been a disaster because Hawai'i's heavy rains would have reduced the structures to the consistency of wet sponge cake.

16. Construction Division, Officer of the Quartermaster General, Plan 6517–240, "Wheeler Field, T.H., Layout Plan," 17 November 1939, updated to February 1941 (hereinafter "Wheeler Field Layout"), entry E393, box 280, folder 7, RG 77, NARA II; War Department, QMC Form 111, "Record of Equipment and Condition of Buildings" (hereinafter "Wheeler/Buildings"), Record of T.H., 30 June 1941, Wheeler Field, 30 June 1941, sheet 2, Records of the Chief of Engineers, entry 391, box 328, binder 1, RG 77, NARA II; "Completion Report, Construction of NCO Quarters," 2, 5. The second wing of the NCO BOQ was never built. Early construction priorities—quarters and barracks first, and the hangar line and industrial buildings afterward—contrasted sharply with the order of construction at Hickam later in the decade. See J. M. Wenger, R. J. Cressman, and J. F. Di Virgilio, *They're Killing My Boys: The History of Hickam Field and the Attacks of 7 December 1941* (Annapolis: Naval Institute Press, 2019), chap. 1.

17. Headquarters, Hawaiian Department, "Completion Report on Construction of Five Sets of Quarters for Married Field Officers, Thirty-Seven Sets of Quarters for Married Company Officers and One Building for Sixteen Bachelor Officers, Together with Certain Roads, Walks and Other Utilities Therefor at Wheeler Field, Schofield Barracks, T.H.," n.d., 1–3, Records of the Chief of Engineers, entry 391, box 328, binder 1, RG 77, NARA II; photograph 324-FH-3B-21828, Still Picture Branch, NARA II; "Record of Buildings," 30 June 1941, sheet 3; War Department, QMC Form 117, "Officers' Garage," Records of the Chief of Engineers, entry E393, box 280, folder 6, RG 77, NARA II.

18. "Landscaping at Wheeler Field," *Air Corps News* 16, no. 12 (18 October 1932): 409; "Landscaping of Wheeler

Field's Quarters Ready," *Honolulu Star-Bulletin*, 20 August 1932; "Wheeler Field to Be Planted," *Honolulu Star-Bulletin*, 10 October 1931, latter two clippings from Jessie Higa.

19. "Completion Report on Barracks"; photograph of Barracks 303 at Albrook Field, 26 October 1931, authors' files; "Wheeler Field Layout"; *Wheeler Field History*, 15, 17. The nomenclature of the barracks is inconsistent on different plans of the base, switching the designations of Barracks Nos. 1 and 2. The authors have used the plan from 1941 as the final authority.

20. Notes on features of Wheeler Field's buildings by architectural historian Mark R. Wenger.

21. Authors' analysis; "Completion Report on Hangars and Shops," 1–2; War Department, QMC Form 117, "Hangar No. 1 (Wheeler Field)," Records of the Chief of Engineers, entry E393, box 280, folder 1, RG 77, NARA II; email correspondence, JMW and Jessie Higa, 29 August 2019; interpretation of photography in RG 77, Textual Branch, and in RG 342-FH, Still Picture Branch, NARA II. See photographs of Hickam Field's hangars in Wenger, Cressman, and Di Virgilio, *They're Killing My Boys*. Architect Louis Bontya provided technical descriptions of the Albrook/Wheeler hangar design.

22. War Department, QMC Form 117, "Warehouse (Wheeler Field)," Records of the Chief of Engineers, entry E393, box 280, folder 1, RG 77, NARA II; War Department, QMC Form 117, "Machine Shop (Wheeler Field)," Records of the Chief of Engineers, entry E393, box 280, folder 2, RG 77, NARA II; War Department, QMC Form 117, "Assembly Shop (Wheeler Field)," Records of the Chief of Engineers, entry E393, box 280, folder 2, RG 77, NARA II.

23. "Completion Report on Hangars and Shops," 1; Headquarters, Hawaiian Department, "Completion Report on Construction of 1 Dispensary Building, 1 Radio Building, 1 Parachute Building, 1 Fire Station and Guard House, 1 Paint, Oil and Dope House, 1 Quartermaster Garage Building, [and] 1 Quartermaster Utilities Shops Building at Wheeler Field, Schofield Barracks, T.H." (hereinafter "Completion Report on Dispensary"), n.d., 4, 1–2, Records of the Chief of Engineers, entry 391, box 328, binder 1, RG 77, NARA II, and photography therein; "Record of Buildings," 30 June 1941, sheet 3.

24. Headquarters, Hawaiian Department, "Completion Report on Construction of One Administration Building and One Photographic Laboratory, Together with Certain Roads and Utilities Therefor at Wheeler Field, Schofield Barracks, T.H." (hereinafter "Completion Report on Administration Building"), n.d., 5, 1–2, Records of the Chief of Engineers, entry 391, box 328, binder 1, RG 77, NARA II; "Wheeler Field Layout." The completion reports for Wheeler Field are almost devoid of descriptions regarding layout and compartmentalization. The report on Wheeler's Administration Building is a notable, though rare, exception.

25. Headquarters, Hawaiian Department, "Completion Report on Construction of Wash Racks, Runways, Aprons, Conduits and Drains at Wheeler Field, Schofield Barracks, T.H." (hereinafter "Completion Report on Construction of Wash Racks, Runways, Aprons"), n.d., 1–2, Records of the Chief of Engineers, entry 391, box 328, binder 1, RG 77, NARA II.

26. Headquarters, Hawaiian Department, "Completion Report on Installation of a Night Light System for Wheeler Field, Schofield Barracks, T.H.," n.d., 1–2, Records of the Chief of Engineers, entry 391, box 328, binder 1, RG 77, NARA II.

27. Headquarters, Hawaiian Department, "Completion Report on Signal Light Installation at Wheeler Field, Schofield Barracks, T.H.," n.d., 4, 1–2, Records of the Chief of Engineers, entry 391, box 328, binder 1, RG 77, NARA II; Headquarters, Hawaiian Department, "Completion Report on Floodlight Installations at Wheeler Field, Schofield Barracks, T.H.," n.d., 1, entry 391, box 329, binder 2, RG 77, NARA II.

28. Analysis, aerial photography of Wheeler Field: 342-FH-3B-21805, -21808, and -21824, Still Picture Branch, NARA II; photography in "Completion Report on Dispensary," RG 77, NARA II; photography in "Completion Report on Administration Building."

29. Analysis, aerial photography of Wheeler Field: 342-FH-3B-21425, Still Picture Branch, NARA II; War Department, "Completion Report for Dismantling Two Airplane Hangars at Wheeler Field and Salvaging All Structural Steel and Transporting Same to Hickam Field, T.H.," 1936, 4, 1, Records of the

Chief of Engineers, entry 391, box 122, binder 1, RG 77, NARA II.

30. "Construction Activities at Wheeler," 6–7, 3.

31. War Department, "Completion Report on Construction of 300-Man Cantonment at Wheeler Field, T.H.," 1939, 1, 4, Records of the Chief of Engineers, entry 391, box 329, binder 2, RG 77, NARA II.

32. War Department, "Completion Report on Grading and Leveling on Officers' and N.C.O. Quarters Area at Wheeler Field, T.H.," 1939, 1, Records of the Chief of Engineers, entry 391, box 329, binder 2, RG 77, NARA II; War Department, "Completion Report on Construction and Completion of Thirty-Eight Double, Type Eight, Non-Commissioned Officers' Quarters and All Utilities Thereto at Wheeler Field, T.H.," 1940, 6, 1–2, Records of the Chief of Engineers, entry 391, box 329, binder 2, RG 77, NARA II; authors' analysis.

33. Authors' analysis; War Department, "Completion Report on Construction and Completion of One Control Tower on A.C. Operations Hangar at Wheeler Field, T.H." (hereinafter "Completion Report, Control Tower"), 1940, 1–3, and photographs, Records of the Chief of Engineers, entry 391, box 329, binder 2, RG 77, NARA II.

34. War Department, "Completion Report on Construction and Completion of a New Air Corps Gasoline Fueling System at Wheeler Field, T.H.," 1940, 1–4, Records of the Chief of Engineers, entry 391, box 329, binder 2, RG 77, NARA II. See Wenger, Cressman, and Di Virgilio, *They're Killing My Boys*, 20–22. Although Wheeler's earlier fuel system is of uncertain origin and date, it is likely the array of underground tanks on the eastern end of the apron area. See Constructing Quartermaster, Hawaiian Department, Hickam Field, T.H., Plan 6812-822-2732, "Water Map, Wheeler Field, T.H." (hereinafter "Wheeler Field Water Map"), 28 November 1940, copy supplied by Jessie Higa. This contention seems to be supported further in "Wheeler Record of Buildings," and War Department, "List of Buildings at Wheeler Field," Records of the Chief of Engineers, entry E393, box 280, folder 1, RG 77, NARA II. This listing was a cross-index of the old Schofield Barracks building numbers and new numbers assigned to Wheeler's structures, effective 9 February 1940.

35. Headquarters, Wheeler Field, "Completion Report on Flagpole," 18 December 1940, Records of the Chief of Engineers, entry 391, box 329, binder 2, RG 77, NARA II; War Department, QMC Form 117, "Administration Bldg. (Wheeler Field)," Records of the Chief of Engineers, entry E393, box 280, folder 3, RG 77, NARA II; "Wheeler Field Water Map;" War Department, QMC Form 117, "Flagpole," Records of the Chief of Engineers, entry E393, box 280, folder 3, RG 77, NARA II.

36. *Wheeler Field History*, 32, 35; "Construction Activities at Wheeler," 3; Headquarters, Wheeler Field, "Completion Report on Construction of Temporary Mess Hall, Latrines and Tent Floors," 18 February 1941, 1, Records of the Chief of Engineers, entry 391, box 329, binder 2, RG 77, NARA II; "Administration Bldg. (Wheeler Field)," photo 80-G-279360, Still Picture Branch, NARA II; "Wheeler Field Water Map." Chapter 3 covers the expansion of pursuit aviation.

37. "Construction Activities at Wheeler," 3; War Department, QMC Form 117, "Barracks (AC)," Records of the Chief of Engineers, entry E393, box 280, folder 3, RG 77, NARA II; "Wheeler Field Layout"; *Wheeler Field History*, 36; authors' analysis; photo 80-G-279373, Still Picture Branch, NARA II.

38. "Wheeler Field Water Map"; authors' analysis; "Construction Activities at Wheeler," 3; photo 80-G-279360, Still Picture Branch NARA II; notes from telephone conversation, JMW and Jessie Higa, 15 August 2019. For further discussion concerning the quarters at Hickam Field, see *They're Killing My Boys*. Per Jessie Higa, for a time Fenander Avenue was designated "Fernander," requiring intervention of the namesake's family to correct it.

39. 804th Engineer Battalion's Avn microfilmed morning reports, 1941, RG 64, NARA, St. Louis; testimony of Frederick L. Martin before the Army Pearl Harbor Board (hereinafter Martin testimony, Army Board), 29 August 1944, *Pearl Harbor Attack: Hearings before the Joint Committee on the Investigation of the Pearl Harbor Attack* (hereinafter *PHA*) (Washington, D.C.: GPO, 1946), pt. 28, 967; Honolulu District Public Affairs, "Army Engineers Fought and Lived through the Attack on Pearl Harbor," 7 December 2012, https://www.army.mil/article/92634/army_engineers_fought_and_lived_through_the_attack_on_pearlharbor,

accessed 22 August 2019; *VII Fighter Comd. History, 1 Nov. 1940–7 Dec. 1941 incl.* (hereinafter *VII Fighter Command History*), AFHSO, reel A7586, file 741.01, 6; 804th Engineers Avn., "Progress Map, Bunker Const[*sic*] Wheeler Field," file DR1 M2, 21 August 1941, *PHA*, pt. 25, Exhibits of the Roberts Commission, Exhibit 1 (Army), item 89; photograph 80-G-279372, Still Picture Branch, NARA II.

40. Analysis of aerial photography of Wheeler Field: photos 80-G-279360, -279368, -279372, and 342-FH-3B 48707, Still Picture Branch, NARA II; "Completion Report on Construction of Wash Racks, Runways, Aprons," 1.

CHAPTER 2. "NOTHING BUT A PROFUSE GROWTH OF SUGAR CANE AND GUAVA BUSHES"

1. Thomas A. Bailey, *The American Pageant: A History of the Republic* (Boston: D. C. Heath, 1961), 722–23.

2. Waimanalo Neighborhood Board No. 32, "Draft Regular Meeting Minutes, Monday, July 19, 2009," http://www.honolulu.gov/rep/site/nco/nb32/09/32200907min.pdf, accessed 20 January 2020, 7; Bailey, *The American Pageant*, 724.

3. *History of Bellows Field from Time of Inception to 31 March 1944* (hereinafter *Bellows Field History*), 1–2, AFHSO, reel A0031, file AAFLD-Bellows-Hi (Jul41–Mar44).

4. Belt Collins Hawaii, *Final Environmental Impact Statement for Land Use and Development Plan, Bellows Air Force Station, Waimanalo, Hawaii* (hereinafter Bellows EIS) (Honolulu: Belt Collins Hawaii, 1995), 9; "New Gunnery Range Opened in Hawaii," *Air Service News* 10, no. 9 (8 June 1926): 8.

5. "Lieut. Wisehart Qualifies as a Long Distance Swimmer," *Air Service News* 10, no. 9 (8 June 1926): 9.

6. "Summer Rest Camps for Hawaiian Air Corps Personnel," *Air Corps News* 12, no. 14 (6 October 1928): 368.

7. Hawaiian Air Depot, Luke Field, "Completion Report, Air Corps Range Camp at Waimanalo, Oahu, T.H." (hereinafter "Completion Report, Air Corps Range Camp"), 31 August 1931, 2, Records of the Chief of Engineers, entry 391, box 318, binder 1, RG 77, NARA II.

8. War Department, QMC Form 117, "Waimanalo Air Corps Camp, Oahu, T.H.," Records of the Chief of Engineers, entry E393, box 269, folder 2, RG 77, NARA II; War Department, QMC Form 117, "Tent Frames," Records of the Chief of Engineers, entry E393, box 269, folder 2, RG 77, NARA II; War Department, QMC Form 117, "Officers Building," Records of the Chief of Engineers, entry E393, box 269, folder 2, RG 77, NARA II; War Department, QMC Form 117, "Kitchen & Mess Hall," Records of the Chief of Engineers, entry E393, box 269, folder 2, RG 77, NARA II; War Department, QMC Form 117, "Latrine," Records of the Chief of Engineers, entry E393, box 269, folder 2, RG 77, NARA II; "Completion Report, Air Corps Range Camp," photograph, 3.

9. "50th Observation Squadron Goes into Camp," *Air Corps News* 15, no. 11 (18 September 1931): 324.

10. War Department, QMC Form 117, "Airplane Runway," Records of the Chief of Engineers, entry E393, box 269, folder 3, RG 77, NARA II; War Department, QMC Form 117, "Shop & Storeroom," Records of the Chief of Engineers, entry E393, box 269, folder 2, RG 77, NARA II.

11. Arakaki and Kuborn, *The Air Force Story*, 199; *Bellows Field History*, appendage 1, Headquarters, Bellows Field, Rex K. Estudillo to F. L. Bellows, 31 January 1942; "War Pilots Honored in Naming Hawaiian Landing Fields," *Air Corps News* 17, no. 9 (30 September 1933): 219.

12. "For Immediate Release," [Air Service] *Weekly News Letter* 1, no. 5 (20 October 1918): 4.

13. *Bellows Field History*, 2.

14. Photographs in file 740.08-2, AFHRA; photographs 80-G-279365 and -279366, Still Picture Branch, NARA II; Headquarters, Hawaiian Department, "Construction at Bellows Field, T.H. [extracts]," 5 April 1941, *PHA*, pt. 24, Exhibits of the Roberts Commission, Exhibit 1B (Army), 1856–57.

15. War Department, QMC Form 117, "N.C.O.'s Quarters," Records of the Chief of Engineers, entry E393, box 269, folder 2, RG 77, NARA II; War Department, QMC Form 117, "Dispensary," Records of the Chief of Engineers, entry E393, box 269, folder 2, RG 77, NARA II; War Department, QMC Form 117, "Operations Office," Records of the Chief of Engineers, entry E393, box 269, folder 2, RG 77, NARA II; War Department, QMC Form 117, "Post Exchange," Records of the Chief of Engineers, entry E393, box 269, folder 3, RG 77,

NARA II; War Department, "Completion Report on WPA Official Project No. 513-2-121 at Bellows Field, T.H.," 1937, 1–2, 4–5, Records of the Chief of Engineers, entry 391, box 329, binder 2, RG 77, NARA II.

16. War Department, QMC Form 117, "Entrance Gate," Records of the Chief of Engineers, entry E393, box 269, folder 3, RG 77, NARA II; War Department, QMC Form 117, "Storehouse, Main Camp," Records of the Chief of Engineers, entry E393, box 269, folder 3, RG 77, NARA II; War Department, QMC Form 117, "Detachment Barracks," Records of the Chief of Engineers, entry E393, box 269, folder 3, RG 77, NARA II; War Department, QMC Form 117, "Control Tower," Records of the Chief of Engineers, entry E393, box 269, folder 3, RG 77, NARA II.

17. "Construction at Bellows Field, T.H.," 5 April 1941, *PHA*, pt. 24, 1856–1857.

18. 86th Observation Squadron's microfilmed morning reports, January and March 1941, RG 64, NARA, St. Louis; 58th Bombardment Squadron's microfilmed morning reports, March and May 1941, RG 64, NARA, St. Louis.

19. *Bellows Field History*, 3.

20. *Bellows Field History*, Chronology; Headquarters, Hawaiian Department, General Orders 42, 22 July 1941; photographs 80-G-279365 and 80-G-279366, Still Picture Branch, NARA II; General Plan, "Bellows Field, Oahu, T.H.," April 1941, *PHA*, pt. 25, Exhibits of the Roberts Commission, Exhibit 12, item 99.

21. Telephone conversation, JMW and Jessie Higa, 16 January 2020; *Historic American Buildings Survey*, HABS no. HI-573, "Oahu Railway & Land Company Terminal," http://lcweb2.loc.gov/master/pnp/habshaer/hi/hi1000/hi1028/data/hi1028cap.pdf, 8. Alternate translations of *haleʻiwa* include "home of the iwa" (frigate bird), and "home of beautiful people."

22. Telephone conversation, JMW and Jessie Higa, 16 January 2020; "Organizational History [of Haleiwa Field]," VI Air Service Area Command, 1 June 1944 (hereinafter "Haleiwa Field History"), AFHSO, reel A0047, file AAFLD-Haleiwa-Hi (Nov41-Mar44), 1; photograph of Haleiwa Landing Field, 27 April 1933, 15th Wing History Office.

23. "The Hawaiian Department Maneuvers," *Air Corps News Letter* 18, no. 15 (15 August 1935): 15; "Hawaiian Department," *Air Corps News Letter* 22, no. 7 (1 April 1939): 6.

24. "The Soldier's Medal," *Air Corps News Letter* 21, no. 4 (15 February 1938): 4; "Soldier's Medal Awards," *U.S. Army Recruiting News* 20, no. 11 (November 1938): 10–11; "The Soldier [*sic*] Medal Award to Corporal Stone," *Air Corps News Letter* 21, no. 23 (1 December 1938): 12; "Soldier's Medal Awards," *U.S. Army Recruiting News* 23, no. 4 (April 1941): 11.

25. Headquarters, Hawaiian Department, "Improvement of Airfield at Haleiwa, Oahu, T.H.," n.d., and 4th indorsement dated 25 June 1941, *PHA*, pt. 24, Exhibits of the Roberts Commission, Exhibit 1B (Army), 1862–1863.

26. "Haleiwa Field History," 1.

27. "*Group History of the 15th Pursuit Group (F),*" AFHSO, reel B0080A, file GP-15-Hi, 59; Paul W. Blanchard Jr., Archie L. Roberts Jr., Jerome R. Sawyer, Fred B. Shifflet, Individual Flight Records (hereinafter IFRs), November 1941, RG 64, NARA, St. Louis; "Haleiwa Field History," enclosure no. 1, Headquarters, 18th Air Base Group, Special Orders No. 89, 14 November 1941. The 72nd Pursuit Squadron was new to the group, having only been activated on 5 October. Existing records do not reveal whether the unit was to be incorporated into the squadron rotation schedule at Haleiwa.

CHAPTER 3. "FERRYING OF NEW AIRCRAFT . . . ASSUMED THE PROPORTIONS OF A MAJOR PROBLEM"

1. *Wheeler Field History*, 3–27; "18th Fighter Group (USAAF)," http://www.historyofwar.org/air/units/USAAF/18th_Fighter_Group.html, accessed 24 February 2020; "Farewell to the 26th Attack Squadron," *Air Corps News Letter* 23, no. 3 (1 February 1940): 8, AFHRA.

2. P-12B/C/E aircraft history cards, AFHRA.

3. Peter M. Bowers, *Boeing Aircraft since 1916* (Annapolis: Naval Institute Press, 1989), 162, 164, 179, 184, 186.

4. P-12B/C/E aircraft history cards, AFHRA; Bowers, *Boeing Aircraft since 1916*, 83.

5. Peter M. Bowers, *The Boeing P-12E* (Leatherhead, Engl.: Profile Publications, 1965), 8; "The Air Battle over Shanghai—1932," http://www.republicanchina.org/Air-Battle-over-Shanghai-Suzhou-Hangzhou-1932.pdf, accessed 30 May 2019.

6. P-12B/E aircraft history cards, AFHRA.

7. Wesley F. Craven and James L. Cate, *The Army Air Forces in World War II,* vol. 1: *Plans and Early Operations, January 1939 to August 1942* (Chicago: University of Chicago Press, 1948), 171; P-12B/C/E aircraft history cards, AFHRA.

8. P-26A/B aircraft history cards, AFHRA; Peter M. Bowers, *The Boeing P-26A* (Leatherhead, Engl.: Profile Publications, 1965), 3; Robert Guttman, "Boeing's Trailblazing P-26 Peashooter," *Aviation History* 6, no. 6 (July 1996): 23, 26–28. "Selfridge Field, Mich.," *Air Corps News Letter* 21, no. 2 (15 January 1938): 18, AFHRA.

9. P-26A aircraft history cards, AFHRA; *Wheeler Field History*, 26.

10. P-26A/B aircraft history cards, AFHRA; Milo N. Clark, Armin F. Herold, Norman D. Sillin, and Phineas K. Morrill Jr., IFRs, January–March 1938, RG 64, NARA, St. Louis. Although the authors were unable to reconstruct complete schedules and rosters for the P-26 ferrying operations of 1938, all available evidence points to the scenarios as presented in the text.

11. P-26A/B aircraft history cards, AFHRA.

12. P-26A/B aircraft history cards, AFHRA; Bowers, *The Boeing P-26A*, 8–9; P-36A aircraft history cards, AFHRA.

13. Clay, *US Army Order of Battle*, vol. 3, 1311; "Noted Airmen Assigned Here," *Honolulu Star-Bulletin*, 12 September 1938, 9.

14. "Major General William E. Lynd" (hereinafter USAF Lynd bio), https://www.af.mil/DesktopModules/ArticleCS/Print.aspx?PortalId=1&ModuleId=858&Article=108567, accessed 24 May 2019.

15. USAF Lynd bio.

16. P-26A/B and P-12E aircraft history cards, AFHRA; Bowers, *The Boeing P-12E*, 9.

17. *Wheeler Field History*, 28–29.

18. *Wheeler Field History*, 30.

19. P-36A aircraft history cards, AFHRA.

20. *18th Fighter Group, 11 Jan 1927–30 Jun 1944*, AFHSO, reel B0083, file GP-18-Hi (Jan/27–Jun/44), 6; "P-36A Airplanes Appear Plenty Fast," *Air Corps News Letter* 22, no. 23 (1 December 1939): 22, AFHRA.

21. Craven and Cate, *AAF in World War II*, vol. 1, 171.

22. *History of the 26th Bombardment Squadron (H)*, AFHSO, reel A0544, file SQ-BOMB-26-Hi, 5–6; "Farewell to the 26th Attack Squadron," 8.

23. *Administrative History of Headquarters, Seventh Air Force* (hereinafter *Administrative History, 7th Air Force*), APO953, AFHSO, reel A7532, file 740.01-2, 7–10.

24. *VII Fighter Command History*, 2–3.

25. Wenger, Cressman, and Di Virgilio, *They're Killing My Boys*, 30; Martin testimony, Army Board, 29 August 1944, *PHA*, pt. 28, 978.

26. Wenger, Cressman, and Di Virgilio, *They're Killing My Boys*, 32; Martin testimony, Army Board, 29 August 1944, *PHA*, pt. 28, 978; P-36A aircraft history cards, P-26A/B aircraft history cards, AFHRA; authors' analysis.

27. Martin testimony, Army Board, 29 August 1944, *PHA*, pt. 28, 978.

28. Craven and Cate, *AAF in World War II*, vol. 1, 172.

29. Martin testimony, Army Board, 29 August 1944, *PHA*, pt. 28, 978; AG Historical Section, 4th Air Force Headquarters, *Processing and Ferrying Functions of the Fourth Air Force through the Year 1941, Fourth Air Force Historical Study No. IV-1*, vol. 1: *Narrative*, AFHSO, reel A4153, file 450.01-10 (hereinafter *4th Air Force Historical Study No. IV-1, Narrative*), 19, 21–22; Secretary of War to Secretary of the Navy, "Air Defense of Pearl Harbor, Hawaii," 7 February 1941, *PHA*, pt. 24, Exhibits of the Roberts Commission, Exhibit 22 (Army), 2013.

30. OpNav to CinCPac, dispatch 061730 CR899, 6 February 1941, CNO/OpNav dispatch files (photostats), Records of the Crane Group (hereinafter CNO dispatch files), NARA II, RG 38. The *Wasp* transported to sea and launched twenty-four P-40s from the 8th Pursuit Group and nine O-47As from the 2nd Observation Squadron.

31. *4th Air Force Historical Study No. IV-1, Narrative*, 6–8.

32. All pilots, 47th Pursuit Squadron, IFRs, November 1941, RG 64, NARA, St. Louis.

33. *4th Air Force Historical Study No. IV-1, Narrative*, 18–19; authors' analysis.

34. HQ, Southwest Air District GHQ Air Force to Maj. George R. Tourtellot, "Orders," 10 February 1941 (hereinafter Tourtellot orders), in *4th Air Force*

Historical Study No. IV-1, vol. 2, *Appendix*: Supporting Documents, AFHSO, reel A4153, file 450.01–10; *4th Air Force Historical Study No. IV-1, Narrative*, 18–19. The figures in the *Historical Study* regarding planes, pilots, and crew chiefs are unclear and contradictory.

35. *4th Air Force Historical Study No. IV-1, Narrative*, 20; various pilots' IFRs, RG 64, NARA, St. Louis.

36. *4th Air Force Historical Study No. IV-1, Narrative*, 20.

37. *4th Air Force Historical Study No. IV-1, Narrative*, 21.

38. Tourtellot orders.

39. George R. Tourtellot, IFRs, 1918–41, RG 64, NARA, St. Louis.

40. Letter, George A. Whiteman, to "Mom and Dad," 6 February 1941, Whiteman papers, courtesy Gayle Kent, grandniece of George A. Whiteman.

41. Frank Taylor, "WWII Pilot Downs Plane," newspaper clipping, circa 1981, 1–2, courtesy John W. Lambert.

42. P-36A aircraft history cards, AFHRA; authors' analysis. Discrepancies in the numbers of aircraft transferred from Selfridge and Hamilton are probably due to confusion at the time and constant changes in aircraft availability at those locations. The authors have calculated the final figures based on the P-36A aircraft history cards, which although imperfect, appear more authoritative.

43. Various IFRs, January–February 1941, RG 64, NARA, St. Louis; P-36A aircraft history cards, AFHRA; authors' analysis.

44. Various IFRs, January–February 1941, RG 64, NARA, St. Louis; *4th Air Force Historical Study No. IV-1, Narrative*, 21–22.

45. *Enterprise* movement cards, February 1941, Naval History and Heritage Command, courtesy Mark Evans; *4th Air Force Historical Study No. IV-1, Narrative*, 19, 21–22; *Enterprise* deck logs, 15–21 February 1941, RG 24, NARA II, via Robert Cressman.

46. Everett W. Stewart interview with Ronald Marcello, 24 February 1976 (hereinafter Stewart, NTU interview), OH 0309, University of North Texas Oral History Collection, Denton, Tex. (hereinafter UNTOHC), 4; Mack Matthews, "30 Army Pursuit Planes Make Dramatic, Unannounced Arrival," *Honolulu Advertiser*, 22 February 1941, 8; various IFRs, January–February 1941, RG 64, NARA, St. Louis; authors'

analysis; "*Enterprise* VII (CV-6) 1938–1956," https://www.history.navy.mil/research/histories/ship-histories/danfs/e/enterprise-cv-6-vii.html, accessed 17 February 2020; George R. Tourtellot, IFRs, 1918–1941, RG 64, NARA, St. Louis.

47. OpNav to CinCPac, dispatch 032132 CR109, 3 March 1941, CNO dispatch files, NARA II, RG 38; authors' analysis and correspondence.

48. Authors' analysis; CinCPac to OpNav, dispatch 082200 CR192, 8 March 1941, CNO dispatch files, NARA II, RG 38; *Enterprise* movement cards, March 1941; "*Saratoga* V (CV-3)," https://www.history.navy.mil/content/history/nhhc/research/histories/ship-histories/danfs/s/saratoga-v.html, accessed 19 February 2020; George R. Bickell, Ingram C. Connor Jr., James J. Flood, Raymond K. Gallagher IFRs (hereinafter Mitchel Field IFRs), March 1941, RG 64, NARA, St. Louis; Fred C. Wilson, Pearl Harbor Survivors Association (hereinafter PHSA) application, 27 August 1971; microfilmed officer roster, 18th Pursuit Group, 31 March 1941, RG 64, NARA, St. Louis. Although Wilson maintained that eight pilots from Mitchel Field accompanied the aircraft and maintenance crews on board the *Lexington*, only four officers were attached to the 15th and 18th Pursuit Groups on 25 March 1941. No officer rosters for the 14th Pursuit Wing headquarters exist for this period.

49. P-40B aircraft history cards, AFHRA; *4th Air Force Historical Study No. IV-1, Narrative*, 22; Fred C. Wilson, PHSA application, 27 August 1971; Mitchel Field IFRs, March 1941.

50. *Lexington* (CV 2) deck logs, 18 March 1941, RG 24, NARA II; Fred C. Wilson, PHSA application, 27 August 1971.

51. *Lexington* deck logs, 25 March 1941, RG 24, NARA II; authors' analysis; photos 80-G-279385 and 80-G-279375, Still Picture Branch, NARA II.

52. Mitchel Field IFRs, March 1941; microfilmed officer roster, 18th Pursuit Group, 31 March 1941, RG 64, NARA, St. Louis; *Lexington* deck logs, 25 March 1941, RG 24, NARA II; microfilmed enlisted roster, 18th Pursuit Group, 30 November 1941, RG 64, NARA, St. Louis.

53. Mitchel Field IFRs and Woodrow B. Wilmot IFRs, March 1941, RG 64, NARA, St. Louis.

54. OpNav to CinCPac, dispatch 122037 CR466, 12 March 1941, CNO dispatch files, NARA II, RG 38; CinCPac to OpNav, dispatch 132357 CR317, 13 March 1941, CNO dispatch files, NARA II, RG 38; *Enterprise* movement cards, March 1941.

55. P-40B/C aircraft history cards, AFHRA; Peter M. Bowers, *Curtiss Aircraft, 1907–1947* (Annapolis: Naval Institute Press, 1979), 483; Ray Wagner, *The Curtiss P-40 Tomahawk* (Leatherhead, Engl.: Profile Publications, 1965), 9.

56. OpNav to CinCPac, dispatch 282358 CR296, 28 March 1941, CNO dispatch files, NARA II, RG 38; *Enterprise* movement cards, March 1941; CinCPac to OpNav, dispatch 020345 CR77, 2 April 1941, CNO dispatch files, NARA II, RG 38.

57. *Enterprise* movement cards, April 1941; *Enterprise* deck logs, 3, 21, and 27 April 1941, RG 24, NARA II; OpNav to CinCPac, dispatch 022300 CR108, 2 April 1941, CNO dispatch files, NARA II, RG 38.

58. Various IFRs, April 1941, RG 64, NARA, St. Louis; "Douglas [C-33] DC-2: Commercial Airliner/Military Transport Aircraft," https://www.militaryfactory.com/aircraft/detail.php?aircraft_id=833, accessed 22 February 2020; "Grumman Goose (G-21): Multirole Flying Boat Aircraft," https://www.militaryfactory.com/aircraft/detail.asp?aircraft_id=833, accessed 22 February 2020.

59. Martin testimony, Army Board, 29 August 1944, *PHA*, pt. 28, 978.

60. P-26A/B, P-36A, P-40B/C aircraft history cards, AFHRA; Martin testimony, Army Board, 29 August 1944, *PHA*, pt. 28, 978.

61. Com 14 to CinCPac et al., "Operation Plan No. 1-41," 27 February 1941, *PHA*, pt. 24, Exhibits of the Roberts Commission, Exhibit 45 (Navy Packet 2), 1622–24.

62. ComPatWing 2, "Annex Baker to Commander Naval Base Defense Operation Plan No. 1-41 Dated February 27, 1941," 28 February 1941, *PHA*, pt. 24, Exhibits of the Roberts Commission, Exhibit 45 (Navy Packet 2), 1629.

63. ComPatWing 2 and Commanding General (hereinafter CG), Hawaiian Air Force, "Addendum I to Naval Base Defense Air Force Operation Plan No. A-1-41," 31 March 1941, *PHA*, pt. 24, Exhibits of the Roberts Commission, Exhibit 45 (Navy Packet 2), 1633. For other discussion of the Naval Base Defense Force, see J. M. Wenger, R. J. Cressman, and J. F. Di Virgilio, *This Is No Drill: The History of NAS Pearl Harbor and the Japanese Attacks of 7 December 1941* (Annapolis: Naval Institute Press, 2018), 31–32. For a full understanding of the complex expectations of the Naval Base Defense Force, consult the full range of plans, annexes, addenda, and correspondence contained in *PHA*, pt. 24, 1622–46.

64. "Brigadier General Harvey S. Burwell," https://www.af.mil/About-Us/Biographies/Display/Article/108034/brigadier-general-harvey-s-burwell/, accessed 26 February 2020; Charles N. Branham, ed., *Biographical Register of the Officers and Graduates of the U.S. Military Academy at West Point, New York since Its Establishment in 1802 by Brevet-Major-General George W. Cullum, Colonel of Engineers, U.S. Army Retired* (hereinafter *Biographical Register, USMA*), supplement, vol. 8 (unknown publisher, 1950), 175; Headquarters, Hickam Field to CG, Hawaiian Air Force, "Autobiography [Col. Howard C. Davidson]" (hereinafter Davidson autobiography), 20 January 1941, AFHSO, reel A0086, file AAFLD-Wheeler-Hi (1922–1944), 1.

65. Davidson autobiography, 1–2; Wirt Robinson, ed., *Biographical Register, USMA*, supplement, vol. 6-B: *1910–1920* (Saginaw, Mich.: Seemann & Peters, 1920), 1660; telephone conversation and correspondence, JMW and Daniel Martinez, 26 February 2020.

66. Davidson autobiography, 2–5.

67. William H. Donaldson, ed., *Biographical Register, USMA*, supplement, vol. 7: *1920–1930* (Chicago: Lakeside Press, 1930), 1000; Elbert E. Farman Jr., ed., *Biographical Register, USMA*, supplement, vol. 8, *1930–1940*, 271; Branham, *Biographical Register, USMA*, supplement, vol. 8: *1940–1950* (unknown publisher, 1950), 175.

68. HQ, HD, Special Orders No. 269, 27 October 1941 (hereinafter HD Special Orders No. 269), Exhibits of the Roberts Commission, Exhibit No. 5 (Army), *PHA*, pt. 24, 1769; "William J. Flood," USAF Historical Division, U.S. Air Force Historical Study 91, *Biographical Data on Air Force General Officers, 1917–1952*, vol. 1: *A–K*, AFHRA, file 101-91 (1917–1952) K1011. It is almost certain that the field commanders reported directly to the CG, HAF.

69. HQ, HD, General Orders No. 68, 27 October 1941, Exhibits of the Roberts Commission, Exhibit 5 (Army), *PHA*, pt. 24, 1767; testimony of William E. Farthing before the Army Pearl Harbor Board (hereinafter Farthing testimony, Army Board), 15 August 1944, *PHA*, pt. 27, 435–436; HD Special Orders No. 269.

70. CG, Hawaiian Interceptor Command to CG, HAF, "Records Requested in Telegram Dated 22 December 1941," 23 December 1941, Exhibits of the Roberts Commission, Exhibit 8 (Army), *PHA*, pt. 24, 1935; microfilmed officer roster, 18th Air Base Group, 30 November 1941, RG 64, NARA, St. Louis; microfilmed officer roster, HAF Base Command, Hickam Field, T.H., 26 December 1941, RG 64, NARA, St. Louis.

CHAPTER 4. "IT WAS A PARADISE . . . A QUIET PEACEFUL LIFE"

1. Ernest A. Brown, interview with Peggy Rouh, 2 October 1996, OH 1145 (hereinafter Brown, NTU interview), 1–6.

2. Henry C. Brown, interview with Ronald Marcello, 6 July 1974, OH 0232 (hereinafter Henry Brown, NTU interview), 1–3.

3. Clarence W. Kindl, interview with Ronald Marcello, 4 May 1984, OH 0641 (hereinafter Kindl, NTU interview), 1–3.

4. Fred R. Runce, interview with Ronald Marcello, 6 July 1974, OH 0219 (hereinafter Runce, NTU interview), 2–3.

5. Milroy L. Richardson, interview with Ronald Marcello, 5 June 2002, OH 1463 (hereinafter Richardson, NTU interview), 1–5.

6. Will Roy Sample, interview with Ronald Marcello, 27 March 1978, OH 0408 (hereinafter Sample, NTU interview), 1–4, 21.

7. John J. Springer, interview with Ronald Marcello, 12 June 1976, OH 0334 (hereinafter Springer, NTU interview), 1–2.

8. Stewart, NTU interview, 1–3; Everett W. Stewart, IFRs, RG 64, NARA, St. Louis.

9. Henry Brown, NTU interview, 3.

10. Richardson, NTU interview, 11–12.

11. Richardson, NTU interview, 12, 14–15.

12. Richardson, NTU interview, 11–13.

13. Kindl, NTU interview, 6.

14. Stephen J. Koran, interview with Ronald Marcello, 18 February 1974, OH 0236 (hereinafter Koran, NTU interview), 6, 11–12; marriage certificate, Stephen Jack Koran and Flora Belle Miles, 29 January 1941, via Jessie Higa.

15. Stewart, NTU interview, 3–4.

16. Phillip L. Willis, interview with Ronald Marcello, 16 August 1974, no number (hereinafter Willis, NTU interview), 9–11.

17. Howard C. Davidson, Prange interview, 6 July 1962 (hereinafter Davidson, Prange interview, 6 July 1962), 1–2, Prange Papers in the Goldstein Collection, Archives Service Center, University of Pittsburgh (hereinafter Prange Papers, Goldstein Collection), UA-90/F-78, box 23, ff-23; William J. Flood, Prange interview, 8 July 1962 (hereinafter Flood, Prange interview), 1–2, Prange Papers, Goldstein Collection, UA-90/F-78, box 23, ff-44.

18. Runce, NTU interview, 18; Kindl, NTU interview, 11.

19. Koran, NTU interview, 14–16.

20. Koran, NTU interview, 28.

21. Koran, NTU interview, 7, 16.

22. Stewart, NTU interview, 7–9; Jessie Higa analysis; authors' analysis.

23. Signal Corps, Hawaiian Department, *Telephone Directory: Military Telephone Systems of the Hawaiian Department*, July 1941, 52; "Wheeler Field Water Map"; Stewart NTU interview, 8.

24. Sample, NTU interview, 4, 10; Stewart, NTU interview, 3.

25. Mannie E. Siegle, interview with Ronald Marcello, 7 December 1978, OH 0464 (hereinafter Siegle, NTU interview), 5–6; Runce, NTU interview, 11; Stewart, NTU interview, 3.

26. Byron W. Kolbert, interview with Ronald Marcello, 25 February 1978, OH 0411 (hereinafter Kolbert, NTU interview), 10; testimony of Leonard D. Weddington before the Army Board, 12 September 1944, *PHA*, pt. 28, 1574.

27. Kolbert, NTU interview, 10, 19.

28. *Wheeler Field History*, 15–16.

29. *Wheeler Field History*, 8; Maurer Maurer, *Aviation in the U.S. Army, 1919–1939* (Washington, D.C.: GPO, 1987), 256–57.

30. Maurer, *Aviation in the U.S. Army*, 258; "The Hawaiian Flight."

31. "Hawaiian Flight Authorized," *Air Corps News* 11, no. 6 (27 June 1927): 196, AFHRA; Maurer, *Aviation in the U.S. Army*, 258; *Wheeler Field History*, 8; "The Hawaiian Flight," *Air Corps News 11*, no. 6 (27 June 1927): 181.

32. National Museum of the U.S. Air Force, "Atlantic-Fokker C-2 'Bird of Paradise,'" https://web.archive.org /web/20110913055923/http://www.nationalmuseum .af.mil/factsheets/factsheet.asp?id=3239, accessed 26 April 2020; Maurer, *Aviation in the U.S. Army*, 258; "Hawaiian Flight a Remarkable Achievement," *Air Corps News* 11, no. 9 (19 July 1927): 205–6, AFHRA.

33. "Hawaiian Flight a Remarkable Achievement," 206; Maurer, *Aviation in the U.S. Army*, 258.

34. Maurer, *Aviation in the U.S. Army*, 260; "Hawaiian Flight a Remarkable Achievement," 206; U.S. Department of Commerce, *United States Coast Pilot: The Hawaiian Islands, 1933* (Washington, D.C.: GPO, 1933), 77; U.S. Department of Commerce, *Supplement to United States Coast Pilot: The Hawaiian Islands* (Washington, D.C.: GPO, 1946), 5.

35. *Wheeler Field History*, 8; "Landing of the Dole Flyers in Hawaii," *Air Corps News* 11, no. 13 (15 October 1927): 304, AFHRA.

36. Frederick Howard, "Kingsford Smith, Sir Charles Edward (1897–1935)," *Australian Dictionary of Biography*, http://adb.anu.edu.au/biography/kingsford -smith-sir-charles-edward-6964, accessed 27 April 2020; *Wheeler Field History*, 11, 21. Maitland and Hegenberger had flown a heavily modified American-made version of the Fokker one year before.

37. *Wheeler Field History*, 11, 21; "New Zealand Citizens Express Gratitude to U.S.," *Air Corps News Letter* 18, no. 3 (15 February 1935): 56, AFHRA; Golden Years of Aviation, "Civil Aircraft Register—Australia," www.airhistory.org.uk/gy/reg_VH-U1.html, accessed 28 April 2020; "Weather Bureau Believes Squalls North of Hawaii Will Clear by Sunday," *Honolulu Star-Bulletin*, 1 December 1934, 1, https://www .newspapers.com/newspage/275038279/, accessed 28 April 2020; National Library of Australia, caption for photograph PIC/8392/386-423, https://nla.gov.au/nla .obj-147721912/view, accessed 28 April 2020; "Planes, Submarines, Ships Seek Ulm," *Nevada State Journal* (Reno), 5 December 1934, 1, https://www.newspapers .com/newspage/78824482/, accessed 28 April 2020; "Lost and Out of Gasoline," *St. Louis Star-Times*, 4 December 1934, 1, https://www.newspapers.com /newspage/205507631/, accessed 28 April 2020.

38. Passenger manifest, Honolulu arrival, *Lurline* voyage 38, Los Angeles to Honolulu, 22–27 December 1934, microfilmed publication A4156, roll 229, RG 85, NARA DC, via Jessie Higa; Hawaii Aviation, "Amelia Earhart," https://aviation.hawaii.gov/aviation -pioneers/amelia-earhart/, accessed 30 April 2020. This material was extracted from William J. Horvat, *Above the Pacific* (Fallbrook, Calif.: Aero Publishers, 1966).

39. William H. Ewing, "Few on Hand to See Start of Great Hop," *Honolulu Star-Bulletin*, 12 January 1935, 1–2; "Amelia Earhart"; Amelia Earhart Original Photo Archive, photo caption for "Amelia Earhart in Hawaii, #613," https://www.ameliaarchive.org/index.aspx?year =1934#&gid=1&pid=1, accessed 5 May 2020.

40. "Amelia Earhart"; Jean L. Backus, ed., *Letters from Amelia: An Intimate Portrait of Amelia Earhart* (Boston: Beacon Press, 1982), 165.

41. Ewing, "Few on Hand," 1–2.

42. Ewing, "Few on Hand," 2; "Miss Earhart Off on Pacific Flight; Heard about 3 Hours Out," *New York Times*, 12 January 1935, 1, https://archive.nytimes.com/www .nytimes.com/learning/aol/onthisday/big/0111.html, accessed 5 May 2020.

43. Ewing, "Few on Hand," 2.

44. *Wheeler Field History*, 25; Ray Panko, "Amelia Earhart's Crash on Ford Island, March 20, 1937," 16 November 2009, https://www.pearlharboraviationmuseum.org /blog/amelias-earharts-crash-on-ford-island-may-20 –1937/, accessed 30 April 2020.

45. "Amelia Earhart."

46. "Amelia Earhart"; passenger manifest, Honolulu departure, *Malolo*, Honolulu to San Francisco, 20–27 March 1937, microfilmed publication A3510, roll 116, RG 85, NARA DC, via Jessie Higa; "Hawaiian Air Depot, Luke Field, T.H., April 14," *Air Corps News Letter* 20, no. 9 (1 May 1937): 25, AFHRA; *Wheeler Field History*, 25.

47. Kindl, NTU interview, 15–16; correspondence, JMW and Jessie Higa; Wenger, Cressman, and Di Virgilio, *They're Killing My Boys*, 67.

48. Springer, NTU interview, 11; Melvin L. Miller, oral history, 25 February 2003 (hereinafter, Miller, TLM oral history), Tropic Lightning Museum (hereinafter TLM), 1; Kindl, NTU interview, 10; Sample, NTU interview, 12–13; Kolbert, NTU interview, 14–15.

49. Springer, NTU interview, 11; Kolbert, NTU interview, 11–13.

50. Richardson, NTU interview, 19; John P. Conlon, "Chevrons and Rockers," in "Letters" section, *Army: The Magazine of Landpower* 34, no. 4 (April 1984); 9; Sample, NTU interview, 11.

51. Runce, NTU interview, 23; Springer, NTU interview, 8.

52. Siegle, NTU interview, 9, 11; authors' analysis; Runce, NTU interview, 23–24.

53. Runce, NTU interview, 25–26.

54. Koran, NTU interview, 14–16.

55. Stewart, NTU interview, 9–10.

56. Runce, NTU interview, 13–14; Henry Brown, NTU interview, 24; Kindl, NTU interview, 12.

57. Kindl, NTU interview, 11; Runce, NTU interview, 23; Henry Brown, NTU interview, 20.

58. Henry Brown, NTU interview, 22; Runce, NTU interview, 23; Kolbert, NTU interview, 29.

59. Henry Brown, NTU interview, 25; Kindl, NTU interview, 14–15; Springer, NTU interview, 7; Brown, NTU interview, 20–21.

60. Kindl, NTU interview, 12; Richardson, NTU interview, 32.

61. Siegle, NTU interview, 10; Munn, NTU interview, 10; Henry Brown, NTU interview, 20–21; Kindl, NTU interview, 12–14.

62. Kindl, NTU interview, 12; Siegle, NTU interview, 11.

63. Kindl, NTU interview, 13; Henry Brown, NTU interview, 24; Siegle, NTU interview, 10; Munn, NTU interview, 9.

64. Springer, NTU interview, 7; Siegle, NTU interview, 16; Sample, NTU interview, 19; authors' analysis.

65. Siegle, NTU interview, 16–17.

66. Richardson, NTU interview, 31.

67. Willis, NTU interview, 17–18, 20.

68. Kolbert, NTU interview, 30–31.

69. Passenger manifest, Honolulu arrival, *Matsonia*, Los Angles to Honolulu, 8–14 October 1941, RG 85, NARA DC, via Jessie Higa; Marcelina Saclausa, "Tourist Tattler," *Honolulu Advertiser*, 18 October 1941, 13, https://www.newspapers.com/image/259335728, accessed 26 September 2020, via Jessie Higa; 47th Pursuit Squadron, morning reports, October–November 1941, NARA, St. Louis; passenger manifest, Honolulu departure, *Lurline*, Honolulu to San Francisco, 7 November 1941, RG 85, NARA DC, via Jessie Higa; George S. Welch, flight logs, 1941, entry for 7 November 1941, Aiken Collection, National Museum of the Pacific War, Fredericksburg, Texas (hereinafter Aiken Collection, NMPW), Welch folder; George S. Welch, IFRs, 7 November 1941, NARA, St. Louis.

CHAPTER 5. "A RATHER CAREFREE LOT WHO HAD TO BE KEPT IN CHECK"

1. Authors' analysis of unit rosters and duty codes at NARA, St. Louis; Edward J. White, oral history, 16 October 1986 (hereinafter White, 15WHO oral history), 15th Wing History Office, Hickam AFB (hereinafter 15WHO), 4. The authors thank James Tobias at the U.S. Army Center of Military History, Fort McNair, for his assistance in locating a copy of Army Regulation No. 615-26 from 3 September 1940, "Index and Specifications for Occupational Specialists and Index to Military Occupational Specialists."

2. Richardson, NTU interview, 22–23; Weddington testimony, Army Board, *PHA*, pt. 28, 1572; Henry Brown, NTU interview, 26–27.

3. Authors' analysis; Miller, TLM oral history, 2; Richardson, NTU interview, 28.

4. Miller, TLM oral history, 1; Richardson, NTU interview, 33; Henry J. Straub, oral history, circa 1991 (hereinafter Straub, 15WHO oral history), 1.

5. Miller, TLM oral history, 1; Richardson, NTU interview, 20, 27, 33–34.

6. Kindl, NTU interview, 21.

7. Bowers, *Curtiss Aircraft, 1907–1947*, 348, 350.

8. Bowers, *Curtiss Aircraft, 1907–1947*, 474.

9. Bowers, *Curtiss Aircraft, 1907–1947*, 474–75, 477–78.

10. Dana Bell, *P-40 Warhawk* (Tucson, Ariz.: Classic Warships, 2013), 21, 62–63. The authors thank Dana Bell for his generosity in sharing information and photography regarding the P-40.

11. General Plan, "Bellows Field, Oahu, T.H.," April 1941, *PHA*, pt. 25; O-47B aircraft history cards, AFHRA; telephone conversation and correspondence, JMW and Louis Bontya, 9 May 2020. The number of aircraft

present on 7 December 1941 is uncertain, but the aircraft parking diagram provided to the Roberts Commission shows six machines present, indicating that one aircraft was out of service apart from the three undergoing overhaul at the Hawaiian Air Depot.

12. National Museum of the U.S. Air Force, "North American O-47B," https://www.nationalmuseum.af .mil/DesktopModules/ArticleCS/Print.aspx?PortalId =7&ModuleId=1155&Article=198091, accessed 9 May 2020.

13. Kolbert, NTU interview, 5; Willis, NTU interview, 12.

14. Runce, NTU interview, 5–7.

15. "Recruit Training at Wheeler Field," *Air Corps News Letter* 22, no. 22 (15 November 1939): 15–16, AFHRA.

16. "Recruit Training," 16; authors' analysis; see Wenger, Cressman, and Di Virgilio, *They're Killing My Boys*, 56.

17. *VII Fighter Command History*, 5–6.

18. Histories , flight records, and morning reports and histories of Wheeler's pursuit squadrons, 1941, in AFHRA and RG 64, NARA, St. Louis; *History of the 47th Fighter Squadron*, AFHSO, reel A0741, file Sq-Fi-47-Hi, 3; authors' analysis. Interestingly, there is no mention in the morning reports and histories of *any* such deployments in 1941 until June.

19. Microfilmed morning reports, 47th Pursuit Squadron, June 1941, RG 64, NARA, St. Louis; *VII Fighter Command History*, "Training Memorandum No. 1," 1 July 1941, AFHSO, reel A7586, file 741.01, 1–8.

20. "Training Memorandum No. 1," 1–2.

21. "Training Memorandum No. 1," 2–4.

22. "Training Memorandum No. 1," 5–6.

23. Testimony of Howard C. Davidson before the Roberts Commission, 23 December 1941 (hereinafter Davidson, Roberts testimony), *PHA*, pt. 22, 106, 118.

24. *VII Fighter Command History*, "Trainee Discipline," 13 August 1941, AFHSO, reel A7586, file 741.01, 1; authors' analysis.

25. Davidson, Roberts testimony, 23 December 1941, *PHA*, pt. 22, 106–7, 118.

26. P-26A, P-26B, P-36A, P-40B, P-40C aircraft history cards, AFHRA.

27. Various Aircraft Accident Reports, Wheeler pilots, 1941, AFHRA.

28. Judge Advocate, Hawaiian Department, General Court-Martial, Record of Trial, Henry C. Brown, September 1941–February 1942 (hereinafter Brown Court-Martial), testimony of Pvt. Henry C. Brown, 14 November 1941, 16; Brown Court-Martial, statement of Pvt. John H. Wilberding, n.d., NARA, St. Louis.

29. Brown Court-Martial, statement of Cpl. James E. Driver Jr., n.d.; Brown Court-Martial, statement of Pfc. Nelson A. Vona, n.d. (hereinafter Vona statement); Brown Court-Martial, testimony of Pfc. Nelson A. Vona, 14 November 1941 (hereinafter Vona testimony), 6.

30. Brown Court-Martial, Vona statement; Vona testimony, 6; Brown Court-Martial, statement of Pvt. Lorimer Peterson, n.d., Brown Court-Martial Records.

31. Brown Court-Martial, Gordon H. Austin statement.

32. Brown Court-Martial, memorandum to accompany record of trial; Headquarters Hawaiian Department, General Court-Martial Orders No. 13, 14 February 1942, 1.

33. *VII Fighter Command History*, "Hawaiian Air Force Training Directive, 1941–1942 (1st Quarter)" (hereinafter "HAF Training Directive"), 13 August 1941, 1; "Trainee Discipline," 1; IFRs of new pilots, RG 64, NARA, St. Louis.

34. Morning reports of the squadrons and IFRs of pilots involved, RG 64, NARA, St. Louis; "HAF Training Directive," 1–2.

35. Histories, flight records, and morning reports of Wheeler's pursuit squadrons, 1941, in AFHRA and RG 64, NARA, St. Louis; "Haleiwa Field History," enclosure no. 1, Headquarters, 18th Air Base Group, Special Orders No. 89, 14 November 1941; *Group History of the 15th Pursuit Group (F)*, AFHSO, reel B0080A, file GP-15-Hi, 59; authors' analysis. There is no record of any deployment by the 73rd Pursuit Squadron to either Bellows or Haleiwa. The 72nd Pursuit Squadron did not receive its aircraft until 6 December, so there is no record of a deployment for that squadron either.

36. 46th Pursuit Squadron, Operations Order No. 86, 31 October 1941, AFHRA, via Randall Asherbranner; microfilmed officer roster, 15th Pursuit Group, 30 September 1941, RG 64, NARA, St. Louis; IFRs, various pilots.

37. Operations Order No. 86; William J. Flood to CG Hawaiian Air Force, "Aircraft Status," 14 December 1941 (hereinafter Flood, "Aircraft Status"), *PHA*, pt. 24, Exhibits of the Roberts Commission, Exhibit 1 (Army), 1763–65.

38. Operations Order No. 86; IFRs, various pilots.

39. Aircraft Accident Report, William J. Feiler, P-36A, 38-108, 31 October 1941; "2 Planes Crash at Kahuku; 1 Pilot Missing," *Honolulu Star-Bulletin*, 31 October 1941, 1, via Jessie Higa; "Organizational History, 46th Fighter Squadron, 21st Fighter Group, VII Fighter Command, Seventh Air Force," AFHSO, reel A0741, file Sq-Fi-46-Hi, 2; "Army Airman Killed as 2 Planes Crash," *Honolulu Advertiser*, 1 November 1941, 8, via Jessie Higa; authors' analysis; Operations Order No. 86.

40. 44th Pursuit Squadron IFRs, 3–7 November 1941, RG 64, NARA, St. Louis; various historical materials, 78th Pursuit Squadron, AFHSO; microfilmed morning reports, 44th Pursuit Squadron, November 1941, RG 64, NARA, St. Louis.

41. 44th Pursuit Squadron IFRs, RG 64, NARA, St. Louis.

42. 44th and 46th Pursuit Squadron IFRs, RG 64, NARA, St. Louis.

43. Microfilmed morning reports, 45th and 46th Pursuit Squadrons, November 1941, RG 64, NARA, St. Louis; authors' analysis; "Hawaiian Islands, Oahu," map, *PHA*, pt. 21, Exhibits of the Joint Committee, Exhibit 6, item 14.

44. 46th Pursuit Squadron IFRs, November 1941, RG 64, NARA, St. Louis. The authors were unable to locate the IFRs for 2nd Lt. Dewitt S. Spain and 2nd Lt. George L. Wirt.

45. 46th Pursuit Squadron IFRs, 17–26 November 1941, RG 64, NARA, St. Louis.

46. Martin testimony, Army Board, 29 August 1944, *PHA*, pt. 28, 982–83; Wenger, Cressman, and Di Virgilio, *They're Killing My Boys*, 46.

47. HQ, 14th Pursuit Wing, memorandum re: Ground Defense Units, Wheeler Field, T.H., 8 April 1941, *Wheeler Field History*, Ground Defense, AFHSO, reel A0086, file AAFLD-Wheeler-Hi (1918); Wenger, Cressman, and Di Virgilio, *They're Killing My Boys*, 46.

48. Headquarters, 14th Pursuit Wing (S-4) to CG, 14th Pursuit Wing, "Delays and difficulties resulting from ground defense training," 1 August 1941, 1–2, *VII Fighter Command History*, AFHSO, reel 7586, file 741.01.

49. Headquarters, Wheeler Field, "Ground Defense Training Memorandum No. 2," 10 November 1941, 1–2, *Wheeler Field History*, Ground Defense, AFHSO, reel A0086, file AAFLD-Wheeler-Hi (1918).

50. Kindl, NTU interview, 19–20.

51. Koran, NTU interview, 25.

CHAPTER 6. "CONCERNED WITH PREPARING OURSELVES, AND COME WHAT MAY"

1. Stewart, NTU interview, 11.

2. Willis, NTU interview, 28–29.

3. Stewart, NTU interview, 13.

4. Willis, NTU interview, 29–31.

5. Kindl, NTU interview, 22–23; Runce, NTU interview, 22.

6. Stewart, NTU interview, 12; authors' analysis.

7. Microfilmed morning reports for 86th Observation Squadron, September and November 1941, RG 64, NARA, St. Louis; Willis, NTU interview, 13; aircraft history card, O-47B, A.C. Serial No. 39-84, AFHRA; "Two Bellows Field Fliers Die in Crash," *Honolulu Advertiser*, 18 November 1941, 7, via Jessie Higa; Joe McCarthy, "Bellows Field Observations," *Honolulu Star-Bulletin*, 26 June 1942, 6, via Jessie Higa.

8. HQ, HD to CG, HAF, "Records Requested in Telegram Dated 22 December 1941," 23 December 1941, *PHA*, pt. 24, 1935.

9. Testimony of William J. Flood before the Army Pearl Harbor Board, 11 September 1944 (hereinafter Flood testimony, Army Board), *PHA*, pt. 28, 1490–91.

10. Passenger manifest, Honolulu departure, *Matsonia* voyage 94, Honolulu to San Francisco, 15 October 1941, microfilm publication A3510, roll 142, RG 85, NARA DC, via Jessie Higa; Howard C. Davidson, IFRs, 20–22 October 1941, RG 64, NARA, St. Louis.

11. "*Lurline* in with Second Largest Passenger List" (hereinafter "Lurline In"), *Honolulu Star-Bulletin*, 3 December 1941, via Jessie Higa; "General Davidson, Visiting Here, Lauds New Air Service Command," *Dayton Daily News* (Dayton, Ohio), 9 November 1941, 1, 6, via Jessie Higa.

12. "General Davidson, Visiting Here," 1; Howard C. Davidson, IFRs, 20–22 October 1941, RG 64, NARA,

St. Louis; Wesley F. Craven and James L. Cate, *The Army Air Forces in World War II*, vol. 6: *Men and Planes* (Washington, D.C.: Office of Air Force History, 1983), 366; Flood, "Aircraft Status," 14 December 1941, *PHA*, pt. 24, 1763.

13. Howard C. Davidson, IFRs, 2–23 November 1941, RG 64, NARA, St. Louis; Davidson testimony, Army Board, 27 September 1944, *PHA*, pt. 29, 2118; passenger manifest, Honolulu arrival, *Lurline* voyage San Francisco to Honolulu, 3 December 1941, microfilmed publication A3422, roll 235, RG 85, NARA DC, via Jessie Higa.

14. CinCPac to ComAirBatFor and ComPatWing 2, "Naval Air Station Wake and Naval Air Station Midway—Basing of Aircraft at," Serial 01825, 10 November 1941, Operational Plans & Orders, CinCPac, box 19, RG38, NARA II; OpNav to CinCPac, Secret Dispatch 270038, Serial 11-822, 27 November 1941 (hereinafter Secret Dispatch 270038), CinCPac dispatches, Pearl Harbor Liaison Office (hereinafter PHLO); OpNav to CinCPac, Secret Dispatch 270040, Serial 11-830, 27 November 1941 (hereinafter Secret Dispatch 270040), CinCPac dispatches, PHLO; authors' analysis.

15. Secret Dispatch 270038; Secret Dispatch 270040; testimony of Walter C. Short before the Joint Committee (hereinafter Short testimony, Joint Committee), 22 January 1946, *PHA*, pt. 7, 2942; testimony of William F. Halsey before the Hart Inquiry (hereinafter Halsey testimony, Hart Inquiry), 12 April 44, *PHA*, pt. 26, 321; testimony of Charles H. McMorris before the Hart Inquiry (hereinafter McMorris testimony, Hart Inquiry), 1 April 44, *PHA*, pt. 26, 258; testimony of James A. Mollison before the Army Pearl Harbor Board (hereinafter Mollison testimony, Army Board), 15 August 1944, *PHA*, pt. 27, 412; testimony of Charles H. McMorris before the Roberts Commission, 30 December 1941, *PHA*, pt. 27, 526.

16. Mollison testimony, Army Board, 15 August 1944, *PHA*, pt. 27, 411; authors' analysis; McMorris testimony, Hart Inquiry, 1 April 44, *PHA*, pt. 26, 259; *4th Air Force Historical Study No. IV*-I, *Narrative*, 19–22.

17. Testimony of William F. Halsey before the Roberts Commission (hereinafter Halsey testimony, Roberts Commission), 2 January 1942, *PHA*, pt. 23, 607;

testimony of William W. Smith before the Hewitt Inquiry (hereinafter Smith testimony, Hewitt Inquiry), 2 June 1945, *PHA*, pt. 36, 207; Mollison testimony, Army Board, 15 August 1944, *PHA*, pt. 27, 412.

18. Halsey testimony, Hart Inquiry, 12 April 44, *PHA*, pt. 26, 322; McMorris testimony, Hart Inquiry, 1 April 44, *PHA*, pt. 26, 259.

19. McMorris testimony, Hart Inquiry, 1 April 44, *PHA*, pt. 26, 259; Short testimony, Joint Committee, 22 January 1946, *PHA*, pt. 7, 2942; Mollison testimony, Army Board, 15 August 1944, *PHA*, pt. 27, 412.

20. Smith testimony, Hewitt Inquiry, 2 June 1945, pt. 36, 207; Halsey testimony, Hart Inquiry, 12 April 44, *PHA*, pt. 26, 322.

21. McMorris testimony, Hart Inquiry, 1 April 44, *PHA*, pt. 26, 258; Halsey testimony, Hart Inquiry, 12 April 44, *PHA*, pt. 26, 322; Wenger analysis; OpNav to CinCPac, Secret Dispatch 282054, serial 11-944, 28 November 1941, CinCPac dispatches, PHLO.

22. List of papers under 370.5, "Transfer of Two (2) Pursuit Squadrons," serial 4, "Building Materials for Midway Island," and "Materials for 23 Pyramidal Tent Frames," AFHSO, reel A7551, file 740.229-3, 1–2; "Transfer of Two (2) Pursuit Squadrons," serial 5, "Memorandum to the Chief of Staff, Hawaiian Air Force, Hickam Field, T.H.," AFHSO, reel A7551, file 740.229-3, 1–2.

23. PHSA applications: Liston A. Coomer, 16 June 1979, Harold C. Hitt, 29 July 1978, Harold J. Moore, 19 December 1964, Bertram E. Swarthout, 14 March 1992, Fred C. Wilson, 27 August 1971; Munn, NTU interview, 5, 9; Ronald F. Norton, oral history, 5 November 1991 (hereinafter Norton, 15WHO oral history), 15WHO, 1.

24. Halsey testimony, Hart Inquiry, 12 April 44, *PHA*, pt. 26, 322; William J. A. Bowen and Charles H. MacDonald, IFRs, February and November 1941, RG 64, NARA, St. Louis; microfilmed officer rosters, 18th Pursuit Group, 30 November 1941, NARA, St. Louis; *Enterprise* deck log, 27 November 1941, *PHA*, pt. 16, Exhibits of the Joint Committee, Exhibit 101 (hereinafter *Enterprise* deck log), 2033–35.

25. *Enterprise* deck log, 28 November 1941, *PHA*, pt. 16, 2039; William J. A. Bowen and Charles H. MacDonald, IFRs, February and November 1941, RG 64, NARA, St.

Louis. The aircraft carrier *Wasp* (CV 7) had conducted a practice launch of P-40s and O-47s on 12 October 1940. On 6 August 1941, in an operational (not practice) mission, *Wasp* launched thirty Curtiss P-40Cs (and three Stearman PT-17 trainers) from the 33rd Pursuit Squadron, 8th Air Group, Air Force Combat Command, Mitchel Field, to fly in to Reykjavik, Iceland, to provide fighter cover for the arrival of U.S. Army troops.

26. Affidavit of Robert H. Dunlop, 28 February 1945 (hereinafter Dunlop affidavit), Clausen Investigation, *PHA*, pt. 35, 33; WD to CG, HD, Secret Radiogram 472/27th, 27 November 1941, *PHA*, pt. 30, Exhibits of the Army Pearl Harbor Board, Exhibit 1 (incl. Short Exhibit B), 2486–87.

27. Short testimony, Joint Committee, 22 January 1946, *PHA*, pt. 7, 2942; testimony of Walter C. Short before the Army Pearl Harbor Board, 11 August 1944 (hereinafter Short testimony, Army Board), *PHA*, pt. 27, 157; authors' analysis; Short testimony, Joint Committee, 22 January 1946, *PHA*, pt. 7, 2941.

28. HQ, HD, "Standard Operating Procedure," 5 November 1941, *PHA*, pt. 24, Exhibits of the Roberts Commission, Exhibit 32 (Army), 2110–13, italics added.

29. Dunlop affidavit, 34; testimony of Walter C. Phillips before the Roberts Commission, 24 December 1941, *PHA*, pt. 22, 134; Short testimony, Joint Committee, 22 January 1946, *PHA*, pt. 7, 2941; authors' analysis.

30. Short testimony, Joint Committee, 22 January 1946, *PHA*, pt. 7, 2941; Martin testimony, Army Board, 29 August 1944, *PHA*, pt. 28, 956–57; Wenger analysis; Short testimony, Army Board, 11 August 1944, *PHA*, pt. 27, 157–58; Martin testimony, Roberts Commission, 24 December 1941, *PHA*, pt. 22, 197.

31. Flood testimony, Army Board, 11 September 1944, *PHA*, pt. 28, 1485–86, 1488–89, italics added. Flood's question implies that Wheeler's aircraft were already dispersed in the revetments prior to the alert.

32. Donald M. Arras, PHSA application, 28 November 1964; Kindl, NTU interview, 18; Richardson, NTU interview, 25, 30, 37; Miller, TLM oral history, 2; Melvin L. Miller, PHSA application, 25 June 2004; Straub, 15WHO oral history, 1.

33. HQ, Hawaiian Air Force to distribution, "Alert No. 1," 2 December 1941, 1–2, *Wheeler Field History*,

"Ground Defense," AFHSO, reel A0086, file AAFLD-Wheeler-Hi (1918).

34. "Alert No. 1," 1.

35. Authors' analysis; Martin testimony, Army Board, 29 August 1944, *PHA*, pt. 28, 957; testimony of Patrick N. L. Bellinger before the Joint Committee (hereinafter Bellinger testimony, Joint Committee), 31 January 1946, *PHA*, pt. 8, 3457, 3480.

36. Authors' analysis; IFRs, 46th Pursuit Squadron and 42nd Bombardment Squadron, November–December 1941, RG 64, NARA, St. Louis; 86th Observation Squadron (C&D) AC to CG, HD, "Flight Operations of 86th Obsn Sq (C&D) AC during the period 15 November 1941 to 7 December 1941, Inclusive," 22 December 1941 (hereinafter "Flight Operations of 86th Observation Squadron"), *PHA*, pt. 24, Exhibits of the Roberts Commission, Exhibit 11 (Army), 1938–58; Patrol Wing 2 to Patrons, Seaplane Tenders, "Operation Schedule No. 45-41 (Week of Nov. 26–Dec. 2, 1941)," 25 November 1941, *PHA*, pt. 17, Exhibits of the Joint Committee, Exhibit 113C, 2549–50; Patrol Wing 2 to Patrons, "Watch and Duty Schedule for December 1, 1941, to January 1, 1942," 25 November 1941, *PHA*, pt. 17, Exhibits of the Joint Committee, Exhibit 113C, 2547–48.

37. Straub, 15WHO oral history, 1; microfilmed morning reports for 44th, 46th, and 47th Pursuit Squadrons, November–December 1941, RG 64, NARA, St. Louis; authors' analysis; Kindl, NTU interview, 1; Donald M. Arras, PHSA application, 28 November 1964; Richardson, NTU interview, 25, 30, 37; Miller, TLM oral history, 2; Melvin L. Miller, PHSA application, 25 June 2004. Although there are no documents that indicate the locations of the 45th and 73rd Pursuit Squadrons, they probably deployed to the revetments.

38. Kindl, NTU interview, 16–17; microfilmed morning reports, 46th Pursuit Squadron, August, November–December 1941, and 47th Pursuit Squadron, November 1941, RG 64, NARA, St. Louis; Springer NTU interview, 17.

39. "*Lurline* In," 1; Davidson testimony, Roberts Commission, 23 December 1941, *PHA*, pt. 22, 110.

40. Wenger, Cressman, and Di Virgilio, *They're Killing My Boys*, 83; authors' analysis.

41. Authors' analysis; Straub, 15WHO oral history, 1–2; annotated vertical photograph of Wheeler Field, *PHA*, pt. 25, Exhibits of the Roberts Commission, Exhibit 1 (Army), item 88 (hereinafter Wheeler aircraft parking diagram); Spangler, TLM oral history, 1; Richardson, NTU interview, 30; Davidson, Prange interview, 6 July 1962, 4, Prange Papers, Goldstein Collection.

42. Richardson, NTU interview, 25, 37; authors' analysis; Wheeler aircraft parking diagram.

43. Springer, NTU interview, 17–18; Siegle, NTU interview, 18.

44. Miller, TLM oral history, 2; Straub, 15WHO oral history, 2; Norton, 15WHO oral history.

45. Lewis M. Sanders to John W. Lambert, handwritten account of air action on 7 December 1941, n.d., transcription by Wenger circa 1990 (hereinafter Sanders account), 1.

CHAPTER 7. "THE TOWN WAS JUMPING!"

1. Runce, NTU interview, 26; Norton, 15WHO oral history, 1; Brown, NTU interview, 25.

2. Runce, NTU interview, 26–28; Brown, NTU interview, 26–27.

3. Kolbert, NTU interview, 16–17, 32, 34–37.

4. Willis, NTU interview, 14–15.

5. Willis, NTU interview, 15, 19, 34.

6. Kenneth M. Taylor, National Park Service interview, USAR no. 179, 4 December 1986 (hereinafter Taylor, USAR oral history), 2–3, courtesy Daniel Martinez, WWII Valor in the Pacific National Monument; authors' analysis; George S. Welch, testimony before the Roberts Commission, 26 December 1941 (hereinafter Welch, Roberts testimony), *PHA*, pt. 22, 255.

7. Kindl, NTU interview, 23; Gordon H. Sterling Jr. and Eldon E. Stratton, IFRs, December 1941, RG 64, NARA, St. Louis.

8. Testimony of Stephen G. Saltzman before the Roberts Commission, 26 December 1941 (hereinafter Saltzman, Roberts testimony), *PHA*, pt. 22, 276; Koran, NTU interview, 33.

9. Springer, NTU interview, 18; Sample, NTU interview, 24.

10. Vladamir "William" M. Shiflette III, interview with Ronald Marcello, 8 March 1974, OH 0297 (hereinafter Shiflette, NTU interview), 24, UNTOHC; Siegle,

NTU interview, 18–19; Edmund H. Russell, TLM oral history, 5 December 1981, 2.

11. Munn, NTU interview, 1; Straub, 15WHO oral history, 2.

12. Stewart, NTU interview, 18.

13. Koran, NTU interview, 31.

14. Richardson, NTU interview, 37–38.

15. Charles L. Hendrix, 15WHO oral history, 12 December 1941, 1; Davidson, Prange interview, 6 July 1962, 5, Prange Papers, Goldstein Collection; Flood testimony, Army Board, 11 September 1944, *PHA*, pt. 28, 1487.

16. Carroll T. Andrews, questionnaire, n.d. (hereinafter Andrews, Lord questionnaire), 1, 3, Lord Collection HAD, NHHC.

17. Springer, NTU interview, 24.

18. Siegle, NTU interview, 20; Koran, NTU interview, 34.

19. Wenger, Cressman, and Di Virgilio, *They're Killing My Boys*, 93–94; Fuchida Mitsuo chart, "Flying Formation on [sic} Pearl Harbor Attack, First Attack Force (183 Planes)," Prange Collection, University of Maryland, box 35. Takahashi did not exercise direct command over a *chūtai*. Takahashi's "Special Command *Shōtai*" fronted the 3rd Chūtai, composed of six aircraft under Lt. Hira Kuniyoshi.

20. Genda Minoru, Prange interview 25, 28 December 1947 (hereinafter Genda, Prange interview 25), 1, Prange Collection, University of Maryland, box 19; Opana radar plot chart, Treasure Vault, NARA DC; authors' analysis; Fuchida Mitsuo, Prange interview 19, 6 January 1949 (hereinafter Fuchida, Prange interview 19), 1, Prange Collection, University of Maryland, box 19. Two accounts document the transmission of the code word ト-ツ-レ (to-tsu-re), or "assume preliminary charge formation." See Yoshino Haruo, "Kaga Dengekitai, Senkan Okurahoma Ni Shiro-o Tore," in Fujita Iyozō, comp., *Shōgen Shinjuwan Kōgeki* (Tōkyō: Kōjin-sha, 1991), 42; and Matsuda Norio, "To Renso," *Rekishi-to Jinbutsu* (Tōkyō: Chūō Kōron-sha, 20 January 1983), 246. Reconstruction of coded messages based on fragmentary codebooks recovered from Japanese aircraft wreckage (hereinafter Japanese codebooks, NARA II). See Pearl Harbor Liaison Office, entry 167F, RG 80, NARA II. Dr. Timothy P. Mulligan provided copies to the authors.

21. Fuchida Mitsuo, Prange interview 14, 10, Prange Papers, Goldstein Collection, UA-90/F-78, box 21; Fuchida Mitsuo, Prange conference 3, 11 December 1963 (hereinafter Fuchida, Prange conference 3), 1, Prange Collection, University of Maryland, box 19; authors' analysis; Genda, Prange interview 25, 2.

22. Fuchida, Prange conference 3, 1; Genda, Prange interview 25, 3; Fuchida, Prange interview 14, 9–10; *Shōkaku* detailed action report (hereinafter *Shōkaku* DAR, Atene Shobō), in Yamagata Tsunao, comp., *Kaigun: Kūbo-Kan Sentō Kiroku* (Atene Shobō, 2002), 200.

23. *Shōkaku* DAR, Atene Shobō, 200; authors' analysis.

24. Fuchida, Prange conference 3, 1; chart of first-wave deployment and tactical analysis by Di Virgilio; Fuchida, Prange interview 14, 10.

25. Di Virgilio analysis; *Shōkaku* DAR, Atene Shobō, 200; Genda, Prange interview 25, 3; chart of first-wave deployment and tactical analysis by Di Virgilio.

26. Genda, Prange interview 25, 4; chart of first-wave deployment and tactical analysis by Di Virgilio; authors' analysis; *Hikōkitai Sentō Kōdōchōsho* (hereinafter *kōdōchōsho*), War History Office, Japan Defense Agency, *Zuikaku*, 8 December 1941; *Shōkaku* DAR, Atene Shobō, 200.

27. Ema Tamotsu, Prange interview 1 (hereinafter Ema, Prange interview 1), 3, Prange Collection, University of Maryland, box 19.

28. Hori Kenji, "99-Shiki Kanjō Bakugekiki," *Maru Mechanic*, no. 5 (1982): 63.

29. Okajima Kiyokuma, Prange statement, 19 January 1951 (hereinafter Okajima, Prange statement), 2; Muranaka Kazuo, Prange questionnaire, 17 December 1949 (hereinafter Muranaka, Prange questionnaire), 3; authors' tactical analysis; *kōdōchōsho, Sōryū*, 8 December 1941.

30. *Shōkaku* DAR, Atene Shobō, 199, 207.

31. *Shōkaku* DAR, Atene Shobō, 199–200.

32. Letter and map, Matsumura Hirata to John F. Di Virgilio, 15 July 1993; chart of first-wave deployment and tactical analysis by Di Virgilio.

33. Matsumura Hirata, Di Virgilio interview, 8 November 1991, 4.

34. Yoshioka Masamitsu, "16.12.08 Sentō Kiroku," *Kōkū Bokan Sōryū-no Kiroku* (Japan: *Sōryū-kai*, 1992), 166; Mori Jūzō, *Kiseki-no Raigekkitai* (Tōkyō: Kōjin-sha,

1994), 161; statement, Nakajima Tatsumi, 28 January 1951, 1, Prange Collection, University of Maryland, box 19; Mori Jūzō, "Raigekki Shutsudo," in Fujita, *Shōgen Shinjuwan Kōgeki*, 154; Mori Jūzō, "We Will Attack Pearl Harbor!" *Cavalier* 12, no. 103 (January 1962): 78.

35. Harold J. Moore, PHSA application 19 December 1964; Christopher Ward, PHSA application, 10 September 1990.

36. Authors' analysis; *Shōkaku* DAR, Atene Shobō, 200.

37. *Shōkaku* DAR, Atene Shobō, 199–200; Satō Zen'ichi attack photography, Pearl Harbor Air Museum; authors' analysis. Very few documents address Sakamoto's deployment over Wheeler Field. Fortunately, the *Shōkaku*'s action report—the only such report from the Hawaiian Operation known to exist—provided an operational order for the Wheeler attack unit regarding target selection and a diagram that documents the alternating pinwheel movement of Sakamoto's three *chūtai*s. The *Shōkaku*'s report probably included those details only because Lt. Cdr. Takahashi Kakuichi was the overall commander of the first-wave dive-bombers.

38. Wenger, Cressman, and Di Virgilio, *They're Killing My Boys*, 98–100, 106; authors' analysis; Genda, Prange interview 25, 4.

39. *Kōdōchōsho, Zuikaku*, 8 December 1941; Di Virgilio analysis; *Shōkaku* DAR, Atene Shobō, 200. The direction from which Lieutenant Hayashi's 3rd Chūtai attacked is uncertain, but it is reasonable to assume that he turned right, following Sakamoto. Such a movement is consistent with the admittedly vague deployment diagram presented in the *Shōkaku* action report. See *Shōkaku* DAR, Atene Shobō, 200.

40. Ema, Prange interview 1, 3–4.

41. Hendrix, 15WHO oral history, 1; David B. Stephenson, 15WHO oral history, 15 September 1963 (hereinafter Stephenson, 15WHO oral history), 1.

CHAPTER 8. "DEAR GOD, WHAT DID WE DO TO DESERVE THIS?"

1. Di Virgilio analysis; *kōdōchōsho*s, *Zuikaku* and *Sōryū*, 8 December 1941.

2. Authors' tactical analysis; photographs 111-SC-176604 and -176605, Still Picture Branch, NARA II; "Wheeler

Field Water Map;" *kōdōchōsho*, *Zuikaku*, 8 December 1941.

3. *Kōdōchōsho*, *Zuikaku*, 8 December 1941; White, 15WHO oral history, 5.

4. White, 15WHO oral history, 5–6; Harold C. Hitt, PHSA application, 29 July 1978.

5. Authors' tactical analysis; photographs 111-SC-176606, -176607, and -176608, Still Picture Branch, NARA II.

6. Fuchida Mitsuo's handwritten aircrew roster for the Hawaiian Operation (hereinafter Fuchida roster, Hawaiian Operation), folder of original documents in the Prange Collection, University of Maryland, box 35. This note applies to the two succeeding *chūtais* as well. The definitive sources for almost all of the Japanese strike units from the 7 December 1941 attack on Oʻahu are the aircraft group *kōdōchōsho* volumes held in the War History Office of the Japan Defense Agency. *Zuikaku*'s first-wave *kōdōchōsho* is fragmentary with only its fighter unit and the first five carrier bomber crews intact. Fortunately, Fuchida preserved his original copy of the Hawaiian Operation strike roster and furnished it to Prange. The nature of the document suggests that Fuchida compiled it during the war from the action reports of the aircraft carriers in *Kidō Butai*. Fuchida's document is the only known source for the *Zuikaku* roster, although over the span of two generations historians have attempted to reconstruct it. Without question, the "Fuchida roster," rendered here in *romaji* for the first time, is one of the most significant Japanese document discoveries in recent years.

7. Carl W. Shrader, questionnaire, 18 June 1956 (hereinafter Shrader, Lord questionnaire), 1, 3, Lord Collection, HAD, NHHC.

8. Hendrix, 15WHO oral history, 1; Stephenson, 15WHO oral history, 1.

9. Spangler, TLM oral history, 1; George V. Biggs, PHSA application, 7 April 1980; Stephenson, 15WHO oral history, 1.

10. Russell, TLM oral history, 1. The school was Leilehua High School.

11. Straub, 15WHO oral history, 2.

12. William J. Young, PHSA application, 24 March 1982.

13. Koran, NTU interview, 36–37.

14. Bess Lalumendier, questionnaire, n.d. (hereinafter Lalumendier, Lord questionnaire), 1, Lord Collection, HAD, NHHC.

15. Francis S. Gabreski, *Gabby: A Fighter Pilot's Life* (New York: Orion Books, 1991), 39–40.

16. Sanders account, 1–2.

17. Flood, Prange interview, 9 July 1962, 3–5, Prange Papers, Goldstein Collection; Flood testimony, Army Board, 11 September 1944, *PHA*, pt. 28, 1487; Davidson, Prange interview, 6 July 1962, 5–8, Prange Papers, Goldstein Collection.

18. Donald D. Flickinger, questionnaire, 18 June 1956 (hereinafter Flickinger, Lord questionnaire), 1, Lord Collection, HAD, NHHC.

19. Ema, Prange interview 1, 4–5; Hori Kenji, "Machini Matta X-Bi," *Rekishi-to Jinbutsu* (Tōkyō: Chūō Kōron-sha, 20 January 1983), 240.

20. *Kōdōchōsho*, *Sōryū* fighter unit, 8 December 1941; Okajima Kiyokuma, map and questionnaire to John W. Lambert, circa March 1981; Okajima, Prange statement, 2; Muranaka, Prange questionnaire, 3–4.

21. Charles D. Boyer, PHSA application, 7 December 1978; William F. Winzenburg, PHSA application, 28 July 1987; Ray E. Hadwick, PHSA application, 15 November 1966.

22. Kenneth E. Krepps, questionnaire, n.d. (hereinafter Krepps, Lord questionnaire), 1, Lord Collection, HAD, NHHC; John F. Plassio, questionnaire, 31 May 1956 (hereinafter Plassio, Lord questionnaire), 1, Lord Collection, HAD, NHHC; microfilmed morning reports, 46th Pursuit Squadron, December 1941, RG 64, NARA, St. Louis.

23. Andrews, Lord questionnaire, 1, 3.

24. Norton, 15WHO oral history, 1–2.

25. Norton, 15WHO oral history, 2.

26. Gordon F. Smith, questionnaire, n.d. (hereinafter Smith, Lord questionnaire), 1–2, Lord Collection, HAD, NHHC.

27. Lalumendier, Lord questionnaire, 1–2.

28. Testimony of Mobley L. Hall before the Roberts Commission, 26 December 1941, *PHA*, pt. 22 (hereinafter Hall testimony, Roberts Commission), 257–58, 260.

29. Miller, TLM oral history, 3; Arakaki and Kuborn, *The Air Force Story*, 192.

30. Morton Kamm, PHSA application, 11 February 1977; Arakaki and Kuborn, *The Air Force Story*, 125–26; Joe K. Harding, PHSA application, 1 November 1975.

31. George S. Welch, Interview with Lieutenant George S. Welch, Serial Number 398557, 46th Pursuit Group–Wheeler Field, 19 May 1942 (hereinafter Welch, AAF interview), 1, AFHRA, file 142.052 Welch Geo. S. 19 May 1942, copy in Aiken Collection, NMPW, Welch folder; Taylor, USAR oral history, 1; Robert L. Scott Jr., *Damned to Glory* (Garden City, N.Y.: Blue Ribbon Books, 1944), 122–23.

32. Scott, *Damned to Glory*, 123; Welch, Roberts testimony, 26 December 1941, *PHA*, pt. 22, 254; Taylor, USAR oral history, 1–2. The movie *Tora! Tora! Tora!* (dir. Fleischer, Masuda, and Fukasaku, 1970, 20th Century Fox) portrays Taylor's Buick sedan as a convertible. See Taylor, USAR oral history, 10.

33. Harry W. Brown, interview with John W. Lambert, n.d. (hereinafter Brown, Lambert interview), courtesy of Mark Stevens, 1–2; Welch testimony, Roberts Commission, 26 December 1941, *PHA*, pt. 22, 255; testimony of Kenneth M. Taylor before the Roberts Commission, 26 December 1941 (hereinafter Taylor testimony, Roberts Commission), *PHA*, pt. 22, 251; George E. Kovak, letter, n.d. (hereinafter Kovak, Lord letter), 1, Lord Collection, HAD, NHHC.

34. Stewart, NTU interview, 23–24.

35. Paul R. Cipriano, PHSA application, 14 October 1977; James R. Piggott, PHSA application, 20 October 1984.

36. Miller, TLM oral history, 2; Charles D. Boyer, PHSA application, 7 December 1978.

37. Keith E. Cragg, PHSA application, n.d.; Raeburn D. Drenner, questionnaire, 23 March 1956 (hereinafter Drenner, Lord questionnaire), 1, Lord Collection, HAD, NHHC.

38. 7th Air Force Base Command, GO 17, 5 May 1942 (hereinafter 7th AFBC, GO 17), citations for Kraig L. Van Noy and Ralph C. Riddle; John W. Lambert, *The Pineapple Air Force: Pearl Harbor to Tokyo* (St. Paul, Minn.: Phalanx, 1990), 17.

39. 7th AFBC, GO 17, citations for Kraig L. Van Noy and Milton J. Dunn; microfilmed morning reports, 24th Material Squadron, 25th Material Squadron, 14th Quartermaster Company (Trk), Quartermaster Detachment, 46th Pursuit Squadron, and 72nd Pursuit Squadron, 7–8 December 1941, RG 64, NARA, St. Louis; 7th AFBC, GO 17, citation for George J. Van Gieri.

40. Henry C. Brown, NTU interview, 32–33, 40.

41. Henry C. Brown, NTU interview, 34–35, 46.

42. 7th AFBC, GO 17, citations for Daniel A. Mahoney, Bruce Harlow, and Gottlieb J. Kaercher.

43. Fuchida roster, Hawaiian Operation; Ema, Prange interview 1, 4. The reference to "the tower" probably does not refer to the Control Tower, as no weapons are known to have fired from that position.

44. Ema, Prange interview 1, 4; Fuchida roster, Hawaiian Operation; Christopher Ward, PHSA application, 10 September 1990.

45. Authors' analysis of photography in record group 111-SC, Still Picture Branch, NARA II; *Shōkaku* DAR, Atene Shobō, 200; authors' analysis and personal inspection of surviving bomb crater impacts at Wheeler Field; *Wheeler Field History*, 50.

46. Bertram E. Swarthout, PHSA application, 14 March 1992; photograph 111-SC-127020, Still Picture Branch, NARA II; David L. Crabtree, PHSA application, 14 October 1991. David L. Crabtree does not appear in extant rosters from any of Wheeler Field's units, although in his application to the Pearl Harbor Survivors Association he designated the 6th Pursuit Squadron as his unit. Many of the 6th Pursuit's records (including *all* morning reports) were lost in the raid. It was not unusual for men to be carried as temporarily attached to particular units, a circumstance that makes it difficult to determine actual assignments on given dates, *particularly* in the absence of morning reports.

47. Francis A. White, PHSA application, 14 January 1984; Glen F. Heller, PHSA application, 11 March 1982.

48. Norton, 15WHO oral history, 2.

49. Winston S. Jones, PHSA application, 19 June 1970; Joseph T. Pawlowski, PHSA application, 25 April 1981.

50. *Wheeler Field History*, 50; Kindl, NTU interview, 26.

51. Hori, "Machini Matta X-Bi," 240; authors' analysis; photo 111-SC-128339, Still Picture Branch, NARA II; Ema, Prange interview 1, 4.

52. Stanley J. Jaroszek, PHSA application, 14 January 1988; HQ, 18th Air Base Group, General Orders No. 1, 2 January 1942; HQ, 7th Interceptor Command, General

Orders No. 3, 16 February 1942, Silver Star citation for Charles A. Fay.

53. Kindl, NTU interview, 27.

54. 7th AFBC, GO 17, citations for Vernon C. Rider, Ethelbert E. Lovell, John J. Ostrum, and Ford E. Dodd; authors' analysis. Other firefighters listed in the 18th Air Base Group's General Orders No. 1 are Pfc. Robert T. Mineau, Pfc. Adrian S. Black, Pvt. Joseph Berlinski, Pfc. Henry E. Zenzer, Pfc. Edwin Rakocy, Pfc. John Cena, and Pvt. Carl W. Wunderlin.

55. Drenner, Lord questionnaire, 1–2.

56. "Wheeler Gets a New Fire Chief," *Honolulu Star-Bulletin*, 6 September 1941, 30, https://www.newspapers.com/newspage/275056805/, accessed 12 September 2020; passenger manifest, Honolulu arrival, *Lurline* voyage 183, San Francisco to Honolulu, 20–26 March 1941, microfilmed publication A3422, roll 228, RG 85, NARA DC; passenger manifest, Honolulu arrival, *Matsonia* voyage 87, San Francisco to Honolulu, 5–10 July 1941, microfilmed publication A3422, roll 231, RG 85, NARA DC; "Assignment of Quarters," *Honolulu Star-Bulletin*, 30 August 1941, 44, https://www.newspapers.com/image/275199381, accessed 12 September 2020; photograph 342-FH-3B-48707, Still Photo Branch, NARA II; "Chief Who Fought Wheeler Field Fires during Blitz, Retires," *Honolulu Star-Bulletin*, 8 October 1946, 17, https://www.newspapers.com/image/282708161, accessed 12 September 2020. Passenger manifests and newspaper articles via Jessie Higa.

57. Arthur W. Fusco, questionnaire, 31 May 1956 (hereinafter Fusco, Lord questionnaire), 1–2, Lord Collection, HAD, NHHC.

58. 7th AFBC, GO 17, citation for Edward I. Pratt Jr.

59. Wallace Bloom, PHSA application, 26 April 1993.

60. William T. Petherbridge, PHSA application, 2 January 1992; Charles A. Zelonis, PHSA application, 4 May 1976.

61. Edward R. Young, PHSA application, 15 November 1987; 7th AFBC, GO 17, citations for Daniel A. Mahoney, William L. Bayham, and John T. Benton.

62. 7th AFBC, GO 17, citations for Hilmer C. Nelson, Carl M. Sidenblad, and Gottlieb J. Kaercher. Although the 30 November officer roster for the 18th Air Base Group lists Nelson as a captain, the morning report for 12 December indicates that he was appointed a major effective 5 December.

63. 7th AFBC, GO 17, citation for Gerald L. Suprise; Donald K. Ross and Helen L. Ross, *"0755": The Heroes of Pearl Harbor* (Port Orchard, Wash.: Rokalu Press, 1988), 84.

64. Leonard T. Egan, questionnaire, 18 June 1956 (hereinafter Egan, Lord questionnaire), 1–2, Lord Collection, HAD, NHHC.

65. Andrews, Lord questionnaire, 1, 3.

66. Stephenson, 15WHO oral history, 1; QMC Form 117, "N.C.O. Garage," Wheeler Field, T.H., 30 August 1932, Records of the Chief of Engineers, entry E393, box 280, folder 7, RG 77, NARA II.

67. Siegle, NTU interview, 21, 24.

68. James W. McAdams, questionnaire, n.d. (hereinafter McAdams, Lord questionnaire), 1–2, Lord Collection, HAD, NHHC.

69. Authors' tactical analysis. Given the location of concrete-filled "crater ghosts" that were still visible on Wheeler's apron during the 1990s, there is little question that Sakamoto's two trailing *chūtai*s strayed from the "bomb the hangars" directive. Regarding the level of experience of aircrews from the 5th Carrier Division, *Shōkaku* and *Zuikaku* had a higher percentage of pilots and crews holding the rank of F1c—relative neophytes just out of flight school. The anvil attack tactic required self-discipline and nerves of steel. Whether some of the less-experienced aircrews had sufficient training in that tactic is an open question. For a comparison of rank distribution among various carrier air groups, see *kōdōchōshos* from *Akagi, Kaga, Shōkaku, Zuikaku*, 8 December 1941. For Genda and Fuchida's thoughts regarding pilot experience in the 5th Carrier Division, see Genda Minoru, "Mr. Genda's Analysis of Pearl Harbor Attack Operation," no. 1, 6, Prange Collection, University of Maryland, box 19; and Fuchida Mitsuo, Prange interview 3, 1, Prange Collection, University of Maryland, box 19.

70. Fuchida roster, Hawaiian Operation; authors' tactical analysis; Leigh Hilderbrant, PHSA application, 7 November 1975.

71. Authors' tactical analysis.

72. Authors' tactical analysis; *Wheeler Field History*, 50; Stephenson, 15WHO oral history, 1.

73. Hendrix, 15WHO oral history, 1.

74. Munn, NTU interview, 14–15.

75. Aiken analysis via Louis Bontya; authors' tactical analysis; photos 111-SC-134875 and 342-FH-3B-48707, Still Picture Branch, NARA II; Donald M. Arras, PHSA application, 28 November 1964; George Seibel, PHSA application, 25 November 1964; *Wheeler Field History*, 45.

76. George Tillett, PHSA application, 25 November 1967.

77. Spangler, TLM oral history, 1–2; photo 111-SC-128339, Still Picture Branch, NARA II; Edward E. Randall (son of MSgt. Flecher S. Randall), "Wheeler Field," undated reminiscence, circa 2013, 2, via Jessie Higa.

78. Donovan S. Ginn, PHSA application, 19 May 1982.

79. Lambert, *The Pineapple Air Force*, 16.

80. Gabreski, *Gabby*, 41.

81. Letter, Henry W. Lawrence to David Aiken, 23 February 1990, 1, Aiken Collection, NMPW, 45th PS folder. Letters from Lawrence show the necessity for evaluating veterans' accounts that change over time.

82. Flood, Prange interview, 9 July 1962, 5, Prange Papers, Goldstein Collection; William J. Flood, questionnaire, n.d. (hereinafter Flood, Lord questionnaire), 1–2, Lord Collection, HAD, NHHC; Davidson, Prange interview, 6 July 1962, 7, Prange Papers, Goldstein Collection; authors' analysis; Lambert, *The Pineapple Air Force*, 16; Straub, 15WHO oral history, 3.

83. Flood testimony, Army Board, 11 September 1944, 1487, 1492; Flood, Prange interview, 9 July 1962, 6.

84. Hall testimony, Roberts Commission, 26 December 1941, 257, 259.

85. Ema, Prange interview 1, 4–5; Hori "Machini Matta X-Bi," 240.

86. Microfilmed officer roster, 18th Air Base Group, 30 November 1941, NARA, St. Louis; Daniel P. Jorgenson, *The Service of Chaplains to Army Air Units 1917–1946* (Washington, D.C.: Office, Chief of Air Force Chaplains, 1961), 84; Robert McEnery, "First of Army's New Chapels Nearly Finished," *Honolulu Advertiser*, 7 October 1941, 9, https://www.newspapers.com/image/259327737, accessed 13 September 2020, via Jessie Higa; Stewart, NTU interview, 25.

87. Jorgenson, *Service of Chaplains to Army Air Units*, 84; Robert L. Gushwa, *The Best and Worst of Times: The United States Army Chaplaincy, 1920–1945* (Washington, D.C.: Office of the Chief of Chaplains, Department of the Army, 1977), 103–4.

88. William J. Feiler, PHSA application, 7 August 1975; John E. Quasnovsky, PHSA application, 7 November 1971; John P. Young, PHSA application, 4 October 1964.

89. Charles D. Boyd, PHSA application, 9 June 1989; Horace G. Moran, PHSA application, 4 April 1982; Danforth P. Miller Jr., PHSA application, 26 October 1981.

90. Yokosuka Naval Air Corps, "Lessons (Air Operation) of the Sea Battle off Hawaii," vol. 1 (trans.) (hereinafter "Lessons of the Sea Battle off Hawaii"), 40, Prange files, authors' collection.

91. *Kōdōchōshos*, *Zuikaku* and *Sōryū* fighter units, 8 December 1941; "Lessons of the Sea Battle off Hawaii," 40; authors' analysis; Office of the Air Force Command, Hickam Field, T.H., to Roberts Commission, Memorandum to Roberts Commission, 26 December 1941, *PHA*, pt. 24, Exhibits of the Roberts Commission, Exhibit 25 (Army), 2019–20.

92. Flood, Prange interview, 9 July 1962, 3–4, Prange Papers, Goldstein Collection.

93. Franklin Hibel, PHSA application, 20 December 1976.

94. Davidson, Prange interview, 6 July 1962, 10, Prange Papers, Goldstein Collection.

CHAPTER 9. "DISPERSE ALL YOUR PLANES AND FLY FULLY LOADED WITH AMMUNITION"

1. Adalbert B. Olack, PHSA application, 5 January 1981.

2. Earl Boone, PHSA application, 3 June 1987.

3. Adalbert B. Olack, PHSA application, 5 January 1981; Lambert, *The Pineapple Air Force*, 17.

4. Officer rosters, 15th Pursuit Group, November 1941, NARA, St. Louis; IFRs for Charles E. Kneen, November–December 1941, NARA, St. Louis; Charles E. Kneen, PHSA application, 11 January 1966; Earl Boone, PHSA application, 3 June 1987; authors' analysis.

5. "Map of Oahu, T.H., showing the disposition, number, types, and operational and readiness condition of U.S. Navy Aircraft on 7 Dec. 1941" (cropped area), *PHA*, pt. 21, Exhibits of the Joint Committee, Exhibit 6, item 14; Scott, *Damned to Glory*, 124; Taylor, USAR oral history, 2; authors' analysis.

6. Brown, Lambert interview, 2; authors' analysis.

7. For a thorough examination of the B-17 flights to Hawai'i, see Wenger, Cressman, and Di Virgilio, *They're Killing My Boys*.

8. Richard H. Carmichael, letter to *LIFE*, 9 March 1956 (hereinafter Carmichael, Lord letter), 1, Lord Collection, HAD, NHHC; Richard H. Carmichael, AFHRA interviews, 8–10 September 1980 and 10–11 November 1980 (hereinafter Carmichael, AFHRA interviews), 63, AFHRA, file K.239.0512-1229.

9. Lt. Walter H. Johnson, Adjutant, "Squadron Diary, Eighty-Eighth Reconnaissance," (H) AFCC, AFHSO, reel A0614, file SQ-BOMB-435-Hi, Dec/41–Nov/42, 11; Pearl Harbor Survivors Association, comp., *The Pearl Harbor Survivors Association Silver Anniversary Commemorative Book*, vol. 1 (Santa Ana, Calif.: Taylor, 1984), 74; authors' analysis.

10. 88th Reconnaissance Squadron (H) AFCC, Fort Douglas, Utah, Annex No. [blank] to Field Order No. 2 (hereinafter 88th Recon. Sq. Annex to Field Order No. 2), 3 December 1941, 7 [*sic*] Bombardment Group Movement Orders, AFHRA, file GP-7-SU-OR-M-(Bomb) 1941–1942. Chaffin's crew did not include a bombardier.

11. Carmichael, Lord letter, 2; Carmichael, AFHRA interviews, 64.

12. 88th Recon. Sq. Annex to Field Order No. 2.

13. Authors' analysis; "Vertical Photograph of Haleiwa Field," *PHA*, pt. 25, Exhibits of the Roberts Commission, Exhibit 1 (Army), item 86; photographs 80-G-279357 and -279358, Still Picture Branch, NARA II. See David Aiken, "Ghosts of Pearl Harbor: The Facts, Figures and Forgotten Heroes," *Flight Journal* 12, no. 3 (June 2007): 26. Photographs 80-G-279357 and 80-G-279358 taken on 4 September 1941 show Haleiwa Field as it appeared at the time of the attacks on O'ahu. Had prepped fighters simply been pulled away from the tree line just below the road leading into the field at center-right, less "runway" would have been available for Taylor and Welch, perhaps by about 20 percent, or 240 feet of the 1,200-foot length. During the war, the strip was extended a considerable distance southwest, so wartime photographs give the illusion of a far less difficult takeoff than actually was the case in 1941.

14. Letter, Don Dawson to David Aiken, 7 January 1990, 1, Aiken Collection, NWPW, Don Dawson folder; Taylor testimony, Roberts Commission, *PHA*, pt. 22, 249; Scott, *Damned to Glory*, 124; War Department, General Orders No. 2, "Awards of Distinguished Service Cross,"

5 January 1942, 1–2, Distinguished Service Cross citation for George S. Welch (hereinafter DSC citation, Welch), AFHSO, reel B0080A, file GP-15-HI. There is an interesting difference between the wording of the decoration citations for the two pilots and Taylor's testimony before the Roberts Commission on 26 December 1941. Welch's citation reads, "At the time of take off he was armed only with a caliber .30 machine guns [*sic*]." Taylor's reads, "At the time of take off his plane was equipped with caliber .30 machine guns only." In his testimony before the Roberts Commission, however, Taylor stated that lack of .50-caliber ammunition was at the root of the problem, not that his aircraft had no .50-caliber machine guns installed.

15. Snowden Steuart, PHSA application, 6 February 1987; Richard A. Mergenthaler, PHSA application, 1 December 1989.

16. Lambert, *The Pineapple Air Force*, 17.

17. Lt. Col. Clyde K. Rich (HQ, Bellows Field) to Lt. Col. Edward M. Raley (HAF G-2), Memorandum to Colonel Raley, 20 December 1941 (hereinafter Rich memo to Raley), AFHSO, reel A7581, file 740.674-1A; Earl L. Bigelow, PHSA application, 16 September 1971.

18. Wayne H. Rathbun, PHSA application, 15 December 1981; John E. Ireland, PHSA application, 10 March 1970.

19. Microfilmed morning reports, 86th Observation Squadron, 7 December 1941, RG 64, NARA, St. Louis; authors' analysis; Elmer J. Steffan, PHSA application, 5 November 1965. It seems that the 0827 alert (as ineffectively as it might have been relayed) was the catalyst for the dispersal of Bellows' aircraft, rather than the first machine-gun attack or the subsequent arrival of the B-17.

20. Letter, Minnie Sliney to an unknown recipient, 12 December 1941 (hereinafter Minnie Sliney letter), 1, excerpted in undated newspaper clipping, courtesy James W. Spinney.

21. *Kōdōchōsho*s, *Shōkaku* and *Zuikaku*, 8 December 1941; *Shōkaku* DAR, Atene Shobō, 209, 211. For a more thorough examination of the attacks on NAS Kaneohe Bay, see J. M. Wenger, R. J. Cressman, and J. F. Di Virgilio, *No One Avoided Danger: NAS Kaneohe Bay and the Japanese Attacks of 7 December 1941* (Annapolis: Naval Institute Press, 2015).

22. Ronald J. Nash, PHSA application, 4 October 1988.

23. Arnold J. Trempler, PHSA application, 7 June 1971; Rich memo to Raley, 1; General Plan, "Bellows Field, Oahu, T.H.," April 1941, *PHA*, pt. 25; Stanley W. Thomas, PHSA application, 1 June 1981; *History of Bellows Field*, 11; Cosmo R. Mannino, PHSA application, 14 October 1991; Kolbert, NTU interview, 40; *Shōkaku*, DAR, *Atene Shobō*, 211.

24. Donald H. Halferty, PHSA application, 19 March 1984; Elmer L. Rund, PHSA application, 28 November 1980.

25. Lyle M. Grover, PHSA application, 20 March 1984; Cosmo R. Mannino, PHSA application, 14 October 1991; authors' analysis.

26. Stanley W. Thomas, PHSA application, 1 June 1981; George F. Keeler, PHSA application, 12 September 1966; Snowden Steuart, PHSA application, 6 February 1987.

27. See Wenger, Cressman, and Di Virgilio, *They're Killing My Boys*.

28. Elmer L. Rund, PHSA application, 28 November 1980; letter, Elmer L. Rund to David Aiken, 26 March 1985, 1–2, Aiken Collection, NMPW, 44th PS folder; George F. Keeler, PHSA application, 12 September 1966. Although Bellows' fire truck supposedly had reported to Hickam Field, Elmer Rund maintained that a fire truck accompanied the ambulance to tend to the B-17C. The sequence of events at Bellows Field regarding aircraft dispersal, Lieutenant Kaneko's attack, and the arrival of 1st Lieutenant Richards' B-17C is unclear. Substantial disagreement among Bellows' survivors presents a muddled timeline and conflicts that are difficult to resolve. One key event for the authors, however, is the 0827 alert, after which aircraft dispersal almost surely commenced, although to what degree and with what sense of urgency is unknown. Without question, the pace of preparations accelerated with Kaneko's attack. The B-17s arriving from California were very low on fuel, which would favor an earlier arrival by Richards, with Kaneko's attack taking place last at 0840, per *Hiryū*'s air group report. It is noteworthy that none of the accounts/statements from Richards' crew mention anything about being fired upon *while landing*, despite statements from one individual on the ground. See letter, Homer Garcia to David Aiken, 15 February 1985 (hereinafter letter, Garcia to Aiken, 15 February 1985), 4, Aiken Collection, NMPW, 44th PS folder.

29. 38th Reconnaissance Squadron, Special Orders No. 1, 4 December 1941, 2, Prange Collection, University of Maryland.

30. Letter, Keith A. Schilling to David Aiken, 15 April 1986, 1, Aiken Collection, NMPW, 44th PS folder.

31. Minnie Sliney letter, 1; Raymond F. McBriarty, "Radio Frequency McBriarty," undated account (hereinafter McBriarty account), 5, Aiken Collection, NMPW, 86th OS folder.

32. Arthur H. Cochran, PHSA application, 22 August 1991; John P. Joyce, PHSA application, 17 December 1964; Joe McCarthy, "New Bellows Field Chaplain Asks for Books for Post Library," *Honolulu Advertiser*, 6 December 1941, 8; George F. Keeler, PHSA application, 12 September 1966.

33. Orris R. Julian, PHSA application, 29 August 1966; Arthur H. Cochran, PHSA application, 22 August 1991.

34. John M. Neuhauser, PHSA application, 9 July 1984.

CHAPTER 10. "IT WAS AN AWFUL LOOKING SITUATION"

1. CG, Headquarters Hawaiian Interceptor Command to CG, HAF, "Report of Enemy Activity over Oahu, 7 December 1941," 18 December 1941, *VII Fighter Command History*, 3, AFHSO, reel A7586, file 741.01; Welch, AAF interview, 1; HQ, 14th Pursuit Wing, map of Oʻahu showing magnetic compass bearings and distances to various points on the coast, in *Tentative Manual of Interceptor Command Organization, Procedure and Operations for Air Defense* (hereinafter map, *Interceptor Command Manual*), 27 October 1941, AFHRA, file 741.01 7 Dec 1941–Jul 1944 vol. 11; DSC citation, Welch; authors' analysis; Detailed Action Report No. 1, CarDiv 5 (trans.), 15, Prange Collection, University of Maryland, box 21 (hereinafter CarDiv 5 DAR).

2. Welch testimony, Roberts Commission, *PHA*, pt. 22, 255; Brown, Lambert interview, 2–3; Aiken, "Ghosts of Pearl Harbor," 26; authors' analysis.

3. Authors' analysis; Brown, Lambert interview, 3; Carmichael, Lord letter, 2. The two B-17s probably landed shortly before the fighter pilots arrived from Wheeler. In his letter to Lord, Carmichael was very clear that both of the bombers were present at the time of the strafing attack, which Brown implied took place while ground crews prepared the P-36s for flight.

Welch asserted that Rogers, and therefore Brown too, were airborne about thirty minutes after he and Taylor took off. For Rogers and Brown to have gotten airborne in time to engage aircraft of the *departing* second wave, it is improbable that the two Americans were *on the ground* at the time those aircraft were retiring from over Oʻahu. The dive-bomber in question was from either the *Shōkaku* or *Zuikaku* rather than from dive-bombing units that had completed their work over Pearl Harbor.

4. Charles H. Leyshock, PHSA application, 12 November 1983; Charles H. Leyshock, 15WHO oral history (hereinafter Leyshock, 15WHO oral history), 3.

5. Spangler, TLM oral history, 2; Henry C. Brown, NTU interview, 38–39.

6. Homer R. Baskin, PHSA application, 10 August 1971; Herbert C. Ward, PHSA application, 4 July 1963.

7. Munn, NTU interview, 16, 20; David C. Cameron, PHSA application, 21 June 1968.

8. Stewart, NTU interview, 25–26.

9. Wenger, Cressman, and Di Virgilio, *They're Killing My Boys*, 141–42.

10. Tom Hutchinson, PHSA application, 12 November 1991.

11. Spangler, TLM oral history, 2.

12. Flood, Lord questionnaire, 2; David I. Walsh, PHSA application, 1 December 1981. It is unclear whether Cooper landed during the lull or during the second wave, but he appears to have reached the ground not long before the Japanese arrived. Similarly, it is uncertain when Cooper flew into Hickam, although documents indicate that the airplane was in service at the field as of 1845 on 8 December. No known photography taken at Wheeler in the aftermath of the raid shows Cooper's aircraft present.

13. 38th Reconnaissance Squadron, Special Orders No. 1, 2–3.

14. Frederick T. Bowen, PHSA application, 8 September 1976, text of Bronze Star citation.

15. Guy Messacar Jr., PHSA application, 19 June 1984; Wilbur S. Carr, PHSA application, n.d.; letter, John E. Sterling to David Aiken, 22 December 1986 (hereinafter letter, Sterling to Aiken), 1, Aiken Collection, NMPW, Sterling folder; Robert S. Turk, PHSA application, 2 February 1974; letter, David Aiken to Robert S. Turk Jr., circa August 1994, 1, Aiken Collection, NMPW, Sterling folder; Sanders account, 2.

16. David Aiken, "Gordon Sterling, BNR [body not recovered] 7 Dec 1941, Pearl Harbor," review draft of journal article, circa 1994 (hereinafter Aiken, "Gordon Sterling, BNR"), 2, Aiken Collection, NMPW, Sterling folder; Sanders account, 3. In "Gordon Sterling, BNR," Aiken maintained that Sanders appointed Thacker as leader of the flight's second element owing to his superior experience in P-40s. In fact, Norris had accumulated the most hours flying P-40s, and Thacker was within three hours of being tied with Sterling for dead last. This analysis underscores the importance of using the IFRs at NARA, St. Louis, when attempting to evaluate pilot and crew experience. Sanders chose Thacker to lead the second element based on his trust in Thacker's piloting and leadership skills. Of the five pilots in question, the ranking in P-40 flight hours as of 7 December 1941 was (in descending order): Norris, 52 hours; Sanders, 35 hours; Rasmussen, 34 hours; Thacker, 31 hours; and Sterling, 28 hours.

17. Aiken, "Gordon Sterling, BNR," 2; letter, Sterling to Aiken, 1; Kindl, NTU interview, 29–30; enlisted roster, 46th Pursuit Squadron, 30 November 1941, NARA, St. Louis. Sterling's letter quotes verbatim a passage from Captain Sanders' wartime letter to the Sterling family. As Clarence W. Kindl's account predates Aiken's article by ten years, we have credited the former with Sterling's quote. Then–2nd Lieutenant Rasmussen said that Sterling had not progressed well in gunnery and formation flying. See letter, Philip M. Rasmussen to David Aiken, 27 September 1994, Aiken Collection, NMPW, Sterling folder.

18. Aiken, "Gordon Sterling, BNR," 1; letter, Lawrence to Aiken, 23 February 1990, 1, Aiken Collection, NMPW, 46th PS folder.

19. Letter, Lawrence to Aiken, 23 February 1990, 1; Lambert, *The Pineapple Air Force*, 17; Lewis M. Sanders, "1st Flight, 46th Pursuit Squadron, Red Section" (hereinafter Sanders action report), n.d., in *Wheeler Field History*, S-2, 6; Sanders account, 3. Sanders' takeoff time is unclear. Although one of his postwar accounts states that the flight left Wheeler at about 0840, such a time greatly complicates interpretation of later events near NAS Kaneohe Bay. The time

of 0930 (fifty minutes later!) in his report to Wheeler's S-2 eliminates most of those problems. In that 0930 appeared in his official report, it should be regarded as more authoritative.

20. Letter, Lawrence to Aiken, 23 February 1990. This narrative—as set forth in Lawrence's 1990 letter to David Aiken—illustrates the hazards inherent in presenting detailed accounts of air actions using only logbook entries that clerks typed into the pilots' IFRs. In a subsequent letter to David Aiken dated 2 November 1994, Lawrence backtracked on the composition of the flight, insisting that 2nd Lt. Francis Gabreski was the third pilot rather than 2nd Lt. William Haning Jr. Aiken's later analysis placed squadron commander Capt. Aaron Tyer in the flight. Alternatively, in his autobiography, Gabreski placed 2nd Lt. Fred Shifflet in the flight but did not mention Lawrence. The IFRs do nothing to clarify these conflicts because there are no "time stamps" in IFRs. There are no microfilmed IFRs for Haning, and Shifflet's do not show a flight for 7 December. In addition, it was very common to consolidate multiple flights into single entries. Beyond the personnel involved, even the timing of the flight is in question. Lawrence's account states categorically that he took off immediately after Sanders' foursome, with Wilmot and Haning taking to the air shortly thereafter. Gabreski flatly contradicted this in his application to the Pearl Harbor Survivors Association by saying that he did not take off until *long after* the raid ended. The authors are of the opinion that Gabreski's was probably a later second flight composed of Tyer, Wilmot, Shifflet, and Gabreski.

21. Letter, Lawrence to Aiken, 23 February 1990, 1–2, Aiken Collection, NMPW, 46th PS folder. At the end of August 1941, Shifflet married the daughter of Lt. Col. Leonard D. Weddington, who was the commander of Bellows Field on 7 December 1941.

22. HQ, 7th Interceptor Command, General Orders No. 3, 16 February 1942, 1, Silver Star citation for Malcolm A. Moore (hereinafter SS citation, Moore), AFHRA, file GP-15-Hi (FTR) Dec40–Dec43; Malcolm A. Moore, IFRs, December 1941, RG 64, NARA, St. Louis; Lambert, *The Pineapple Air Force*, 20; Othniel Norris, IFRs, December 1941, RG 64, NARA, St. Louis;

Malcolm A. Moore, "46th Pursuit Squadron, airplane P-36 #91, Commander's Report," n.d., in *Wheeler Field History*, S-2 (hereinafter Moore action report), 7; HQ, 7th Interceptor Command, General Orders No. 3, 16 February 1942, 2, Silver Star citation for John J. Webster (hereinafter SS citation, Webster), AFHRA, file GP-15-Hi (FTR) Dec40–Dec43.

CHAPTER 11. "DISPERSE THE FLYABLE AIRCRAFT AND PREPARE THEM FOR LAUNCH"

1. Letter, Homer Garcia to David Aiken, 12 December 1984, 3, 6, Aiken Collection, NMPW, 44th PS folder (hereinafter letter, Garcia to Aiken, 12 December 1984).

2. Letter, Garcia to Aiken, 15 February 1985, 2; Oscar B. Myers Jr. and George A. Whiteman, IFRs, 1941, RG 64, NARA, St. Louis; letter, Garcia to Aiken, 12 December 1984, 6.

3. Kolbert, NTU interview, 43–45; Paul G. Teegardin, PHSA application, 29 January 1965.

4. *Kōdōchōsho*, *Hiryū*, 8 December 1941.

5. David Aiken, "Pearl Harbor's Lost P-36: Still Missing after 60 Years: 2nd Lt. Gordon Sterling," *Flight Journal* 7, no. 5 (October 2002): 75; "Diagram of Bellows Field, Oahu, T.H., showing numbers and formations of attacking Japanese planes, times of attacks and disposition of U.S. planes in Japanese attack 7 Dec. 1941" (hereinafter Bellows Field attack map), *PHA*, pt. 21, item 7, Exhibits of the Joint Committee, listed as item 7 in Exhibit 5 (Army Exhibit), in *PHA*, pt. 12, 325; untitled and undated report with maps and text outlining the Japanese attacks on Bellows, authors' files, copy provided by William M. Cleveland, circa 1985 (hereinafter undated Bellows report, Cleveland), 2.

6. Undated Bellows report, Cleveland, map 1; letter, Rund to Aiken, 26 March 1985, 2.

7. Letter, Garcia to Aiken, 12 December 1984, 6; letter, Garcia to Aiken, 6 February 1985, 2; Lambert, *The Pineapple Air Force*, 18.

8. Letter, Rund to Aiken, 26 March 1985, 2; Lambert, *The Pineapple Air Force*, 18.

9. Letter, Garcia to Aiken, 12 December 1984, 6–7; *kōdōchōsho*, *Hiryū*, 8 December 1941; Elmer L. Rund, PHSA application, 28 November 1980.

10. Letter, Edward J. Covelesky to David Aiken, circa May 1985 (hereinafter letter, Covelesky to Aiken, circa May 1985), 4, Aiken Collection, NMPW, 44th PS folder.

11. Lambert, *The Pineapple Air Force*, 18; Rich memo to Raley, 2; authors' analysis; letter, Covelesky to Aiken, circa May 1985, 1; telephone conversation, Wenger and Di Virgilio, 12 October 2020; microfilmed morning report, 44th Pursuit Squadron, 13 December 1941, RG 64, NARA, St. Louis; Samuel W. Bishop, IFRs, December 1941, RG 64, NARA, St. Louis.

12. Earl L. Bigelow, PHSA application, 16 September 1971.

13. Willis, NTU interview, 34–35.

14. Kolbert, NTU interview, 46–47, 53.

15. McBriarty account, 5–6; Ross, *"0755,"* 86, 92; testimony of Raymond F. McBriarty before the Roberts Commission, 26 December 1941, *PHA*, pt. 22, 294.

16. Rich memo to Raley, 3; *kōdōchōsho, Hiryū*, 8 December 1941; "The Japanese Fleet Task Organization, 7th December 1941," Prange Collection, University of Maryland, box 14; J. Michael Wenger, "Whitepaper No. 3: Japanese Submarines and the Hawaiian Operation," 1 June 2008, 2, authors' files, prepared for the National Park Service, USS *Arizona* Memorial.

17. Letter, Covelesky to Aiken, circa May 1985, 4.

18. Cosmo R. Mannino, PHSA application, 14 October 1991; letter, Garcia to Aiken, 12 December 1984, 6; letter, Garcia to Aiken, 6 February 1985, 2.

19. Analysis by Tagaya Osamu and David Aiken; email correspondence, JMW and Tagaya Osamu, 25 October 2020; *kōdōchōsho, Hiryū*, 8 December 1941; "Lessons of the Sea Battle off Hawaii," 40. The evaluation and analysis by Tagaya Osamu and David Aiken was particularly valuable to the authors' interpretation regarding the Japanese progress toward Ewa.

20. Authors' analysis; analysis by Tagaya Osamu and David Aiken; Tagaya Osamu, *Aichi 99 Kanbaku "Val" Units 1939–1942* (hereinafter Tagaya, *Aichi 99 Kanbaku*) (Long Island City, N.Y.: Osprey, 2011), 35.

21. Scott, *Damned to Glory*, 124; Welch, AAF interview, 1; author's analysis.

22. Authors' analysis; Welch, AAF interview, 1; Scott, *Damned to Glory*, 124–25. The air battle over Ewa has always presented historiographical problems. Despite references in popular accounts, there were no formal after-action narratives (or at least none that have survived) from the pilots on either side. A plethora of mostly vague accounts, most compiled years after the fact (and Taylor and Welch's DSC citations to an extent), contradict each other or fail to mention key points. Note that details of this and other combats are, generally, a synthesis of the authors' research and analysis, and the analysis, collected documents, and published works of historians John W. Lambert, David Aiken, and Tagaya Osamu, with perhaps greater weight placed on Tagaya's work.

23. Welch, AAF interview, 1; DSC citation, Welch; Scott, *Damned to Glory*, 125; Tagaya, *Aichi 99 Kanbaku*, 35; *kōdōchōsho, Hiryū*, 8 December 1941.

24. Authors' analysis; *kōdōchōsho, Akagi*, 8 December 1941; Abe Zenji, map of Pearl Harbor prepared for John W. Lambert, circa 6 October 1980; Welch, AAF interview, 2; Tagaya, *Aichi 99 Kanbaku*, 35; DSC citation, Welch; Scott, *Damned to Glory*, 125; Iizuka Tokuji, "Kanbaku War Notes," trans. Kawamoto Minoru, courtesy James Lansdale.

25. Scott, *Damned to Glory*, 125–26; *kōdōchōsho, Akagi*, 8 December 1941; Lambert, *The Pineapple Air Force*, 22.

26. Ōbuchi Keizō, questionnaire prepared for John W. Lambert, 1 May 1981, 4, 6; Ibuki Shōichi, "Kaga Kyūkōka Bakugekitai Hawai Jōkū-no Shukun," in Fujita, *Shōgen Shinjuwan Kōgeki*, 454.

27. Tagaya, *Aichi 99 Kanbaku*, 35; Aiken, "Ghosts of Pearl Harbor," 29; John M. Sweeney, keeper, Barbers Point Light Station, "The action as seen from Barbers Point," 10 December 1941, enclosure "GG" to Com14 to CNO, "Report on the Battle of Pearl Harbor, 7 December, 1941," RG 38, NARA II. Sweeney's account has Gotō and Utsuki parachuting onto land close to the Barbers Point Light Station, but analysis by Tagaya Osamu and David Aiken indicates that such was not the case. See their sources noted above.

28. Authors' analysis of reconstructed timeline at Haleiwa; Gillman correspondence, JMW and Charles Gillman, various dates; email correspondence, JMW and Tagaya Osamu, 25 October 2020. The authors contend that the strafing attack on Haleiwa took place much earlier than is generally supposed—that is, just after Taylor and Welch took off around 0840. Dains is thought to have taken off during or just after the strafing attack. The dive-bomber would have departed from the

airfield at close to full speed, while Dains would have climbed to altitude at a slower speed, so pursuit of the attacker—while not impossible—would have been difficult.

Also problematic is the claim in some accounts that the dive-bomber over Haleiwa was from the second wave (see Aiken, "Ghosts of Pearl Harbor," 29). There is testimony that after Dains shot down a dive-bomber off Kaʻaʻawa on the windward shore, he flew back to Wheeler Field for fuel and/or ammunition *just prior to the arrival of Taylor and Welch at about 0930*. Given the timeline, it is unlikely that Dains chased a second-wave aircraft that (1) had finished its attacks over the harbor, (2) had flown all the way out to Haleiwa to strafe, and then (3) attempted to evade a pursuer all the way across Oʻahu to the opposite shore. That scenario does not fit with the evidence that Dains refueled at Wheeler in advance of 0930 and is simply implausible.

29. Questionnaire, Philippe A. Michaud, 18 February 1988 (hereinafter Michaud questionnaire), 1, courtesy of John W. Lambert; "Location of Mobile AWS Stations on Dec. 7, 1941 with Sectors Showing Coverage to the Electrical Horizon," *PHA*, pt. 25, item 36, Exhibits of the Roberts Commission, listed as item 36 in Exhibit 2 (Navy Packet 2) in *PHA*, pt. 24, 1363; interstaff routing slip; "Proposed Installation of Six Mobile RDF Units on Island of Oahu," circa 14 August 1941, Exhibits of the Army Pearl Harbor Board, Exhibit 57, enclosure D, *PHA*, pt. 31, 3136; authors' analysis. The six mobile radar stations were Kaʻaʻawa, Opana, Kawailoa, Waiʻanae, Fort Shafter, and Koko Head.

30. Michaud questionnaire, 1–2; Tagaya, *Aichi 99 Kanbaku*, 31. One troubling aspect of Michaud's account is that he maintained that the dogfight over Kaʻaʻawa took place at 0800, a manifest impossibility.

31. Authors' analysis; Aiken, "Ghosts of Pearl Harbor," 29; Harry W. Brown, Robert J. Rogers, John J. Webster, IFRs, December 1941, RG 64, NARA, St. Louis. Although Rogers' IFRs do not include his 7 December 1941 flight(s), the squadron's P-40Bs were checked out to Taylor, Welch, Dains, and Webster, so it is likely that Rogers flew a P-36A. Taylor indicated in his testimony before the Roberts Commission that the squadron had only four P-40s present at Haleiwa on 7 December (Taylor testimony, Roberts Commission, 26 December

1941, *PHA*, pt. 22, 250). Welch estimated that Rogers (and therefore probably Brown and Webster) took off approximately thirty minutes after he and Taylor took off (Welch, Roberts testimony, *PHA*, pt. 22, 255). However, Brown noted later that, after takeoff, he heard something over his radio regarding Bellows Field, which might have been the exchange between 1st Lt. Lewis Sanders and the Information Center at Fort Shafter. Such would move Brown's takeoff time closer to 0930.

32. Aiken, "Ghosts of Pearl Harbor," 29; Scott, *Damned to Glory*, 126; message, Thomas Leonard to David Aiken, *Pearl Harbor Attacked Message Board*, posted 10 June 2001, http://www.pearlharborattacked.com /cgi-bin/IKONBOARDNEW312a/ikonboard.cgi?act =ST;f=14;t=5, accessed 29 January 2021; microfilmed enlisted roster, 19th Pursuit Squadron, 30 November 1941, RG 64, NARA, St. Louis; authors' analysis. Generally, the authors do not create endnotes for Army rosters or morning reports when documenting a name, rank, or specialty. We do so here to point out the handicaps under which historian David Aiken operated in the decades prior to the release of those microfilmed records by the National Personnel Records Center in August 2009. Prior to that, even the most elementary data relating to a specific veteran's service was beyond the reach of historians. Those circumstances make the breadth of Aiken's research all the more amazing.

33. Aiken, "Ghosts of Pearl Harbor," 29; notes of telephone conversation between William G. Temple Jr. and David Aiken, circa June 2001 (hereinafter phonecon notes, Temple and Aiken), Aiken Collection, NMPW, Welch folder; Scott, *Damned to Glory*, 126; microfilmed enlisted roster, 19th Pursuit Squadron, 30 November 1941, RG 64, NARA, St. Louis; Paul R. Cipriano, PHSA application, 14 October 1977; Harry P. Kilpatrick, PHSA application, 20 July 1970.

34. Harry P. Kilpatrick, PHSA application, 20 July 1970; phonecon notes, Temple and Aiken; Scott, *Damned to Glory*, 127; authors' analysis.

35. David I. Walsh, PHSA application, 1 December 1981.

36. Authors' analysis; Lambert, *The Pineapple Air Force*, 22; Tagaya, *Aichi 99 Kanbaku*, 36; Welch, AAF interview, 2; Aiken, "Ghosts of Pearl Harbor," 29; John L. Palinkas, PHSA application, 18 December 1991; Scott,

Damned to Glory, 127. Taylor and Welch were unable to take off north because of the hangar line and other buildings.

37. Scott, *Damned to Glory*, 127; Lambert, *The Pineapple Air Force*, 22; HQ, HAF, "Combat Reports Furnished by Pilots Engaging the Enemy [on] 7 December 1941," 2 January 1942, report of Kenneth M. Taylor, AFHSO, reel A7572, file 740.335.

38. Welch, AAF interview, 2, 4, authors' analysis; DSC citation, Welch; memorandum to Colonel Blessley; HQ, 24th Infantry Division, CP at Schofield Barracks, T.H., to G-2, Hawaiian Department, Forward Echelon, "Narrative Report of Events of 7 December 1941 in the North Sector," 22 December 1941, 2–3, file 324-0.3.0 (diary), entry 427, box 7672A, RG 407, NARA II; Scott, *Damned to Glory*, 127. Based on contemporary photography and maps, Makino's crash site was closer to 717 Neal Avenue than the 711 Neal "Street" address so often cited. On pages 2 and 4 of his 19 May 1942 AAF interview, George Welch almost certainly mixed two separate descriptions of the same crash site, known variously as 711 Neal Street, the Power Station, and the CCC camp. Additionally, there is a mistaken impression that Kenneth Taylor's kill northwest of Wahiawā crashed near Paul B. Young's laundry at 251 Hiwi Place. The two official documents referenced in this note state unambiguously that the two crash sites (with two bodies each) were in Wahiawā near an electric substation (Welch) and Brodie Camp No. 4 (Taylor), the latter sometimes referred to in error as Brodie Camp No. 2. The Brodie camps were settlements erected for pineapple plantation workers.

39. Welch, AAF interview, 4; Saltzman, Roberts testimony, 273; testimony of Lowell V. Klatt before the Roberts Commission (hereinafter Klatt testimony, Roberts Commission), 26 December 1941, *PHA*, pt. 22, 278.

40. Klatt testimony, Roberts Commission, 278–79.

41. Scott, *Damned to Glory*, 128; Stewart, NTU interview, 33.

42. Kenneth M. Taylor, map prepared for John W. Lambert, circa 1981, attached to letter, John W. Lambert to David Aiken, 17 April 1990, Aiken Collection, NMPW, Don Dawson folder; Tagaya, *Aichi 99 Kanbaku*, 36; Kenneth M. Taylor, IFRs, December 1941, RG 64, NARA, St. Louis; Scott, *Damned to Glory*,

128; Welch, AAF interview, 2; DSC citation, Welch; George S. Welch, IFRs, December 1941, RG 64, NARA, St. Louis. Welch maintained that the aircraft was a carrier bomber in which the rear gunner was either dead or incapacitated. In "Ghosts of Pearl Harbor," however, Aiken claimed that the kill was a Zero from the *Kaga*. The situation is further confused by Welch's blanket observation that all the aircraft he encountered were "Light Bomber[s], *retractable landing gear*, rear gunner," which of course included all of the wheel-spatted *kanbaku*s that he had shot down earlier in the day. Clearly, American pursuit pilots lacked sufficient knowledge of Japanese aircraft types.

43. *Kōdōchōsho*, *Sōryū* fighters, 8 December 1941; Fujita Iyozō, "Kōnnaru Seikan" (hereinafter Fujita, "Lucky Return"), in *Rekishi-to Jinbutsu* (Tōkyō: Chūō Kōron-sha, 20 January 1983), 262–63; *kōdōchōsho*, *Shōkaku*, 8 December 1941; Fujita Iyozō, interview, 2 February 1951 Prange Collection, University of Maryland, box 19 (hereinafter Fujita, Prange interview), 4; Fujita Iyozō, "Kaeranakatta San Ki-no Yōgunki" (hereinafter Fujita, "Three Fighters Never Returned"), in *Mikōkai Shashin ni Miru: Shinjuwan Kōgeki* (Tōkyō: Shin Jinbutsu Ōrai-sha, 12 July 1990), 122; "Lessons of the Sea Battle off Hawaii," 20 (an altitude of two thousand meters appears in this document). For readability the authors have used the approximation six thousand feet as referred to later by Lewis Sanders.

It is curious that the *Sōryū*'s *kōdōchōsho* does *not* mention the firing passes at Bellows. Although the Yokosuka Naval Air Corps' study of the Hawaiian Operation (within its battle results section) fails to indicate the *Sōryū* fighter unit's presence at Bellows, the study does indicate elsewhere that (quoted verbatim) "fighters which, after strafing on the Beroes [*sic*] Field, were about to strafe the Kaneohe airfield, circling at the altitude of 2,000 meters were surprised by nine enemy interceptors. This attributed lack of attention to the air." The study thus appears to support Fujita's narrative, although possible confusion in the report with the *Hiryū* fighter unit cannot be ruled out. The extended interval from Iida's first attacks on Kaneohe at 0915 until his loss at 0942 seems to allow sufficient time for the short flight down to Bellows and back, particularly if Iida only circled the Army base rather than attacking it. For a fuller discussion of the timing of events at NAS Kaneohe Bay, see Wenger, Cressman, and Di Virgilio, *No One Avoided Danger*.

44. Interview, Fujita Iyozō, *Tora, Tora, Tora: The Real Story of Pearl Harbor*, History Channel, circa 2001; Fujita, Prange interview, 5. According to Fujita, Iida's gesture to his men was a hand held straight up, thumb to the face, and waved to the left and right—the same gesture used in Japan today to signify one's discomfort and/or inability to render assistance. It is uncertain whether the *Sōryū* unit ascended before or after Iida's departure. However, as only three minutes elapsed between Iida's self-destruction and the arrival of the American fighters, the former scenario appears more probable. See *kōdōchōsho, Sōryū* fighter unit, 8 December 1941.

45. Letter, Guy C. Avery, 4 November 1963, 2, Prange Papers, Goldstein Collection, UA-90/F-78, box 23, ff-2. For a fuller story regarding the Iida incident, see the authors' *No One Avoided Danger*, 119–23.

46. *Kōdōchōsho, Sōryū* fighters, 8 December 1941; "Lessons of the Sea Battle off Hawaii," 20; Fujita, "Lucky Return," 263; authors' analysis.

47. Sanders action report, 6; Aiken, "Pearl Harbor's Lost P-36," 75; Sanders account, 3; John M. Thacker, map provided to John Lambert; authors' analysis; Gillman correspondence. Given Wheeler's roughly east-north-easterly–west-southwesterly orientation, a left-hand turn toward Bellows would have required a course change of approximately 130 degrees. Such a turn would have set a course north of the columns of smoke climbing out of Pearl Harbor, which was Sanders' supposed objective before Fort Shafter instructed him to fly toward Bellows Field.

48. Sanders account, 3; authors' analysis; map, *Interceptor Command Manual*; Lambert, *The Pineapple Air Force*, 17; Gillman correspondence; Aiken, "Pearl Harbor's Lost P-36," 75. Tindal had commanded the 15th Pursuit Group until the previous September.

49. Gillman correspondence; Philip M. Rasmussen, "Take Off at Pearl Harbor," lecture at National Museum of the U.S. Air Force (hereinafter Rasmussen lecture, USAF Museum), 26 September 1998, https://www.nationalmuseum.af.mil/Portals/7/av/take_off_at_pearl_harbor.mp3?ver=2015-08-27-145311–720, accessed 14 December 2020; Philip M. Rasmussen,

speech at the USS *Arizona* Memorial, circa April 2003 (hereinafter Rasmussen speech, *Arizona* Memorial), 2, transcript in TLM; "US Air Force Museum—WWII—Pearl Harbor—Philip Rasmussen's P-36 Diorama & P-35" (hereinafter Rasmussen's P-36 Diorama), http://www.williammaloney.com/Aviation/USAFMuseum/WWII/PearlHarbor/PearlHarbor.htm, accessed 30 November 2020.

50. Sanders account, 3; Lambert, *The Pineapple Air Force*, 18.

51. Sanders account, 3; letter, Philip M. Rasmussen to David Aiken, 27 September 1994, 1, Aiken Collection, NMPW, Sterling folder; Othniel Norris, Gordon H. Sterling Jr., IFRs, 1941, RG 64, NARA, St. Louis.

52. Gillman correspondence; Sanders account, 3; Aiken, "Pearl Harbor's Lost P-36," 76; authors' analysis; Lambert, *The Pineapple Air Force*, 18. The Silver Star citations for Sanders, Thacker, and Rasmussen all state that only six enemy aircraft were engaged, indicating that, initially, the flight intercepted Iida's 1st and 2nd Shōtais. See 7th Interceptor Command, General Orders No. 8, 30 March 1942, 1, Silver Star citation for Lewis M. Sanders; 7th Interceptor Command, General Orders No. 3, 16 February 1942, 2, Silver Star citation for John M. Thacker; 7th Interceptor Command, General Orders No. 6, 18 March 1942, 1, Silver Star citation for Philip M. Rasmussen, all in AFHRA, file GP-15-Hi (FTR) Dec40–Dec43. Sanders' accounts conflict with one another regarding the discovery that Sterling had taken Norris' place; one narrative has the incident occurring to the southeast over Bellows Field, but in his other accounts it took place well to the northwest, *after* Sanders sighted the Japanese fighters and signaled his men to close in for attack instructions. See Betty Osborne, "Pearl Harbor Veteran at Lillian Recalls Japanese Attack 32 Years Ago," 7 December 1973, *Mobile Press*, 9A.

53. Fujita, "Lucky Return," 263; Aiken, "Pearl Harbor's Lost P-36," 76; authors' analysis. The reason for Matsuyama's appearance is unclear. He and Makinoda suppressed American takeoffs from Bellows Field while the balance of the *Hiryū*'s fighters strafed the base. It is plausible that while Matsuyama and Makinoda chased 1st Lieutenant Bishop out to sea, the balance of the *Hiryū* unit formed and flew toward the rendezvous area. In his earlier analysis David Aiken stated that

both pilots joined the *Sōryū* fighters, but he backed away from that assertion in "Pearl Harbor's Lost P-36." References to a lesser number of "six enemy aircraft [or planes]" in the Silver Star citations of Rasmussen, Sanders, and Thacker might have justified this change. While we defer to certain details in Aiken's analysis regarding the air battle over Kāneʻohe Bay, the authors feel that Japanese pilots generally adhered to the doctrine of maintaining contact with a flight leader and have concluded that only extraordinary circumstances would have prevented Makinoda from accompanying his chief. Aiken also speculated that the two *Hiryū* pilots were low on ammunition (the supposed cause for their departure from Fujita), but we have found no hard evidence of that.

54. Rasmussen speech, *Arizona* Memorial, 2; authors' analysis; letter and map, John M. Thacker to David Aiken, 26 June 1985 (hereinafter letter, Thacker to Aiken, 26 June 1985), Aiken Collection, NMPW, Sterling folder.

55. Gillman correspondence; Sanders action report; authors' analysis; Sanders account, 3; Aiken, "Pearl Harbor's Lost P-36," 76. Okamoto's carrier fighter sustained damage twice in action over Oʻahu, and it is uncertain whether the gunfire came from Sterling or from ground defenders at NAS Kaneohe Bay. Extreme caution is called for in assigning credit for specific damage, because the Japanese air group reports seldom provide sufficient detail for such attribution. Aiken's schematic of the Japanese formation shows Fujita continuing straight ahead and Okamoto turning left, which (with regard to Fujita) is at odds with Sanders' after-action report.

56. Sanders account, 5; letter, Thacker to Aiken, 26 June 1985, 2; Lambert, *The Pineapple Air Force*, 19; "Gordon Sterling, BNR," 1; authors' analysis. The dilemma Thacker and Rasmussen faced is reminiscent of Jefferson's analogy likening slavery to holding a wolf by the ears: "we can neither hold him, nor safely let him go." See Abraham Lincoln Online: Speeches and Writings, "Eulogy on Henry Clay," http://www.abrahamlincolnonline.org/lincoln/speeches/clay.htm, accessed 21 January 2021.

57. Sanders account, 3–4; authors' analysis; Gillman correspondence; "West Hartford Man Fought Even with

Plane in Flames," undated clipping from the family of Gordon H. Sterling Jr., Aiken Collection, NMPW, Sterling folder; Thacker to Aiken, 26 June 1985, 1–2; letter, Philip M. Rasmussen to David Aiken, 18 August 1981, 1, Aiken Collection, NMPW, 46th PS folder; Lambert, *The Pineapple Air Force*, 19.

58. Lambert, *The Pineapple Air Force*, 18; Aiken, "Pearl Harbor's Lost P-36," 76; Sanders account, 4; *kōdōchōsho*, *Sōryū* fighters, 8 December 1941; authors' analysis.

59. Authors' tactical analysis; John B. Lundstrom, *The First Team: Pacific Naval Air Combat from Pearl Harbor to Midway* (Annapolis: Naval Institute Press, 1984), 486–89.

60. Authors' analysis; Aiken, "Pearl Harbor's Lost P-36," 76; letter and attached map, John M. Thacker to David Aiken, 7 December 1985, Aiken Collection, NMPW, Sterling folder; Lambert, *The Pineapple Air Force*, 20; Bōeichō Kenshūjo Senshishitsu, *Senshi Sōsho* [*War History*], vol. 10: *Hawai Sakusen* [*Hawaiian Operation*] (hereinafter *Hawai Sakusen*) (Tōkyō: Asagumo Shimbun-sha, 1967), 615. The reference to Sterling's natural metal aircraft comes from Thacker's direct statement to John Lambert. Oda's role in this portion of the engagement over Kāneʻohe Bay is something of a blank, as no known documents apart from the roster in the *Sōryū kōdōchōsho* link him to the action.

61. Rasmussen lecture, USAF Museum; Rasmussen speech, *Arizona* Memorial; authors' analysis; *kōdōchōsho*, *Sōryū* fighters, 8 December 1941; Aiken, "Pearl Harbor's Lost P-36," 78.

62. Authors' analysis; Rasmussen speech, *Arizona* Memorial, 2; Fujita, Prange interview, 5; Fujita, "Three Fighters Never Returned," 127.

63. Rasmussen speech, *Arizona* Memorial, 2; authors' analysis; Fujita, "Three Fighters Never Returned," 127; Fujita, Prange interview, 5. The action in which Rasmussen's P-36 sustained such heavy damage was particularly difficult for the authors to interpret because much of the supporting documentation is vague or contradictory. Earlier accounts of this combat rendered by John Lambert in *The Pineapple Air Force* (p. 19) and by David Aiken in "Pearl Harbor's Lost P-36" (p. 78) assert that additional aircraft were involved in the attack on Rasmussen. Lambert

presented an extended quotation from Rasmussen but made no attempt to interpret it. Aiken ventured out on a limb and offered interpretation, although the authors reached different conclusions based on (1) study of the damage to Rasmussen's aircraft; (2) Rasmussen's failure to observe any other attacking fighters; (3) the probability that Oda's damaged fighters arrived singly; (4) Fujita's failure to mention involvement of other aircraft in the incident; (5) Oda and Takashima's failure to claim a kill; and (6) timing problems. While any single issue noted above might be dismissed, taken together they appear to support Rasmussen's being attacked by Fujita alone. The authors are deeply grateful to Capt. Charles B. Gillman (call sign "Sid Vicious"), USN (Ret.), without whose assistance and analysis the story of this combat would not have taken its present (and much improved) form.

64. Lambert, *The Pineapple Air Force*, 19; authors' analysis; photography from the collection of Philip M. Rasmussen; Rasmussen lecture, USAF Museum. A photograph of Rasmussen's badly damaged P-36A shows that the rudder is clearly jammed and/or frozen slightly to the left. See the illustration and caption on page 228.

65. Lambert, *The Pineapple Air Force*, 19; Gillman correspondence.

66. Lambert, *The Pineapple Air Force*, 18; Sanders account, 4; Gillman correspondence. "Walking the rudder" is synonymous with "changing nose position" and is effective only at slower speeds, particularly in a turning fight wherein the aircraft are losing energy.

67. Gillman correspondence; *kōdōchōsho*, *Sōryū* fighters, 8 December 1941; Lambert, *The Pineapple Air Force*, 18. David Aiken was of the opinion that Sanders once again encountered Fujita, who engaged him in a head-on pass. See Aiken, "Pearl Harbor's Lost P-36," 78. The authors have concluded that Fujita's engine damage would have precluded any aggressive turning fight with Sanders.

68. Brown, Lambert interview, 3–4; Stan Cohen, *East Wind Rain* (Missoula, Mont.: Pictorial Histories, 1991), 84; authors' analysis.

69. Brown, Lambert interview, 4; authors' analysis; Cohen, *East Wind Rain*, 84; HQ, 7th Interceptor Command, General Orders No. 3, 16 February 1942, 1, Silver Star citation for Robert J. Rogers (hereinafter SS citation,

Rogers), AFHRA, file GP-15-Hi (FTR) Dec40–Dec43; HQ, 7th Interceptor Command, General Orders No. 8, 30 March 1942, 1, Silver Star citation for Harry W. Brown (hereinafter SS citation, Brown), AFHRA, file GP-15-Hi (FTR) Dec40–Dec43. The identity of the Japanese aircrews in this combat is uncertain, although Brown's description suggests that Japanese carrier bombers were involved rather than fighters. Some accounts mention the *Sōryū*, although *Kaga* bombers retiring from Wheeler Field cannot be ruled out. The Aichi Type 99s were surprisingly maneuverable with no bomb load and gave the Americans all that they could handle. Had Brown and Rogers been outnumbered by carrier fighters, it is difficult to imagine that the Zeroes would have disengaged with such a numerical advantage as supposedly existed.

70. Brown, Lambert interview, 5–6; Cohen, *East Wind Rain: A Pictorial History of the Pearl Harbor Attack*, 84; authors' analysis; letter, Harry W. Brown to David Aiken, 9 August 1971, 1, Aiken Collection, NMPW, Brown folder; letter, Harry W. Brown to David Aiken, 22 June 1970, Aiken Collection, NMPW, Brown folder. The tentative crew identity is by process of elimination. The *Sōryū* lost only two carrier bombers over Oʻahu, with the other plane being shot down by Dains over Kaʻaʻawa. Brown, whose memories of the combats appear to be quite good, stated that he had "an impression of a single blue band" on the fuselage. See letter, Brown to Aiken, 9 August 1971, 1.

71. Brown, Lambert interview, 6; authors' analysis.

72. Moore action report, 7; Brown, Lambert interview, 6–7; SS citation, Moore; SS citation, Brown; letter, Harry W. Brown to David Aiken, circa 7 July 1987, Aiken Collection, NMPW, Brown folder; fragmentary letter, Fujita Iyozō to David Aiken, n.d. Aiken Collection, NMPW, 46th PS folder; Fujita, "Three Fighters Never Returned," 127. The evidence for Brown's kill over Atsumi is strong, particularly regarding the timelines of the air battles over the eastern and western shores of Oʻahu. In addition, Brown's accounts are voluminous and very consistent. In a fragment of undated correspondence with Aiken, Fujita stated that Atsumi's aircraft went down in flames "3–5 miles southwest of Kahuku Point," which would be consistent with his being lost en

route to the two assembly areas west and north of O'ahu. As for FPO2c Ishii Saburō, that same piece of correspondence states that after Fujita returned to the *Sōryū*, a radioman overheard Ishii's distress call requesting that the carrier transmit a radio signal to guide him back. Ishii sent another message stating that his fuel was exhausted. Admittedly, other surviving records are vague and often contradictory. In "Pearl Harbor's Lost P-36," Aiken claimed that the pair joined Fujita, flew to the rendezvous off Ka'ena Point, engaged in another dogfight, escaped, but then ran out of fuel and ditched in the channel between Ni'ihau and Kaua'i. On the other hand, Fujita indicated that only his wingmen Takahashi and Okamoto formed with him for the return flight. In "Three Fighters Never Returned," Fujita also claimed that Atsumi's engine backfired and ignited the fuel. A more likely scenario is that the aircraft succumbed to damage accumulated over the island.

Apart from Fujita's fragmentary letter noted above, the curator at the National Museum of the Pacific War was unable to locate Aiken's correspondence with Fujita. In a documentary on the Type 0 carrier fighter, squadronmate Harada Kaname (who flew in the combat air patrols over *Kidō Butai* during 7 December) confirmed details of the Ishii incident to which Fujita referred in his correspondence with Aiken. See Harada Kaname, interview, n.d., in *Reisen* [The A6M Zero fighter documentary], pt. 2, "The Design," https://www.youtube.com/watch?v=9b-dEEtGkJW8, courtesy Charles Gillman, accessed 1 January 2021.

73. John J. Webster, IFRs, December 1941, RG 64, NARA, St. Louis; SS citation, Webster; David Aiken, "In Defense of the Fleet: The Amazing Response to the Total Surprise," *Flight Journal* 22, no. 6 (December 2016): 51–52.

74. Sanders account, 4; photographs from the collection of Philip M. Rasmussen. Unfortunately, there is no thorough photographic documentation of the damage to Rasmussen's P-36A. To the authors' knowledge no photographs of damage to the underside and wings exist. The damage visible in the photographs that do exist, while certainly extreme, is nowhere near the "544 holes" Sanders described. Indentations in (and partial penetrations of) the interior of the aircraft skin (due to fragmentation from the 20-millimeter detonations) may have been counted as holes. It is also possible that damage to the wings (apparently not photographed) was severe.

75. Rasmussen speech, *Arizona* Memorial, 2.

76. Rasmussen speech, *Arizona* Memorial, 2; Rasmussen lecture, USAF Museum; Sanders action report, 6. The damage to Sanders' aircraft probably occurred during his passage over Schofield Barracks. According to all available accounts' no Japanese aircraft brought him under fire.

77. Authors' analysis; "Combat Reports Furnished by Pilots Engaging the Enemy [on] 7 December 1941," 2 January 1942, combat reports of Philip M. Rasmussen, Lewis M. Sanders, and John M. Thacker, 2 January 1942, AFHSO, reel A7572, file 740.335; Lambert, *The Pineapple Air Force*, 19. The elongated "greenhouse" of the Type 0 carrier fighter probably created the illusion that it was a bomber with a rear gunner.

78. Fujita, "Lucky Return," 263.

79. Fujita, "Lucky Return," 263; email correspondence, Tagaya Osamu to JMW, 18 January 2021; Fujita, Prange interview, 6; authors' analysis.

80. Fujita, Prange interview, 6; Fujita, "Three Fighters Never Returned," 127; Fujita, "Lucky Return," 262; Gillman correspondence. The anecdote referring to a piston falling onto the *Sōryū*'s flight deck is either a bit of hyperbole or a mistranslation.

81. John L. Dains, IFRs, December 1941; Aiken, "In Defense of the Fleet," 55; letter, Harry Brown to Mr. and Mrs. Roy L. Dains (hereinafter letter, Brown to parents of John L. Dains), circa December 1941, John L. Dains Individual Death Personnel File (hereinafter Dains IDPF), RG 64, NARA, St. Louis; John C. Wretschko, IFRs, December 1941, RG 64, NARA, St. Louis; Arakaki and Kuborn, *The Air Force Story*, 79; Irwin W. Henze Jr., PHSA application, 20 November 1973.

82. Aiken, "In Defense of the Fleet," 55; letter, Kenneth M. Taylor to Brian W. Wretschko, 21 August 1993, Aiken Collection, NMPW, 47th PS folder; authors' analysis; Irwin W. Henze Jr., PHSA application, 20 November 1973; letter, Brian W. Wretschko to Leatrice R. Arakaki and John R. Kuborn, 7

December 1993, Aiken Collection, NMPW, 47th PS folder.

83. Aiken, "In Defense of the Fleet," 55; John C. Wretschko, logbook entry, 7 December 1941, Aiken Collection, NMPW, 47th PS folder; letter, Brown to parents of John L. Dains.

84. Telegram, Walter Short to Adjutant General, "Second Lt John L Dains," 7 December 1941, Dains IDPF; letter, Harry W. Brown to Vince Travens, circa September 1990, courtesy John Di Virgilio; Gushwa, *The Best and Worst of Times*, vol. 1, 103.

CHAPTER 12. "LOOKS LIKE WE'VE HAD IT FOR NOW"

1. Runce, NTU interview, 43; Miller, TLM oral history, 2; Siegle, NTU interview, 29; Stewart, NTU interview, 36–37.

2. Kolbert, NTU interview, 65–66; Brown, NTU interview, 32, 36; Rich memorandum to Raley, 2.

3. Harry E. Fitzgibbon, PHSA application, 21 November 1992.

4. Walter Zaharevitz, PHSA application, 5 May 1979; letter, Charles B. Stewart to David Aiken, 20 April 1992, Aiken Collection, NMPW, 86th OS folder; McBriarty account, 6; "Flight Operations of 86th Observation Squadron," *PHA*, pt. 24, 1956; authors' analysis. In his narrative, McBriarty said that the radio operator was named Baranimo, but no man so named appears in the 86th Observation Squadron's roster from 30 November 1941 or the morning report from 1–10 December.

5. Letter, Wayne H. Rathbun to David Aiken, 24 September 1988 (hereinafter letter, Rathbun to Aiken), Aiken Collection, NMPW, 86th OS folder.

6. "Flight Operations of 86th Observation Squadron," *PHA*, pt. 24, 1956; Robert E. Henry, PHSA application, 28 October 1998.

7. Authors' analysis; letter, Rathbun to Aiken; Wayne H. Rathbun, PHSA application, 15 December 1981; "Flight Operations of 86th Observation Squadron," *PHA*, pt. 24, 1956.

8. "Flight Operations of 86th Observation Squadron," *PHA*, pt. 24, 1956.

9. Evidence suggests that more than sixty Army pursuit pilots were airborne on 7 December, with most taking off after the raid. Pilots who flew on 7 December 1941 (but known *not* to have entered combat) include: 1st Lt. Teuvo A. Ahola, 2nd Lt. Ross C. Baker Jr., 1st Lt. George R. Bickell, 1st Lt. Floyd D. Colley, 1st Lt. Howard H. Cords, 1st Lt. James A. Cox, 1st Lt. John S. Evans, 2nd Lt. John B. Farrar Jr., 2nd Lt. Francis S. Gabreski, 2nd Lt. William F. Haney, 2nd Lt. William F. Haning Jr., 2nd Lt. Franklin A. Harrison, 1st Lt. Norval K. Heath, 2nd Lt. Irwin W. Henze Jr., 2nd Lt. Samuel L. Hitchcock, 2nd Lt. Besby F. Holmes, 1st Lt. Jack M. Hounsom, 1st Lt. Gordon R. Hyde, 2nd Lt. Albert L. Johnson, Capt. Arthur R. Kingham, 2nd Lt. Lawrence M. Kirsch, 2nd Lt. Floyd E. Lambert, 2nd Lt. Henry W. Lawrence Jr., 1st Lt. Cecil J. Looke Jr., 2nd Lt. Victor M. Mahr, 2nd Lt. Harry E. McAfee, 2nd Lt. Robert F. McCabe, 2nd Lt. John L. McGinn, 1st Lt. Joseph A. Morris, 2nd Lt. Othniel Norris, 1st Lt. Maurice C. Phillips, 1st Lt. Kenneth R. Powell, 1st Lt. Owen M. Seaman, 2nd Lt. Fred B. Shifflet, 2nd Lt. John B. Simonton, 2nd Lt. Bill Southerland, 2nd Lt. DeWitt S. Spain, 1st Lt. Everett W. Stewart, 1st Lt. Fred C. Stoffel, 1st Lt. Charles E. Taylor, 1st Lt. John Thogerson, 2nd Lt. Richard A. Toole, Capt. Aaron W. Tyer, 1st Lt. William F. Underwood, 2nd Lt. William A. Waldman, 1st Lt. James R. Watt, 1st Lt. John C. Wilkins, 1st Lt. Woodrow B. Wilmot, 1st Lt. John C. Wretschko. The authors compiled this listing from the microfilmed IFRs in NARA, St. Louis for pilots assigned to the 14th Pursuit Wing and from other records and accounts. Most of the men who flew on 7 December are named here for the first time. Some 10 percent of the flight records were unavailable or lost. Other individuals who undoubtedly flew had IFRs but no entries for 7 December (such as Fred C. Shifflet and Robert J. Rogers). Other pilots combined multiple landings/missions into single entries, making proper interpretation of the IFRs almost impossible.

10. "Lewis M. Sanders, 2nd Flight," n.d., *Wheeler Field History*, S-2, 6; "Malcolm A. Moore, 2nd Mission," n.d., *Wheeler Field History*, S-2, 7; Wenger, Cressman, and Di Virgilio, *They're Killing My Boys*, 190–92.

11. "Time of Take-offs by Airfield after Beginning of Attack, 7 Dec. 1941," *PHA*, pt. 12, Exhibits of the Joint Committee, Exhibit 5, sect. VI, 324; letter, Homer Garcia to David Aiken, 11 September 1985, 4, Aiken Collection, NMPW, 44th PS folder; analysis of IFRs of 44th Pursuit Squadron pilots, RG 64, NARA, St. Louis.

There is the possibility that the two flights might be in reverse order, with defensive fire over Pearl Harbor forcing one of the groups to cut short its patrols. Bad weather later in the day may have influenced pursuit pilots as well.

12. Besby F. Holmes, interview, American Fighter Aces Association, Museum of Flight, Seattle (hereinafter Besby F. Holmes, interview), circa 1980s, 8; Besby F. Holmes and John D. Voss, IFRs, August–December 1941, RG 64, NARA, St. Louis.

13. Besby F. Holmes, interview, 9–10.

14. Besby F. Holmes, interview, 11–12.

15. Brown, NTU interview, 30–31.

16. Kolbert, NTU interview, 53–54.

17. Kolbert, NTU interview, 64; Snowden Steuart, PHSA application, 6 February 1987; Arthur H. Cochran, PHSA application, 22 August 1991.

18. Willis, NTU interview, 38, 35; Richard A. Mergenthaler, PHSA application, 1 December 1989.

19. Malcolm W. Pettet, PHSA application, 13 August 1971.

20. David I. Walsh, PHSA application, 1 December 1981; "Organizational History, 46th Fighter Squadron, 21st Fighter Group, VII Fighter Command, Seventh Air Force," 4, AFHSO, reel A0741, file Sq-Fi-46-Hi Dec/40–Mar/44.

21. Miller, TLM oral history, 2; Straub, 15WHO oral history, 4; White, 15WHO oral history, 1; authors' analysis.

22. Thomas A. Bromund, PHSA application, 15 January 1972; microfilmed morning reports, 804th Engineer Battalion (Avn), 7–31 December 1941, RG 64, NARA, St. Louis; Leroy J. Smith, PHSA application, 26 February 1978; microfilmed officer roster, 804th Engineer Battalion (Avn), 30 November 1941, RG 64, NARA, St. Louis; authors' analysis. Ironically, 1st Lt. Jones had been warned by his neighbor and fellow engineer 1st Lt. John C. Geffel that "all the Army families should be evacuated [from the Hawaiian Islands] because talks in Washington [with the Japanese] seemed to be failing." See U.S. Army Corps of Engineers Headquarters, "Historical Vignette 128—Pearl Harbor," https://www.usace.army.mil/about/history/historicalvignettes/military constructioncombat/128pearlharbor/, accessed 9 February 2021.

23. William H. Roach Jr., PHSA application, 1 June 1982.

24. Russell, TLM oral history, 1–3.

25. Siegle, NTU interview, 28; Spangler, TLM oral history, 2–3.

26. James R. Piggott, PHSA application, 20 October 1984; John L. Palinkas, PHSA application 18 December 1991.

27. Hendrix, 15WHO oral history, 2; Runce, NTU interview, 46–47; Henry C. Brown, NTU interview, 55.

28. Hendrix, 15WHO oral history, 2; Henry C. Brown, NTU interview, 55.

29. Kindl, NTU interview, 36–37; authors' analysis.

30. Andrews, Lord questionnaire, 3; Richardson NTU interview, 46.

31. Spangler, TLM oral history, 2–3; Wenger, Cressman, and Di Virgilio, *This Is No Drill*, 200–208.

32. Spangler, TLM oral history, 3; admission records of the General Hospital, Schofield Barracks, 7 December 1941, courtesy of Ray Emory.

33. Henry C. Brown, NTU interview, 48; Krepps, Lord questionnaire, 3.

34. Leonard T. Egan, Lord questionnaire, 3A–3B.

35. Richardson, NTU interview, 47; Siegle, NTU interview, 33; Russell, TLM oral history, 2; Flickinger, Lord questionnaire, 3.

36. Leyshock, 15WHO oral history, 2, 4; Robert B. Williams, questionnaire, n.d. (hereinafter Williams, Lord questionnaire), 3, Lord Collection HAD, NHHC; Egan, Lord questionnaire, 3B; Siegle, NTU interview, 17.

37. Richardson, NTU interview, 47; Egan, Lord questionnaire, 3A; Andrews, Lord questionnaire, 3; Siegle, NTU interview, 33.

38. Brown, NTU interview, 30–31.

39. Willis, NTU interview, 47–48.

40. Stewart, NTU interview, 37, 41; microfilmed morning reports, 73rd Pursuit Squadron, December 1941, RG 64, NARA, St. Louis.

41. Stewart, NTU interview, 37, 41–43; IFRs, 73rd Pursuit Squadron, December 1941.

42. Stewart, NTU interview, 37, 42–44, 46; IFRs, 73rd Pursuit Squadron, December 1941. Although it is unclear whether the 73rd's entire complement of pilots reported to Haleiwa, the 1st lieutenants and the sole senior 2nd lieutenant (John L. McGinn) shouldered nearly all the flight duty during 7–8 December.

43. Letter, Victor H. Peterson to David Aiken, 20 January 1986, 4, Aiken Collection, NMPW, 44th PS folder; John A. Moore, IFRs, December 1941, RG 64, NARA, St. Louis; photographs 111-SC-127000 and -127012, Still Picture Branch, NARA II; authors' analysis; microfilmed Aircraft Accident Report, George A. Whiteman, P-40C, 41-13337, 22 July 1941, AFHRA.

44. "Bellows Field History," 12.

45. Letter, Jean K. Lambert to David Aiken, 6 April 1992 (hereinafter letter, Lambert to Aiken, 6 April 1992), 2, Aiken Collection, NMPW; Arakaki and Kuborn, *The Air Force Story*, 142.

46. James T. Lewis, IFRs, December 1941, RG 64, NARA, St. Louis; Arakaki and Kuborn, *The Air Force Story*, 142.

47. Arakaki and Kuborn, *The Air Force Story*, 142; microfilmed officer roster, 298th Infantry Regiment, RG 64, NARA, St. Louis; "298th/299th Infantry," http://encyclopedia.densho.org/298th/299th_Infantry/, accessed 18 November 2020.

48. Journal of 2nd Lt. Paul C. Plybon (hereinafter Plybon journal), entries from 7–8 December 1941, 4–5, courtesy of son Robert B. Plybon.

49. Plybon journal, 5–7; Arakaki and Kuborn, *The Air Force Story*, 144.

50. Arakaki and Kuborn, *The Air Force Story*, 142; letter, Lambert to Aiken, 6 April 1992, 2; Plybon journal, 7.

51. Plybon journal, 8.

52. Letter, Lambert to Aiken, 6 April 1992, 2; Arakaki and Kuborn, *The Air Force Story*, 142; letter, Wallace B. Thomas to David Aiken, circa October 1996, Aiken Collection, NMPW, 86th Observation Squadron folder; authors' analysis.

53. Lalumendier, Lord questionnaire, 3.

54. Authors' analysis; Henry C. Brown, NTU interview, 55; Hendrix, 15WHO oral history, 2.

55. Authors' analysis; Charles E. Kneen, Karl F. Harris, Joseph Oblak IFRs, November–December 1941, RG 64, NARA, St. Louis. Although obsolete, the eight P-26s on hand after the raid were assigned to the 73rd Pursuit Squadron, which had lost all its P-40Bs. See "Organizational History 73rd Fighter Squadron, AAF," 2, AFHSO, reel A0754, file Sq-Fi-73-Hi Oct/41–Mar/44.

56. Authors' analysis; "Memorandum to Roberts Commission," 26 December 1941, *PHA*, pt. 24, 2019–20.

57. Authors' analysis; Hawaiian Air Force, War Diary, 7–31 December (hereinafter HAF War Diary), entry for 17 December 1941, AFHSO, reel A7554, file 740.3051-1.

58. IFRs of various pilots, December 1941, RG 64, NARA, St. Louis; "History, Air Depot, APO #953, VII Air Force Service Command, VII Air Force from 7 December 1941 to March 1944" (hereinafter "Hawaiian Air Depot History"), 91–92, AFHSO, reel A7374, file 723.401, vol. II.

59. "Hawaiian Air Depot History," 92; IFRs of various pilots, December 1941, RG 64, NARA, St. Louis; HAF War Diary, entry for 17 December 1941.

60. DPW Environmental Cultural Resources, annotated aerial photograph, "WWII Bomb Craters and Battle Damage, WAAF, Oahu," 29 July 2010, authors' files; authors' observations at Wheeler Army Airfield, 1991–2016.

61. Photograph 342-FH-3B-48707, Still Picture Branch, NARA II; photograph 2094, 15th Wing History Office, Joint Base Pearl Harbor–Hickam.

62. Davidson, Prange interview, 5 July 1962, 1–4, Prange Papers, Goldstein Collection.

63. Kolbert, NTU interview, 68–69.

64. Stewart, NTU interview, 54.

65. Runce, NTU interview, 48; Drenner, Lord questionnaire, 3.

66. Kolbert, NTU interview, 66–67.

67. Davidson, Prange interview, 6 July 1962, 12, 4, Prange Papers, Goldstein Collection.

68. Brown, NTU interview, 37.

69. Munn, NTU interview, 19; Stewart, NTU interview, 53–54.

70. USAF Historical Division, Research Studies Institute, *A Preliminary List of U.S. Air Force Aces 1917–1953*, USAF Historical Study 73, AFHRA; Office of Air Force History, Headquarters, USAF, *USAF Credits for the Destruction of Enemy Aircraft, World War II*, USAF Historical Study 85, AFHRA. The twelve "Wheeler" aces (alphabetically, with official victories indicated) are Harry W. Brown (8), Francis S. Gabreski (31), Ernest A. Harris (10), Besby F. Holmes (6), Verl

E. Jett (7), Charles H. MacDonald (27), William F. McDonough (5), John L. McGinn (5), Joseph T. McKeon (6), Franklin A. Nichols (5), Everett W. Stewart (8), and George S. Welch (16), together accounting for 134 aircraft destroyed. Forty-four other pilots received credit for 73 victories, for a total of 207 among all Wheeler survivors.

71. Richard A. Mergenthaler, PHSA application, 1 December 1989.

72. Letter, Roy L. Dains to CO, 18th Pursuit [sic] Group, 19 December 1941, Dains IDPF; letter, Capt. Emil W. Geitner to Roy L. Dains, 19 December 1941, Dains IDPF.

73. Letter, Harry W. Brown to parents of John L. Dains, Dains IDPF.

74. Letter, John L. Dains to Bea, n.d., Dains IDPF.

75. Letter, William J. Flood to John C. Whiteman, 15 December 1941, courtesy Gayle Kent.

76. Arakaki and Kuborn, *The Air Force Story*, 191–95. The figures for the killed and wounded reflect—with minor alterations—the listing in the 1991 book on the Hawaiian Air Force by Arakaki and Kuborn. That work remains, at present, the authority regarding the casualties of the 14th Pursuit Wing. Historian Ray Emory consulted with Arakaki regarding the list, which is as accurate as practicality allowed in 1991. Access to the Army's microfilmed muster rolls and morning reports will help to refine the casualty figures further. In particular, the count of those men wounded in action will almost surely increase.

77. Lawrence Gross, PHSA application, 18 March 1991; White, 15WHO oral history, 7.

78. Vernon C. Rubenking, questionnaire, n.d., 4, Lord Collection, HAD, NHHC.

BIBLIOGRAPHY

MILITARY RECORDS

U.S. Air Force Reports, Histories, Correspondence Files, Action Reports (U.S. Army Air Forces), and Interviews, Air Force Historical Research Agency, Maxwell Air Force Base, Montgomery, Alabama

Aircraft Accident Reports, various pilots, groupings, and locations.

Aircraft History Cards: DH-4A, O-47B, O-49, P-12B/C/E, P-26A/B, P-36A, P-40B/C.

Carmichael, Richard H. Interviews 8–10 September 1980 and 10–11 November 1980.

88th Reconnaissance Squadron (H) AFCC, Fort Douglas, Utah, Annex No. [blank] to Field Order No. 2, 3 December 1941.

46th Pursuit Squadron, Operations Order No. 86, 31 October 1941.

Tentative Manual of Interceptor Command Organization, Procedure and Operations for Air Defense, 27 October 1941. AFHRA, file 741.01 7 Dec 1941–Jul 1944 vol. 11.

U.S. Air Force Historical Study 73. *A Preliminary List of U.S. Air Force Aces 1917–1953.*

U.S. Air Force Historical Study 85. *USAF Credits for the Destruction of Enemy Aircraft, World War II.*

U.S. Air Force Historical Study 91. *Biographical Data on Air Force General Officers, 1917–1952.* Vol. 1: A–K.

Welch, George S. Interview, 19 May 1942. Copy in Aiken Collection, National Museum of the Pacific War.

U.S. Air Force Reports, Histories, Correspondence Files, and Action Reports (U.S. Army Air Forces) (microfilm), Air Force History Support Office, Bolling Air Force Base, Washington, D.C.

Administrative History of Headquarters, Seventh Air Force. APO953.

AG Historical Section, 4th Air Force Headquarters. *Processing and Ferrying Functions of the Fourth Air Force through the Year 1941. Fourth Air Force Historical Study IV-1*, vol. 1: *Narrative*; vol. 2: *Documents.*

Combat Reports Furnished by Pilots Engaging the Enemy [on] 7 December 1941, 2 January 1942.

[History of] 18th Fighter Group, 11 Jan 1927–30 Jun 1944.

Group History of the 15th Pursuit Group (F).

Hawaiian Air Force War Diary, 7–31 December.

"History, Air Depot, APO #953, VII Air Force Service Com-mand, VII Air Force from 7 December 1941 to March 1944."

History of Bellows Field from Time of Inception to 31 March 1944.

History of the 26th Bombardment Squadron (H).

History of the 47th Fighter Squadron.

History, Wheeler Field, T.H. 1922–1944. A host of critical documents are appended to this history, including two pilot after-action reports and documents bearing on ground defense.

Johnson, Walter H., "Squadron Diary, Eighty-Eighth Recnnaissance," (H) AFCC.

Memorandum. Clyde K. Rich [Bellows HQ Detachment] to Edward M. Raley, 20 December 1941. AFHSO, reel A7581, file 740.674-1A.

"Organizational History, 46th Fighter Squadron, 21st Fighter Group, VII Fighter Command, Seventh Air Force."

"Organizational History, 73rd Fighter Squadron, AAF."

"Organizational History [of Haleiwa Field]."

"Report of Enemy Activity over Oahu, 7 December 1941," 18 December 1941.

VII Fighter Comd. History, 1 Nov. 1940–7 Dec. 1941 incl.

"Transfer of Two (2) Pursuit Squadrons." List of Papers under 370.5, file 740.229-3.

U.S. Army Miscellaneous Documents,
National Archives and Records Administration

Dains, John L. Individual Death Personnel File, RG 64, NARA, St. Louis.

"Narrative Report of Events of 7 December 1941 in the North Sector," 22 December 1941, NARA II.

Opana radar plot chart, NARA DC Treasure Vault.

Deck Logs (U.S. Navy), NARA II, RG 24

Enterprise (CV 6), 15–21 February 1941; 3, 21, 27 April 1941; 27 November 1941.

Lexington (CV 2), 18–25 March 1941.

Movement Cards (U.S. Navy), Naval History
and Heritage Command

Enterprise (CV 6), 15–21 February–April 1941.

Action Reports (U.S. Navy), NARA II, RG 38

John M. Sweeney. "The action as seen from Barbers Point," 10 December 1941. Enclosure "GG" to Com14, "Report on the Battle of Pearl Harbor, 7 December, 1941."

Decoration Citations, Air Force History Support Office

7th Interceptor Command, General Orders No. 3,
16 February 1942

Charles A. Fay

Malcolm A. Moore

Robert J. Rogers

John M. Thacker

John J. Webster

7th Interceptor Command, General Orders No. 6,
18 March 1942

Samuel W. Bishop

Philip M. Rasmussen

George A. Whiteman

7th Interceptor Command, General Orders No. 8,
30 March 1942

Harry W. Brown

John L. Dains

Lewis M. Sanders

War Department, General Orders No. 2, 5 January 1942

Kenneth M. Taylor

George S. Welch

Decoration Citations, NARA, St. Louis

7th Air Force Base Command, General Orders No. 17.

William L. Bayham

John T. Benton

Ford E. Dodd

Milton J. Dunn

Bruce Harlow

Gottlieb J. Kaercher

Ethelbert E. Lovell

Daniel A. Mahoney

Hilmer C. Nelson

John J. Ostrum

Edward I. Pratt Jr.

Ralph C. Riddle

Vernon C. Rider

Carl M. Sidenblad

Gerald L. Suprise

George J. Van Gieri

Kraig L. Van Noy

18th Air Base Group, General Orders No. 1

Joseph Berlinski

Adrian S. Black

John Cena

Robert T. Mineau

Edwin Rakocy

Carl W. Wunderlin

Henry E. Zenzer

CinCPac Operational Plans and Orders, RG 38

"Naval Air Station Wake and Naval Air Station
Midway—Basing of Aircraft at." Serial 01825, 10
November 1941.

CinCPac Dispatch Files, 1941 (Originals and Photostats), NARA II, Records of the Pearl Harbor Liaison Office, RG 80

OpNav to CinCPac, dispatch 061730 CR899, 6 February
1941.

OpNav to CinCPac, dispatch 032132 CR109, 3 March
1941.

CinCPac to OpNav, dispatch 082200 CR192, 8 March
1941.

OpNav to CinCPac, dispatch 122037 CR466, 12 March
1941.

CinCPac to OpNav, dispatch 132357 CR317, 13 March
1941.

OpNav to CinCPac, dispatch 282358 CR296, 28 March
1941.

CinCPac to OpNav, dispatch 020345 CR77, 2 April 1941.

OpNav to CinCPac, dispatch 022300 CR108, 2 April
1941.

OpNav to CinCPac, Secret Dispatch 270038, Serial 11-822,
27 November 1941.

OpNav to CinCPac, Secret Dispatch 270040, Serial 11-830,
27 November 1941.

OpNav to CinCPac, Secret Dispatch 282054, Serial 11-944,
28 November 1941.

Engineering Records (U.S. Army), NARA II, Records of the Chief of Engineers, RG 77

Completion Reports, Bellows Field

Air Corps Range Camp at Waimanalo, Oahu, T.H., 1931.

WPA Official Project No. 513-2-121 at Bellows Field, T.H.,
1937.

Completion Reports, Wheeler Field

Construction and Completion of a New Air Corps
Gasoline Fueling System at Wheeler Field, T.H., 1940.

Construction and Completion of One Control Tower on
A.C. Operations Hangar at Wheeler Field, T.H., 1940.

Construction and Completion of Thirty-Eight Double,
Type Eight, Non-Commissioned Officers' Quarters
and All Utilities Thereto at Wheeler Field, T.H., 1940.

Construction of Five Sets of Quarters for Married Field
Officers, Thirty-Seven Sets of Quarters for Married
Company Officers and One Building for Sixteen
Bachelor Officers, Together with Certain Roads, Walks
and Other Utilities Therefor at Wheeler Field, Schofield
Barracks, T.H., n.d.

Construction of Forty-Two (42) Sets of Married N.C.O.
Quarters, One Building for Bachelor N.C.O.s, Together
with Roads, Walks and Other Utilities Therefor at
Wheeler Field, Schofield Barracks, T.H., n.d.

Construction of One Administration Building and One
Photographic Laboratory, Together with Certain Roads
and Utilities Therefor at Wheeler Field, Schofield
Barracks, T.H., n.d.

Construction of 1 Dispensary Building, 1 Radio Building,
1 Parachute Building, 1 Fire Station and Guard House,
1 Paint, Oil and Dope House, 1 Quartermaster Garage
Building, [and] 1 Quartermaster Utilities Shops
Building at Wheeler Field, Schofield Barracks, T.H.,
n.d.

Construction of Six Steel Hangars, 1923.

Construction of Temporary Mess Hall, Latrines and Tent
Floors, 1941.

Construction of 300-Man Cantonment at Wheeler Field,
T.H., 1939.

Construction of Wash Racks, Runways, Aprons,
Conduits and Drains at Wheeler Field, Schofield
Barracks, T.H., n.d.

Dismantling Two Airplane Hangars at Wheeler Field and
Salvaging All Structural Steel and Transporting Same
to Hickam Field, T.H., 1936.

Flagpole, 1940.

Floodlight Installations at Wheeler Field, Schofield
Barracks, T.H., n.d.

Four Air Corps Barrack Buildings Together with Certain
Roads, Walks and Other Utilities Therefor at Wheeler
Field, Schofield Barracks, T.H., n.d.

[Four] Air Corps Double Hangars, 1 Air Corps Machine
 Shop, 1 Air Corps Assembly Shop, 1 Air Corps
 Warehouse, n.d.
Grading and Leveling on Officers' and N.C.O. Quarters
 Area at Wheeler Field, T.H., 1939.
Installation of a Night Light System for Wheeler Field,
 Schofield Barracks, T.H., n.d.
Signal Light Installation at Wheeler Field, Schofield
 Barracks, T.H., n.d.

QMC Form 111—Records of Equipment and Condition of Buildings
Wheeler Field, T.H., 30 June 1941

QMC Form 117—Data Card and Building Portraiture, Bellows Field
Airplane Runway
Control Tower
Detachment Barracks
Dispensary
Entrance Gate
Kitchen & Mess Hall
Latrine
N.C.O. Quarters
N.C.O.s' Garage
Officers Building
Operations Office
Post Exchange
Shop & Storeroom
Storehouse, Main Camp
Tent Frames
Waimanalo Air Corps Camp, Oahu, T.H.

QMC Form 117—Data Card and Building Portraiture, Wheeler Field
A.C. Bomb Storage Warehouse
Administration Bldg. (Wheeler Field)
Assembly Shop (Wheeler Field)
Barracks (AC)
Flagpole
Hangar No. 1
Machine Shop
Officers' Garage (Wheeler Field)
Warehouse (Wheeler Field)

Plans and Miscellaneous
Plan 6517-240. "Wheeler Field, T.H., Layout Plan."
Report on Construction Activities at Wheeler Field,
 Territory of Hawaii, Covering the Period 1935–January
 6, 1941, 24 February 1941.

General Court-Martial Records, NARA, St. Louis
Record of Trial, Henry C. Brown, September 1941–
 February 1942.

Individual Flight Records (IFRs), NARA, St. Louis
George R. Bickell
Samuel W. Bishop
Paul W. Blanchard Jr.
William J. A. Bowen
Harry W. Brown
Milo N. Clark
Ingram C. Connor Jr.
John L. Dains
Howard C. Davidson
James J. Flood
Raymond K. Gallagher
Karl F. Harris
Armin F. Herold
Besby F. Holmes
Charles E. Kneen
James T. Lewis
Charles H. MacDonald
John A. Moore
Malcolm A. Moore
Phineas K. Morrill Jr.
Oscar B. Myers Jr.
Othniel Norris
Joseph Oblak
Archie L. Roberts Jr.
Robert J. Rogers
Jerome R. Sawyer
Fred B. Shifflet
Norman D. Sillin
Gordon H. Sterling Jr.
Everett W. Stewart
Eldon E. Stratton

Kenneth M. Taylor
George R. Tourtellot
John D. Voss
John J. Webster
George S. Welch
George A. Whiteman
Woodrow B. Wilmot
John C. Wretschko

Japan Defense Agency Reports, Tokyo
Detailed Action Reports
Aircraft Carrier *Shōkaku*, 8 December 1941

Hikōkitai Sentō Kōdōchōshos
(Aircraft Group Battle Action Reports)
Akagi
Hiryū
Kaga
Shōkaku
Sōryū
Zuikaku

Keirekis (Japanese Naval Officer Career Summaries)
Ema Tamotsu
Hayashi Chikahiro
Iida Fusata
Nōno Sumio
Okajima Kiyokuma
Sakamoto Akira
Suganami Masaji

Morning Reports and Rosters (U.S. Army), NARA, St. Louis, RG 64
6th Pursuit Squadron
14th Pursuit Wing
14th Quartermaster Company (Trk)
15th Pursuit Group
18th Air Base Group
18th Pursuit Group
19th Pursuit Squadron
24th Material Squadron
25th Material Squadron
42nd Bombardment Squadron

44th Pursuit Squadron
45th Pursuit Squadron
46th Pursuit Squadron
47th Pursuit Squadron
58th Bombardment Squadron
72nd Pursuit Squadron
73rd Pursuit Squadron
78th Pursuit Squadron
86th Observation Squadron
298th Infantry Regiment
804th Engineer Battalion (Avn)
Hawaiian Air Force Base Command
Quartermaster Detachment

Reports and Documents in the Prange Collection, University of Maryland
Fuchida Mitsuo. Chart of "Flying Formation on [*sic*] Pearl Harbor Attack, First Attack Force (183 Planes)."
CarDiv 5. Detailed Action Report No. 1, 8 December 1941 (translation).
CarDiv 5. War Diary, 1 December 1941–31 December 1941 (translation).
Yokosuka Naval Air Corps. "Lessons (Air Operation) of the Sea Battle off Hawaii," vol. 1.

Reports and Documents from Authors' Files
Admission records of the General Hospital, Schofield Barracks, 7 December 1941.
Chart of Japanese first-wave air deployment.
Fujita Iyozō. *Tora, Tora, Tora: The Real Story of Pearl Harbor.* The History Channel, circa 2001, authors' notes.
Journal of 2nd Lt. Paul C. Plybon, entries from 7–8 December 1941.
Letter, Harry W. Brown to Vince Travens, circa September 1990.
Matsumura Hirata, interview notes.
Matsumura Hirata, letter and map.
Untitled and undated report with maps and text outlining the Japanese attacks on Bellows. Copy provided by William M. Cleveland, circa 1985.
Wenger, J. Michael. "Whitepaper No. 3: Japanese Submarines and the Hawaiian Operation," 1 June 2008.

CORRESPONDENCE, INTERVIEWS, AND MISCELLANEOUS MATERIAL

Authors' General Correspondence

David Aiken

Ernest Arroyo

Louis Bontya

William M. Cleveland

Jessie Higa

Charles B. Gillman

Kamada Minoru

John W. Lambert

James Lansdale

Daniel Martinez

Timothy P. Mulligan

Shimizu Ikuo

Mark Stevens

Tagaya Osamu

John M. Thacker

Mark R. Wenger

Accounts and Statements Attached to Applications to the Pearl Harbor Survivors Association

Donald M. Arras

Homer R. Baskin

Earl L. Bigelow

George V. Biggs

Wallace Bloom

Earl Boone

Frederick T. Bowen

Charles D. Boyd

Charles D. Boyer

Thomas A. Bromund

David C. Cameron

Wilbur S. Carr

Paul R. Cipriano

Arthur H. Cochran

Liston A. Coomer

Harry E. Cornelius

Michael T. Cossack

David L. Crabtree

Keith E. Cragg

William J. Feiler

Harry E. Fitzgibbon

Francis S. Gabreski

Donovan S. Ginn

Lawrence Gross

Lyle M. Grover

Ray E. Hadwick

Donald H. Halferty

Joe K. Harding

Glen F. Heller

Robert E. Henry

Irwin W. Henze Jr.

Franklin Hibel

Leigh Hilderbrant

Harold C. Hitt

Tom Hutchinson

John E. Ireland

Stanley J. Jaroszek

Winston S. Jones

John P. Joyce

Orris R. Julian

Morton Kamm

George F. Keeler

Harry P. Kilpatrick

Charles E. Kneen

Charles H. Leyshock

Cosmo R. Mannino

Richard A. Mergenthaler

Guy Messacar Jr.

Danforth P. Miller Jr.

Melvin L. Miller

Harold J. Moore

Horace G. Moran

Ronald J. Nash

John M. Neuhauser

Adalbert B. Olack

John L. Palinkas

Joseph T. Pawlowski

William T. Petherbridge

Malcolm W. Pettet

James R. Piggott

John E. Quasnovsky

Wayne H. Rathbun

William H. Roach Jr.

Elmer L. Rund

George Seibel

Leroy J. Smith

Elmer J. Steffan

Snowden Steuart

Bertram E. Swarthout
Paul G. Teegardin
Stanley W. Thomas
George Tillett
Arnold J. Trempler
Robert S. Turk Jr.
David I. Walsh
Christopher Ward
Herbert C. Ward
Francis A. White
Fred C. Wilson
William F. Winzenburg
Edward R. Young
John P. Young
William J. Young
Walter Zaharevitz
Charles A. Zelonis

Interviews, Statements, and Documents
Papers of John W. Lambert
Abe Zenji
Harry W. Brown
Philippe A. Michaud
Ōbuchi Keizō
Lewis M. Sanders
Kenneth M. Taylor

Papers of Walter Lord, Naval History and Heritage Command,
Washington Navy Yard
Carroll T. Andrews
Richard H. Carmichael
Raeburn D. Drenner
Leonard T. Egan
Donald D. Flickinger
William J. Flood
Arthur W. Fusco
George E. Kovak
Kenneth E. Krepps
Bess Lalumendier
James W. McAdams
John F. Plassio
Vernon C. Rubenking
Carl W. Shrader
Gordon F. Smith
Robert B. Williams

Oral History Collection of World War II Valor in the Pacific
National Monument
Philip M. Rasmussen
Kenneth M. Taylor

University of North Texas Oral History Collection, Denton, Texas
Ernest A. Brown
Henry C. Brown
Clarence W. Kindl
Byron W. Kolbert
Flora Koran
Stephen J. Koran
Thomas Leonard
John P. Munn
Milroy L. Richardson
Fred R. Runce
Will Roy Sample
Vladamir "William" M. Shiflette III
Mannie E. Siegle
John J. Springer
John E. Sterling
Everett W. Stewart
William G. Temple Jr.
Wallace B. Thomas
Robert S. Turk Jr.
Phillip L. Willis
Brian W. Wretschko

Collection of David Aiken, National Museum of the Pacific War,
Fredericksburg, Texas
Aiken, David. "Gordon Sterling, BNR [body not recov-
    ered] 7 Dec 1941, Pearl Harbor." Review draft of
    journal article, circa 1994.
Leatrice R. Arakaki
Harry W. Brown
Edward J. Covelesky
Don Dawson
Fujita Iyozō
Homer Garcia
Jean K. Lambert
Henry W. Lawrence Jr.
Raymond F. McBriarty
Victor H. Peterson
Philip M. Rasmussen
Wayne H. Rathbun

Elmer L. Rund
Keith A. Schilling
John E. Sterling
Charles B. Stewart
William G. Temple Jr.
John M. Thacker
Robert S. Turk Jr.
George S. Welch (photostats of flight logs)
Brian W. Wretschko

Papers of Gordon W. Prange, Goldstein Collection, Archives Service Center, University of Pittsburgh; or Prange Collection, Hornbake Library, University of Maryland
Guy C. Avery
Howard C. Davidson
Ema Tamotsu
William J. Flood
Fuchida Mitsuo
Fujita Iyozō
Genda Minoru
"Japanese Fleet Task Organization," 7th December 1941
Truman H. Landon
Muranaka Kazuo
Nakajima Tatsumi
Okajima Kiyokuma
38th Reconnaissance Squadron, Special Orders No. 1, 4 December 1941.

Authors' Correspondence with Families of the Following American Veterans
Carroll T. Andrews
Wallace Bloom
Henry C. Brown
Charles C. Cunningham
Franklin Hibel
Besby F. Holmes
Stephen J. Koran
Jean K. Lambert
Guy Messacar Jr.
Hilmer C. Nelson
Paul C. Plybon
Edmund H. Russell
Robert S. Turk Jr.
George A. Whiteman

Authors' Interviews with Japanese Veterans
Abe Zenji
Fujita Iyozō
Hori Kenji
Matsumura Hirata

Miscellaneous Documents, U.S. Army Center of Military History Wing History, Fort McNair, Washington, D.C.
Army Regulation No. 330-40, Machine Records Codes, Code 40
Army Regulation No. 330-63, Machine Records Codes, Code 63
Army Regulation No. 345-400, Military Records, Morning Reports
Army Regulation No. 345-900, Military Records, Personnel Rosters
Army Regulation No. 615-26, Enlisted Men, Index and Specifications for Occupational Specialists and Index to Military Occupational Specialists

Miscellaneous Documents and Materials, 15th Wing History Office, Joint Base Pearl Harbor–Hickam, Interviews and Oral Histories, Various
Charles L. Hendrix
Charles H. Leyshock
Ronald F. Norton
David B. Stephenson
Henry J. Straub
Edward J. White

Miscellaneous Documents and Materials, Tropic Lightning Museum, Schofield Barracks, Interviews and Oral Histories, Various
Melvin L. Miller
Jack M. Spangler
Edmund H. Russell

Miscellaneous Documents and Materials from Jessie Higa
Correspondence with family of Charles C. Cunningham
Correspondence with family of George A. Whiteman
Hawaiian Department, *Telephone Directory*, 25 July 1941
Passenger manifest, SS *Lurline*, 22–27 December 1934
Passenger manifest, SS *Lurline*, 20–26 March 1941
Passenger manifest, SS *Lurline*, 7 November 1941
Passenger manifest, SS *Lurline*, 3 December 1941

Passenger manifest, SS *Lurline*, 20–26 December 1941

Passenger manifest, SS *Malolo*, 20–27 March 1937

Passenger manifest, SS *Matsonia*, 5–10 July 1941

Passenger manifest, SS *Matsonia*, 8–14 October 1941

Passenger manifest, SS *Matsonia* 15 October 1941

Plan 6812-822-2732. "Water Map, Wheeler Field, T.H."

Randall, Edward E. "Wheeler Field," reminiscence

Sliney, Minnie (sister of Edmund C. Sliney), letter, 12
    December 1941

Study of Wheeler Field residents as of 7 December 1941

Various newspaper articles and clippings

PHOTOGRAPHS

National Archives and Records Administration (NARA II), Still Picture Branch

RG 18: Records of the Army Air Forces

RG 77: Records of the Corp of Engineers

RG 80: Records of the Department of the Navy

RG 111: Records of the Signal Corps

RG 342: Records of the U.S. Air Force

Other Government Agencies

Joint Base Pearl Harbor–Hickam, 15th Wing History
    Office

Maxwell Air Force Base, Air Force Historical Research
    Agency

Pearl Harbor Air Museum

World War II Valor in the Pacific National Monument,
    Honolulu, Hawai'i, Historian's Office, Photo Archives

Private Collections

David Aiken Collection, National Museum of the Pacific
    War, Fredericksburg, Texas

Dana Bell

Robert J. Cressman

John F. Di Virgilio

Maru magazine

Timothy P. Mulligan

Pearl Harbor Aviation Museum

Todd Pederson

Gordon W. Prange Papers, Goldstein Collection, Archives
    Service Center, University of Pittsburgh

Gordon W. Prange Papers, University of Maryland,
    Hornbake Library

Gordon W. Prange Papers, via Wenger

Satō Zenichi, via Pearl Harbor Aviation Museum

Philip M. Rasmussen

J. Michael Wenger

Yoshino Yasutaka

CONGRESSIONAL RECORDS

*Congressional Record: Proceedings and Debates of the First
Session of the Seventieth Congress of the United States of
America.* Washington, D.C.: GPO, 1928.

CONGRESSIONAL HEARINGS

*Pearl Harbor Attack: Hearings before the Joint Committee
on the Investigation of the Pearl Harbor Attack.* 79th
Congress, 1st Session. 39 parts, plus Joint Committee
Report and General Index. Washington, D.C.: GPO, 1946.

Testimonies

Patrick N. L. Bellinger

Howard C. Davidson

William E. Farthing

William J. Flood

Mobley L. Hall

William F. Halsey

Lowell V. Klatt

Frederick L. Martin

Raymond F. McBriarty

Charles H. McMorris

James A. Mollison

Walter C. Phillips

Stephen G. Saltzman

Walter C. Short

William W. Smith

Kenneth M. Taylor

Leonard D. Weddington

George S. Welch

Exhibits and Other Documents

"Addendum I to Naval Base Defense Air Force Operation
    Plan No. A-1-41," 31 March 1941. Exhibits of the
    Roberts Commission, Exhibit 45 (Navy Packet 2).

Affidavit of Robert H. Dunlop, 28 February 1945. Clausen
    Investigation.

"Air Defense of Pearl Harbor, Hawaii," 7 February 1941.
    Exhibits of the Roberts Commission, Exhibit 22
    (Army).

"Aircraft Status." 14 December 1941. Exhibits of the Roberts Commission, Exhibit 1 (Army).

Annex Baker to Commander Naval Base Defense Operation Plan 1-41. Exhibits of the Roberts Commission, Exhibit 45 (Navy Packet 2).

Annotated vertical photograph of Wheeler Field. Exhibits of the Roberts Commission, Exhibit 1 (Army), item 88.

"Construction at Bellows Field, T.H. [extracts]," 5 April 1941. Exhibits of the Roberts Commission, Exhibit 1B (Army).

"Diagram of Bellows Field, Oahu, T.H., showing numbers and formations of attacking Japanese planes, times of attacks and disposition of U.S. planes in Japanese attack 7 Dec. 1941." Exhibits of the Joint Committee, Exhibit 5 (Army), item 7.

Enterprise deck log, 27–28 November 1941. Exhibits of the Joint Committee, Exhibit 101.

"Flight Operations of 86th Obsn Sq (C&D) AC during the period 15 November 1941 to 7 December 1941, Inclusive," 22 December 1941. Exhibits of the Roberts Commission, Exhibit 11 (Army).

General Orders No. 68, 27 October 1941. Exhibits of the Roberts Commission, Exhibit 5 (Army).

General Plan. "Bellows Field, Oahu, T.H.," April 1941. Exhibits of the Roberts Commission, Exhibit 12, item 99.

"Hawaiian Islands, Oahu." Exhibits of the Joint Committee, Exhibit 6, item 14.

"Improvement of Airfield at Haleiwa, Oahu, T.H.," n.d.; and 4th indorsement dated 25 June 1941. Exhibits of the Roberts Commission, Exhibit 1B (Army).

"Location of Mobile AWS Stations on Dec. 7, 1941 with Sectors Showing Coverage to the Electrical Horizon." Exhibits of the Roberts Commission, Exhibit 2 (Navy Packet 2), item 36.

"Map of Oahu, T.H., showing the disposition, number, types, and operational and readiness condition of U.S. Navy Aircraft on 7 Dec. 1941." Exhibits of the Joint Committee, Exhibit 6, item 14.

"Memorandum to Roberts Commission," 26 December 1941. Exhibits of the Roberts Commission, Exhibit 25 (Army).

"Operation Plan No. 1-41," 27 February 1941. Exhibits of the Roberts Commission, Exhibit 45 (Navy Packet 2).

"Operation Schedule No. 45-41 (Week of Nov. 26–Dec. 2, 1941)," 25 November 1941. Exhibits of the Joint Committee, Exhibit 113C.

"Progress Map, Bunker Const [*sic*] Wheeler Field." File DR1 M2, 21 August 1941. Exhibits of the Roberts Commission, Exhibit 1 (Army), item 89.

"Proposed Installation of Six Mobile RDF Units on Island of Oahu," circa 14 August 1941. Exhibits of the Army Pearl Harbor Board, Exhibit 57, enclosure D.

"Records Requested in Telegram Dated 22 December 1941," 23 December 1941. Exhibits of the Roberts Commission, Exhibit 8 (Army).

Secret Radiogram 472/27th, 27 November 1941. Exhibits of the Army Pearl Harbor Board, Exhibit 1 (incl. Short Exhibit B).

Special Orders No. 269, 27 October 1941. Exhibits of the Roberts Commission, Exhibit 5 (Army).

"Standard Operating Procedure," Hawaiian Department, 5 November 1941. Exhibits of the Roberts Commission, Exhibit 32.

"Time of Take-offs by Airfield after Beginning of Attack, 7 Dec. 1941." Exhibits of the Joint Committee, Exhibit 5, section VI.

"Vertical Photograph of Haleiwa Field." Exhibits of the Roberts Commission, Exhibit 1 (Army), item 86.

"Watch and Duty Schedule for December 1, 1941, to January 1, 1942," 25 November 1941. Exhibits of the Joint Committee, Exhibit 113C.

PUBLICATIONS

Books

Arakaki, Leatrice R., and John R. Kuborn. *7 December 1941: The Air Force Story.* Washington, D.C.: GPO, 1991.

Backus, Jean L., ed. *Letters from Amelia: An Intimate Portrait of Amelia Earhart.* Boston: Beacon Press, 1982.

Bailey, Thomas A. *The American Pageant: A History of the Republic.* Boston: D. C. Heath, 1961.

Bell, Dana. *P-40 Warhawk.* Tucson, Ariz.: Classic Warships, 2013.

Belt Collins Hawaii. *Final Environmental Impact Statement for Land Use and Development Plan, Bellows Air Force Station, Waimanalo, Hawaii.* Honolulu: Belt Collins Hawaii, 1995.

Bōeichō Kenshūjo Senshishitsu. *Senshi Sōsho.* Vol. 10: *Hawai Sakusen.* Tōkyō: Asagumo Shimbun-sha, 1967.

Bowers, Peter M. *Boeing Aircraft since 1916.* Annapolis: Naval Institute Press, 1968.

———. *The Boeing P-12E.* Leatherhead, England: Profile Publications, 1965.

———. *The Boeing P-26A.* Leatherhead, England: Profile Publications, 1965.

———. *Curtiss Aircraft, 1907–1947.* Annapolis: Naval Institute Press, 1979.

Branham, Charles N., ed. *Biographical Register of the Officers and Graduates of the U.S. Military Academy at West Point, New York since Its Establishment in 1802 by Brevet-Major-General George W. Cullum, Colonel of Engineers, U.S. Army Retired.* Supplement, vol. 8. Unknown publisher, 1950.

Cohen, Stan. *East Wind Rain: A Pictorial History of the Pearl Harbor Attack.* Illus. Mary Beth Percival. Missoula, Mont.: Pictorial Histories, 1991.

Clay, Steven E. *US Army Order of Battle 1919–1941.* Vol. 3: *The Services: Air Service, Engineers, and Special Troops, 1919–41.* Fort Leavenworth, Kans.: Combat Studies Institute Press, 2010.

Craven, Wesley F., and James L. Cate. *The Army Air Forces in World War II.* Vol. 1: *Plans and Early Operations, January 1939 to August 1942.* Chicago: University of Chicago Press, 1948.

———. *The Army Air Forces in World War II.* Vol. 6: *Men and Planes.* Washington, D.C.: Office of Air Force History, 1983.

Cressman, Robert J. *A Magnificent Fight: The Battle for Wake Island.* Annapolis: Naval Institute Press, 1995.

Donaldson, William H., ed. *Biographical Register, USMA.* Supplement, vol. 7: *1920–1930.* Chicago: Lakeside Press, 1930.

Farman, Elbert E. Jr., ed. *Biographical Register, USMA.* Supplement, vol. 8: *1930–1940.* Chicago: Lakeside Press, 1940.

Fujita Iyozō, comp. *Shōgen Shinjuwan Kōgeki.* Tōkyō: Kōjin-sha, 1991.

Gabreski, Francis S. *Gabby: A Fighter Pilot's Life.* New York: Orion Books, 1991.

Gushwa, Robert L. *The Best and Worst of Times: The United States Army Chaplaincy, 1920–1945.*

Washington, D.C.: Office of the Chief of Chaplains, Department of the Army, 1977.

Jorgenson, Daniel P. *The Service of Chaplains to Army Air Units 1917–1946.* Washington, D.C.: Office of the Chief of Air Force Chaplains, 1961.

Lambert, John W. *The Pineapple Air Force: Pearl Harbor to Tokyo.* St. Paul, Minn.: Phalanx, 1990.

Lord, Walter. *Day of Infamy.* New York: Henry Holt, 1957.

Lundstrom, John B. *The First Team: Pacific Naval Air Combat from Pearl Harbor to Midway.* Annapolis: Naval Institute Press, 1984.

Matsuda Norio. "To Renso." In Rekishi-to Jinbutsu. Tōkyō: Chūō Kōron-sha, 20 January 1983.

Maurer, Maurer. *Aviation in the U.S. Army, 1919–1939.* Washington, D.C.: GPO, 1987.

Mori Jūzō. *Kiseki-no Raigekkitai.* Tōkyō: Kōjin-sha, 1994.

———. "Raigekki Shutsudo." In *Shōgen Shinjuwan Kōgeki,* comp. Fujita Iyozō. Tōkyō: Kōjin-sha, 1991.

O'Neill, P. G. *Japanese Names: A Comprehensive Index by Characters and Readings.* New York and Tōkyō: John Weatherhill, 1972.

Pearl Harbor Survivors Association, comp. *The Pearl Harbor Survivors Association Silver Anniversary Commemorative Book.* Vol. 1. Santa Ana, Calif.: Taylor, 1984.

Prange, Gordon W. *At Dawn We Slept: The Untold Story of Pearl Harbor.* New York: McGraw-Hill, 1981.

Robinson, Wirt, ed. *Biographical Register, USMA.* Supplement, vol. 6-B: *1910–1920.* Saginaw, Mich.: Seemann & Peters, 1920.

Ross, Donald K., and Helen L. Ross. *"0755": The Heroes of Pearl Harbor.* Port Orchard, Wash.: Rokalu Press, 1988.

Scott, Robert L. Jr. *Damned to Glory.* Garden City, New York: Blue Ribbon Books, 1944.

Tagaya Osamu. *Aichi 99 Kanbaku "Val" Units 1939–1942.* Long Island City, N.Y.: Osprey, 2011.

U.S. Department of Commerce. *United States Coast Pilot: The Hawaiian Islands, 1933.* Washington, D.C.: GPO, 1933.

———. *Supplement to United States Coast Pilot: The Hawaiian Islands.* Washington, D.C.: GPO, 1946.

U.S. War Department. *Army Directory, Reserve and National Guard Officers on Active Duty, July 31, 1941.* Washington, D.C.: GPO, 1941.

———. *Official Army Register, January 1, 1942.* Washington, D.C.: GPO, 1942.

———. *Official Army Register, January 1, 1945.* Washington, D.C.: GPO, 1945.

Wagner, Ray. *The Curtiss P-40 Tomahawk.* Leatherhead, England: Profile Publications, 1965.

Wenger, J. Michael, Robert J. Cressman, and John F. Di Virgilio. *"No One Avoided Danger": NAS Kaneohe Bay and the Japanese Attacks of 7 December 1941.* Annapolis: Naval Institute Press, 2015.

———. *"They're Killing My Boys": The History of Hickam Field and the Attacks of 7 December 1941.* Annapolis: Naval Institute Press, 2019.

———. *"This Is No Drill": The History of NAS Pearl Harbor and the Japanese Attacks of 7 December 1941.* Annapolis: Naval Institute Press, 2018.

Yamagata Tsunao, comp. *Kaigun: Kūbo-Kan Sentō Kiroku.* Tōkyō: Atene Shobō, 2002.

Articles

Air Corps News Letters

"Barksdale Field, La., January 24th." *Air Corps News Letter* 21, no. 3 (1 February 1938): 21.

"Changes in Air Service Organizations in Hawaii." *Air Service News Letter* 7, no. 19 (12 October 1923): 3.

"Death of Major Sheldon H. Wheeler, Air Service." *Air Service News Letter* 5, no. 28 (28 July 1921): 3.

"Farewell to the 26th Attack Squadron." *Air Corps News Letter* 23, no. 3 (1 February 1940): 8, 10.

"50th Observation Squadron Goes into Camp." *Air Corps News* 15, no. 11 (18 September 1931): 324.

"For Immediate Release." [*Air Service*] *Weekly News Letter* 1, no. 5 (20 October 1918): 4.

"Free Ballooning over Texas." *Air Service News Letter* 7, no. 13 (22 March 1920): 16–18.

"Greetings from Wheeler Field, H.T. [*sic*]." *Air Service News Letter* 7, no. 5 (5 March 1923): 7.

"Hawaiian Air Depot, Luke Field, T.H., April 14." *Air Corps News Letter* 20, no. 9 (1 May 1937): 25.

"Hawaiian Department." *Air Corps News Letter* 22, no. 7 (1 April 1939): 6–7.

"The Hawaiian Department Maneuvers." *Air Corps News Letter* 18, no. 15 (15 August 1935): 15–16.

"The Hawaiian Flight." *Air Corps News* 11, no. 6 (27 June 1927): 181.

"Hawaiian Flight a Remarkable Achievement." *Air Corps News* 11, no. 9 (19 July 1927): 205–7.

"Hawaiian Flight Authorized." *Air Corps News* 11, no. 6 (27 June 1927): 196.

"Hqrs. 5th Group (Obs.) Luke Field, H.T. [*sic*], Jan. 14." *Air Service News Letter* 6, no. 5 (9 March 1922): 20.

"Landing of the Dole Flyers in Hawaii." *Air Corps News* 11, no. 13 (15 October 1927): 303–4.

"Landscaping at Wheeler Field." *Air Corps News* 16, no. 12 (18 October 1932): 409.

"Lieut. Wisehart Qualifies as a Long Distance Swimmer." *Air Service News* 10, no. 9 (8 June 1926): 9.

"New Gunnery Range Opened in Hawaii." *Air Service News* 10, no. 9 (8 June 1926): 8.

"New Zealand Citizens Express Gratitude to U.S." *Air Corps News Letter* 18, no. 3 (15 February 1935): 56.

"P-36A Airplanes Appear Plenty Fast." *Air Corps News Letter* 22, no. 23 (1 December 1939): 22.

"Parachute and Life Vest Prevent Casualty." *Air Corps News Letter* 22, no. 21 (1 November 1939): 7.

"Recruit Training at Wheeler Field." *Air Corps News Letter* 22, no. 22 (15 November 1939): 15–16.

"Selfridge Field, Mich." *Air Corps News Letter* 21, no. 2 (15 January 1938): 18, 26–27.

"The Soldier [*sic*] Medal Award to Corporal Stone." *Air Corps News Letter* 21, no. 23 (1 December 1938): 12.

"The Soldier's Medal." *Air Corps News Letter* 21, no. 4 (15 February 1938): 3–4.

"Summer Rest Camps for Hawaiian Air Corps Personnel." *Air Corps News* 12, no. 14 (6 October 1928): 368.

"Tow Target Operator Whisked out of Plane." *Air Corps News Letter* 22, no. 22 (15 November 1939): 17.

"20th Pursuit Group Loses Its P-26's." *Air Corps News Letter* 21, no. 3 (1 February 1938): 6.

"War Pilots Honored in Naming Hawaiian Landing Fields." *Air Corps News* 17, no. 9 (30 September 1933): 219.

Other Articles

Aiken, David. "Ghosts of Pearl Harbor: The Facts, Figures and Forgotten Heroes." *Flight Journal* 12, no. 3 (June 2007): 24–32.

———. "In Defense of the Fleet: The Amazing Response to Total Surprise." *Flight Journal* 22, no. 6 (December 2016): 49–55.

———. "Pearl Harbor's Lost P-36, Still Missing after 60 Years: 2nd Lt. Gordon Sterling." *Flight Journal* 7, no. 5 (October 2002): 72–76, 78.

"Army Airman Killed as 2 Planes Crash." *Honolulu Advertiser*, 1 November 1941.

Conlon, John P. "Chevrons and Rockers" [in "Letters" section]. *Army: The Magazine of Landpower* 34, no. 4 (April 1984): 9.

Ewing, William H. "Few on Hand to See Start of Great Hop." *Honolulu Star-Bulletin*, 12 January 1935.

Fujita Iyozō. "Kaeranakatta San Ki-no Yōgunki [Three Fighters Never Returned]." In *Mikōkai Shashin ni Miru: Shinjuwan Kōgeki*. Tōkyō: Shin Jinbutsu Ōrai-sha, 12 July 1990, 124–26.

———. "Kōnnaru Seikan [Lucky Return]." In *Rekishi-to Jinbutsu*. Tōkyō: Chūō Kōron-sha, 20 January 1983, 262–63.

"General Davidson, Visiting Here, Lauds New Air Service Command." *Dayton (Ohio) Daily News*, 9 November 1941.

Guttman, Robert. "Boeing's Trailblazing P-26 Peashooter." *Aviation History* 6, no. 6 (July 1996): 22–28, 73.

Hori Kenji. "Machini Matta X-Bi." In *Rekishi-to Jinbutsu*. Tōkyō: Chūō Kōron-sha, 20 January 1983, 240–41.

———. "99-Shiki Kanjō Bakugekiki." *Maru Mechanic*, no. 5 (1982): 62–65.

Ibuki Shōichi. "Kaga Kyūkōka Bakugekitai Hawai Jōkū-no Shukun." In Fujita Iyozō, comp., *Shōgen Shinjuwan Kōgeki*. Tōkyō: Kōjin-sha, 1991, 450–55.

Iizuka Tokuji and Kawamoto Minoru (trans.). "Kanbaku War Notes." Courtesy James Lansdale.

"Landscaping of Wheeler Field's Quarters Ready." *Honolulu Star-Bulletin*, 20 August 1932.

"*Lurline* in with Second Largest Passenger List." *Honolulu Star-Bulletin*, 3 December 1941.

Matsuda Norio. "To Renso." In *Rekishi-to Jinbutsu*. Tōkyō: Chūō Kōron-sha, 20 January 1983.

Matthews, Mack. "30 Army Pursuit Planes Make Dramatic, Unannounced Arrival." *Honolulu Advertiser*, 22 February 1941.

McCarthy, Joe. "Bellows Field Observations." *Honolulu Star-Bulletin*, 26 June 1942.

———. "New Bellows Field Chaplain Asks for Books for Post Library." *Honolulu Advertiser*, 6 December 1941.

Mori Jūzō. "We Will Attack Pearl Harbor!" *Cavalier* 12, no. 103 (January 1962): 28–31, 76–79, 81.

"Noted Airmen Assigned Here." *Honolulu Star-Bulletin*, 12 September 1938.

Osborne, Betty. "Pearl Harbor Veteran at Lillian Recalls Japanese Attack 32 Years Ago." *Mobile Press*, 7 December 1973.

"Soldier's Medal Awards." *U.S. Army Recruiting News* 20, no. 11 (November 1938): 10–11.

"Soldier's Medal Awards." *U.S. Army Recruiting News* 23, no. 4 (April 1941): 11.

Taylor, Frank. "WWII Pilot Downs Plane." Newspaper clipping.

"Two Bellows Field Fliers Die in Crash." *Honolulu Advertiser*, 18 November 1941.

"2 Planes Crash at Kahuku; 1 Pilot Missing." *Honolulu Star-Bulletin*, 31 October 1941.

"Wheeler Field to Be Planted." *Honolulu Star-Bulletin*, 10 October 1931.

Yoshioka Masamitsu. "16.12.08 Sentō Kiroku." In *Kōkū Bokan Sōryū-no Kiroku*. Japan: *Sōryū-kai*, 1992, 164–68.

Internet Articles

"The Air Battle over Shanghai—1932." http://www.republicanchina.org/Air-Battle-over-Shanghai-Suzhou-Hangzhou-1932.pdf.

"Amelia Earhart." Hawaii Aviation. https://aviation.hawaii.gov/aviation-pioneers/amelia-earhart/.

"Amelia Earhart in Hawaii, #613." Amelia Earhart Original Photo Archive. https://www.ameliaarchive.org/index.aspx?year=1934#&gid=13&pid=2.

"An Army Engineer at Pearl Harbor." U.S. Army Corps of Engineers Headquarters https://www.usace.army.mil/about/history/historicalvignettes/militaryconstructioncombat/128pearlharbor/.

"Army Engineers Fought and Lived through the Attack on Pearl Harbor." Honolulu District Public Affairs, 7 December 2012. https://www.army.mil/article/92634/army_engineers_fought_and_lived_through_the_attack_on_pearl_harbor/.

"Assignment of Quarters." *Honolulu Star-Bulletin*, 30 August 1941. https://www.newspapers.com/image/275199381.

"Atlantic-Fokker C-2 'Bird of Paradise.'" National Museum of the United States Air Force. https://web.archive.org/web/20110913055923/http://www.nationalmuseum.af.mil/factsheets/factsheet.asp?id=3239.

"Brigadier General Harvey S. Burwell." https://www.af.mil/About-Us/Biographies/Display/Article/108034/brigadier-general-harvey-s-burwell/.

"Chief Who Fought Wheeler Field Fires during Blitz, Retires." *Honolulu Star-Bulletin*, 8 October 1946. https://www.newspapers.com/image/282708161.

"Civil Aircraft Register—Australia." Golden Years of Aviation. www.airhistory.org.uk/gy/reg_VH-U1 .html.

"Douglas [C-33] DC-2: Commercial Airliner/Military Transport Aircraft." https://www.militaryfactory.com /aircraft/detail.asp?aircraft_id=809.

"18th Fighter Group (USAAF)." http://www.historyofwar .org/air/units/USAAF/18th_Fighter_Group.html.

"*Enterprise* VII (CV-6) 1938–1956." https://www.history .navy.mil/research/histories/ship-histories/danfs/e /enterprise-cv-6-vii.html.

"Eulogy on Henry Clay." Abraham Lincoln Online: Speeches and Writings. http://www.abrahamlincolnonline.org /lincoln/speeches/clay.htm.

"Grumman Goose (G-21): Multirole Flying Boat Aircraft." https://www.militaryfactory.com/aircraft/detail .php?aircraft_id=833.

Howard, Frederick. "Kingsford Smith, Sir Charles Edward (1897–1935)." *Australian Dictionary of Biography*. http://adb.anu.edu.au/biography/kingsford -smith-sir-charles-edward-6964.

"Lost and Out of Gasoline." *St. Louis Star-Times*, 4 December 1934. https://www.newspapers.com /newspage/205507631/.

"Major General William E. Lynd." https://www.af.mil /DesktopModules/ArticleCS/Print.aspx?PortalId =1&ModuleId=858&Article=108567.

"Major Sheldon Harley Wheeler." Hawaii Aviation. https: //aviation.hawaii.gov/airfields-airports/oahu/wheeler -field/major-sheldon-harley-wheeler/.

McEnery, Robert. "First of Army's New Chapels Nearly Finished." *Honolulu Advertiser*, 7 October 1941. https://www.newspapers.com/image/259327737.

"Miss Earhart Off on Pacific Flight; Heard about 3 Hours Out." *New York Times*, 12 January 1935. https://archive .nytimes.com/www.nytimes.com/learning/aol /onthisday/big/0111.html.

National Library of Australia, caption for photograph PIC/8392/386–423. https://nla.gov.au/nla.obj -147721912/view.

"North American O-47B." National Museum of the United States Air Force. https://www.nationalmuseum .af.mil/Visit/Museum-Exhibits/Fact-Sheets/Display /Article/198091/north-american-o-47b/.

"Oahu Railway & Land Company Terminal." *Historic American Buildings Survey,* HABS No. HI-573. http://lcweb2.loc.gov/master/pnp/habshaer/hi/hi1000 /hi1028/data/hi1028cap.pdf.

Panko, Ray. "Amelia Earhart's Crash on Ford Island, March 20, 1937," 16 November 2009. https://www. pearlharboraviationmuseum.org/blog/amelias-earharts -crash-on-ford-island-may-20-1937.

"Planes, Submarines, Ships Seek Ulm." *Nevada State Journal* (Reno), 5 December 1934. https://www .newspapers.com/newspage/78824482/.

Rasmussen, Philip M. Speech at the USS *Arizona* Memorial, circa April 2003. http://www.williammaloney .com/Aviation/USAFMuseum/WWII/PearlHarbor /PearlHarbor.htm.

———. "Take Off at Pearl Harbor," 26 September 1998. https://www.nationalmuseum.af.mil/Portals/7/av/take _off_at_pearl_harbor.mp3?ver=2015–08–27–145311–720.

Reisen [The A6M Zero fighter documentary]. Part 2: "The Design." https://www.youtube.com/watch?v =9bdEEtGkJW8.

Saclausa, Marcelina. "Tourist Tattler." *Honolulu Advertiser*, 18 October 1941. https://www.newspapers.com/image /259335728.

"*Saratoga* V (CV-3)." https://www.history.navy.mil/content /history/nhhc/research/histories/ship-histories/danfs/s /saratoga-v.html.

"298th/299th Infantry." http://encyclopedia.densho.org /298th/299th_Infantry/.

Waimanalo Neighborhood Board No. 32. "Draft Regular Meeting Minutes, Monday, July 19, 2009." http://www .honolulu.gov/rep/site/nco/nb32/09/32200907min.pdf.

"Weather Bureau Believes Squalls North of Hawaii Will Clear by Sunday." *Honolulu Star-Bulletin*, 1 December 1934. https://www.newspapers.com/newspage /275038279/.

"Wheeler Gets a New Fire Chief." *Honolulu Star-Bulletin*, 6 September 1941. https://www.newspapers.com /newspage/275056805/.

INDEX

Page numbers in *italics* refer to images, tables, or maps.

OA-9 Goose, *61*; destroyed, at Wheeler Field, *236*; and ferrying aircraft to Wheeler, 60; rescue activity, 99; training on, 101

Oahu Railway and Land Company: delivery of construction material to Wheeler Field, 3, 8; and Haleiwa Hotel, 39; rail spur extended to Wheeler Field, 3, 12, *26*

Oblak, Joseph, 256

Ōbuchi Keizō, 205–6

Oda Kiichi, *216*, 219, 221–22

Officers' Club, 98th Coast Artillery, 122

Okajima Kiyokuma (fighter unit commander), *142*; aborts strafing attacks on Wheeler Field, 142; flies to Ewa Mooring Mast Field, 142; unit roster, *141*

Okamoto Takashi, 215, *216*, *219*, 220–21, *221*, 230

Olack, Adalbert B., 176–77

Olson, Ross, 176

opinions on Japanese attack, 258–59; as failure of U.S. government, 258; and failure of U.S. to anticipate attack, 259; on Japanese invasion following attacks, likely success of, 259; on Japanese mistakes and failures during attack, 259; as long-term benefit to U.S., 258; as part of Roosevelt's supposed plan to push U.S. into war, 258–59

Ostrum, John J., 155–56

Ōtsuka Reijirō, 128, 154, *154*

Owen, Ernest W., 169

P-12B/C/E Hawk: attrition rate, 44; at Bellows field, *30*; design characteristics, 44; at Haleiwa Field, 41; obsolescence, 45; replacement with P-26A Peashooters, 45, 48; as standard equipment in 1930s, 44; at Wheeler Field, 43, *43*, 44, *44*, 45

P-26A Peashooter: deliveries to Hawaiian Department, 45–47, 48; engines in, 47; numbers available, before and after attack, *257*; performance characteristics, 45; replacement by P-36As, 46, 48; replacement of P-12 variants, 45, 48; at Wheeler Field, *45*

P-26Bs: in gunnery training, 101; numbers available, before and after attack, *257*

P-36: fuel requirements, 22; numbers available, before and after attack, 257

P-36A Hawk, *49*, *88*; armament, 89; as Army's principle fighter before 1941, 89; delivery to Hawaiian Department, fall 1939, 48; design characteristics and development, 88; impending obsolescence of, 48; landing gear issues, 96; numbers available, before and after attack, *257*; performance, 48; replacement by P-40, 89; as replacement for Boeing P-26 Peashooter, 46, 48; in revetments, *87*, 88; rotation schedule for Haleiwa Field, 42; at Wheeler Field, 88

P-36A Hawk, ferried to Hawaiian Department, February 1941, 52–56; condition of aircraft as concern, 53; ferry flights to San Diego, complexity of, 53–55, *55*; flight from *Enterprise* to Wheeler Field, 56; March Field, modifications to aircraft at, 54; pilot inexperience, as concern, 52, 53; pilots transferring with aircraft, 56; replacement of damaged aircraft, 54

P-38 Lightning, delays in delivery to 15th Hawaiian Air Force, 60–61

P-39Ds (Bell), arrival in mid-late December as replacement aircraft, 257

P-40: armament, 87; armorers, responsibilities of, 87; at Bellows Field, *38*; bore sighting of, *93*, *94*; design shortcomings, 90; fuel requirements, 22; large numbers available, 90; numbers available, before and after attack, 257; as obsolete before production, 89–90; performance, 90; production of, 58; as re-engineered P-36, 90; in revetments, *87*, 88; view from cockpit, *93*; at Wheeler Field, 88

P-40 Conference on sending Army fighters to Wake and Midway Islands, 107–11; Army fighters' limited range and, 109; command

of fighters as issue in, 109; decision to send VMF-211, 109; and discounting of attack on Hawai'i, 108–9; and *Enterprise*, test launch of P-40s from, 110–11; extraction of P-40s from Wake impossible, 107; Kimmel's intent to move MAG-21, 107; manpower and supplies required for, 109–10; officers in attendance, 108; as option for future, 109–10

P-40B Tomahawk, 89; armament, *89*, *90*, 90–91, *91*; numbers available, before and after attack, *257*

P-40B Tomahawk, ferried to Hawaiian Department, March 1941, 56–58; delivery of planes to NAS San Diego, 56; departure for Hawai'i, 56–57; *Enterprise* in overhaul, thus unavailable, 56, 58; flight from Ford Island to Wheeler Field, 57–58; flying off of *Lexington*, impracticality of, 56; *Lexington* selected for ferry mission, 56, 57; pilots and crew accompanying, to train Wheeler personnel, 56, 57; unloading of planes from *Lexington*, moored at Ford Island, 57

P-40B/C Tomahawk, armament, *90*, 90–91, *91*

P-40B/C Tomahawk, ferried to Hawaiian Department, April 1941, 58–60; arrival at Ford Island, Hawai'i, 59, *59*; Curtiss plant delivery of fifty-three aircraft, 58; *Enterprise* available for mission following overhaul, 58; flight from Ford Island to Wheeler Field, 60; Kimmel pressured by Stark to ferry a third group of Army fighters, 58; transport from Curtiss plant to San Diego, 58, 59

P-40C Tomahawk: characteristics of, 58; cockpit, *89*; numbers available, before and after attack, *257*

P-40D/Es, arrival in mid-late December as replacement aircraft, 257

Pacific Fleet. *See* U.S. Pacific Fleet

Pali Pass, *119*, 120

Palinkas, John L., 209, 248

ABOUT THE AUTHORS

Military historian **J. Michael Wenger** lives in Raleigh, North Carolina, and has conducted research since the 1970s at repositories in the United States, from St. Louis, Missouri, to Washington, D.C., and also in Tōkyō, Berlin, and London. He has cowritten twelve books and numerous journal articles, newspaper features, and reviews. His main interest is Japanese carrier aviation and doctrine in World War II.

Naval historian **Robert J. Cressman** lives in Silver Spring, Maryland. His *The Official Chronology of the United States Navy in World War II* received a John Lyman Book Award in 1999, and his body of work on U.S. naval aviation history was recognized with the Admiral Arthur W. Radford Award in 2008.

Military historian **John Di Virgilio** lives in Honolulu, Hawaiʻi. He has conducted research for forty years in repositories across the United States and Japan. He is the author of two groundbreaking articles related to Pearl Harbor and is recognized for his extensive research on Japanese naval ordnance and for his illustrated Pearl Harbor battleship damage profiles.